Valerio Alfonso Bruno, Antonio Campati, Paolo Carelli,
Anna Sfardini (Eds.)

Dystopian Worlds Beyond Storytelling

Representations of Dehumanized Societies in Literature, Media, and
Political Discourses: Multidisciplinary Perspectives

With a foreword by Damiano Palano and
an afterword by Massimo Scaglioni

Valerio Alfonso Bruno, Antonio Campati,
Paolo Carelli, Anna Sfardini (Eds.)

DYSTOPIAN WORLDS BEYOND STORYTELLING

Representations of Dehumanized Societies in Literature,
Media, and Political Discourses:
Multidisciplinary Perspectives

With a foreword by Damiano Palano and
an afterword by Massimo Scaglioni

Bibliographic information published by the Deutsche Nationalbibliothek
Die Deutsche Nationalbibliothek lists this publication in the Deutsche Nationalbibliografie; detailed bibliographic data are available on the Internet at http://dnb.d-nb.de.

Bibliografische Information der Deutschen Nationalbibliothek
Die Deutsche Nationalbibliothek verzeichnet diese Publikation in der Deutschen Nationalbibliografie; detaillierte bibliografische Daten sind im Internet über http://dnb.d-nb.de abrufbar.

Cover picture: ID 31785090 © Yorkberlin | Dreamstime.com

ISBN (Print): 978-3-8382-1830-4
ISBN (E-Book [PDF]): 978-3-8382-7830-8
© *ibidem*-Verlag, Hannover • Stuttgart 2024
All rights reserved.

No part of this publication may be reproduced, stored in or introduced into a retrieval system, or transmitted, in any form, or by any means (electronic, mechanical, photocopying, recording or otherwise) without the prior written permission of the publisher. Any person who commits any unauthorized act in relation to this publication may be liable to criminal prosecution and civil claims for damages.

Alle Rechte vorbehalten. Das Werk einschließlich aller seiner Teile ist urheberrechtlich geschützt. Jede Verwertung außerhalb der engen Grenzen des Urheberrechtsgesetzes ist ohne Zustimmung des Verlages unzulässig und strafbar. Dies gilt insbesondere für Vervielfältigungen, Übersetzungen, Mikroverfilmungen und elektronische Speicherformen sowie die Einspeicherung und Verarbeitung in elektronischen Systemen.

Printed in the United States of America

Table of Contents

Damiano Palano
Foreword 9

Valerio Alfonso Bruno, Antonio Campati, Paolo Carelli, Anna Sfardini
Introduction
Dystopian Worlds: A Multidisciplinary Approach to
Analyse Transformations in Literature, Media and Politics 25

Part 1:
Political Orders and Techno-Dystopias: Debates and Models

Manuela Ceretta
From *Darwin among the machines* to *Black Mirror*: Rise and
Fall of a Technological Paradigm 37

Vassilis Galanos
Between Monstrous Dystopias and Policy Utopias in
Artificial Intelligence: *Reporting on a ten-year journey into
the AI-topia* 51

Paola Dalla Torre
Transhuman Dystopias: Cinematographic Science Fiction and
Biorthical Issues 69

Enrico Reggiani
"A happy congruence of myth and politics".
Mike McCormack's Biopolitical Dystopia in
Notes from a coma 85

Romina Perni
The Space of Full Transparency. Contemporary Dystopian
Scenarios 99

Marco Milani
A Dystopian Reality: Social Inequality and Dystopian
Narratives in Korea's Contemporary Cultural Production 113

Part 2:
De-Humanized Worlds and Contaminations

Ivana Mette
La terra dei figli. From the Graphic Novel to the Movie.
Dehumanization and Reconfiguration of Imaginaries and
Identities through Landscapes 135

Matteo Quinto
Hybridizations and Interspecies Relations:
Turning Dystopias into Potential Assets 145

Raffaele Chiarulli
To Dystopia and Beyond. Escape from the Techno-Economic
Paradigm with *Wall•E* 159

Alessandro Dividus
The Coming of Machines: Dystopian Visions of Society in
Samuel Butler and George Dyson 173

Ivo Stefano Germano and Massimiliano Panarari
The Retrotopia Science Fiction, Cacotopy, and Not Only
Distopy: Scattered Notes on the "cold science fiction of
the 21st century" 185

Part 3:
Literary and Performing Arts

Patricia Chiantera-Stutte
Out of Sight and beyond Speech: State of Nature and
Morality in Saramago 203

Emiliano Marra
Comparing Two Italian Alternative History Novels:
Asse pigliatutto by Lucio Ceva and *Contro-passato prossimo*
by Guido Morselli 221

Luca Gendolavigna
Walls, Camps, State of Exception, Sweden-Enemies, and Gang-Related Individuals. A Journey into the Dystopian Sweden of Johannes Anyuru and Jens Lapidus 235

Silvia Leonzi, Fabio Ciammella, Grazia Quercia
From Natural to Cyber. A Transmedia Approach to Body Representation in Techno-Dystopias 255

Jovana Malinarić
Beyond Fiction and Reality. Contemporary Performance Discovers Fairy Tales in the Works of Lina Majdalanie and Rabih Mroué 269

Maria Teresa Zanola
Clothes and Costumes: Dystopian Storytelling through Fashion 281

Part 4:
Transmedia Narratives

Luca Barra
Sliding Towards an Uncertain Future. *Years and Years* and the Ever-Closer Dystopia 293

Stefania Antonioni
Sisters in Arms against the Pandemic. Female Figures in the TV Series *The Rain* and *Anna* 307

Daniela Cardini
Dystopian Nostalgia. Oxymorons in Pandemic Television. 317

Miriam Petrini
The Potential and the Use of the Radio in the Construction of a Dystopian Imaginary 329

Gianni Sibilla
Walls, Animals and Drones: Concept Albums and Transmedia Dystopic Narratives in Popular Music 339

Andrea Piano
Build Your Own Dystopian Nightmare: The Case of Civilization VI 351

Part 5:
Catastrophic and Apocalyptic Imaginaries

Joe Trotta
Loving the Futures We Hate: The Ubiquity of Dystopias in Popular Culture* 363

Mario Tirino and Lorenzo Denicolai
Dystopia in Your Eyes! Retro-Mediation as Retroactive Remediation of Pandemic Visual Imaginaries 387

Anja Boato
Our Dystopian World. Catastrophic Storytelling in Virtual Reality 407

Giovanni Bernardini
"The end times may really be night". Science Fiction and Nuclear Dystopia between the 1950s and 1960s 421

Mariangela La Manna
A Close Enough Dystopia? International Law and Climate Change in Kim Stanley Robinson's
The Ministry for the Future 435

Massimo Scaglioni
Afterword 449

About the Autors 451

Foreword

Damiano Palano

Reflecting on Alfonso Cuarón's *The Children of Men* (2006), Mark Fisher wrote that the film, which brought D. James' novel to the big screen, eloquently displayed the hallmark of the new dystopian imagination. Fisher observed that "Once, dystopian films and novels were exercises in such acts of imagination—the disasters they depicted acting as narrative pretext for the emergence of different ways of living" (Fisher 2009, 9). In contrast, the world foreshadowed by Cuarón's film "seems more like an extrapolation or exacerbation of ours than an alternative to it", a scenario that reflects "the suspicion that the end has already come, the thought that it could well be the case that the future harbors only reiteration and re-permutation" (*ibidem*). Not all contemporary dystopias can be traced back to what Fisher claims is the hallmark of capitalist realism. Consider a film like James McTeigue's *V for Vendetta*, which depicts a world dominated by a ruthless despotic regime. Nevertheless, it is quite likely that the genre's fortunes are linked to a famous phrase attributed to Fredric Jameson and Slavoj Žižek, that at the beginning of the 21st century, "it is easier to imagine the end of the world than it is to imagine the end of capitalism" (*ibidem*). "From the moment the division of the world into two 'blocs' ends and the alternative between capitalism and communism falls," wrote Francesco Muzzioli fifteen years ago, "the collective imagination becomes incapable of thinking of the future, except in terms [..] of the end of the world," in the sense that triumphant capitalism "is also a capitalism left 'alone in the world,' which in its solitude cannot avoid mirroring itself in the nightmare of its own collapse" (Muzzioli 2007, 12).

Since they began to define the canon of a new genre at the end of the 19th century, 20th-century dystopian narratives assumed a critical role concerning the promises of progress, the great utopian projects of social transformation, and the utopias that materialised in 20th-century totalitarianisms (Arciero 2005; Baccolini and Moyland 2003; Battaglia 1998; Battaglia 2006; Brooker 1994; Ceretta 2001; Claeys 2010; 2017; Guardamagna 1980; Kumar 1995; Stock 2019). The aim of 20th-century dystopia—often openly and visibly political—was therefore above all to warn against the illusions of progress and the promises of utopias, although dystopian scenarios took on a different profile depending on the specific utopian horizon toward which the polemic was directed. Instead, the fascination that dystopias exert on the world in the 21st century is probably connected to our perception of the future, one that underwent a radical reorientation after 1989 as compared to the 20th-century. In 1989, Norberto Bobbio wrote that there was not simply the crisis of a few authoritarian regimes founded on a socialist ideology, but it revealed "the total reversal of a utopia, of the greatest political utopia in history [...] into its exact opposite. [...] The first utopia that tried to enter history, to pass from the realm of 'discourses' to the realm of things, [...] not only did not come true but is being overturned, has almost been overturned, in the countries in which it has been put to the test, into something that has come increasingly to resemble the negative utopias, which have also existed so far only in discourses" (Bobbio 1989, 1). Because of the collapse of socialist regimes, even the very image of historical progress underwent a radical transformation from which any promise of future palingenesis was expunged, as well as the idea that the future could be significantly better than the present. Placed within this perception of the future, contemporary dystopias continue playing the critical role that marked the birth of this genre, starting with the classic novels of Zamjatin, Huxley, and Orwell. At the same time, they update the maps of fears and anxieties, broadening the spectrum well beyond the nightmare of a new totalitarian power.

When Francis Fukuyama, over three decades ago, saw the end of the Cold War as a sign of the "end of History," he was not referring to the end of history as a succession of events, conflicts, crises, and scientific discoveries, but, more specifically, to history as a "single, coherent, evolutionary process, when taking into account the experience of all peoples in all times" (Fukuyama 1992, xii). The endpoint of History, in this perspective, is therefore not the end of events, but the achievement of that condition in which the fundamental principles and institutions, capable of solving humanity's problems, have finally been conquered. It was precisely in this sense that Fukuyama was able to claim that History had come to a halt during the months in which the Soviet bloc had dissolved, collapsing the last great antagonist of the liberal democratic project. Hegel had argued that History had ended in 1806, on the day of the Battle of Jena, because with that battle, the ideals of the American and French revolutions had defeated the old aristocratic world and, above all, had made a new social model triumph — one based on a universal and reciprocal recognition, according to which each citizen recognises the dignity as a human being of all other citizens, and this dignity is in turn recognised by the state through the granting of rights (Fukuyama 1992). Fukuyama merely updated the Hegelian formula, shifting the date of the conclusion of History to 1989, because it was at that very moment that Western liberal democracy was indeed revealed as the "end point of mankind's ideological evolution" and the "final form of human government" (Fukuyama 1992, xi). The defeat of authoritarian regimes — based on nationalist ideologies or variants of Marxist-Leninist ideology — signified something more than the mere attrition of the conditions of existence of strong states — i.e., centralised states endowed with a sizeable bureaucracy and capable of exercising strict control over society. That defeat effectively meant the victory of liberal democracy over every other contender. "As mankind approaches the end of the millennium, the twin crises of authoritarianism and socialist central planning," Fukuyama wrote, "have left only one competitor standing in the ring as an ideology of potentially universal validity: liberal democracy, the doctrine of individual freedom and popular sovereignty" (ivi, 63). It was not simply a political victory because Western liberal democracy had won the ideological contest that had marked the 20th century, clearing the field of all ideologies that had portrayed the future in different terms. After that victory, liberal democracy — in the form established by Western experience — could become the only alternative in which the future of humanity was conceivable, as well as desirable. "In our grandparents' time, many reasonable people could foresee a radiant socialist future in which private property and capitalism had been abolished," Fukuyama observed, whereas today, "by contrast, we have trouble imagining a world that is radically better than our own, or a future that is not essentially democratic and capitalist" (Fukuyama, 1992, 67). "We can also imagine future worlds that are significantly worse that what we know now," but "we cannot picture to ourselves a world that is *essentially* different from the present one, and at the same time better" (Fukuyama 1992, 68).

In the more than thirty years since it was first formulated, Fukuyama's thesis—often reduced by critics to a caricature—has been challenged and refuted dozens, perhaps even hundreds of times, and on several occasions—after 11 September, 2001, after the outbreak of the global financial crisis of 2008 or the Covid-19 pandemic, or more recently, on the occasion of Russia's military aggression against Ukraine—the "return of History" has been hailed. On the other hand, the first two decades of the 21st century have seriously undermined the optimism of the 1990s, because the difficulties encountered by the democratisation process have revealed how the planetary victory of Western liberal democracy was much less solid than was hoped for at the time, since a veritable global democratic recession has taken shape, and autocratic powers old and new have once again come to play a leading role on the world stage (Palano 2019a). In spite of such striking signs, which seem to testify that History has begun once again, it is indeed difficult to deny that the West has not continued to live, or at least to perceive itself, within a post-historical—and, for this reason, a largely post-political—world. In the thirty years since the Cold War ended, the West has never really ceased to live at the "end of history." In our eyes as Westerners, the ideological evolution of mankind is really over, while progress seems to have found its definitive political form in liberal democracy. Politically, the West can only think of progress in terms of preservation of the present institutional form. That is, it can conceive of it as a kind of expansion of the present conditions of well-being, an extension of the potential for consumption, or in terms of a lengthening of the average lifespan. But it cannot really conceive it outside the political-institutional-cultural perimeter of liberal democracy, nor can it project in a more or less distant future the attainment of true democracy, as the 20th-century ideological families — not only those of a socialist stamp — tended to do. Progress is in essence understood — more or less explicitly — only in terms of a preservation of present conditions, or at most as an adjustment aimed at preserving the condition we have achieved. The idea of the "end of History" thus restores, in a paradigmatic way, the ideological and emotional condition of a West able to perceive the future either as the preservation of the present in the face of growing internal and external threats, or in terms of catastrophe, of environmental and political apocalypse. Orphans of any idea of radical social transformation, of any hope of progress other than the perpetuation of the present, we Westerners are unable to conceive the future except with the contours of a difficult preservation of liberal democracy, or in those of the end of the world, cataclysm, barbarian invasions, and apocalypse. And it is probably within this post-historical horizon that one can recognise both the roots of today's fortune of dystopian narratives and the reasons that make them at least in part different from those of the past.

After all, it is not so surprising that old classics of the dystopian genre, such as George Orwell's *Nineteen Eighty-four*, Aldous Huxley's *Brave New World*, Margaret Atwood's *The Handmaid's Tale*, and even Nobel Prize winner Sinclair Lewis' *It Can't Happen Here*, have returned to bookshops, sometimes reaching the top of bestseller lists. The political rise of disruptive figures such as Donald Trump, the electoral success of the far right, and the growth of political polarisation in general, have suggested to some political scientists the hypothesis that some Western democracies are deconsolidating or that they are now even threatened by collapse (Levitsky and Ziblatt, 2019; Mounk 2018; Runciman, 2018). Those events, however, delivered a new fortune to those old dystopias that had imagined during the 20th century that democracy could give way to some form of despotism, or that moulded the sinister outlines of totalising powers, authoritarian regimes, and capillary control apparatuses. The interest in Orwell's old novel and in all the classics of 20th-century dystopian literature can indeed be considered an eloquent demonstration of the new attitude, which — not only in the United States — induces one to glimpse on the horizon a possible collapse of democratic regimes, or at least to look at the future of democracy with much more disquiet than in the recent past. In the same direction, it can be argued that some great dystopian and uchronic novels, such as *The Plot Against America, The Man in the High Castle, The Handmaid's Tale* and *Brave New World*, have given rise to television series with a greater impact, in some cases, on popular culture than older films produced for the big screen, such as Michael Radford's *Nineteen Eighty-Four* (1984) or François Truffaut's *Fahrenheit 451* (1966).

Nevertheless, the success of the dystopian genre cannot only be explained by evoking the conjuncture experienced by American politics, or by considering the pessimism with which the fate of liberal democracies has begun to be viewed. In fact, the repertoire of dystopian narratives has been considerably enriched compared to that of the 20th century, even long before the Covid-19 pandemic prompted Western governments to adopt exceptional measures in the early 2020s, making European and American metropolises resemble the sets of films such as *28 Days Later* or *I Am Legend*, thus rendering the gloomy scenarios of dystopian narratives increasingly realistic. In a recent book, the British political scientist David Runciman observed that our political imaginations of the crisis of democracy "are stuck with outdated images of what democratic failure looks like" and that we "are trapped in the landscape of the twentieth century" (Runciman 2018, 2). That is, we are stuck in a scenario shaped by the ways in which the collapse of liberal democratic institutions materialised in the years between the two world wars in Italy and Germany, or if anything, by the ways in which the armed forces seized power in Latin America, Africa, and Asia between the 1950s and 1970s. Updating such an imaginary requires relativising the 20th-century experience without forgetting history, but bearing in mind that today's societies have very different characteristics—demographic, cultural, economic, and technological— from those that Europe had a century ago. Responses to tensions are likely to take very different directions from those experienced during the twenty years between the two World Wars. Similarly, confronting dystopian imaginaries today—and also grasping their political significance at different levels—means recognising the radical changes that have occurred in the languages with which dystopian narratives are articulated, and in the recipients to whom these productions are addressed. Although the political climate following Trump's rise in the United States has contributed to the revival of old dystopian narratives and the dystopias of the past continue to play a significant role in the contemporary imagination, it would be superficial to crush the prevalent dystopias in 21st-century popular culture into the silhouette of an Orwellian Big Brother. By relativising the weight of those old dystopian scenarios, we can succeed in recognising the political role of contemporary dystopias—their capacity to shape imaginaries and to play an implicit political role, not confined to pure entertainment but also not ascribable to the register of committed criticism, which was the hallmark of 20th-century dystopian production.

In reconstructing the trajectories followed by dystopian narratives, it is essential to identify criteria that make it possible to establish, as far as possible, the genre's distinctive characteristics (Abdelbaky 2016). In general, every dystopia describes a future society marked by an accomplished and relatively stable internal organisation, as well as various forms of oppressive control, that contribute to a strongly negative representation of such a society. According to a recent proposal, a typical dystopian narrative is characterised by the presence of a controlling power (usually an authoritarian government, but it can also be a global corporation, a church, or another entity) that oppresses citizens and intervenes in their lives in various ways, including—but not necessarily—through the exploitation of their labour (Trotta, Filipovic and Sadri 2021, 4). Apocalyptic narratives are also often intertwined with dystopian narratives but have qualifying features that clearly distinguish them: the classic apocalyptic narrative envisages that a catastrophic event—or a series of catastrophic events—causes (or has caused) the collapse of social structures to such proportions that mankind is plunged into a ruthless struggle for survival and into a world in which each individual has to cope alone with all vital needs (Trotta, Filipovic and Sadri 2021, 4-5). Moreover, there are frequent intersections between the two genres: a great catastrophe may, for instance, give rise to the construction of a new social organisation with dystopian features, while a dystopian society may collapse, materialising an apocalyptic scenario (Giuliani 2015; Haldaway and Scaglioni 2017; Palano 2017).

In schematic terms, one can identify some major stages in the development of dystopian literature, distinguishing between three phases. First, during the season of modern dystopia (1800-1950), narratives focus on the problems triggered by industrialisation and collectivism. Second, the season of postmodern dystopia (1950-2000) is marked by the emergence of significant themes, such as the relationship between the self and others and, more generally, the disconnect between reality and perception. Finally, the season of contemporary dystopia (from 2000 to the present) defines a world often marked by apocalyptic traits in which leading female figures frequently emerge (Barton 2016). Beyond these stages, it is important to bear in mind that dystopian imaginaries, as Manuela Ceretta points out, have undergone a series of radical transformations in recent decades, making today's dystopian narratives markedly different from those of the twentieth century. First, a macroscopic transformation concerns the audience, for whom very heterogeneous media products are addressed, which include—in addition to novels—TV series, comics, manga, or video games. If the first generation of dystopian authors (Evgenij Zamjatin, Aldous Huxley, Katharine Burdekin, Karin Boye, Ayn Rand, George Orwell, and Ray Bradbury) had written for the adult world, contemporary dystopian production is aimed at a very different audience. The dystopian turn of the 21st century has opened up to young adults, creating a form of trans-generational literature (Attimonelli and Susca 2020; Carluccio and Ortoleva 2010; Ilardi 2016; 2018). Striking examples include Suzanne Collins' *The Hunger Games* tetralogy, Veronica Roth's *Divergent* trilogy, and Lois Lowry's *The Giver*. Another change has been the emergence of critical dystopias and the increasing role of female writers in dystopian fiction, such as Ursula K. Le Guin, Octavia E. Butler, Naomi Alderman, and Christina Dalcher. Additionally, dystopian fiction aimed at young adults has incorporated themes related to the depletion of the planet's resources and the Anthropocene crisis. A more recent change has delved into the issue of power, especially the growing role of technology and artificial intelligence in governing economic and social organisations.

The dystopian imagination continues to emphasise fear, showing how it is the lever through which despotic power can impose control over individuals. This is evident in classic dystopias like Zamjatin's, Orwell's, and Bradbury's, as well as in Burdekin's *The Night of the Swastika*, Rand's *Anthem*, Boye's *Kallocain*, Moore's *V for Vendetta*, Collins' *The Hunger Games*, and Sansal's *2084*. Examining the serial production of the early 21st century from a geopolitical perspective, Dominique Moïsi has highlighted how fear — more specifically, a multifaceted fear — serves as the central theme in many of the most well-known TV series, including non-dystopian ones. This encompasses "the fear of chaos and a return to barbarism, […] the fear of decline linked to the crisis of democracy, […] the fear of terrorism and the question of the nature of the threat and the identity of the enemy, […] the fear of descending into another world order, accompanied by nostalgia for a bygone order, […] [and] the fear of Russian occupation" (Moïsi 2017, 44-45). Alongside this predominant theme, there is also a minority thread that traces its origins to *Brave New World* and extends to novels such as Michel Houellebecq's *Submission*. It is characterised by dystopias that "imagine and represent the process of individualization, atomization, and infantilization of society," encompassing "materialistic, hedonistic dystopias of opulence, satiety, tedium, boredom, and anxiety rather than fear" (Ceretta 2018b, 185). In any case, due to this complex set of transformations in audiences, registers, and themes, contemporary dystopias "investigate not only the 'who' but the 'what,' focusing on the mechanisms accompanying the process as well as the decision-makers" (Ceretta 2022b, 83). In engaging with social contexts where the mechanisms of exercising power take on unprecedented forms compared to the past, the new dystopias, as Ceretta observes, strive to "give a face to the threats looming over democracies, centering their imaginaries on the commitment to rethink power beyond the dichotomies of violence-fear, dominators-dominated, culprits-victims, masters-servants, in order to look beyond the specter of totalitarianism that haunted much of 20th-century dystopian literature" (Ceretta 2022b, 83).

Although political scholars have rarely focused on these aspects, such an investigation could likely provide valuable insights into key phenomena of contemporary politics, particularly the dynamics of public opinion polarisation and the methods of mobilisation within the context of the "bubble democracy," wherein the audience fragments into largely separate and self-referential niches (Palano 2020; 2022). Despite the long-recognised deep interpenetration between entertainment and political information, the discourse has only partially expanded to consider the role of fictional narratives in shaping political behaviours during an era marked by the weakening of traditional ideological coordinates and the emergence of more flexible representations of society and its conflicts compared to those provided by 20th-century ideologies. The success experienced by neopopulist movements over the past decade has led many scholars to acknowledge that ideologies tend to re-emerge as thin-centered: loosely structured narratives with a thin conceptual core, yet still capable of delineating lines of conflict and often closely connected to portrayals of future scenarios. Various studies have shown, for instance, that the ability to politically mobilise perceptions of risk (economic, cultural, social) plays a crucial role in determining the success of outsider candidates and formations. However, contemporary reflection has not yet adequately considered how representations of the future—optimistic, pessimistic, utopian, or dystopian—influence contemporary thin ideologies, nor has it sufficiently explored the channels that help direct risk perception, shape expectations, and define models of society.

By intersecting the paths of political science reflection on neo-populism and drawing from Cultural Studies, it may be possible to focus on the clash of narratives in popular culture and political communication. This approach could identify continuities and discontinuities with Western modernity and develop comparative elements with non-European contexts. Several studies have shown that many users tend to treat fictional narratives and non-fictional information similarly, incorporating information from both into their cognitive structure of the real world and resulting behaviour. Precisely because they are so widespread in the contemporary imagination, dystopian narratives—while not performing the function that more structured ideologies fulfilled in the past — provide a stylised representation of society and its distortions. In this sense, they can play a political role and feed contemporary ideologies, even if configured as thin-centered ideologies. Adopting a minimalist conception, one can conceive of ideology as "a more or less coherent set of ideas that provides the basis for organized political action, whether this is intended to preserve, modify or overthrow the existing system of power" (Heywood 2007, 11). Furthermore, ideologies typically exhibit three main characteristics: "a) They offer an account of the existing order, usually in the form of a 'world view'; b) They advance a model of a desired future, a vision of the 'good society'; c) They explain how political change can and should be brought about — how to move from a) to b)" (Heywood 2007, 11-12). Of course, dystopias cannot fulfill all these tasks, but by depicting a sinister world, they help identify present enemies. Some 20th-century dystopias — starting with 1984 — contributed significantly to redefining the democratic imagination, sculpting the silhouette of a totalitarianism capable of nullifying individual autonomy. Today, that role becomes even more significant, as contemporary dystopias help shape political visions of the present and future.

As Charli Carpenter has shown, in political debates and battles over limiting the use of fully automatic armaments, the imagery of science fiction plays a constitutive role, with arguments drawing on representations of the human-machine relationship provided by science fiction narratives (Carpenter 2012; 2014). Dystopian narratives could also direct specific political behaviour or foster specific attitudes. As Calvert W. Jones and Celia Paris have demonstrated, dystopias such as *The Hunger Games* and *Divergent* do not seem to foster attitudes of political cynicism but rather orient towards legitimising protest against perceived injustices. "Dystopian fiction appears to subtly expand the political imagination of viewers and readers to encompass a range of scenarios outside the normal realm of democratic politics," they noted, "and what people then consider reasonable and thinkable appears to expand accordingly" (Jones and Paris 2018, 983). Beyond the implications dystopian imaginaries may have on democratic politics, these authors highlight an interesting area of study. They invite consideration of how fictional representations—especially dystopian ones—feed into political imaginaries and integrate within contemporary thin-centered ideologies, even surrogating the role that 20th-century heavy ideologies no longer fulfill. As representations of the good society of the future tend to lose political grip—with the good society projected more into the past or present—the battle over the representation of the future shifts. Dystopias, while not able to say what goal to pursue positively, can define what a good society should not be, identifying present threats to avoid a hellish future.

The importance of dystopian narratives in contemporary imaginaries is reason enough to map the multiple forms this transmedia genre has taken over the past thirty years. However, it is also time to consider dystopian narratives from another perspective to grasp the relevance that dystopias have progressively gained: a relevance that is political and can no longer be circumscribed only to the critical function vis-à-vis the (imagined or realised) utopias of the 20th century. On the terrain of the politicalness of the dystopian imaginary, extraordinary possibilities for fruitful collaboration between different disciplinary fields, such as media studies and political investigation, are emerging. Based on these insights, a heterogeneous group of researchers from different disciplines launched the project titled *The Clash of Narratives. The representation of the future in popular culture and traditional media and their political use*, financed by the Università Cattolica del Sacro Cuore and carried out by a large group of scholars. I would particularly like to highlight the teams from the Certa Research Center, directed by Massimo Scaglioni, and Polidemos (Center for the Study of Democracy and Political Change), which I direct. This volume, edited by Valerio Alfonso Bruno, Antonio Campati, Paolo Carelli, and Anna Sfardini, is a result of our work and, in particular, the rich discussions that took place during the international conference *Dystopian Worlds Beyond Storytelling. Representations of Dehumanized Societies in Literature, Media, and Political Discourses. Multidisciplinary Perspectives*, held at the Università Cattolica del Sacro Cuore in Milan on September 15-16, 2022.

Our objectives in developing the project were twofold: first, to investigate the dynamics through which the old models of the good society adopted by 20th-century ideological families are being replaced — or integrated — with materials mediated by popular culture; and second, to explore how representations of the future influence elites and political choices. Specifically, the project aimed to study the transformations in representations of the future in traditional media and the narratives that coalesce through digital media, focusing on mutations and negations of the relationship with the past, human-machine and interindividual relationships, transformations of power, global dynamics, and environmental conditions. In general, the focus has been on the representations of the future present in the ideological heritage of 20th-century cultures and political families (utopias, dystopias, past futurisms, declinism, etc.) and the role of popular culture (genre fiction, cinema, comics, TV series) in defining contemporary socio-political imaginaries.

The work we have initiated, which traverses an important milestone in this volume, is still in its early stages. The mapping of contemporary dystopian narratives is still in its beginning, as is the investigation into the interactions between contemporary political ideologies and dystopian imaginaries. For this reason, besides attempting to account for the pervasive penetration of dystopian narratives in the 21st-century imagination, this volume aims to encourage further investigation and to take seriously the political role that dystopias can play in the contemporary world.

References

Abdelbaky, Ashraf. 2016. "A Perfect World or an Oppressive World. A Critical Study of Utopia and Dystopia as Subgenres of Science". *International Journal of English Language, Literature and Humanities* 3, 17-33.

Arciero, Angelo. 2005. *George Orwell: «contro il totalitarismo e per un Socialismo democratico»*. Milan: Franco Angeli.

Attimonelli, Claudia, and Susca, Vincenzo. 2020. *Un oscuro riflettere. Black Mirror e l'aurora digitale*. Milan: Mimesis.

Baccolini, Raffaella, and Moylan, Tom. 2003. *Dark Horizon. Science Fiction and the Dystopian Imagination*. New York-London: Routledge.

Barton, Riven. 2016. "Dystopia and the Promethean Nightmare", in MacKay Demerjian, 5-18.

Battaglia, Beatrice. 1998. *Nostalgia e mito nella distopia inglese. Saggi su Oliphant, Wells, Forster, Orwell, Burdekin*. Ravenna: Longo Editore.

Battaglia, Beatrice. 2006. *La critica alla cultura occidentale nella letteratura distopica inglese*. Ravenna: Longo Editore.

Bobbio, Norberto, 1989. "L'utopia capovolta". *La Stampa*, 9 June, 1.

Brooker, M. Keith. 1994. *The Dystopian Impulse in Modern Literature*. Greenwood: Wesport.

Carluccio, Giulia Anastasia and Ortoleva, Giuseppe. 2010. *Diversamente vivi. Zombi, vampiri, mummie, fantasmi*. Milan: Il Castoro.

Carpenter, Charli. 2012. "Game of Thrones as Theory", Foreign Affairs, (available online at https://www.foreignaffairs.com/articles/2012-03-29/game-thrones-theory).

Carpenter, Charli. 2014. 'Lost' Causes: Agenda-Vetting in Global Issue Networks and the Shaping of Human Security. Ithaca New York: Cornell University Press.

Ceretta, Manuela. 2018a. "Non è un paese per bambini? Cenni su alcune recenti trasformazioni della letteratura distopica". *Cosmopolis. Rivista di filosofia e teoria politica*, 1-2.

Ceretta, Manuela. 2018b. "Tra Huxley e Tocqueville: *Sottomissione* di Michel Houellebecq", in Ilardi, Loche e Marras (eds.), 175-203.

Ceretta, Manuela. 2022a. "Il «profumo» della servitù. Universi distopici e «servitù fai da te»". *Filosofia politica*, 1, 69-84.

Ceretta Manuela. 2022b. "Immaginario distopico e crisi europea. Riflessioni a partire da *Soumisson* di Houellbecq". *Storia del pensiero politico*, 1, 81-89.

Ceretta, Manuela. 2001. "Contro Bellamy. Le distopie americane di fine Ottocento: fra conservatorismo, realismo politico e critica della progettazione utopica", in B. Bongiovanni and G.M. Bravo (eds) *Nell'anno 2000. Dall'utopia all'ucronia*. Firenze: Olschki, 149-165.

Claeys, Gregory. 2017. *Dystopia. A Natural History. A Study of Modern Dispotism, Its Antecendents, and Its Literary Diffractions*. Oxford: Oxford University Press.

Claeys, Gregory. 2010. "The origins of dystopia: Wells, Huxley and Orwell", in *The Cambridge Companion to utopian literature*. Cambridge: Cambridge University Press.

Fisher, Mark. 2009. *Capitalist Realism: Is There No Alternative?* London: John Hunt Publishing.

Fukuyama, Francis. *The End of History and the Last Man*. New York: The Free Press, 1992.

Giuliani, Gregory. 2015. *Zombie, alieni e mutanti. Le paure dall'11 settembre a oggi*. Firenze: Le Monnier.

Guardamagna, Daniela. 1980. *Analisi dell'Incubo. L'utopia negativa da Swift alla fantascienza*. Rome: Bulzoni Editore.

Heywood, Andrew. 2007. *Political Ideologies. An Introduction*. New York: Palgrave.

Holdaway, Dom and Scaglioni, Massimo. 2017. *The Walking Dead. Contagio culturale e politica post-apocalittica*. Milan-Udine: Mimesis.

Ilardi, Emiliano. 2016. "L'adolescenza è morta. Serialità e transmedialità nelle saghe fantascientifiche del XXI secolo: Hunger Games, Divergent, La Trilogia del Silo, Maze Runner". *Mediascapes Journal*, 7, 62-69.

Ilardi, Emiliano. 2018. "Adolescenti di tutto il mondo armatevi. La paura per la guerra civile nelle distopie fantascientifiche del XXI secolo", in E. Ilardi, A. Loche and M. Marras (eds), 225-254.

Ilardi, Emiliano,. Loche, Annamaria,. and Marras, Martina. 2018. *Utopie mascherate. Da Rousseau a «Hunger Games»*. Milan: Meltemi.

Jones, Calvert V. and Paris, Celia. 2018. "It's the End of the World and They Know It: How Dystopian Fiction Shapes Political Attitudes", *American Political Science Association*, 16(4), 969-989.

Kumar, Krishan. 1995. *Utopia e Antiutopia. Wells, Huxley, Orwell*. Ravenna: Longo Editore.

Levitsky, Steven and Ziblatt, Daniel. 2019. *Come muoiono le democrazie*. Rome-Bari: Laterza.

Mackay Demerijan, L. 2016. *The Age of Dystopia. One Genre, Our Fears and Our Future*. Newcastle upon Tyne: Cambridge Scholars Publishing.

Moïsi, Dominique. 2017. *La geopolitica delle serie tv. Il trionfo della paura*. Rome: Armando (ed. or. 2016).

Mounk, Yascha. 2018. *The People vs. Democracy: Why Our Freedom is in Danger and how to Save it*. Cambridge: Harvard University Press.

Moylan, Tom. 2000. *Scraps of the Untained Sky: Science Fiction. Utopia, Dystopia*. Boulder: Westview.

Muzzioli, Francesco. 2007. *Scritture della catastrofe*. Milan: Meltemi.

Palano, Damiano. 2017. "Apocalisse zombie. La metamorfosi della paura nell'immaginario «postpolitico» contemporaneo". *Rivista di Politica*, 2, 161-176.

Palano, Damiano. 2019a. "The «Democratic Recession» and the Crisis of Liberalism", *in* A. Colombo and P. Magri (eds.), *The End of a World. The Decline of the Liberal Order*. Milan: Ledi, 37-50.

Palano, Damiano. 2019b. "The Truth in a Bubble. The end of «audience democracy» and the rise of «bubble democracy»". *Soft Power*, 2, 37-52.

Palano, Damiano. 2019c. "La fin du «public», la bubble democracy et la nouvelle polarisation", in C. Delsol and G. De Ligio (eds), *La démocratie dans l'adversité. Enquête internationale*. Paris: Cerf, 699-715.

Palano, Damiano. 2020. "Apocalisse democratica. Pensare la «fine della democrazia» dopo la pandemia". *Power and Democracy*, 2, 4-28.

Palano, Damiano. 2022. *Towards a Bubble Democracy? Notes for a Theoretical Framework*. Milan: Educatt.

Runciman, David. 2018. *How Democracy Ends*. London: Profile Books.

Stock, Adam. 2019. *Modern Dystopian Fiction and Political Thought. Narratives of World Politics*. London: Routledge.

Trotta, Joe,. Filipovic, Zlatan,. and Sadri, Houman. 2020. "Introduction: Welcome to the Begining of the End of Everything", in J. Trotta, Filipovic, Z., and Sadri, H. (eds.), *Broken Mirrors. Representations of Apocalypses and Dystopias in Popular Culture*. London: Routledge, 1-14.

Introduction

Dystopian Worlds: A Multidisciplinary Approach to Analyse Transformations in Literature, Media and Politics

Valerio Alfonso Bruno, Antonio Campati, Paolo Carelli, Anna Sfardini

In the last several decades, political and social discourses as well as media and cultural productions have been characterized by a growing emphasis on dystopian worlds and "possible universes" (Moylan and Baccolini 2013; Trotta, Filipovic and Sadri 2020; Palano 2022) as tools to describe the fears and contradictions human beings face regarding the uncertainty of the future and the reworkings of the past and memory. The Covid-19 pandemic and climatic emergencies have accentuated this process, not only in the direction of health and epidemiological and environmental topics but, more generally, towards a reconfiguration of new imaginaries about catastrophes and other social, cultural and technological upheavals (McKenzie and Patulny 2022).

A multidisciplinary approach to the issue of dystopias and their representations in political debates and popular culture took shape in 2020 at Universita Cattolica del Sacro Cuore through a wide research project, "The clash of narratives. The representation of the future in popular culture and traditional media and its political use", directed by Professor Damiano Palano as principal investigator. As part of this project, also carried out through an interesting *Atlas of dystopian storytelling* (www.unicatt.it/atlante distopiemediali), this book adopts a strong multidisciplinary perspective, including media, political, literary, linguistic, sociological and cultural studies, to focus on the various ways the theme of dystopia has become relevant and pervasive in contemporary popular culture, both in traditional and digital forms, highlighting how it has changed across different languages and formats and also in the direction of a strong transmediality (novels, comics, movies, TV series, video games, digital and social platforms, political discourses and so on).

Dystopian societies have always been present in literature, film and media studies, but they undeniably emerged in abundance in recent cultural productions as a result of deep social and political transformations that occurred in Western and non-Western societies after the collapse of twentiethcentury ideologies (Moisi 2015) and traumatic events, such as the 9/11 attack and the pandemic crisis. Thus, as part of the rise of what Wojtyna (2018) called a "dystopian turn", new narratives have emerged, often representing neopopulist or conspiracy theories on one hand and an apocalyptic future or "parallel present" on the other. The scenario of popular culture products reflects and also stokes contemporary fears and anxieties within a society characterized by the domain of the technique, migrations and nomadic processes, democratic and environmental crises and health emergencies—all aspects that underline the fragility of our societies and reconfigure the concepts of space (productions and representations of places, both real and fictional) and time (the roles of the past, present and future in dystopian media narratives)—providing a cartography of complex trajectories and hybridizations of media, genres and discourses of dystopia in popular culture and social practices.

As Lyman Tower Sargent stated, dystopian narratives represent a sort of "negative utopia" and primarily refer to "a non-existent society described in detail and normally located in time and space, which the author wants the contemporary reader sees as considerably worse than the society in which the reader lives" (Sargent 1994: 9). Therefore, the representation of dystopian worlds aims at projecting into an apocalyptic future what happened in the past and reading events through the lens of new fears of contemporary times (Giuliani 2016). On these continuous fluctuations between real and non-real on one hand and the past and the future on the other, this book aims to answer crucial questions about the representation of contemporary societies in political and cultural theory and practice.

Structure of the Book

This collected book contains the proceedings of a conference held at Universita Cattolica del Sacro Cuore of Milan in September 2022. The conference was an occasion of dialogue and discussion among several disciplines involved in the study of dystopias and their relevance in the contemporary scenario. The "Dystopian Worlds beyond Storytelling" project—involving political theorists, sociologists, historians, linguists, literature scholars, media, communications and performing arts researchers, and many others—was born around the convergence of multiple fields of analysis, signalling the heterogeneity and richness of the phenomena underlying the fears of contemporary societies and their representations and discourses in public debate and popular culture. The book is structured in five parts, each one expressing a particular point of view on the role of dystopias in the twenty-first century. These parts are not sectorial, since our aim is to provide a transdisciplinary focus on the issue of dystopia in reading through the lens of a wide range of perspectives and extracting a pluralistic vision of such a complex theme.

The first part of the book, as the title suggests, presents contemporary debates about and models of political orders and techno-dystopias. In the first essay, Manuela Ceretta compares nineteenth–twentieth century technological dystopias and contemporary digital dystopias, arguing that we are witnessing the demise of the technological paradigm established by these nineteenth–twentieth century dystopias. In the second essay, Vassilis Galanos guides readers on a journey into artificial intelligence (AI), connecting six key arguments "concerned with the experiential interplay between expectations about exponential growth, expanding experts and expatriated researchers, most of them explorers but not exploiters". In the third essay, Paola Dalla Torre argues that bioethics, a science that addresses the questions posed by the techno-human condition in contemporary times, finds in science fiction films a popular way to reach the public and make its questions known, and identifies the different perspectives with which it addresses them. In the fourth essay, Romina Perni examines three contemporary dystopian works—two episodes of the *Black Mirror* series and Dave Eggers' novel *The Circle*—arguing that when transparency becomes more pervasive, the possibility of its erosion becomes more concrete, bringing out its extreme fragility, and as inner/private and public spaces become totally transparent, human freedom seems to be resized and its limits redefined. In the fifth essay, Enrico Reggiani analyses the novel *Notes from a Coma* (2005) by Irish writer Mike McCormack, showing how it can be seen as generating a twenty-first-century narrative actualization of the sub-genre of "biopolitical dystopia". In the sixth essay, Marco Milani analyses the historical, political and economic causes of the rising inequality in South Korea and related cultural products, focusing specifically on how inequalities have been represented in films and TV shows, to grasp the origins of the conflicts and tensions of contemporary Korean society, why they have influenced cultural production so much and how they have been represented on screen.

The second part investigates how the rise of technologies on one hand and the apocalyptic societies emerging from catastrophes on the other could lead to a progressive weakening of human beings and their relationships and connotations. Dehumanization is a process that we can retrace in audiovisual representations (animated movies and series fall under this label by definition) and, in the worst imaginary, is tied to some technological shifts during the history of humanity and societies. In the first essay of this section, Ivana Mette explores a specific case of adaptation—that is, *La terra dei figli*, an Italian graphic novel that was subsequently adapted into a movie. The author underlines the difference between the two products, emphasizing how the landscapes represented in them act as narrative tools for reconfiguring identities completely dehumanized by catastrophic scenarios. Matteo Quinto and Raffaele Chiarulli, respectively, in the second and the third chapters of this part, focus on the specific language of animation. Quinto analyses how the hybridization of humans and robots takes form in some recent products, while Chiarulli provides a critical reading of the animated movie *Wall•E*, an example of a future society subjugated to the dominance of a new techno-economic paradigm. Alessandro Dividus investigates the "coming of machines" and the connection between nineteenth-century British writer Samuel Butler and contemporary American writer George Dyson in an essay adopting a philosophical and techno-scientific approach to show that the thoughts of two writers so distant in time must be considered in a line of continuity. Then, in the fifth chapter of this second section, Ivo Stefano Germano and Massimiliano Panarari focus on the concept of "retrotopia", as defined by Zygmunt Bauman (2017) as a sort of idealization of the past. The authors apply this concept to the genre of science fiction, highlighting some cases of film remakes as paradigmatic of this drift and striving to read this process through the cultural trend of "collapsology" to thematize the decomposition of urban spaces and its impact on human relationships in civil society and the way people cope with the uncertainty of the future.

The third part contains six essays reflecting upon the contrast between real and unreal within literary and dramatic products. Literary novels, theatre works, aesthetic representations of bodies and costumes in media and audiovisual storytelling are all ways to conceive of dystopia as a creative form of narrating the world's contradictions. In the first essay of this section, Patricia Chiantera-Stutte provides a detailed account of the process of refoundation of individual and collective moralities in Saramago's *Blindness*, observing the interdependence of the individual's and the group's regenerations of a moral world in a state of nature. In the second essay, Lorenzo Marra compares two Italian alternative history novels—*Asse Pigliatutto* (1973) by Lucio Ceva and *Contro-passato prossimo* (1975) by Guido Morselli—and argues that the two should be considered modern nexus stories as her topic reflects a postmodern point of view with the link between subtle satire and a detailed analysis of war events, which is not comparable to the works of the previous century. In his essay, Luca Gendolavigna focuses on the recent trend in Swedish literature of describing a drift and future scenarios where debates on migration, tolerance, climate change and democratic crises are taken to their extremes, analysing in depth the works of two authors: Johannes Anyuru and Jens Lapidus. The issue of body representation in a dystopian frame is introduced in

Silvia Leonzi, Fabio Ciammella and Grazia Quercia's essay aimed at interpreting the role of the body within technodystopian narratives (e.g. cyberpunk) characterized by the overcoming of nature/culture and mind/body dualisms in order to narrate the contradictions of postmodern society. In the fifth essay, Jovana Malinarić approaches the concept of dystopia as an umbrella term encompassing thematically close concepts that often intertwine in artistic works which utilize dystopia to investigate the mechanisms of reality, analysing in which way they are employed in the performative writings of two artists from Lebanon: Lina Majdalanie and Rabih Mroue. This section closes with Maria Teresa Zanola's essay focusing on the capacity of fashion throughout history to anticipate the dystopian anxieties of any specific time as well as to announce the common trends in fears and anxieties. The author offers some examples taken from the eighteenth century and the "extreme contemporary" to illustrate the linguistic and semiotic functions of fashion as a creator of anticipatory signs of dystopian visions.

The fourth part of the book takes an in-depth look at "transmedia narratives" through six essays that examine different media and how dystopian themes are developed through their specific language. The first contribution, by Luca Barra, is dedicated to the TV miniseries *Years and Years* (BBC, 2019), an original mix of science fiction and crime drama with the narrative structure of a family drama and the distinctive tone of a black comedy and political satire. Set in the future, the series portrays a dystopian world buffeted by wars, pandemics, conspiracy theories and populist politics. The next two essays are also dedicated to TV series and examine a particular moment in recent history, the Covid-19 pandemic, which led to a focus on health emergency fears. Stefania Antonioni's essay analyses two TV series, *The Rain* (Netflix, 2018–2020) and *Anna* (Sky Italia, 2021), showing several points of similarity, starting with the common backdrop of a dystopian, apocalyptic future caused by the spread of an epidemic. Daniela Cardini explores the link between dystopia and nostalgia by highlighting the fundamental role of sitcoms and classic series in daily life during the lockdown as a means of escaping the uncertainties of our dystopian present, taking refuge in this nostalgic TV world. The fourth essay shifts the focus to radio and its ability to construct dystopian imaginary. Miriam Petrini delves into radio dystopia in the Italian cultural panorama, analysing two of Primo Levi's radio dramas, *Il versificatore* (1960) and *La bella addormentata nel frigo* (1961), and focusing on a more recent Teatro Valle project, *Scienza e fantascienza* (2021). Gianni Sibilla's essay offers an analysis of one of the most interesting expressions of transmedia musical narratives, the so-called "dystopic concept album": a group of songs with recurring characters and connected events used to represent dehumanized societies. His essay proposes examples such as Pink Floyd's *Animals* (1977, based on George Orwell's *The Animal Farm*), *The Wall* (1981) and, more recently, Muse's *Drones* (2015). The sixth and last essay of this section is dedicated to video games with a focus on one of the most influential and popular franchises, *Civilization VI* (Firaxis Games, 2016). Andrea Piano points out the dystopian nature of this game which forces the player to strive for victory, implying competition either with AI or other human players, showing how the pursuit of world domination can lead to starvation, devastation, war and ecological decadence.

In the fifth and last part of the book, we confront catastrophic and apocalyptic imaginaries. In the first essay, Joseph Trotta scrutinizes the term *dystopia/n*, assessing its substantive usage and questioning whether over-flexibility in its application to an expanding variety of imagined and reallife scenarios has caused a kind of semantic inflation, resulting in a depreciation of its essential meaning. In the second essay, Mario Tirino and Lorenzo Denicolai focus on "retro-mediation", defined as a media logic of reimagining the past, operating as retroactive remediation, through which users project symbols, icons and dystopian elements and conceivable as the "embodiment of a mass dystopian gaze on pre-pandemic cultural products, experienced in the light of the emotional experience of viral catastrophe and its aesthetics". In the third essay, Anja Boato attempts to provide a comprehensive overview of the applications of virtual reality to the narrative arts and describe the medium's peculiarities in creating dystopian worlds. In the fourth essay, Giovanni Bernardini analyses science fiction and nuclear dystopia between the 1950s and 1960s, and shows how the former contributed more than other genres of speculation to shaping atomic dystopia through characters, images and dynamics destined to remain in the collective imagination well beyond the boundaries of the literary genre. In the fifth essay, Mariangela La Manna critically assess, through the lens of international law and using a *law and literature* perspective, Kim Stanley Robinson's *The Ministry for the Future* (2020), focusing on the depiction of the structural limitations of international organizations before the climate challenge and on the inefficient enforcement mechanisms provided for under international law to react to internationally wrongful acts.

Acknowledgements

At the end of this collective effort, the editors wish to thank, first, all the authors of this collection for their fruitful and inspiring contributions to fully understand a multifaceted issue, spread through many disciplines and perspectives, and strongly topical for comprehending the past, present and future of our societies. Thanks also go to all the speakers who attended the conference "Dystopian Worlds beyond Storytelling. Representations of Dehumanized Societies in Literature, Media and Political Discourses: Multidisciplinary Perspectives" in September 2022 at Universita Cattolica del Sacro Cuore in Milan.

The conference from which these proceedings derive was made possible by the support of Universita Cattolica del Sacro Cuore. Therefore, the editors are grateful to Rector Magnificus Professor Franco Anelli and to the Deans of the Faculties of Political and Social Sciences and Foreign Languages and Literature, respectively, Professor Guido Merzoni and Professor Giovanni Gobber.

In addition, this book would not have been possible without the efforts of Damiano Palano and Massimo Scaglioni, who enriched these pages with a preface and an afterword. Together with them, the editors wish to thank the other members of the Scientific Committee of the International Conference, some of whom are also active participants in the research already mentioned above in this introduction: Gabriele Balbi, Giovanni Boccia Artieri, Luca G. Castellin, Arturo Cattaneo, Fausto Colombo, Chiara Continisio, Ruggero Eugeni, Guido Gili, Giacomo Manzoli, Alberto Marinelli, Federica Missaglia, Andrea Minuz, Francesca Pasquali, Enrico

Reggiani, Nicoletta Vittadini and Maria Teresa Zanola. Lastly, thanks to the local organizing committee of the conference (Edoardo Maria Castelli, Maria Grazia Contu, Nicola Crippa, Joyce Faelli and Mattia Galli) and all the friends and colleagues who supported us in the realization of this book.

References

Bauman, Zygmunt. 2017. *Retrotopia*. Polity Press, Cambridge.

Giuliani, Gaia. 2016. *Zombie, alieni e mutanti. Le paure dall'11 settembre a oggi*. Le Monnier, Firenze.

McKenzie, Jordan and Patulny, Roger (eds.). 2022. *Dystopian Emotions. Emotional Landscapes and Dark Futures*. Bristol University Press, Bristol.

Moisi, Dominique. 2015. *La géopolitique des émotions*. Flammarion, Paris, 2nd edition.

Moylan, Tom and Baccolini, Raffaella (eds). 2013. *Dark Horizons. Science Fiction and the Dystopian Imagination*. Rouledge, New York.

Palano, Damiano (ed.). 2022. *Il futuro capovolto. Per una mappa degli immaginari distopici del XXI secolo*. Polidemos-Educatt, Milan.

Sargent, Lyman Tower. 1994. *The Three Faces of Utopianism Revisited*. "Utopian Studies", 5(1), 1- 37.

Trotta, Joseph, Filipovic, Zlatan and Sadri, Houman (eds.). 2020. *Broken Mirrors. Representations of Apocalypses and Dystopias in Popular Culture*. Routledge, New York.

Wojtyna, Miłosz. 2018. *Solidarity, Dystopia, and Fictional Worlds in Contemporary Narrative TV Series*. "Beyond Philology", 15, 3, 163-180.

***

Università Cattolica del Sacro Cuore contributed to the funding of this research project and its publication. This publication is made within the project "The clash of narratives. The representation of the future in popular culture and traditional media and its political use" – D.3.2 – 2020 – PI: prof. Damiano Palano.

Part 1:
Political Orders and Techno-Dystopias: Debates and Models

From *Darwin among the machines* to *Black Mirror*: Rise and Fall of a Technological Paradigm

Manuela Ceretta

Introduction

About twenty years ago, Raymond Trousson, an authoritative scholar of the dystopian tradition, wrote: "Dystopia found the same difficulties of bringing itself up to date after Zamjatin, Huxley and Orwell had defined its paradigms. Fifty years later, writers described the same obsessions and terrors of a threatening future" (Trousson 2000, 184). At the time of that statement, the Belgian scholar was probably right, but does his thesis still hold today? Are the dystopias of the third millennium recounting "the same obsessions and terrors" of half a century ago or are they introducing changes and perhaps even discontinuities with respect to the themes addressed by the dystopian tradition of the nineteenth and twentieth centuries?

It is my belief that contemporary dystopias are: 1. raising some original themes (I am thinking especially of all the issues related to the relationship among bodies, genders, generations, cultures and systems of domination); 2. proposing themes that were barely touched upon in the past, with completely new emphases and with unprecedented declensions (I am thinking in particular of eco-dystopias); 3. addressing 'old' problems which have been at the center of the dystopian narrative since its origins, but doing so from a radically innovative standpoint (I am thinking of the relationship among humans, technology and society).

This article addresses the last of the above three aspects. It does so by comparing the nineteenth-twentieth century technological dystopias and contemporary digital dystopias to argue that we are witnessing the demise of the technological paradigm established by nineteenth-twentieth century dystopia.

Before going into details, however, it is useful to clarify the meaning of the question relative to the changes and discontinuities introduced by contemporary dystopian narratives. The question does not concern measurement of the 'novelty' of contemporary dystopias in and of themselves; rather, it concerns determining whether the dystopias of the third millennium are still able to perform the function exercised by their forebears: that is, whether they are still able to express themselves with a critical voice with respect to society or not (Runciman 2018). The question that lies behind inquiry into the transformations of the dystopian technological paradigm therefore concerns the actual capacity to "historicize the present" of the dystopias of the third millennium (Jameson 2010).

In a dystopian-philiac era like ours, where dystopian worldviews are embraced by both mass culture and Nobel laureates or Goncourt prize-winners (such as José Saramago, Kazuo Ishiguro and Michel Houellebecq), asking whether such dystopian visions are helping us to penetrate more deeply into the problems of our time and to look at them with farsightedness is a problem worthy of interest. In fact, dystopias shape fictitious worlds that have a real impact on our attitudes and beliefs (Palano 2022). Moreover, as Dominique Moïsi has rightly observed, the images of a film or a television series "can prepare minds to understand the world much more than a book or an article" to the extent that they "render it concrete by making it visible"; but "they can also act in the direction opposite to understanding by fostering disinformation, denial of reality, or a shift of attention to what is irrelevant" (Moïsi 2017, 25). If this is the case, the imaginaries that interpenetrate our societies are a matter of major importance (Zizek 2018).

The Rise of the Dystopian Technological Paradigm

Between the second half of the 19th century and the beginning of the 20th, dystopia defined its technological paradigm. As a *quo* term for the definition of this paradigm, which looks with suspicion at the relationship among humans, technology and society, we can take the work of Simon Butler (1835-1902), author of a famous articled entitled *Darwin among the Machines* (1863), and of a satirical dystopia, *Erewhon* (1872). Instead, as the *ad quem* term we can identify the work by Edward Morgan Forster (1879-1970), *The Machine Stops* (1909). The theoretical principle on which this paradigm is based is the reversal of what has been called "Aristotle's dream" (Mari 2020).

In Book I of *Politics*, Aristotle had imagined that one day men, thanks to machines, would be able to re-appropriate for themselves a time 'freed' from the slavery of work and 'freed' from relationships of subordination (Aristotle, I, 4). Nineteenth-century dystopias no longer believed in this dream, which had been the vision of Francis Bacon and of the industrialist utopias of Robert Owen, Etienne Cabet, and Bellamy.

Since its inception, dystopian literature has expressed the demise of the belief that machines and technology are instruments of mankind's liberation. Aristotle's dream is reversed and, as Butler writes, the machines that we are endowing with the power to self-regulate and act autonomously, and which we already conceive as living creatures—as testified by the fact that we use the verb 'to feed' to describe the process of recharging—will sooner or later take the place of humans by wresting their supremacy on earth away from them (Butler, 1863). In *Erewhon*, an anagram of the word 'Nowhere' or perhaps, more suggestively, an anagram of the words 'here' and 'now' (Deleuze and Guattari, 1996) Butler imagined that sooner or later machines would be powered by patient slaves; they would have their doctors and when they died they would enter a new phase of existence (the circular economy!), at which point humans would be to them what dogs or horses are to humans (Butler, 1872).

It is difficult to find exceptions to this paradigm, which, on the one hand, conceives technology as a threat, a source of malaise and decadence and, on the other hand, seeks freedom outside it. Thus, in *Darwin among the Machines* Butler declares war without quarter against machines. With technophobic features and with overt or covert Luddite ambitions, all nineteenth and twentieth century dystopias imagined that technology, instead of being an instrument of liberation, would eventually become an instrument of domination and control of mankind by mankind and that it would develop its capacities against mankind itself. With different variations on the theme, and expressing different fears from time to time, dystopias have described the menacing nature of a technology that operates in both the body and the mind. In Zamjatin's *We* (1922), bio-technologies enabled the "great operation" which would definitively erase the human imagination; ten years later, *Brave New World* used a bio-genetic technique to weaken human capacity to produce the Epsilons (the exact opposite of what had cruelly tempted the infamous Doctor Moreau). During the second world war the Swedish writer Karin Boye imagined that pharmacological research would develop a truth drug able to make the minds of men and women finally transparent to the gaze of power, etc etc.

In this critical posture, which is by no means a prerogative of dystopian literature, but which distinguishes dystopia from science fiction — which remained imbued with a faith in science until the 1930s — many different factors converge. They concern the decline of the idea of progress, the fears generated by the rapid and profound changes caused by the first and second industrial revolutions, fears about the stability of the social order under the pressure of socialism and feminism, the new discoveries in biology, thermodynamics, and the impact of Darwinian evolutionism. Added to these is the precocious awareness exhibited by dystopian literature of what Günther Anders called the 'Promethean gap': the divide between the human capacity to produce ever more refined and deadly technologies and the parallel inadequate development of the ethical and judgmental skills necessary to keep those technologies under control (Anders 2007). In nineteenth and twentieth century dystopias, humanity appears caught between the sin of *hubris*, embodied by the science of Victor Frankenstein, and the risks of the age of machinery.

Even Forster, who with his ability to imagine the frontiers of technological development is perhaps the most visionary of all the authors mentioned, remains entirely within this paradigm. In a world totally controlled by the Machine, the inhabitants shun physical contacts, and the human being is destined to progressively lose contact with reality, which is gradually replaced by simulacra:

> The clumsy system of public gatherings had been long since abandoned; neither Vashti nor her audience stirred from their rooms. Seated in her armchair she spoke, while they in their arm-chairs heard her, fairly well, and saw her, fairly well (Forster 2011, 7).

The technological invasion of individual life is recounted with images that closely resemble the morning awakening of many adolescents or the end of a meeting that has disconnected us from the world:

> And there were of course the buttons by which she communicated with her friends. The rom, though it contained nothing, was in touch with all that she cared for in the world. Vashti's next move was to turn off the isolation-switch, and all the accumulations of the last three minutes burst upon her (Forster 2011, 6-7).

And yet, the tragic ending of *The Machine Stops* confirms that despite his visionary energy, Forster adhered to the technological paradigm that envisages a struggle between mankind and machinery in which freedom is at stake: the last words of Kuno (the rebellious son of Vashti), spoken after the Machine stopped, are in fact "Humanity has learnt its lesson" (Forster 2011, 55).

The Dystopias of the Digital Society: Sunset of the Technological Paradigm

At the centre of the dystopias that today focus on the transformations of digital society—I am thinking in particular of the *Black Mirror* TV series—there is the same issue as raised by the dystopias of the nineteenth and twentieth centuries: the problematic relationship among humans, technology and society. Moreover, they are flanked by the same apprehension about the Promethean gap that characterizes humans in their relationship with technology. Hence, at first sight, there is no discontinuity. Yet, upon closer inspection, this is not the case.

It is not the case for two reasons. Firstly, the dystopias of the digital society observe the same problem, but they do so by entering through a different 'front door'. The Promethean gap between the exceptional nature of the machine and the mediocrity of humans is mainly considered in terms of its anthropological effects: that is to say, the effects that it produces on individuals more than on society as a whole; or rather, on society, but through the grip that digital technologies exert on individuals taken individually. At the core of the narrative is the individual, not society.

Secondly, it is not the case because in the television series created by Charlie Brooker and broadcast between 2011 and 2019, mankind's titanic struggle against the machine has disappeared (Brooker, Jones and Arnopp, 2018). The armed resistance that Butler urges his readers to raise in *Darwin among the Machines*; the struggle waged by the son of Vashti to see the light of the stars; Winston Smith's struggle to evade the watchful eye of the cathode tube; the rejection by John the Savage of Soma, and his struggles to suffer, love, make mistakes: all these struggles—which are against technology, and in which physical freedom and that of thought, of judgement are at stake—are no longer apparent in *Black Mirror*.

Together with them, almost disappeared are the robots, which were the protagonists of the best-known films thematizing the risks of technological drift. The *Black Mirror* universe is imbued by Apps and microchips, not by robots. The latter functioned throughout the twentieth century as a mirror of mankind (Telotte 2016). As mirrors, they reproduced the same human dynamics: they rebelled, they tried to overturn power relations, to become masters of humans instead of their slaves. Whether they succeeded or failed was immaterial. They waged a titanic struggle against mankind: the two enemy fronts saw human beings drawn up in battle order on one front, and machines on the other: freedom was at stake. All this has almost disappeared in *Black Mirror*.

Certainly, some episodes lend themselves to a 'technophobic' reading which remains within the nineteenth-twentieth century paradigm. Consider the episode entitled "Metalheads", which presents an updated version of the mechanical hounds of *Fahrenheit 451*; hounds whose homicidal behaviour (it can be presumed) is the unwanted outcome of an incorrect programming which originally conceived them as guarantors of individual safety. And yet, most of the series episodes look in a completely different direction. In this respect, *Black Mirror* marks a decisive discontinuity with the "obsessions and terrors" of the dystopian literature to which Raymond Trousson referred.

Black Mirror episodes are constructed around the theme of the effects of the invention of futuristic digital technologies and the pressure of social media. These themes are intertwined with the discourse on the development of Artificial Intelligence and the one relative to the weight of social conformism under the pressure of the 'revolution of the gaze' that has given renewed impetus to the spectacularization of society and the need for social recognition in an era which continues to be marked by the culture of narcissism (Lasch 2020; Byung-Chul Han 2015, 37-38). These phenomena are observed against the backdrop of processes that no-one seems able to control (Saignes, 2021).

Black Mirror eschews the 'antagonistic' technological paradigm posited by *Darwin among the Machines*, *Erewhon*, *The Machine Stops*, etc., and propounds the human capacity to submit "with resignation if not with assent" (Bazin, 2019). It conveys imaginaries drawn from advanced, performative, and persuasive digital forms built on nudges and gamification processes that exploit people's socialization needs, their frailties, their competitive or infantile instincts. It recounts user-friendly apps and games which require people's active participation and partly their complicity. *Black Mirror* does not describe the implacable grasp of power exercised through technology, as Zamjatin, Huxley, Boye, Orwell, Bradbury, etc., did. Rather, it tells of the impossibility, or at least the difficulty, of escaping the camera's gaze, to detach oneself from video games, to relate to people of flesh and blood, and to inhabit a world that cannot be extinguished. In short, it narrates the dynamics of voluntary servitude to digital technologies, not those of forced servitude to them (Bauman, Lyon 2015).

Black Mirror takes to its extreme consequences the process of reflection on the transhuman already begun by the cult film *Blade Runner*, where the replicants had evolved to the point that they were indistinguishable from human beings (Della Torre, 2012), urging us to imagine invisible technologies, incarnated in our own bodies. In so doing, it gradually shifts the paradigm. The act of rebellion of mankind against technology does not appear on the scene (except for the episode entitled *The Entire History of You*), nor is space given to forms of technological anthropomorphisation (with the sole exception of *Be Right Back*). The representation of technology as something massive and external to humans no longer exists. The digital technologies depicted by *Black Mirror* enter humans, envelop them, adapt to them, caress them, invite them, shape them, and tame them by means of an infinite number of small daily routines. It is the Web 2.0 technologies and the smartphone—invented, it should be remembered, only in 2008—that allow and solicit constant possibilities for interaction between the media and people, and vice versa.

Whilst in *Blade Runner* the replicants rebelled and tried to subvert power relations, and whilst in films like *AI* or *Wall-e* the robots are represented with human psychological and/or physical features, in *Black Mirror* the technologies are stripped down: they do not carry any anthropomorphic surplus because they no longer need it. Unlike a valuable film like *Ex machina*, where the robot women rebel by establishing gender solidarity, and unlike McEwan's *Machines like me*, where the robot Adam, the real co-protagonist of the story, resists its buyer's attempt to shut it down, in *Black Mirror* the individual remained alone in front of his/her screen (Turckel, 2011).

The microchips, games, apps, computers, and cell phones of *Black Mirror* do not turn against their manufacturers or threaten their users; they are totally indifferent to them. The scriptwriters of *Black Mirror* seem to suggest that the entire technological paradigm that has conceived machines as evil bearers of desires, ambitions, and feelings capable of being used against humans is a huge and despicable lie, a gigantic form of self-absolution. What *Black Mirror* depicts, therefore, is not the heterogenesis of ends, nor the reversal of roles between machines and humans, but rather the univocal impulse that drives contemporary humans to their mobile phones, their video games, their computers—machines endowed with such seductive characteristics that they induce people to project themselves and immerse themselves in them, abandoning everything else. As Byung-Chul Han wrote: "The inhabitants of the digital panoptic are not prisoners, they live in the illusion of freedom", they "develop an obsessive and forced relationship with digital technologies" (Byung-Chul Han, 2015, 50-51).

The themes of deception and surveillance are the litmus papers of this sunset of the technological paradigm. Deception, which dominated dystopian fiction until about twenty years ago, is a residual, if not completely absent, theme in Charlie Brooker's television series. It is not under the sign of the lies imposed by the regime that the relationship with technologies described by the television series develops, but instead under the sign of voluntariness — proof of which is that in some episodes (*The Entire History of You*, *Be Right Back*), the protagonists autonomously rip out the devices they have installed in their bodies or cease to use them (but without being able to do without them altogether). As regards surveillance, this too is significantly rethought in *Black Mirror*. As Peter Marks observed, even if it is "difficult to overestimate the impact that Orwell's novel *Nineteen Eighty-Four* has on the popular and academic imaginations", surveillance scholars "regularly complain that the concept of Big Brother is "out of date" and that no single Orwellian big brother oversees the massive monitoring effort that is surveillance in the twenty-first century" (Marks 2015, 3). Although, our imagination is still largely shaped by the surveillance model described in *1984* (and is still hegemonized by the '1984 paradigm', as evidenced by the protests during the Covid-19 pandemic against physical distancing, masks, the green pass, vaccines) surveillance scholars believe it is a partially outdated model. The glass and steel city of Zamjatin, the screens of Oceania, the interactive televisions of the America in *Fahrenheit 451* were technological devices able to impose total surveillance and domination, and to extort a consensus unimaginable in previous centuries. But in the age of data mining, machine learning and AI, individuals are much less interesting than their 'doubles': that is, their data and their digital profiles, which, in turn, are of interest as a whole and not as individuals. Finally, as pointed out by Slavoj Zizek, contributing to the outdatedness of Big Brother is the consideration that today "what frightens and produces anxiety is the fact that someone stops watching us or stops following us" (Zizek 2001, 271).

Conclusions: Happy Sisyphus?

To conclude: the digital dystopian imagery conveyed by *Black Mirror* questions where the capacity for self-determination of men and women has gone in contemporary digitalized and globalized society. Upstream of this television series is reflection on the impact exerted in contemporary societies by the predictive analysis of behaviours, by probabilistic calculation, and by the fear that these innovations are pushing in the direction of a post-disciplinary, but not therefore freer, society where significant amounts of the capacity for self-institution—typical of modern societies—are gradually eroded. In what sense, then, does *Black Mirror* pertain to the demise of the technological paradigm that took shape between the works of Butler and Forster? It does so in the sense that it weaves together a discourse on the co-responsibility of the dominated in the process of domination that depicts different degrees of voluntariness, ranging from full compliance to a gradual lapse into total unawareness—a discourse within which it is difficult to see where one can go to find freedom. Its episodes focus on the fundamental anthropological inadequacy experienced by men and women in contact with a digital revolution which is transforming their mode of relating to the world and to themselves. In deconstructing an optimistic narrative about emancipated people being 'connected', in deconstructing the celebratory rhetoric that places utopian hopes in the digital revolution, the authors of *Black Mirror* denounce the scant transformative scope of smart cities and their Apps, exploring the forms of unfreedom that threaten the look-down generation for which the Aristotelian concept of 'liberated' time has lost its meaning. *Black Mirror* represents digital technologies as constituting an arsenal available to the happiness industry and as deadly weapons of mass distraction, which reveal the entirely human passion for distraction and play, for what is neither true nor false but just pure entertainment (Postman, 1985; Byung-Chul Han 2022). Charlie Brooker's series convey the conviction that there is a tangible risk that "the omnipotence of the virtual" will develop in the shadow of "the sense of impotence over the real" (Schmit, Benasayag, 2013). *Black Mirror* recounts a world in which the traditional figures of power have disappeared. A world in which the thirst for freedom of individuals has dried up and with it their oppositional drive against technologies because of the disappearance of the belief that freedom is still attainable. Or, perhaps, that freedom is still worth pursuing beyond the illusion of agency which is the deceptive promise of video games (Domsch, 2013). Video games give players a strong sense of choice, give them the illusion that they can change things, that they are the protagonist of their environment, but as Colin explains to Stefan in Bandersnatch, the interactive movie in the Black Mirror series: "There are messages in every game. Like Pac-Man, do you know what PAC stands for? P-A-C. Programme and Control. He's programmed and controlled. The whole thing is a metaphor. He thinks he's got a free will but really, he's trapped in a maze, in a system" (Attimonelli, Susca 2020, 202).

Assuming that a different technologic paradigm is rising, a paradigm at the hearth of which lies the concept of voluntary servitude and not that of slavery (even if as George Orwell once wrote: "each age lives on into the next" (Orwell 1942) — then we can borrow an image proposed by Michel Houellebecq, to get an idea of how it works:

> I have never quite understood how one can 'imagine Sisyphus happy'; Sisyphus seems to me obviously unhappy since he performs vain, repetitive, and painful gestures; but the being who performs vain, repetitive, and pleasant gestures seems to me obviously happy. You only must compare Sisyphus pushing his boulder to a puppy playing ball on the stairs to understand what I mean (Houellebecq 2020, 319).

References

Anders, Günther. 2007. *L'uomo è antiquato*. Torino: Bollati Boringhieri.

Aristotle. 1996. *The Politics and the Constitution of Athens*. Cambridge: Cambridge University Press.

Attimonelli, Claudia, Susca Vincenzo. 2019. *Un oscuro riflettere. Black Mirror e l'aurora digitale*. Milano-Udine: Mimesis.

Bauman, Zygmunt, Lyon, David. 2013. *Liquid Surveillance. A Conversation*. Cambridge: Polity Press.

Bazin, Laurent. 2019. *La dystopie*. Clermont-Ferrand: Presses universitaires Blaise Pascal.

Brooker Charlie, Jones Annabel, Arnopp, Jason. 2018. *Inside Black Mirror*. London: Ebury Publishing.

Butler, Simon. 1863. *Darwin among the Machines*. The Press, 13th June 1863.

Butler, Samuel. 1872. *Erewhon or Over the Range*. London: Trübner & Co.

Dalla Torre, Paola. 2012. *Sognando il futuro. Da 2001 Odissea nello Spazio a Inception*. Soveria Mannelli: Rubbettino.

Deleuze, Gilles, Guattari, Felix. 1996. *Che cos'è la filosofia*. Torino: Einaudi.

Domsch, Sebastian. 2013. *Storyplaying. Agency and Narrative in Videogames*. Berlin: De Gruyter.

Fisher, Mark. 2009. *Capitalist Realism. Is there no Alternative?.* London: Zero Books.

Forster, Edward Morgan. 2011. *The Machine Stops*. London: Penguin Books.

Han, Byung-Chul. 2015. *Nello sciame*. Milano: nottetempo.

Han, Byung-Chul. 2021. *Sano intrattenimento*. Milano: nottetempo.

Hartog, François. 2003. Régimes d'historicité. Présentisme et expérience du temps. Paris: Seuil.

Houellebecq, Michel. 2020. *Interventions, 2020*. Paris: Flammarion.

Jameson, Frederic. 2010. *Utopia as Method, or the Uses of the Future*, in Gordin, M.D. – Prakash, G. (eds.). *Utopia/Dystopia. Conditions of Historical Possibility*, Princeton: Princeton University Press: 21-44.

Kumar, Krishan. 1987. *Utopia & Anti-utopia in Modern Times*. Oxford and New York: Basil Blackwell.

Mari, Giovanni. 2020. *Dominio, Sottomissione e lavoro*. Teoria Politica, 10, X: 435-439.

Marks, Peter. 2015. *Imagining Surveillance. Eutopian and Dystopian Literature and Film*. Edinburgh: Edinburgh University Press.

Martinez Mesa, Francisco José. 2022. *Years and Years. La vertiente gratificadora de la distopía*. in Solanilla M.U. – Mesa-Villar, J. M. – Filhol, B. (eds). *Imágenes distópicas. Representaciones culturales*. Madrid: Catarata.

Moïsi, Dominique. 2016. *La géopolitique des séries ou le triomphe de la peur*. Paris: Stock.

Orwell, George. 1942. *The Rediscovery of Europe*. "Listener", 19 March 1942.

Palano, Damiano. 2022. *Il futuro capovolto. Per una mappa degli immaginari distopici del XXI secolo*. Milano: EduCatt.

Runciman, David. 2018. *How Democracy Ends*. New York: Basic Books.

Saignes, Anne. 2021. *La pensée politique de l'anti-utopie*. Paris: Honoré Champion.

Telotte, Jay P. 2016. *The Persistence of the Robot*. In *Endangering Science Fiction Film*. New York and London: Routledge: 243-257.

Tirino, Mario, Tramontana Antonio. 2018. *I riflessi di Black Mirror. Glossario su immaginari, culture e media della società digitale*. Roma: Rogas edizioni.

Trousson, Raymond. 2000. *Dystopia* in Fortunati, V.—Trousson, R. (eds). *Dictionary of the Literary Utopias*. Paris: Honoré Champion.

Turkle, Sherry. 2011. *Alone Together. Why We Expect More from Technology and Less from Each Other*. New York: Basic Books.

Zizek, Slavoj. 2001. *Vous avez dit totalitarisme? Cinq interventions sur le (més)usages d'une notion*. Paris: Amsterdam Poches.

Zizek, Slavoj. 2009. *The Plague of Fantasies*. London: Verso.

Between Monstrous Dystopias and Policy Utopias in Artificial Intelligence: *Reporting on a ten-year journey into the AI-topia*

Vassilis Galanos

Introduction: Journey into the AI-Known

This is a narcissistic paper. I have been interested in the field of artificial intelligence (AI) for over a decade as a researcher coming from an information science and media studies background with an interest in cybernetic thinking. Upon receiving my MSc diploma in 2014, my child hero, Stephen Hawking, in a series of public statements, raised concerns about the future of AI. This alarmed me, but it also coincided with my entry into the territory of science and technology studies (STS), eventually leading me to a doctoral research concerned with the dialectic relationship between expertise and expectations in the shaping of whatever we might call AI in different eras of the field's long historical development since the 1950s (Galanos 2023). Due to my interest in experimenting with various approaches to theoretical and empirical exploration, I found myself publishing various papers about the sociology of AI, however, as some commentators suggested, they seemed to have been written by entirely different people. In this paper, I aim at synthesising these steps towards telling an autobiographical research story about AI as monsterised in the mass media landscape, enabling a chain reaction that led to an idolisation of AI in national governance. Nonetheless, and as argued below, not every use of the term "AI" is the same. It is a concept that is flexible enough to interpret for different causes and meet certain self-fulfilling expectations and specific enough to sound defined by those who negotiate their AI expertise and thus shape expectations.

With a nod to Gregory Bateson (Bateson 1987, 1-2), I therefore realised that the different, seemingly disparate pieces of work (only very tiny portions of them made it to my doctoral thesis), were "steps" towards understanding AI's evolution and ecosystem in the last decade. Therefore, the sections below will be presented as such: steps. Yet, because linearity is well-known to carry its fallacies, they will not be presented in a chronological order but in a conceptual, sense-making one, akin to Julio Cortázar's hopscotch approach (1968), as some of my earlier attempts towards explaining AI as a social endeavour made more sense after additional research. This is why the present article is narcissistic (what humanities publication really is not?). It is also a journey into AI as something that is well-known to many people, as it expresses fears and hopes about technoscientific dystopias and utopias that might be promising but also unsettling — a grand unknown. Hence, this is a journey into the AI-known.

What we Mean by AI? Mission Impossible

The typical way to begin one's exploration of a technological or scientific field is to delineate it by seeking its definition(s). AI's case is so unique that just by attempting to do that, I found myself conducting primary and secondary historical research about its definitions. These have changed a lot: from before its terminological inception (when scholars, technologists, novelists, and priests spoke about automata, robots, machines, Golems and homunculi, animist spirits, analytical engines, or electronic brains), throughout its establishment as "AI" (a more "flashy term" than the previously proposed "automata studies" and "complex information processing" according to McCarthy who coined the term in 1955 in order to get sponsorship for a summer school; BBC 1973), and up until its latest resurgence whereby the military-industrial-academic complex equated AI with its applications, after mandating that sponsorship for AI research should aim at practical applications (chiefly militaristic or commercial, with healthcare being a reverse scapegoat).

AI's meaning progressively changed from being "the conjecture that every aspect of learning or any other feature of intelligence can in principle be so precisely described that a machine can be made to simulate it" (McCarthy et al. 1955, 14) and "the science of making machines do things that would require intelligence if done by men [sic]" (Minsky 1968, v) to a very narrow practical application "'artificial intelligence system' (AI system) means software that is developed with one or more of the techniques and approaches listed in [the EU's AI Act draft's] Annex I and can, for a given set of human-defined objectives, generate outputs such as content, predictions, recommendations, or decisions influencing the environments they interact with" (European Commission 2021, 39). For several AI scientists I have interviewed between 2019 and 2021, such definitions obscure the importance of AI as a scientific field — however, several younger scholars admit that this is what is meant by AI today.

For one, my occasional involvement with cognitive science and the philosophy of social science as well as elements of Shintoism, led me to suggest that AI does not exist (Galanos 2018). The more one mediates on the term and examines it critically through the lessons learned from schools of thought such as constructivism, naturalism, or shared cognition, the more AI appears as a poor terminological choice. It is not just that AI was meant to be a study *of* intelligence and since we have no good definition of intelligence, therefore AI cannot be defined. It is also that if intelligence is viewed as a shared and social practice, an emerging property of systems of interaction and collective endeavour rather than an essentialist property of the brain within a body, then, defining intelligence in AI becomes senseless. By the same token, constructivist STS as well as other branches of social science and philosophy have argued for decades about the arbitrary distinction between the "artificial" (or "cultural" or "nurtured") as opposed to "natural." Constructivists would suggest that drawing the line is an exercise of power and dominance — as much as drawing a line about what counts as intelligence or not. But even from a naturalist perspective (if one considers Whitehead or the Marquis de Sade), if, for the sake of conversation, we agree on the hypothesis that intelligence "exists" within bodies (organic or mechanic) it is a product of the same nature, and therefore natural. This binary boundary-work, however, denoting at the personal, subjective, and species level what counts as natural or artificial, intelligent or unintelligent, lies at the core of inner working processes that construct the dystopian AI-phobia.

What We Fear in AI? Automation, Automatism, and Uncanny Monsters

The social narrative shaping AI's scientific and public understanding embedded in a vast number of popular culture that predated or co-evolved with AI: Pinocchio, Dr Frankenstein's monster, humanity's artificial successors in Samuel Butler's *Erehwon*, Karel Čapek's *Rossum's Universal Robots* (first appearance of the term "robot" in 1919), Maria in Lang and von Habou's *Metropolis*, Asimov's four laws of robotics, Philip K. Dick's androids, C3PO and R2D2 in *Star Wars*, HAL in *2001: A Space Odyssey*, B-9 in *Lost in Space*, Kraftwerk's music, an immense amount of robots in popular comicbooks and videogames (from Marvel's Vision to Tekken's Yoshimitsu).

By now, the way in which these narratives matter by what they express has been well documented (Royal Society 2018, Szollosy 2016): the eternal recurrence of the same fear about humanity's hubris aiming to replicate its own self through science with its unintended consequences paired to possibilities of being surpassed by its own creation (a Saturnine fear) on the one end, and on the other, a hope for robots that can alleviate humanity from routinisable tasks and the very notion of work. This latter hope, however, comes with two reverse narratives: that of work deskilling and progressive elimination of humanity's relevance as workforce with significant economic and political underlying motives and consequences on the one hand, and on the other, the realisation that many human tasks that can be performed by machines confirm that humans are being treated and find their value *as* machines (for the latter case, consider Kraftwerk's song *We Are the Robots*; in their typically arbitrary lyrical style, Kraftwerk do not specify whether the robot singers stress the word "robots," thus being robots who come to take over human jobs, or the word "we," thus being humans realising their robotic life).

This latter dual fear led me to an expression of it as a post-psychoanalytical framework (Galanos 2019b). In classical Freudianism, human mind is typically divided between conscious and unconscious states that extend to the performance of automatic acts (psychical automatisms such as linguistic slips, unintentional gestures, certain ticks, and more). Such acts of the Freudian unconscious consist part of everyday life that if repeated consistently, might signify reason for concern, conventionally (and psychoanalytically) speaking, as the individual is thought to be unable to control their conscious side of the mind that makes them more "human" in a Cartesian mindset (could not think of a better word here). I suggested, thus, that in machines (AI, computers, robots, or otherwise), the opposite is observed, as expressed in the following table. Machines' "regular" or "conventionally acceptable" state is being unconscious and automatic. Irregular behaviour on behalf of a machine would consist of breaking the automatism/automation and thus act in way that is perceived as conscious.

	Regularly performing state	Unconventionally performing state
Human	Conscious, thus not automatic	Unconscious, thus automatic
Machine (AI, robot, software, computer)	Automated, thus unconscious	Not automated, thus (?) conscious

During the time composing that piece of work, I was unaware of its similarity with the concept of the uncanny valley, a theory proposed in 1970 by Japanese roboticist and practicing animist Buddhist Masahiro Mori, suggesting that the closer a machine resembles the behaviour of a living being, the more likely that is to cause feelings of eeriness to a perceiving individual. I was also unaware of Sigmund Freud's work on the concept of the uncanny, as well as the confusion caused by several scholars who published as valid the assumption that Mori's theory was based on Freud's. This led to my historical, translational, and geographical biography of the "uncanny" and the "uncanny valley," from Scotland's root of the "uncanny," to the German and Austrian explorations of the "unheimlich," to Japan and the "不気味の谷" ["bukimi no tani" — the "uncanny valley"] (Galanos 2020. Freud 1925, Mori 1970).

Elsewhere (Galanos 2019c), I suggested that this critical distinction between humans and machines should not be treated only as a psychological form of fear, but as an extension of sociological activity. In particular, I argued that the fear of AI or robots exhibiting emergent consciousness or signifying risks of deskilling, bears sufficient homology with previous forms of social discrimination, hierarchical ordering, or even the justification of slavery — in which case, the term "AI" signifies a type of intelligence that justified its lower value, since it is artificial, pretty much as human categorisations of species, races, genders, ages, or classes (among others) extended assumptions about degrees of intelligence exhibited by different members within those sets. Such processes of othering or monsterisation are embedded in the anthropomorphisation or zoomorphisation of AI/robotic technologies, as shown in the case of the uncanny valley, through an increasing will to recognise the familiar within the strange that is being broken up as soon as what has been thought of as sufficiently strange becomes overly familiar. It is in the virtue of the present paper that I get the chance to synthesise this inner contradiction between (a) a hope to identify the self within the machine and (b) a fear that this self is actually identifiable, by contextualising this within a broader social contradiction I explored before.

What We Hype in AI? A Double Bind of Hope and Horror

This step refers to a paper called "Singularitarianism and Schizophrenia" (Galanos 2017) reflecting my immersion to the works (a) by Gregory Bateson (1973, 206-207) who explained individual schizophrenia as the outcome of persistent repetition of contradictory commands he termed "double binds" (similar to catch-22s), and (b) Deleuze and Guattari's (1988) "capitalism and schizophrenia" who, among many other proposals, focused on the schizophrenic condition not just as an individual's one, but also as social/collective and environmental, produced by capitalist contradictory commands. I borrowed the term "singularitarianism" from Luciano Floridi (2015) who suggested the religious undertone behind believers of the singularity argument (that a machine can reach a point of outsmarting humans), either by looking at it as path to salvation or road to condemnation.

I therefore suggested that the then still emerging latest round of AI hype consists of a collective form of "double bind" where the different rhetorical uses of the term "AI" (see step 1) serve different modes of capitalist production of value, interest, and alienation around the resources that make "AI" while this is effectuated at massive scale through a series of contradictory commands. As a parent who may be equally responsible for offering care as well as punishment to a child, news consumers, vendors, marketplaces, universities, and other social domains, are repeatedly facing the contradictory commands concerned with (a) the mandate to adopt, produce, research, support, use, get excited about AI (or any related application) because of its operational, financial, and prestige gains, and (b) the warning that doing so will result to unemployment/deskilling, self-aware robots that will evolve as to displace humans, carbon emissions with massive environmental effects, and algorithmic discrimination. Interestingly, while the word "hype" is chiefly associated with positive hype, there is a flavour of negative hype serving a similar purpose, that I later termed counter-hype (Galanos 2019a) and what further later Lee Vinsel termed "critihype" (Vinsel 2021 in Phan et al. 2022).

At the time, my only suggestion in that article was to import more holistic and relational (and non-Western) frameworks in our analyses of AI-related dichotomies, such as the Shintoist model, that is historically dealing successfully with contradictions by enlightenment about them which allows moving beyond them. Becoming aware of the historical, sociological, economic, and political production of such contradictions and dichotomies (optimism/pessimism, natural/artificial, conscious/unconscious), allows for reexamination of situations in more pragmatic fashion (return to the things themselves) in a post-Nietzschean transvaluation of good/evil values.

What We Regulate in AI? Dystopian Thinking in the Press Triggering Utopian Thinking in Policy

While I was thus preparing for a doctoral investigation of the social dimensions of AI, Stephen Hawking's initial 2014 warning about the future of AI was repeated throughout 2015 and in this he was joined by another public figure whose name is associated with science and technology, although his expertise in AI programming is questionable: Elon Musk. It was in October 2016 that three key policy documents were published in the United States, the United Kingdom, and the European Union, concerned with the future and potential need to regulate AI. For a person who never thought that the word "policymaking" would ever be of interest, I found it fa-Sci-Fi-nating that governments commissioned policy experts to conduct research on the topic. Reading them, revealed that Hawking and Musk's statements, as well as references to the singularity argument were common across all three documents, not necessarily being taken into serious consideration, but not entirely dismissed either—what surprised me the most was the lack of sufficient (if any) AI practitioners representation as part of the writing teams, consultations committees, and auditing processes.

I proceeded by carefully chronicling all public statements by Hawking, Musk, as well as Bill Gates who, despite his computer science expertise, took the other two commentators' side, only to change his mind in 2018, suggesting that AI can mean longer vacations. The process involved the initiation of numerous "future" or "risk" studying institutes (Future of Life Institute, Future of Humanity Institute, Centre for the Study of Existential Risk) of which several futurist affiliates have been overlapping across. My observations became a chronicle that showcased the interface between mass media statements about AI and policy perceptions about AI with public science and technology commentators acting as "expanding experts," whose prestige based on their expert credentials in one field allows them to extend their expertise to other fields and influence decision making through counter-hype or criti-hype. The paper was accepted for publication five days after Hawking's passing.

The result of this media-policy interplay paired to industry's continuous aggregation of user data for online services, was that AI policy and AI regulation became established as a field with an increasing amount of AI-related policy documents being published around the world with the 2021 draft of the EU's AI Act being the first attempt to comprehensively regulate AI (Unlicane 2022, Schiff 2023, von Ingersleben-Seip 2023). Since 2019, the process was a learning curve: more AI practitioners became involved (still not as many as some of us wished for), and less references to imagined dangers were made—instead of them, arbitrary classifications of data-driven machine learning application risks were proposed. In continuation of the previously mentioned vagueness in AI terminology, it seemed that in order to regulate something as broad as AI, policymakers had to limit its scope, thus crystalising more practical and application-based technical definitions of AI (again: step 1). By doing so, they (a) miss the point of what the initial warnings suggested requires regulation (an imagined out-of-control version of ultraintelligent machine), and (b) establish a research path for AI that misses its initial intellectual purpose, something that is discussed in the following step.

The Future of Life Institute published in 2015 the open letter "Research Priorities for Robust and Beneficial Artificial Intelligence," with over 10.000 signatories, displaying the names of several "expanding experts" on the top of the list. The letter influenced the early policy documents from 2016 I referred to. As the present paper is written, the same institute has published their "Pause Giant AI Experiments: An Open Letter" currently signed by over 26.000 people, after receiving immense media publicity but also gaining the support of more AI practitioners, in light of recent advances in publicly available generative AI software such as OpenAI's ChatGPT. While it is early to report on this round of counter-hype's influence of public commentary on AI governance, it is surprising to recognise the pattern repetition in just eight years. It is likely that this may be a case akin to what Parviainen and Coeckelbergh (2021) termed political choreography in social robotics in their study of Sophia the robot and the public debates around AI and robotic citizenship in 2014-5, parts of which migrated into AI debates. The authors suggest that this political choreography "boosts the rise of the social robot market, rather than [making] a statement about robot citizenship or artificial intelligence" and "argue that the media performances of the Sophia robot were choreographed to advance specific political interests" (Parviainen and Coeckelbergh 2021). One has to consider, after all, the intellectual rivalry between OpenAI's Ilya Sutskever and Meta's Yann LeCun, both pioneering figures in the earlier and latter applications of machine learning: back in 2015, hours after OpenAI was unveiled, according to Metz (2021, 166), LeCun warned Sutskever during a Facebook party that his idealism would guarantee his failure. LeCun, features as a signatory for both Open Letters, but this time, against OpenAI's type of open-ended-ness.

In the next section, I am going to show how this AI-phobia and lack of historical AI awareness influences AI research that avoids curiosity-oriented trajectories on the basis of an AI-phobia-phobia, to paraphrase Arie Rip in examination of "exaggerated interpretation of public concerns" on behalf of nanotechnology policymakers and funders that are "seen as an indication of fear, even phobia of the new technology" that then causes within scientific communities a "nanophobia-phobia — the phobia that there is a public phobia" (Rip 2006, 358). While the key fear about AI was concerned with the unintended outcomes of exponential growth of computation power, what actually proliferated exponentially was dystopian press warnings followed utopian AI-first policy statements and regulations about a beneficial AI. I am not against the notion of a "beneficial AI" — I am against the technologically deterministic belief that a technology can be, as presented in such documents, beneficial or not without sufficient examination of researchers, designers, sponsors, and users' motives.

What We Research in AI? Nomadic Exploration and State Exploitation

Conversation about values in AI design, however, was generally missing during that period of early post-2010 AI hype. It was the period when an army of prospective doctoral candidates submitted almost simultaneously PhD proposals to study the views and doings of AI practitioners — myself being one of them. I therefore embarked on a half-historical, half-interview-based study of AI during which I managed to speak extensively with 25 AI practitioners (leading research figures, senior or early career researchers, everyday AI workers) and gain informal insights from many more while attending numerous events, conferences, and visiting laboratories during the course of this study, asking about their perception of AI expectations and expertise — who counts as an AI expert and what shapes AI expectations, as well as what are the outcomes of putting too much trust/faith into different types of AI experts and expectations.

The research journey offered unexpected findings, beyond confirmations that Musk and Hawking knew little about AI. When asked about what interests them in the field and what they think about promising, interviewees' responses revealed very different motives for conducting AI research and I described this taxonomy in two different ways based on different theoretical lenses, however suggesting the same division between a tendency towards romanticism and a tendency towards opportunism. I did this by employing Deleuze and Guattari's (1988) terminology about nomadic/State science (Galanos 2022a) and a metaphor from biology also used in organisational studies concerned with the exploration/exploitation survivability trade-off (Laureiro-Martínez et al. 2015, Galanos 2023, 161-165).

I referred, thus, to two modes of AI research: (a) nomad scientists who, being curiosity-driven, are seeking to explore uncharted venues of AI and intelligence at large, and (b) State serving scientists who, being grant-driven, are seeking to exploit available funding opportunities, chiefly offered by the State (including the military), but also the industry (if one perceives the latter as sufficiently different from the State). For Deleuze and Guattari, State science is also static science, and therefore, in order to find shelter for conducting original work, scientists have to expatriate, become nomads, in order to meet better conditions. This has happened a few times in AI's history, especially during the times of perceived "AI winters," where loss of governmental trust to AI research led to fund stagnation after times of overpromising and unrealisability of promises, or in the case of competing approaches to AI creating rivalries within AI departments, leading to proponents of less established approaches to depart and establish their own laboratories elsewhere (Galanos 2023, 75, 125-126).

The historical differentiation between AI-as-science and AI-as-application described above (step 1) was also apparent in the generational gap across different interviewees—most nomad-explorers who expressed interest and nostalgia about an AI that explores the features of intelligence happened to be senior in age, while most State-serving or grant-oriented exploiters happened to be of a younger age. There have been overlaps, of course, and that allowed me to input nuances in the framework as to include the ability to recognise profitability out of curiosity-driven research or unexpected intellectual novelties during the conduct of fund-driven (and more mundane) type of research. Nevertheless, this feature is not unique to AI only and is expressed in the establishment of the so-called "new university" infrastructure where profit-driven educational settings and the threat of funding starvation minimise the posibility and value of basic/blue sky or curiosity-driven research (Sørensen and Traweek 2022). To employ a double wordplay, the dilemma as to whether fashion is following funds or funds are following fashion seems to be resolved when cuts kill curiosity.

Hexing AI—Concluding Synthesis and Future Steps

Literary figure Antonin Artaud's play "To Have Done with the Judgement of God" (Artaud and Eshleman 1975) has a very appealing title if one replaces "Judgement of God" with "Debates on AI," further following Bogost who playfully suggested that replacing "algorithm" with "god" in several public debates can give very interesting results. During the 10 years spent researching the complex social settings of AI, I have felt the urge to hex the concept, in a post-occultist fashion, that is, academic (cf. Stanislav Andreski's "Social Sciences as Sorcery," 1973). And that would surmount, to the degree of my witchcraft abilities, to model AI's complex social environment in a shape that is minimalist enough to be useful, yet informationally rich to convey the complexity. I therefore devised, for the purposes of this narcissistic paper, a hexagram model (no etymological connection to the verb "to hex") connecting six key arguments that have been presented throughout the previous steps, concerned with the *ex*periential interplay between *ex*pectations about *ex*ponential growth, *ex*panding *ex*perts and *ex*patriated researchers, most of them *ex*plorers but not *ex*ploiters. The reader is allowed to draw connections as preferable, either by connecting the points peripherally, diagonally, trigonally, or oppositely.

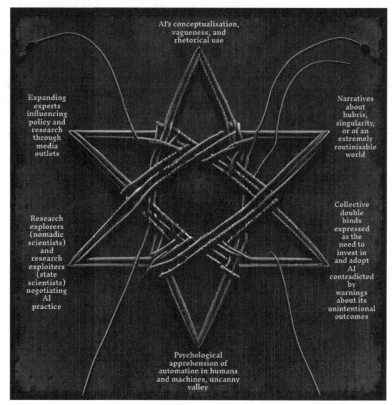

Figure 1 Synthesis of key arguments exemplified above. Produced using Midjourney and Photopea tools.

The seeming symmetry should not be taken as a form of definitive conclusion or necessarily equal weighting in importance. These are just six findings that make more sense being viewed holistically and many more may occur in the future or some can be refuted, depending on historical evolution and conversation. As I mentioned in what will be the final self-reference in the present text (Galanos 2022b) and following Sherry Turkle's 1980 study of computers, AI can be seen as Rorschach: a seemingly symmetrical abstractly shaped inkblot that, once inspected by an individual, evokes feelings of hope and horror, psychic or social forms of utopia and dystopia. Therefore, our journey to the AI-topia cannot but be a simultaneously very personal and collective journey to the AI-known.

References

Andreski, Stanislav. 1972. *Social Sciences as Sorcery*, London: Andre Deutsch.

Artaud, Antonin, and Clayton Eshleman. *To have done with the judgment of God*. Los Angeles: Black Sparrow Press, 1975.

Bateson, Gregory. 1972. *Steps to an ecology of mind: collected essays in anthropology, psychiatry, evolution, and epistemology*. University of Chicago Press, Chicago.

Bogost, Ian. 2015. "The cathedral of computation." *The Atlantic*, January 15, 2015. https://www.theatlantic.com/technology/archive/2015/01/the-cathedral-of-computation/384300/

BBC TV. 1973, June). "The General Purpose Robot is a Mirage. (with Professor Sir James Lighthill, Professor Donald Michie, Professor Richard Gregory and Professor John McCarthy." *Controversy*. Filmed August 1973 at the Royal Institution. http://www.aiai.ed.ac.uk/events/lighthill1973/

Cortázar, Julio. 1963[2020]. *Hopscotch*. London: Random House.

Deleuze, Gilles and Félix Guattari, 1988[2012]. *A Thousand Plateaus: Capitalism and Schizophrenia*. London, New Delhi, New York, Sydney: Bloomsbury Academic.

European Commission. 2021. *Proposal for a Regulation of the European Parliament and of the Council: Laying Down Harmonised Rules on Artificial Intelligence (Artificial Intelligence Act) and Amending Certain Union Legislative Acts*. SEC(2021) 167 final, SWD(2021) 84 final, SWD(2021) 85 final. April 21, 2021.

Floridi, Luciano. 2015. "Singularitarians, AItheists, and Why the Problem with Artificial Intelligence is H.A.L. (Humanity At Large), not HAL." *Philosophy and Computers* 14 no. 2: 8-11.

Freud, Sigmund. 1925[191]. 'The Uncanny'. In *Sigmund Freud: The Standard Edition of the Complete Psychological Works of Sigmund Freud, Volume XVII (1917-1919): An Infantile Neurosis and Other Works*, edited and translated by James Strachey, in collaboration with Anna Freud, assisted by Alix Strachey, 217-256.

Galanos, Vassilis. 2014. "Beyond Information Revolution: Postlude to a Past Future." MSc Diss., University of Copenhagen.

Galanos, Vassilis, 2017. "Singularitarianism and Schizophrenia." *AI & Society* 32, 573-590.

Galanos, Vassilis. 2018. "Artificial Intelligence Does Not Exist: Lessons from Shared Cognition and the Opposition to the Nature/Nurture Divide." In *13th IFIP TC 9 International Conference on Human Choice and Computers. HCC13 2018. Held at the 24th IFIP World Computer Congress. WCC 2018* edited by David Kreps et al, 359-373. Switzerland: Springer Nature.

Galanos, Vassilis. 2019a. "Exploring expanding expertise: artificial intelligence as an existential threat and the role of prestigious commentators, 2014-2018." *Technology Analysis & Strategic Management*, 31 no. 4: 421-432.

Galanos, Vassilis. 2019b. "Blended Automation: The Language-Game of Psychoanalytic Automatism and Cybernetic Automata" In *Blended Cognition: The Robotic Challenge* edited by Jordi Vallverdú and Vincent C. Müller, Springer Series in Cognitive and Neural Systems book series (SSCNS, volume 12), 85-95 Springer, Cham.

Galanos, Vassilis. 2019c. "Teratological Aspects in Artificial Intelligence and Robotics: From Monstrous Threats to Rorschach Opportunities" In *Monsters, Monstrosities, and the Monstrous in Culture and Society* edited by Diego Compagna and Stefanie Steinhart, 103-129. Delaware and Malaga: Vernon Press. pp..

Galanos, Vassilis. 2020. "Towards a Chronological Cartography of the Uncanny Valley and its Uncanny Coincidences" In *Uncanny Bodies* edited by Pippa Goldschmidt, Gill Haddow, and Fadhila Mazanderani. Edinburgh: Luna Press Publishing — Academia Lunace.

Galanos, Vassilis. 2022a. "Nomadic artificial Intelligence and Royal Research Councils: Curiosity-Driven Research Against Imperatives Implying Imperialism." In *The Global Politics of Artificial Intelligence* edited by Maurizio Tinnirello, 173-208 Taylor & Francis — CRC Press.

Galanos, Vassilis. (2022b). "Longitudinal Hype: Terminologies Fade, Promises Stay — An Essay Review on The Robots Are Among Us (1955) and 2062: The World that AI Made (2018)." *Interfaces: Essays and Reviews on Computing and Culture* 3, Charles Babbage Institute, University of Minnesota, 73-87.

Galanos, Vassilis. 2023 "Expectations and expertise in artificial intelligence: specialist views and historical perspectives on conceptualisation, promise, and funding." PhD Diss. University of Edinburgh.

Laureiro-Martínez, Daniella, Stefano Brusoni, Nicola Canessa, and Maurizio Zollo. 2015. "Understanding the exploration–exploitation dilemma: An fMRI study of attention control and decision-making performance." *Strategic Management Journal* 36, no. 3: 319-338.

McCarthy, John, Marvin L. Minsky, Nathaniel Rochester, and Claude E. Shannon. 1955[2006]. "A proposal for the dartmouth summer research project on artificial intelligence, august 31, 1955." *AI Magazine* 27, no. 4 (2006): n.p.

Metz, Cade 2021. *Genius Makers: The Mavericks Who Brought AI to Google, Facebook and the World*. Dublin: Penguin.

Minsky, Marvin. 1968. *Semantic Information Processing*. Cambridge, Massachusetts, and London: The MIT Press.

Mori, Masahiro. 1970. "The uncanny valley [Bukimi No Tani Genshō [不気味の谷現象]]", *Enajii[Energy]*, 7, no. 4: 33-35.

Parviainen, Jaana, and Mark Coeckelbergh. 2021. "The political choreography of the Sophia robot: beyond robot rights and citizenship to political performances for the social robotics market." *AI & Society* 36, no. 3: 715-724.

Phan, Thao, Jake Goldenfein, Monique Mann, and Declan Kuch. 2022. "Economies of virtue: the circulation of 'ethics' in Big Tech." *Science as Culture* 31, no. 1: 121-135.

Rip, Arie. 2006. "Folk theories of nanotechnologists." *Science as Culture* 15 no. 4: 349-365.

Royal Society. 2018. "AI Narratives and Why They Matter." Executive report.

Schiff, Daniel S. "Looking through a policy window with tinted glasses: Setting the agenda for US AI policy." *Review of Policy Research*, (ahead of print).

Sørensen, Knut H., and Sharon Traweek. 2022. *Questing Excellence in Academia: A Tale of Two Universities*. Taylor & Francis.

Szollosy, Michael. 2016. "Freud, Frankenstein and our Fear of Robots: Projection in Our Cultural Perception of Technology." *AI & Society*, 32: 433-439.

Turkle, Sherry. 1980. "Computers as Rorschach: Subjectivity and Social Responsibility." In *Is the Computer a Tool?* edited by Bo Sundin, . 81-99. Stockholm. Almquist and Wiksell.

Ulnicane, Inga. 2022. "Artificial Intelligence in the European Union: Policy, ethics and regulation." In *The Routledge handbook of European integrations*. Taylor & Francis.

von Ingersleben-Seip, Nora. 2023. "Competition and cooperation in artificial intelligence standard setting: Explaining emergent patterns." Review of Policy Research (ahead of print).

Transhuman Dystopias: Cinematographic Science Fiction and Biorthical Issues

Paola Dalla Torre

The Infosphere Revolution in Science Fiction Audiovisual Narratives

> We are now living in the age of the fourth industrial revolution, immersed in an infosphere in which information and communication technologies are having revolutionary effects on the construction of our sense of self as well as the perception of our corporeality (Floridi, 2014).

The changes taking place are leading in the direction of working out answers to new questions on the ethical, philosophical, and anthropological levels, in search of answers for questions that concern not only our present but also, and above all, our future. This takes place through imagining what might happen to the world and the human being in the near future in the face of a technology that is progressing at a dizzying pace, in what now seems to be an autonomous manner (Galimberti, 2002).

In the "synthetic" world, in the "Digital Age", the difference between man and machine becomes increasingly blurred (Benanti, 2020), boundaries get blurred and essential questions arise, such as: what is human and what is not? What distinguishes us from a machine that increasingly resembles us? Also why is the human being seen, studied, and cared for as a "machine" of impulses and information (Benanti, 2016)?

This debate is rich, complex and challenging. And it finds a place not only in academia, among scholars, policymakers and various professionals, but also in newspapers, mass media, and especially in audiovisual narrative products. Films and television series offer themselves as cultural intermediaries: they present these issues and try to make them accessible to all. The genre in which all these elements are reflected par excellence is, of course, that of science fiction, which, by its very nature, is the genre that has always narrated the relationship between man and technology[1].

In particular, contemporary cinematic science fiction is traversed by a strand that we might call the "transhuman dystopias" strand: a subgenre that has transhumanist themes as the main subject of the narrative (Hauskeller, Philbeck, Carbonell 2015). Transhumanism, which we will discuss in detail throughout our essay, is a contemporary philosophical and cultural movement that sees in human-machine hybridization the possibility of an empowerment of the human that will allow the victory of humans over their biological limitations. Its aim is to realize the utopia of man "beyond man" (Miller, Wilsdon, 2006).

"The goal of this movement is expressed in the Central Maxim of Transhumanism, which states that it is ethical and desirable to use technoscientific means to overcome the (given) human condition. In this perspective, human empowerment is realized in the technohuman condition that refuses stasis and is fulfilled by technological evolution. Human enhancement takes on a new and radical significance: from the enhancement of human functions we move to the enhancement of man understood as a posthuman enhanced human" (Palazzani, 2020, 71).

The radical optimistic vision of the transhumanists is of course countered by all the technophobes who see in the world envisaged by the former the annihilation of everything human, the destruction of man and his world (Fukuyama, 2002; Habermas, 2002), the assertion of the artificial against the natural.

This juxtaposition finds a perfect visual form in contemporary transhumanist dystopian films, and their narratives problematize

---

[1] Andrea Tortoreto, in an attempt to define the nature of science fiction, writes that the great science fiction writer Asimov "in his work uses science fiction as a form of social inquiry, considering it as that branch of literature which is concerned with the impact of scientific progress on human beings. Indeed, it arises as a 'literary response to a new intellectual interest' that comes up at the moment when humans, in the very course of their existence, 'are affected by the changes brought about by science and technology and can imagine the future as something profoundly different from the present'" (Tortoreto, ed., 2018, 9).

in popular form concepts that are being addressed in philosophy, anthropology, and especially bioethics.

The hypothesis we want to pursue in our analysis is that bioethics, one of the sciences that addresses the questions posed by the techno-human condition in contemporary times, finds in science fiction films a popular way to reach the general public and to make its questions known, as well as the different perspectives with which it addresses them.

Science Fiction Cinema and Bioethics

Our analysis starts by describing the opening sequences of two films belonging to what we have called the subgenre of transhuman dystopias. The first shows a beautiful yellow flower, a symbol of an earth that is regenerating itself after an electronic blackout, caused by a scientist who, after uploading his brain and consciousness online, has turned into a kind of posthuman cyborg, ending up prey to a mania of omnipotence. It is as if his previously ethically driven consciousness (he was a renowned scientist whose goal was to improve the world) had become morally corrupted in his hybridization with the machine. The film we are talking about is 2013's *Transcendence* starring Johnny Depp, directed by Wally Pfister. A film that saw little success, but which was capable of presenting interesting and topical ideas, even if thwarted by an increasingly complicated and far-fetched plot.

The other sequence, by contrast, shows a close-up of a robot-cyborg opening its eyes and looking through the camera at the viewers, to the beat of a triumphant soundtrack. This new human, or rather more appropriately called post-human, is called Mami. She is a girl who recently died and whose brain was uploaded onto a robotic exoskeleton and reborn to new life. The one who enabled all this was Chappie, a robot who has developed self-awareness and is capable of feeling just like humans. The film we are talking about is 2015's *Humandroid*, directed by Neil Blomkamp, a naturalized Canadian of South African origin. Admittedly, this is not the best film by this interesting auteur, but, like *Transcendence*, it addresses issues and raises topical questions.

The two works have as their subject matter, as we have said, the theme of transhumanism, namely the "cultural, intellectual and scientific movement that affirms the moral duty to improve the physical and cognitive capacities of the human species and to apply new technologies to humans so that we can eliminate unwanted and unnecessary aspects of the human condition such as suffering, disease, aging, and even mortality" to quote Nick Bostrom, one of the leading theorists and president of the World Transhumanist Association[2].

This is a movement that, as we have written, is central to contemporary debate and has taken center stage in contemporary bioethical thinking.

Today we are faced with converging technologies that are developing faster and faster and affecting a wide variety of areas; technologies that manage to connect and create something entirely new in terms of the relationship between human and artificial. Nanotechnology, biotechnology, information technology, cognitive science and neuroscience: their systemic integration has enabled and will enable unpredictable innovations, and one can understand why the themes of the transhumanist movement are increasingly central today. And they find representation on the big screen, as they always have, within the bioethical genre par excellence, which, in our view, is science fiction (Dalla Torre, 2010).

In our view, among the distinctive features of the science fiction genre, which before being cinematic is naturally literary, is that of being ontologically linked to the reflections, naturally presented in popular form, on the relationship between man and machine, between humanity and science, in the increasingly close and vortex-like intertwining that has involved both of them from the late nineteenth century to the present. These themes have since found their reflection in bioethics at the level of social science and philosophy. In a way, it can be said that science fiction anticipated a series of

---

[2] Although Bostrom later completely revised his views and became one of the thinkers who see the development of superintelligences as the greatest danger to humanity's survival (Bostrom, 2018).

questions and reflections on topics that would become the cornerstone of bioethical science[3].

In fact, it can be said that science fiction was born as a literary genre in the late nineteenth century to chronicle the dizzying development of science and machines in those years. Its stories mirror the industrial society that is narrated, explained, made acceptable and exalted. The stories of Jules Verne, a pioneer of the genre, are paradigmatic in this regard—examples of the scientistic optimism of the Belle Epoque.

At the same time, however, science fiction records the anxieties and fears that the arrival of the machine, an unknown "monolith" gives rise to among the social body, concerned about its future and survival. And it warns us from the outset against the use of technology that is not guided by a set of ethical/moral guideposts. Here we can cite the works of H. G. Welles, which, unlike Verne's optimistic and uplifting perspective, are gloomy depictions of future worlds in which social injustice and dehumanization are dominant.

And, in our view, another constitutive characteristic of the genre is that from the very beginning it has had an attitude of framing the world being represented with a humanistic gaze. We can call it a humanistic posture. Indeed, even in Verne's techno-enthusiastic tales, the point of view that governs the narrative and the actions of the characters is that of a universe in which the values of modern humanism, based on the values of dignity, equality, solidarity, and responsibility, must dominate. And which considers man as a moral subject who is self-determining and fulfilled through their conscience. This, at least, is the approach of Western science fiction, while different reflections would certainly be appropriate for that which belongs to the Eastern imagination.

These two founding traits of the genre, its bioethical nature and humanistic posture, run through the entire history of the genre, reaching from its beginnings all the way into contemporary times, in our Western context in particular. As far as cinematic science

---

[3] On the topic of cinema and bioethics, look: Cattorini (2012; 2017), Cosentino (2017), Baccarini (2009; 2012), Dalla Torre (2010), Shapshay (2009).

fiction is concerned, although it was born together with the birth of cinema (take, for instance, *Journey to the Moon* directed by Melies in 1903), it begins its real history, that is, its history as a A-list genre, capable of becoming a landmark for the film industry and the popular imagination, in 1968, when Stanley Kubrick made *2001: A Space Odyssey*. This is not the right space to explain the importance of that world-defining work (for which a separate talk would be warranted in its own right), but it is well established that with that film, Kubrick showed that cinematic science fiction can be the genre par excellence for reflecting on man, human nature and above all on the other element that has always defined human life and evolution, i.e. technology. Simplifying, of course, until that point American science fiction films told stories about alien invasions from the red planet, Mars, clear metaphors for the fear of communism in the Cold War period. With Kubrick, it was understood that the container of science fiction, just as it had been in literature, was the best incubator for developing deeper reflections concerning central issues in society (Chion, 2008).

Then, in 1977, with the worldwide success of *Star Wars* and *Close Encounters*, the genre also conquered the popular imagination, emerging from an elite authorial niche. The last stage we want to recall in this brief account took place in 1982, when Ridley Scott made *Blade Runner*, a film that combines authorial vision and popular vocation, and which for the first time brought to the screen a story by Philip K. Dick, thus inaugurating cyberpunk on the big screen; Dick would become the point of reference for many of the cinematic works to follow. *Blade Runner* is also the first film in which the thoughts and themes that would be developed in transhumanism are most explicitly formulated.

Since then, the silver screen has seen many films dealing with these topics, divided into a few categories:

1. blockbuster entertainment in which transhumanist themes are merely the backdrop for making a high-spectacle, special-effects-filled action film (for instance, *I, Robot*)

2. auteur blockbusters, in which, according to the approach of *Blade Runner,* the pleasure of storytelling is combined with the importance of the subject matter (for instance, Spielberg's films such as *A.I., Minority Report* or *Ready Player One,* or Denis Villeneuve's films, to whom we owe, among others, the sequel to *Blade Runner*)
3. minimalist auteur films, with almost no special effects, all focused on the questions being asked (for instance, Andrew Niccol's films such as *Gattaca* or *Anon,* or even Spike Jonze's *Her*).

These categories of films are different from each other, but, in our view, all share that dual nature that we have defined as constitutive of the science fiction genre: the bioethical nature and the humanistic nature.

Transhuman Dystopias Movies

Let us now return to the two films mentioned at the beginning of this talk. Both investigate the unprecedented relationships that might arise between man and technology in the near present/future that may enhance and improve the former's natural capabilities. And, at the same time, they raise and ask us the question of whether there are ethical limits to the use of these unlimited technological potentialities. And, if so, what are they? They build on the hypothesis that a world that is guided solely by technology is doomed to dehumanization. From a potential utopian world, then, it transforms into a dystopian world. These are films that bring us back to the need "to formulate an ethical framework that can treat the infosphere as a new environment worthy of the moral attention and care of the human inforgs that inhabit it" (Floridi, 2022, 409). An ethical framework capable of addressing and resolving the unprecedented challenges that arise in the new contemporary environment.

All these elements are very clear in *Transcendence*. The world is in danger of catastrophe because of the delusions of omnipotence of Will, the protagonist, who has empowered himself by uploading his consciousness online and has lost sight of all ethical limits in the maddening pursuit of the development of his intelligence alone. The transformation from human being to cyborg[4] has allowed him unimaginable intellectual and cognitive enhancement, but it has not been able to reproduce his consciousness exactly: in the transition, Will has lost his ethical sense, his ability to set a limit for himself, which was at the core of his mode of acting and being as a scientist. In this sense, the film counters the idea coming from transhumanism that the human mind can be reduced to its neural connections and is therefore potentially scannable into an electronic medium.

For transhumanists, the body is a mere machine on par with artificial machines; man is merely matter. His potentiality, his inherent purpose or the possibility of the existence of something immaterial are not taken into account. This is a biologicist reductionism that the film criticizes by showing that man is not just that, but is an ontologically complex subject who finds their meaning beyond matter, in the uniqueness of being capable of making decisions according to their values. The machine corrupts Will; indeed, the machine is an inaccurate copy of Will. A biotechnological monster, as Francis Fukuyama would say (Fukuyama, 2002).

And here we recall the Mephistophelean robot Mary from *Metropolis*, Fritz Lang's 1927 film, one of the prototypes of bioethical science fiction films. Will, once he becomes omniscient thanks to uploading himself to the Internet, just wants to replicate himself in all living beings and nature, to create a world in his image, perfect but also perfectly controllable. And here, too, the film shows the potential slippery slopes of using technology for its own sake: the risk of surveillance, domination, oppression, lack of privacy, subjugation. The world Will would go on to create is a world of slaves following his every command. A world devoid of free choice, a world devoid of humanity. Exactly as Aldous Huxley described in his 1932 *Brave New World*.

---

[4] As Paolo Benanti has written, the cyborg is the science fiction figure that best fits our synthetic and digital age. From the Frankestein-like monster that populated early science fiction stories, an artifact "external" to man, we have come to tell the tale of the cyborg, half man and half artificial machine, which encapsulates the anxieties and hopes of our techno-human time. (Benanti, 2022).

All these aspects underscore the need for a twofold ethical framing of AI: one dealing with its code (the algorithms that oversee its "thinking"), the other broader, requiring political-economic governance of AI development/use. Regarding the first, then, what is needed is an "algorethics" a new universal language that would place human dignity and human rights at the center of machine-sapiens "thinking". Hence, "the fundamental ethical imperative for the machine sapiens: doubt yourself. We must enable the machine to have some sense of uncertainty. Whenever the machine does not know with certainty whether it is protecting human value, it must request human action. This fundamental directive is achieved by introducing statistical paradigms within AI. This capacity for uncertainty must be at the heart of machine decision-making. If the machine asks the human whenever it is in a condition of uncertainty, then what we are achieving is an AI that puts the human at the center, or, as they say among engineers, a human-centered design. The fundamental norm would be one that builds all AI in a human-centered manner" (Benanti, 2021)

As for the second, "the innovative process of artificial intelligences can be evaluated as a positive only if it is characterized as a justified tool, oriented toward progress with a human face, which takes the form of a true and sincere moral commitment by individuals and institutions in the pursuit of the common good. Thus, the management of machine sapiens and their development in the near future requires a political-economic approach: it is necessary to establish international governance for the development of these technologies. In particular, the governance of artificial intelligences becomes, because of its focus on the human person, the means by which to ensure that this synthetic cognition, made possible by technological innovation, does not come to assume dehumanizing forms. Governance is the space where anthropological and ethical considerations must become effective forces and organizational culture to shape and guide technological innovation, making it a genuine source of human development. This space of political-economic action, which constitutes the governance of technologies, thus presents itself as a compelling call to ethics: innovating and developing new technologies must therefore translate into a commitment to governance of artificial intelligence technologies and widespread corporate responsibility" (Benanti, 2018, 56)

The film starring Johnny Depp would seem to be a manifesto of those technophobes who refuse the use of technology altogether. In this perspective, it is no coincidence that in the finale, society, after the general blackout that destroyed the Internet and all related technologies, has returned to a kind of pre-technological state, finally free to live. In reality, this is not exactly the case. The film also shows the beneficial effects that nanotechnology, for example, could bring to humanity, and especially its use for poorer and emerging countries as well. Will builds his new work base in a deprived area and begins his research on regenerative nanotechnology to help the people there. Thus, the view of technology that is on display is not negative for itself, but it is subjected to sharp criticism where the idea of man is reduced to the idea of machine and where the goal of technology becomes its advancement alone, without setting more ethical guideposts to guide its development under the banner of humanism. There must always be man, with his dignity, his morality, to guide the path of science, and man cannot cease being an end and become a means. In this sense, the film also expresses the principle of responsibility or the value of caution, which seems to be the aspect most shared nowadays by the various bioethical theories and anthropologies. And at this point, it is appropriate to make a small digression to clarify a point. When we talk about bioethics, we should actually talk about "bioethicses": that is, there are different anthropologies and philosophical theories underlying bioethics, mirroring the value pluralism of our times. These bioethicses are often at odds with each other on a number of key issues (D'Agostino, Palazzani, 2013; Battaglia, 2022). The great challenge of contemporary bioethicses is to find common points on which to base their decisions, naturally in continuous dialogue with the world of science, politics and the social world. One of these common points today is the principle of responsibility, which draws on the theories of philosopher Hans Jonas, and which postulates a principle of precaution, of focusing on evaluating the beneficial costs in the use/development of certain technologies (Jonas, 2009).

"In summary, precaution is the principle that has as its object the ethical decision (of action or non-action) in the condition of a possible/plausible, unquantifiable, serious, potentially irreversible damage, in the absence of certainty, taking into account the available scientific and technical knowledge, in order to avoid, diminish and control the damage or damages" (Palazzani, 2015, 1052).

Science fiction cinema, as *Transcendence* also demonstrates, has always appealed to this principle of responsibility; however, in our opinion, it connotes it within a very specific anthropological vision: the humanistic and naturalistic vision, as we have argued. Man is a moral agent with essential qualities that distinguish him from the rest of living beings, endowed with self-awareness and capable of identifying his essential purposes, and for these reasons also invested with responsibility towards his fellow human beings and the rest of the world.

At first glance, *Humandroid* seems to go against everything we have said so far. Bolmkamp's film would seem to be a staunch manifesto for transhumanism and its techno-enthusiasm: with the close-up of the cyborg Mami representing the birth of a new human, or, better put, post-human, we are at the dawn of a new world and a new anthropology: exactly as the transhumanists claim and hope. On closer inspection, however, the film argues for this clear techno-enthusiasm in a more complex way. First of all, the setting where the film takes place: a present/future Johannesburg dominated by poverty and violence, in which scientific and technological research has not brought improvements to society and instead has exacerbated inequality and injustice. Only large technological corporations—Chappie's inventor works for one of them—have gained great benefits and can live by certain standards. These corporations are closely linked to political power, with which they establish a vicious interrelationship. The rest of the population lives in conditions of misery, brutality, exploitation. They are continuously surveilled, according to the condition that some have called surveillance capitalism (Zuboff, 2019). Thus, here too the scenario is apocalyptic and dystopian, and hardly reassuring. Chappie lives within this framework, the first Artificial Intelligence to develop an autonomous consciousness, to have feelings, even to make art. The first robot to have, as he himself does not hesitate to claim, a soul. In this regard, the film seems to affirm the reductionist view of transhumanism: man can be reproduced into an artificial being; there is no difference between man and machine. However, this is only the case when the machine takes on the features proper to the human. That is, the model always starts from the human, from that which makes it ontologically valuable in relation to the rest of nature, and which is carried over into the machinic. Not equivalence, then, as with the transhumanist model, but affirmation of the inextricable supremacy of what is human. And it is through the features that characterize it that technology and its development should be guided. We need an ethics of AIs, which should be based on five principles: beneficence, non-maleficence, autonomy and justice, principles elaborated in the field of bioethics, to which a new enabling principle should be added, namely explicability (Floridi, 2022: 80-92). Let us welcome, then, the posthuman, let the "new flesh" be born, as David Cronenberg would say, but never forget that there must be a clear humanistic, personalist and naturalist ethic guiding this anthropological mutation.

As has been argued: "The model, then, is that of a synthetic cognition that is the result of the vision of reality mediated to man by his tool in a transparent manner, and not the passive acquisition of a result obtained in an obscure way. The functional goal, then, is to offer man a better chance of cognition, and never make cognition an algorithmic function instead, taken away from man. This fundamental ethical principle-and the ethical norms derived from it must be translatable to the two poles of the synthetic cognitive relationship: man and machine. On the human side, this means making the algorithmic criteria underlying the machine and its operation transparent and accessible to human cognition. Conversely, on the machine side, this means developing algorithms that can read the human and translate it into machine language" (Benanti, 2018, 51).

To further confirm our interpretation, we only need to look at the previous film made by the same director, *Elysium*: in this film there is no doubt about the humanistic vision and the need not to lose sight of the moral nature of the human subject in the use of technology. We could call *Elysium* a kind of reinterpretation of

Metropolis: here, too, we have two cities, indeed two worlds: one on Earth, overpopulated and now destroyed by pollution (another characteristic theme of science fiction, of course, is the ecological one, which, among others, is a central theme of bioethics as well), an Earth prey to violence and inhabited only by the poor. And then we have another city, in space, where the wealthy few live, a pristine earthly paradise where, thanks to advanced technologies, there is no disease and one can live indefinitely, surrounded by lush vegetation. On Earth, many people, like the protagonist, work for the large corporation that builds the technologies that allow survival on *Elysium*. The others can be divided into thieves, criminals, and destitute people trying to survive. Furthermore, everyone is subjected to a regime of surveillance, where no one is free, continually monitored by robots that oversee every citizen (or it would be more appropriate to call them slaves), including using violence. The rich people of *Elysium* do not want to share their wealth, technological and material, and are locked in a perpetual state of alert, ready for war, against all those who are trying, illegally, to get to that earthly paradise. The situation depicted could not be more dystopian: technologies subservient to the greed of the few have created a world of inequality, repulsive and devoid of all humanity. There is no solidarity, there is no freedom, dignity is trampled upon on a daily basis. The one who ends up subverting this condition will be the protagonist, together with a group of computer hackers, who will succeed in making *Elysium* a city accessible for all. In order to do all this, the protagonist will have to sacrifice himself: it will be his giving up his life, his sacrifice for others, that will finally bring justice — by redressing the balance. What could be more moral than giving one's life for the sake of others? And so, *Elysium*, like science fiction films always warn us, reminds us that those ethical/moral stakes that are inherent in human nature must undergird technological development.

This also leads us to another reflection: science fiction stories are, in the end, reflections on what defines the human being, what is its nature, its purpose, its meaning. And it seems to us that all these stories always affirm a humanistic vision, as we have said. In this sense, the heroes of science fiction films, while showing all their weaknesses and often their disenchanted view of the world, are heroes who affirm a humanistic view of the world. Anti-heroes, as is the case on contemporary screens, but very different from the nihilistic anti-heroes that dominate most noir films and TV series of our time (Dalla Torre, 2022; Bernardelli, 2018).

Comparing it with its quasi-sequel *Elysium*, therefore, *Humandroid* also fits within a vision that is not trivially techno-enthusiastic, but rather within a more complex reflection that has as its ideological backdrop the humanistic paradigm which, in our view, characterizes the entire science fiction genre. In addition, regarding Blomkamp's films, further reflection is warranted on their glocal and colonial dimension, which unfortunately we cannot go into here.

All this being said, two films that at first glance might have seemed to be the opposite of each other, one technophobic, the other techno-enthusiastic, are actually much more similar than one might have imagined, and demonstrate what we have been trying to show from the beginning of our discourse: namely, that science fiction is the bioethical genre par excellence, and that the paradigm that characterizes it is that of the humanistic vision, based on particular values, not least the principle of responsibility. This vision is recounted within dystopian stories that serve as a warning to the audience, urging none other than their caution and their responsibility in the use of certain technologies. These transhuman dystopias are, in our view, a contribution that popular culture offers to bioethical discourse and that aids in the negotiation of concepts, theories, and decisions that are complicated but central to the development of our societies. In fact, as Luciano Floridi writes, "the keys to a correct understanding of our situation and to the development of a sustainable infosphere thus lie not only in communication and transactions, but in the creation, design and management of information. Such understanding requires a new narrative, that is, a new kind of story we tell ourselves about our situation and the human project we wish to pursue" (Floridi, 2022: 408).

To conclude, we would like to recall an image from another movie: *Wall-E*, an animated science fiction masterpiece. The image is from the American poster for the film, in which the little robot

Wall-E looks up at the starry sky. In the film, it is thanks to him that the Earth will be repopulated. Thanks to his curiosity, his dreaming eyes—Wall-E, as Hoderlin would say, "poetically inhabits the earth", a humanly animated machine. And he is the perfect synthesis of the bioethical-humanistic positioning that, in our view, characterizes contemporary Western science fiction films.

References

Baccarini, Franco. 2009. *La tecnoetica nel cinema. Bioetica del futuro*. Roma: Palombi Editore.

Baccarini, Franco. 2012. *Tecnoetica e cinematografia. Un percorso di riflessione sulle tecnologie rappresentate sul grande schermo*. Roma: Edizioni Universitarie Romane.

Battaglia, Luisella. 2022. *Bioetica*. Milano: Editrice Bibliografica.

Benanti, Paolo. 2021. "La necessità di un algoretica per l'Intelligenza artificiale". L'Osservatore Romano. December 20, 2021.

Benanti, Paolo. 2016. *La condizione tecnoumana. Domande di senso nell'era della tecnologia*. Bologna: EDB.

Benanti, Paolo. 2018 *Postumano, troppo postumano. Neurotecnologie e human enhancement*. Roma: Castelvecchi.

Benanti, Paolo. 2019. *Le macchine sapienti. Intelligenze artificiali e decisioni umane*. Bologna: Marietti 1820.

Benanti, Paolo. 2020. *Digital Age. Teoria del cambio d'epoca. Persona, famiglia e società*. Milano; Edizioni San Paolo.

Benanti, Paolo. 2022. *Human in the Loop. Decisioni umane e intelligenze artificiali*. Milano: Mondadori Università.

Bernardelli, Andrea. 2018. *Cattivi seriali. Personaggi atipici nelle produzioni televisive contemporaneo*. Roma: Carocci Editore.

Bostrom, Nick. 2018. *Superintelligenza. Tendenze, pericoli, strategie*. Torino: Bollati Boringhieri.

Cattorini, Paolo. 2012. *Bioetica e cinema. Racconti di malattia e dilemmi morali*. Milano: Franco Angeli.

Cattorini, Paolo. 2017. *CinEtica*. Roma: Maggioli Editore.

Chion, Michael. 2008. *Un'odissea del cinema. Il «2001» di Kubrick*. Torino: Lindau.

Cosentino, Anna Maria. *2017. Bioetica e cinema a confronto*. Roma: IF Press.

D'Agostino, Francesco. Palazzani, Laura. 2013. *Bioetica. Nozioni fondamentali*. Brescia: La Scuola.

Dalla Torre, Paola. 2010. *Cinema contemporaneo e questioni bioetiche*. Roma: Studium.

Dalla Torre, Paola. 2012. *Sognando il futuro. Da 2001 Odissea nello spazio a Inception*. Soveria Manelli: Rubbettino

Dalla Torre, Paola. 2022. *La risata del Joker*. Roma: Studium.

Floridi, Luciano. 2014 *La quarta rivoluzione industriale. Come l'infosfera sta trasformando il mondo*. Milano: Raffaello Cortina Editore.

Floridi, Luciano. 2022. *Etica dell'intelligenza artificiale. Sviluppi, opportunità, sfide*. Milano: Raffaello Cortina Editore.

Fukuyama, Francis. 2002. *Our Posthuman Future. The Consequences of the Biotechnology Revolution*. New York: Farrar Straus & Giroux.

Galimberti, Umberto. 2002. *Psiche e Tecne. L'uomo nell'era della tecnica*. Milano: Feltrinelli.

Habermas, Jurgen. 2002. *Il futuro della natura umana. I rischi di una genetica liberale*, Torino: Einaudi.

Hauskeller, Michael. Philbeck, Thomas. Carbonell, Curtis, ed. 2015. *The Palgrave Hand Book of Posthumanism in Film and Television*. New York: Palgrave and MacMillan.

Jonas, Hans. 2009. *Il principio di responsabilità. Un'etica per la civiltà tecnologica*. Torino: Einaudi.

Miller, Paul. Wilsdon James, ed. 2006. *Better Humans? The Politics of Human Enhancement and Life Extension*. London: Demos.

Palazzani, Laura. 2015. *Il potenziamento umano. Tecnoscienza, etica e diritto*. Torino: Giappichelli.

Palazzani, Laura. 2020. *Tecnologie dell'informazione e intelligenza artificiale. Sfide etiche al diritto*. Roma: Studium.

Shapshay, Sandra ed. 2009. *Bioethics at the Movies*. Baltimore: The John University Press.

Tortoreto, Andrea, ed. 2018. *Filosofia della fantascienza*. Milano: Mimesis.

Zuboff, Shoshana. 2019. *Il capitalismo della sorveglianza*. Roma: LUISS University Press.

"A happy congruence of myth and politics". Mike McCormack's Biopolitical Dystopia in *Notes from a coma*

Enrico Reggiani

Two Premises

Two premises must be formulated before examining the literarization of an Irish experience of dystopia that the Irish writer Mike McCormack (1965-) elaborated in his novel *Notes from a coma* (2005).

Premise n. 1 (shorter): Ireland and Storytelling

It is shared theoretical and hermeneutical awareness that storytelling is "a social practice located in the cultural practices and social actions of a community" (Iseke 2014, 38) and that, as such, it is:

> a complex activity that engages both the teller's and the listener's abilities to use various kinds of semiotic resources (language, body parts), cognitive resources (memory, executive functions), as well as their coordinating abilities (monitoring), particularly for emotional and cognitive attunement (Hydén 2013, 228).

In Irish experience, though being often considered as "the flagship of [Irish] folklore"[1] (Taft 2000, 42), storytelling "involves complex interrelationships between past and present" and, "like much else about contemporary Irish culture" (Hallissy 2016, 30), it is a means of subordinating "such mundane but often crucial matters as taxation, legislation, technology, economics, and ecological conditions to the demands of narrative art" (Hallissy 2016, 65).

---

1   Cf. McCormack 2005, 197 on Irish storytelling: "[JJ O'Malley] once said [to his former girlfriend Sarah Nevin] that just because you can go on at length it doesn't mean you have something to say, it doesn't mean you have a story to tell".

Premise n. 2 (longer): Ireland and Dystopia

When one considers holistically both the frequently negative potentialities of its historical experience and their inexorably negative actualizations, Ireland may be interpreted as the quintessential dystopia. This is exactly what William Butler Yeats (1865-1939) epitomized dystopianly in three celebrated lines (ll. 14-16), sharp as lightning, from *Easter 1916*, a poem on the unfortunate revolutionary events of Easter Rising with an intricate and complicated publishing history: written between May and September 1916, printed privately in 25 copies and, then, in magazines in 1920, but included only in 1921 in the poetry collection *Michael Robartes and the Dancer* (Yeats 1997[2], 182):

> where motley is worn [...]
> all changed, changed utterly:
> a terrible beauty is born.

As genetic paradigms of the Irish quintessential dystopia may be mentioned, for instance, the nightmarish consequences of a non-state, the cruel destiny of underrepresented or unacknowledged citizens, the often apocalyptic future of its deported and/or migrating communities, the catastrophic exploitation of its economic resources, both actual and prospective, by colonizers of any kind and origin. Such paradigms have often been responsible for the genetically dystopian and/or dystopianly-oriented flavour of much autoctonous Irish literature and foreign writers' literarization of Irish experience. Three examples from three different centuries may suffice to illustrate this orientation:

1. the recurrent interpretation of Swift's *Gulliver's Travels* (1726) as the Irish starting-point of "the necessary development of the emergence of the dystopia, or anti-utopian fiction" (Houston 2007, 437);

2. the plausibly Irish reference of the very origin of the term "dystopia", which was probably coined by the English intellectual and politician John Stuart Mill (1806-1873). In a speech delivered in the British House of Commons in 1868, Mill defined as "dys-topians, or cacotopians" (borrowing the latter term from Jeremy Bentham's *Plan of parliamentary reform, in the form of a catechism, with reasons for each article*, 1818) the members of the British Government because, with respect to "the state of Ireland", "what they appear to favour is too bad to be practicable" (Mill 1988, 248);
3. the emblematically high frequency with which political scientists of any theoretical or methodological perspective quote W. B. Yeats's six hyper-dystopian lines from the first stanza of *The Second Coming*, a poem written in 1919, first printed in *The Dial* in November 1920 and, then, included in his 1921 poetry collection *Michael Robartes and the Dancer* (Yeats 1997[2], 189):

> Things fall apart; the centre cannot hold;
> Mere anarchy is loosed upon the world,
> The blood-dimmed tide is loosed, and everywhere
> The ceremony of innocence is drowned;
> The best lack all conviction, while the worst
> Are full of passionate intensity.

Michael Walzer has provided the most authoritative politological interpretation of these lines so far, when he has examined it "to understand passion in politics, or begin to understand it" (Walzer 2002, 618), remarking that "the poem describes the present moment, our own here and now, and what it suggests is that we live in the latter days of some historical process (not necessarily a Yeatsian cycle)" (Walzer 2002, 621).

McCormack's Speculative Approach to Fiction

Perhaps also because of his philosophical studies at the University of Galway with a final thesis on Heidegger and the philosophy of

---

[2] TD stands for Teachta Dála, the Irish denomination of a member of Dáil Éireann, the lower house of the Oireachtas (the Irish Parliament).

technology (McCormack 2021), the Irish fiction writer Mike McCormack (1965-), whom I interviewed on his latest novel *Solar Bones* (McCormack 2016) in one of the events of Milan Book City 2018, thinks that "fiction can be speculative, can conjecture; it's a place for bold ideas and that" (Nolan 2013, 97), and sees "a lot of my work as speculative" (McCormack 2021).

On the one hand, these speculative features and resources make him a perfect incarnation and representative of the Irish aspiration to go "beyond storytelling" (Nolan 2013, 98):

> One of the things that's recognisable about Ireland in the last fifteen or twenty years is our trafficking on this notion that we're great storytellers. Now, recent history [the Celtic Tiger, The Age of Tribunals: The Beef Tribunal, The Hepatitis Tribunal] shows that, not only are we not good storytellers, we have a vested interest in not telling stories, we will do our damndest not to tell stories. [...] It's arguable whether Joyce was a storyteller; it's arguable whether Beckett was a storyteller. [...] It's one of those inherited idiocies, that we're great storytellers. We have to find some way of telling a story, but ... ah, look: Experiment. Experiment or die.

On the other hand, those very same speculative features and resources, joined with a personalistic and communitarian Catholic upbringing and worldview (McCormack 2021), make him refuse an ideological approach to both

a. the anti-real "experimental ethos" (Nolan 2013, 88) — which produces "clubbing zombies with lengths of lead piping" (Nolan 2013, 97) by means of "very schematic" procedures "bound into an irreversible logic" (Nolan 2013, 91) like those in "the video gaming industries" (Nolan 2013, 97)

and

b. the rigidly ideologized dystopia, which refuses "real twenty-first century stuff" (Nolan 2013, 89) and does not forge the literary equivalents of "experimental games or cognitively challenging games" (Nolan 2013, 97).

The Reception of *Notes from a coma*

McCormack's *Notes from a coma* was published by Jonathan Cape in London in 2005 and, only five years later, John Waters, an authoritative literary critic of the *Irish Times*, coined for it the canonically demanding definition of "the greatest Irish novel of the decade just ended" (Waters, 2010). Liam Harte, another literary columnist of the same Irish newspaper, has provided a synopsis of the plot of *Notes from a coma* that may be of some help here, despite its omissions and limitations (Harte 2005):

> the novel charts the progress of JJ [John Joe] O'Malley, born in a Romanian orphanage and adopted by a bachelor farmer from Louisburgh, Co Mayo. Although JJ turns out to be a boy genius, his sense of being "cast out without love or grace" is a constant source of unhappiness. Plagued by "mindrot meditations" and shadowed by misfortune, he volunteers to be the control in a government project [the "Somnos project"] to test the use of deep coma on long-term prisoners. Along with four others, he is sedated in a high-security neurological unit from where his every brainwave is broadcast live to the worshipful gaze of "a generation anxious to move beyond the cowl and the candle".

Immediately after its publication in 2005, McCormack's novel suffered (and still suffers, to be honest) from the typically approximative and manipulative critical readings that move arbitrarily through the literary (in this case, more specifically, narrative) text in search of generic themes and exonogenous ideologemes instead of hermeneutically investigating its endogenous identity by tracing the components and processes of its holistic semiosis. The following exemplary triad can be mentioned as an illustration of such simplistic readings:

1. *Notes from a coma* was hastily described as a genological "cross between *Nineteen Eighty-Four* and the *X Files*" (Harte 2005), although—according to a political character in the novel (Kevin Barret TD[2]) included in its overall actantial orchestration—the "Somnos project" at its narrative core should "not be filed under conspiracy in some sort of paranoid *X-Files* dossier" (McCormack 2005, 111).

2. *Notes from a coma* was also stereotypically pigeonholed as belonging to "the best dystopian fiction" which "combines chillingly credible scenarios with acerbic political commentary" (Harte 2005), although the "speculation" (McCormack's cognitive keyword for his creative procedure) it applies to dystopia does not end up chronotopically in "dystopian accounts of places worse than the ones we live in" (Baccolini and Moylan 2013, 1).
3. More recently, as regards the textual features of *Notes from a coma*, Claire Lynch has simplistically observed that, since "computer technology [is used] as a byword for disorientating change" and "the previously 'only possible' becomes 'achievable reality'", "all former limitations and established markers of stability are deconstructed" (Lynch 2014, 41). Thus, she has extensively, impressionistically and unprovenly applied to McCormack's novel what Baccolini and Moylan consider as the textually genetic procedure of literary dystopias, "hybrid textuality"[3].

Notes from a coma: Tradition and Dystopia

In fact, a semiotic analysis of the text of *Notes from a coma* gives interpretive results on some fundamental issues that are different from those reached by the above-mentioned secondary sources. Firstly, it shows that the intertextual genealogy of *Notes from a coma* does not absorb the influence of dystopian literature (both written and multimedial like *Nineteen Eighty-Four* and the *X Files*) acritically and conformistically. On the contrary, in line with McCormack's speculative orientation, its experimental literary genre tries to recklessly and generously "weld together" (McCormack 2013) the cultural and narrative resources of some seemingly incompatible literary traditions to show the reader how to "become speculative and conjectural about the world" (McCormack 2013) where "chaos and structure are closely aligned" (McCormack 2021). Such traditions can be identified as follows:

---

[3] Cf. Baccolini and Moylan 2013, 6: "the typical dystopian text is an exercise in a politically charged form of hybrid textuality".

1. the quintessentially autoctonous dystopian roots that design the "the publick good of my country" (Swift 2018, 159) in Swift's *A Modest Proposal For preventing the Children of Poor People From being a Burthen to Their Parents or Country, and For making them Beneficial to the Publick* (1729) and reemerge, for instance, in *Revelations of the Dead Alive* (Banim 1824) by the Irish novelist John Banim (1798-1842) with its dystopian "narrator in a state of suspended animation over a period of a year in which he is able to project himself two centuries ahead, to London in 2022-3" (Connolly 2012, 193);
2. "the recklessness and generosity of mind and spirits" of great 20th-century experimental Irish writers like James Joyce (1882-1941), Samuel Beckett (1906-1989), and Flann O'Brien (1911-1966), whose "experimental tradition" "maybe this would be a time we would recover" (McCormack 2013);
3. the Irish domestic realism of John McGahern (1934-2006) and William Trevor (1928-2016) (McCormack 2013), although McCormack confessed that "there wasn't enough of my life" — e.g. his "preoccupation with rock music" and "heavy metal" — in McGahern (McCormack 2021);
4. "a tradition of kind of paranoid science fiction that is more recognizable from — I suppose — James Graham Ballard (1930-2009) and Philip K. Dick (1928-1982)" (McCormack 2013).

Secondly, the idiosyncratically dystopian chronotope of *Notes from a coma* does not portray "apocalyptic and suffocating worlds" (Elices 2016, 73) or "a non-existent society described in considerable detail and normally located in time and space that the author intended a contemporary reader to view as considerably worse than the society in which that reader lived" (Sargent 1994, 9). On the contrary, in emblematic opposition to the innumerable stereotypically retrogressive representations of "rural Ireland" in Irish literature, its dystopian chronotope is unexpectedly rooted in the "augmented realism" (McCormack 2021) of the western area of the Irish County Mayo — which does not turn McCormack into "a spokesman for the [rural] west of Ireland" as many other Irish writers have been in the preceding centuries for literary and political reasons, although he programmatically admits that "there's just that pull in the steering of my pen: every time I put my pen to paper it'll veer off toward West Mayo" (McCormack 2021). Thus, in full coherence with McCormack's speculative genealogy and polyphonic genology, in *Notes from a coma*, West Mayo is his supple and resilient "generative ground", which he elaborates anti-dystopianly as "a place of great innovation" "where the future is being minted" and with "a history of inventing the future", while, in his last novel *Solar Bones*, he maps it dystopianly as "an apocalyptic place [...] that has his kind of end-of-times-thing going on in it" (McCormack 2021).

Thirdly, in *Notes from a coma*, the dystopian polyphony of both its intertextual genealogy and chronotopic conformation does not reproduce "il modello privilegiato di una pratica di meta- e autoriflessione sulle paure, il palcoscenico sul quale inscenare tanto i tabù individuali più scabrosi o inaccettabili [...] quanto i timori collettivi più diffusi" (Ciraci 2018, 36). As a consequence of this, it does not generate the amorphous, dehumanized, and anti-communitarian hybrid textuality, "falling across different semiotic modes" (Borrelli 2017, 218), that "expresses a form of hybrid subjectivity" (Smyth 2017, 405) and literarizes a dystopian "epistemic mode, engendering a never-ending deferral of meaning" (Francesconi 2010, 16). On the contrary, McCormack's textuality in this novel counters dystopian dehumanization and anti-communitarianism by intoning "a hymn to fatherhood, neighborliness, and community" (McCormack 2013), focusing on the "individual as citizen" and "political integer" in a narrative that is "political right from the beginning", and emphasizing his author's "long-running interest in the trans-human and post-human condition" (McCormack 2021).

It is McCormack himself who informs his readers that the textuality of *Notes from a coma* mirrors its author's mind, which is "a mosaic rather than something continuous", whose "bits and pieces and shards and fragments" go "into the structure of *Notes from a coma*" and generate a narrative form that is not a "continuous linear narrative from a coma" (McCormack 2013). However, such textual mosaicality is unified by the magnetic attractiveness of the protagonist JJ O'Malley, who is personally quasi-absent, though verbally hyper-present in all the other characters' thoughts, speeches, and dialogues. As McCormack put it in 2013,

> He's actually never in it. He's the absent vacancy at the heart of the book. It's part of the idea that these people talk him into being. [...] One of the other things that occurred to me, and it's really obvious, is that when we die our biological, existential existence ends but our identity lives on in the minds of those who love us. We are safeguarded by those people. That was the central idea of *Notes From a Coma*; these people keep J.J. alive by talking about him. (Nolan 2013, 92).

Notes from a coma: A Non-ideological Speculative Dystopia

Paradoxically enough, JJ O'Malley's personal quasi-absence, which a semiotics of presence may read as the effect of his dystopian life sentence, instead reflects his utmost dystopian desire of "a break from myself, that's what I need. Just to take myself off somewhere and forget myself for a while" (McCormack 2005, 165). The intimate root of this desire is explicitly stated in the novel: since his "philosophy" "was that he saw signs everywhere, he made too many connections" (McCormack 2005, 46), this "coherent sense of himself in the universe" (McCormack 2005, 47) triggered "a kind of mind-racing — what he called his mindrot meditations" (McCormack 2005, 42) and "flights of fancy he would go off on sometimes" (McCormack 2005, 50), during which "he had this idea that his own mind was eating itself up" (McCormack 2005, 51). According to Jane Evers, the "forensic psychologist at Castlerea Prison" in the novel (McCormack 2005, 104), JJ O'Malley's "elliptic philosophical argument" (McCormack 2005, 105) "points to a kind of dualism which can be interpreted as a wish to achieve a peace of mind independent of thinking" (McCormack 2005, 104) and determines his decision to "take my mind of my mind for a while" (McCormack 2005, 103).

Being "not guilty of anything, [but] just guilty" (McCormack 2005, 50), after having "argued his best friend to death" (McCormack 2005, 80), JJ O'Malley conceives a self-imputed and self-sacrificial dystopia of a kind that the rest of the narrative actants and characters in the novel considers as absurd: he voluntarily adheres to the "penal experiment" of the *Somnos Project* "under the jurisdiction of the European Penal Commission[,] charged with the possibility of using deep coma as a future option in the EU prison system" (McCormack 2005, 102) – i.e., more precisely, "five comatose prisoners on the flat of their backs in Killary harbour exploring something which may or may not prove to be the future of penal incarceration across the EU – incredible" (McCormack 2005, 157).

It is thus almost inevitable and easily predictable that, for this "project that sounded like something out of a fifties sci-fi novel" (McCormack 2005, 157) and that "takes its place amid the gathering iconography of twentieth-century anxiety" (McCormack 2005, 30), "a journalist [...] on the steps of the Dáil" coined the metaphor of "a poisoned chalice right enough" (McCormack 2005, 57), and that JJ O'Malley's self-sacrificial dystopia acquires the aura of "a phenomena of religious fascination" (McCormack 2005, 78). Thus, in the alienating and disintegrating face of dystopianism, thanks to the protagonist's narrative centrality and pragmatics, McCormack succeeds in composing a polymorphous humanized community by means of an organic polyphonic textuality that complementarily combines

    a. the soloistic "ruminations" of the five central characters on JJ O'Malley.

and

    b. a paratextually orchestral "event horizon, a hopeless attempt to inscribe someone as widely as possible in the universe", which the Irish novelist has also defined musically as "contingent riffs [...] on what a specific character is talking about" "in four or five different [micro]languages (Fantasy, Journalese, Philosophical Argument, Hectoring, [...] Mandarin Scientific)" (Nolan 2013, 93).

On the basis of what I have outlined so far, as a conclusion, I propose to interpret McCormack's dystopian approach in *Notes from a coma* as a non-ideological speculative dystopia, in line with the Irish novelist's self-conception "as part of the speculative and conjectural tradition that informs Irish writing" (Nolan 2013, 96). The speculative code of *Notes from a coma* also configures it as a polyphonic "meta-dystopia" that "reflects [dialogically] on the material epistemological premises of the genre" (Brodman–Doan 2017, xi) and distances itself from most dystopian fiction, which "is usually structured in terms of clashing oppositions" and which is almost always set in the chronotope of "an advanced totalitarian state dependent upon a massive technological apparatus, in short, a technotopia" (Elices 2016, 79, 80). As a matter of fact, McCormack's narrative pragmatics releases the quasi-absent protagonist of *Notes from a coma* from such a totalitarian background by transfiguring him into "part of the nation's dreamscape" (McCormack 2005, 25) and "of the nation's dreaming" (McCormack 2005, 33), since "somehow the coma has leaked out through the security perimeter, found its way into the ambience of the nation and once more become the national idiom" (McCormack 2005, 184).

Albeit true, it must also be remarked that JJ O'Malley's is more than just "idiomatic" for his national community. From the very first "contingent riff" that inaugurates *Notes from a coma*, he becomes the perfect incarnation of the metaphor of its body politic and, though "more theatre than politics" (McCormack 2005, 191) according to Kevin Barret TD, his "whole thing" is often elaborated in the novel through the opaque, problematic and highly imaginative brain/mind-associated subsense of the biopolitical register[4] (McCormack 2005, 1; italics mine):

"…he is now both *stimulus* and *qualia*[5]. His name, blurting through the nation's print and electronic media, is also one of those *synapses* at which the

---

[4] Cf. Esposito 2002, 18 on the biopolitical register: "il registro biopolitico si costruisce interno alla […] rinnovata centralità [del corpo individuale e sociale]. È il corpo il terreno più immediato della relazione tra politica e vita perché solo in esso quest'ultima sembra protetta da ciò che minaccia di intaccarla e dalla sua stessa tendenza a oltrepassarsi, ad alterarsi". Kemp 2010, 141 recalls Foucalt's argument that "a fundamental characteristic of the modern era is the inclusion of bare life (the simple fact of living) in the mechanisms of state power, transforming politics into what he calls biopolitics".
[5] On the "stimulus-based approaches to qualia" cf. Northoff 2014, 483: "here, the brain itself and its intrinsic features, the encoding strategy and the spatiotemporal structure, are neglected. Instead, the starting point here is the stimulus-induced activity itself. The association of the purely neuronal stimulus-induced activity with the phenomenal features of qualia remains then unclear and

nation's *consciousness* forms itself. [...] He evokes a *response* and this is to our credit. Contrary to ongoing analysis the nation's *compassion reflex* has not been habituated. There is real concern, a genuine *anxiety* beyond the *compassion* flash fires of the latest crisis de jour. He touches our soul and, in a happy congruence of myth and politics, the public interest is now of interest to the public. *We are not entirely mindful of him but we do bear him in mind…*"

Thus, in total coherence with his "Catholic upbringing" and its "positive reservoir of myth and story and teachings and lore" (McCormack 2021), McCormack can be seen as generating a twenty-first-century narrative actualization of the sub-genre of "biopolitical dystopia" that is unsurprisingly at odds with David Huebert's definition of the latter as taking "place in spaces of carceral and corporeal confinement, often brought about by poverty" (Huebert 2017, 106). In fact, thanks to his speculative narrative and narratological resources, the biopolitical dystopia of *Notes from a coma* embodies "a happy congruence of myth and politics", where the "parole dépolitisé" (Barthes 1957, 216) of the former merges into and harmonizes with the inescapable textual politics of the latter.

References

Baccolini, Raffaella and Tom Moylan. 2013. "Introduction: Dystopia and histories", in *Dark horizons. Science fiction and the dystopian imagination*, edited by Raffaella Baccolini and Tom Moylan, 1-12. New York and London: Routledge.

Banim, John. 1824. *Revelations of the Dead Alive*. London: W. Simpkin – R. Marshall.

Barthes, Roland. 1957. *Mythologies*. Paris: Éditions du Seuil.

Borrelli, Nicola. 2017. "From Travelogues to Travel blogs. Instagram as an Inter-semiotic Travel Journal in the Age of the Web 2.0", in *The many facets of remediation in language studies*, edited by Michela Canepari, Gillian Mansfield, Franca Poppi, 211-229. Beau Bassin: LAP Lambert Academic Publishing.

Broadman, Barbara and James E. Doan. 2017. "Introduction", in *Apocalyptic Chic. Visions of the apocalypse and post-apocalypse in literature and visual arts*, edited by Barbara Broadman and James E. Doan, ix-xvi. Madison-Teaneck: Farleigh Dickinson University Press.

---

purely contingent [...]. There is thus an explanatory gap between neuronal mechanisms and phenomenal features".

Ciraci, Fabio. 2018. "*Metropolis*, apparato del Novecento. La distopia come oggettivazione delle paure urbane". *H-ermes. Journal of communication* 12: 35-62.

Connolly, Claire. 2012. *A cultural history of the Irish novel, 1790-1829*. Cambridge: Cambridge University Press.

Elices, Juan F. 2016. "Othering women in contemporary Irish dystopia: the case of Louise O'Neill's *Only ever yours*". *Nordic Irish Studies* 15 (1): 73-86.

Esposito, Roberto. 2002. *Immunitas. Protezione e negazione della vita*. Torino: Einaudi.

Francesconi, Sabina. 2010. "Negotiation of Naming in Alice Munro's *Meneseteung*". *Journal of the short story in English* 55: 1-30.

Hallissy, Margaret. 2016. *Understanding contemporary Irish fiction and drama*. Columbia: University of South Carolina Press.

Harte, Liam. 2005. "A sedation of the soul". *The Irish Times* May 14, https://www.irishtimes.com/news/a-sedation-of-the-soul-1.442318 (last access: March 14, 2023).

Houston, Chlöe. 2007. "Utopia, Dystopia or Anti-utopia? Gulliver's Travels and the Utopian Mode of Discourse". *Utopian Studies* 18 (3): 425-442.

Huebert, David. 2017. "Biopolitical dystopias, bureaucratic carnivores, synthetic primitives: 'pastoralia' as human zoo", in *Critical essays on George Saunders*, edited by Philip Coleman and Steve Gronert Ellerhoff, 105-120. Basingstoke: Palgrave Macmillan.

Hydén, Lars-Christer. 2013. "Toward and embodied theory of narrative and storytelling", in *The travelling concepts of narrative*, edited by Matti Hyvärinen, Mari Hatavara, and Lars-Christer Hydén, 227-244. Amsterdam-Philadelphia: John Benjamins Publishing Company.

Iseke-Barnes, Judy M. 2014. "Indigenous digital storytelling in video: witnessing with Alma Desjarlais", in *Social justice and the arts*, edited by Lee Ann Bell—Dipti Desai, 25-42. London-New York: Routledge.

Lynch, Claire. 2014. *Cyber Ireland: text, image, culture*. Basingstoke: Palgrave Macmillan.

McCormack, Mike. 2005. *Notes from a coma*. New York: Soho Press.

McCormack, Mike. 2013. *Novelist Mike McCormack on Notes From a Coma and his Irish Roots*. Politics & Prose Bookstore, Washington (D.C.), March 17, https://www.youtube.com/watch?v=1JJojlBLj2c (last access: March 14, 2023)

McCormack, Mike. 2016. *Solar Bones*. Edinburgh: Canongate Books.

McCormack, Mike. 2018. *A conversation with author Mike McCormack*. New York University—Washington (DC), Solas Nua, the Irish Arts Center (New York City), the Embassy of Ireland, and the EU Delegation European Month of Culture, June 13, https://www.youtube.com/watch?v=QB9M6Pzh4IM&t=619s (last access: March 14, 2023)

McCormack, Mike. 2021. *The Word with the Novelist Mike McCormack, in conversation with Alice Lyons*. Sligo Central Library and the BA in Writing & Literature at IT Sligo, November 24, https://www.youtube.com/watch?v=k7M40jJt4FA&t=932s (last access: March 14, 2023)

Mill, John Stuart. 1988. "The State of Ireland", in John Stuart Mill, *Public and parliamentary speeches. Volumes XXVIII-XIX: November 1850 – November 1868*, edited by John M. Robson and Bruce L. Kinzer, 247-261. Toronto—Buffalo: University of Toronto Press.

Nolan, Val. 2013. "Experiment or die: A conversation with Mike McCormack". *Ariel: a review of international English literature* 43 (2), 87-99.

Northoff, Georg. 2014. *Unlocking the brain. Volume II: consciousness*. Oxford: Oxford University Press.

Sargent, Lyman Tower. 1994. "The three faces of utopianism revisited". *Utopian studies* 5 (1), 1-37.

Smyth, Gerry. 2017. "Shanty singing and the Irish Atlantic: Identity and hybridity in the musical imagination of Stan Hugill". *International Journal of Maritime History*, 29 (2): 388-406.

Swift, Jonathan. 2018. *A Modest Proposal For preventing the Children of Poor People From being a Burthen to Their Parents or Country, and For making them Beneficial to the Publick*, in *Irish political writings after 1725: A Modest Proposal and other works*, edited by David Hayton and Adam Rounce, 143-159. Cambridge: Cambridge University Press.

Taft, Michael. 2000. "A proposal for the professionalization of Canadian folklore". *Culture and tradition* 22: 37-44.

Walzer, Michael. 2002. "Passion and politics". *Philosophy and social criticism* 28 (6), 617-633.

Waters, John. 2010. "Core selves go missing in high-tech celeb world". *The Irish Times* January 15, https://www.irishtimes.com/opinion/core-selves-go-missing-in-high-tech-celeb-world-1.1268823 (last access: March 14, 2023).

Yeats, William Butler. 1997². *The Collected Works of William Butler Yeats. Volume I. The Poems*, edited by R.J. Finneran, New York: Scribner.

The Space of Full Transparency. Contemporary Dystopian Scenarios

Romina Perni

Introduction

This essay focuses on transparency in relation to three areas: the personal level, the interpersonal and how it affects human reletionships, and the political. I'm going to do this by examining three contemporary dystopic works: two episodes of *Black Mirror* series, "The Entire History of You" (2011, *EHY* from now on) and "Crocodile" (2017, *Cr* from now on), and Dave Eggers' novel *The Circle* (2017).

On the one hand I would like to show how the idea of full transparency is obtained on a narrative and descriptive level trough the characterization of the inner/private space and the public one. On the other hand, I would like to reflect on its central role. Transparency is seen as a value for an effective control of self and relations with others and as an ideal of right political order, but it cannot be defined and created without considering its possible distortion and the impact on the dimension of human freedom. The dystopian works I'll refer to show us that, when transparency becomes more pervasive, the possibility of its erosion becomes more concrete, bringing out its extreme fragility. Furthermore, if inner/private and public spaces become totally transparent, human freedom seems to be resized and its limits redefined.

Transparency with Oneself and in Interpersonal Relations

In *Black Mirror* episodes transparency with oneself is represented by the opportunity for an individual to keep track of his own memories. In *EHY* Liam discovers that Ffion, his wife, is cheating on him with Jonas. In this parallel reality one can watch his or her own memories on a virtual screen thanks to a technology installed on a microchip called "grain" implanted under one's skin, behind the ear. Individuals can choose to have the grain implanted or not. The impression is that the vast majority of individuals have grains. This use is also associated with certain private and public services. For example airport security involves screening the last 24 hours people's memories. Another example: when Liam attacks Jonas, Hallam, a girl who doesn't have a grain implanted, calls the police but she is not trusted because she hasn't got any footage of the event.

You can select a memory using an interface with a small remote control and watch it again for yourself or share it with others. "Redo" is the term used for this action. It is possible to delete a memory, or a series of memories associated with a particular situation or person or period of life. In this case there will be a visible gap in the footage. That is to say that it should still remain a trace of the operation. In fact Liam, talking about this topic with Ffion, refers to that as the "hole".

A different scenario occurs in *Cr.* in this case you can watch your own memories on a screen thanks to a device called "recaller", a very basic portable television connected wirelessly to microchip implanted in your head. Every thought ones have in any given moment can be displayed on that screen.

Rob and Mia hide the body of a cyclist accidentally hit and murdered by Rob himself with his car. Mia is sitting next to Rob during the accident. Fifteen years later she is now a successful architect, has a family and the tragic event seems to have been forgotten. But Rob returns to Mia with the intention of revealing the truth to the dead cyclist's wife, who is still waiting for her husband's return. Mia doesn't want to and kills Rob. Shazia is a girl who uses the recaller on Mia to reconstruct the dynamics of another accident. She works for an insurance company and the recaller is useful to picture what happened in a certain situation (in this case an accident that Mia had seen the same night of Rob's murder).

Memories are subjective and emotionality-related. In this case the possibility of controlling memories is limited. Mia tries to control her own memories in order to stop them and focus only on what she wants, but she can't. Shazia is a witness and will be another of the woman's victims for this reason.

The grain and the recaller are devices useful to open up and share the inner/private space of memories. But a substantial difference emerges between the two episodes. In *EHY* individuals have control of their memories and of the device. We notice that in this parallel reality people have a hard time doing anything without this technology and accepting, for example, that other people may even refuse to share their memories. However memories are independent from the grain because they exist even if they're no longer viewable thorugh that technology.

In *Cr* individuals can't hide their memories from the recaller's control because this device acts regardless of one's will. It is for this reason that Mia starts her spiral of violence.

First we should take into account the consequences of using memory control devices. In fact memories are no longer memories. Every moment lived, especially in *EHY*, can be subsequently checked, examined, used, deleted, even if only in the grain. As Damiano Garofalo writes, a memory "displayed" is a sort of a different form of life (Garofalo 2020, 1748):

> [...] the individual memory is entirely delegated to the technical device: in a world where I can keep all my memories, without having to distinguish them to store them selectively in my memory, I am therefore authorized to no longer remember anything that happens, to live absently any experience that, in any case, can always be reviewed and analyzed later (Garofalo 2017, 49)[1].

This becomes relevant because in that way it is possible to know something that is impossible to know for a human being generally, "the private memories relived with the eyes of those who have experienced them" (Attimonelli 2020, 1095). In this kind of dystopic society, it is very difficult to have secrets, that are considered limiting or even harmful. Knowing more – knowing everything – is considered an element of progress in interpersonal relationships.

This is closely linked to some possible definitions of transparency that focus on the metaphor of light, as its characterizing

---

[1] My translation.

element[2]. What is made visible and clear, what is shown, is what I can understand in details, and that is a highly positive element. But this is also a dystopian point of view regarding transparency. The possibility to see better — to see everything — becomes also and above a chance for more control, according to a philosophical tradition that originates from Jeremy Bentham *Panopticon*. This project has been interpreted in many different ways[3]. Many famous dystopias have given this idea a material representation: for example, see Zamjatin's *Мы* (1924), describing a world where buildings are made of glass:

> Normally we live surrounded by transparent walls which seem to be knitted of sparkling air; we live beneath the eyes of everyone, always bathed in light. We have nothing to conceal from one another [...] (Zamjatin 1952, 19).

We could also refer to Orwell's *Nineteen Eighty-Four* (1949) and the control carried out by a totalitarian political power also thanks to screens in people's houses:

> "The telescreen received and transmitted simultaneously. Any sound that Winston made, above the level of a very low whisper, would be picked up by it; moreover, so long as he remained within the field of vision which the metal plaque commanded, he could be seen as well as heard. There was of course no way of knowing whether you were being watched at any given moment. [...] You had to live — did live, from habit that became instinct — in the assumption that every sound you made was overheard, and, except in darkness, every movement scrutinized" (Orwell 2012, 7-8).

As we shall see, Eggers' *The Circle* falls under this perspective. In *EHY* e *Cr* transparency affects interpersonal relationships, especially with regard to the possibility of controlling other people's memory. The space of the interpersonal relationships is that of

---

[2] See, for example, Koivisto 2016; Flyverbom 2015; Merloni, Pirni 2021.

[3] The *Panopticon*, or "the inspection-house", is a project for penitentiary houses. But Bentham has a more ambitious claim: "A new mode of obtaining power of mind over mind, in a quantity hitherto without example: and that, to a degree equally without example, secured by whoever chooses to have it so, against abuse" (Bentham 1843). This project has been variously discussed and interpreted, especially referring to a model of power organization based on surveillance and visibility imposed in a one-way direction. Michel Foucault dedicates to "panoptism" the third chapter of *Surveiller et punir. Naissance de la prison* (Foucault 1975).

sharing the inner/private one (the memory): "All men and women with microchips automatically perform the function of surveillance devices of their own memories and that of others" (Garofalo 2017, 66)[4].

In *EHY* the purpose of the grain seems to be the possibility of sharing. At the beginning, this is considered positively, as a vehicle of sincerity, of virtuous behavior. It is also possible to review important episodes of one's own life to evaluate them or live again the emotions connected. As the story goes on, this possibility appears less desirable because there isn't any improvement in interpersonal relations.

In *Cr* transparency is seen positively, but it is not very functional to introduce greater sincerity into interpersonal relationships. The spiral of violence in which Mia falls seems to testify this, although in this case the evaluation is not so clear. The question: "is memory control right and useful or not?" seems not to have an answer. Judgment on it seems more to be suspended. The machine of memories is certainly useful to hold accountability. But the possibility of memory control seems to trigger a storm of violence that otherwise would not have occurred.

Beyond the problem of usefulness or not of the media, there is another interesting aspect related to the use of that technological devices. It concerns the depth of interpersonal relationships that are built through this different way of understanding and "living" memory:

> "Relations in the *grain* age are superficial relations, which can be continually sought in the mnemonic support, this implies a less cognitive commitment (to know the person thoroughly, to strive to remember the words, thoughts, tastes) followed by a necessary emotional detachment (the less you know a person the more difficult it is to establish an emotional relationship with him/her)".

This is the "post-human paradox": "to strengthen the mnemonic media implies the impoverishment (if not the dissolution) of human memory" (Lammoglia, Pastorino 2019)[5].

---

[4] My translation.
[5] My translation.

Political and Institutional Transparency

In *EHY* and *Cr* we can only imagine a world in which transparency is mandatory by law. For example, we don't know what happens to people who don't have the grain. We can generally assume that they don't have the same rights as the other ones. In *Cr* it is difficult to have a general picture of the society based on transparency.

Now I will refer to a dystopic novel built entirely on the concept of transparency — *The Circle*, by Dave Eggers — to talk about the public space of transparency. My idea is that transparency is considered as a value for an effective control of self and relationships with others and as an ideal of right political order, but it create very relevant problems when it is brought to its extreme implementation.

In Eggers' novel Mae Holland lands a job at *The Circle*, a powerful technology company. She starts from the Customer Experience, but quickly climbs the company ladder. Meanwhile, The *Circle* continues to develop technologies, including, for example, *SeeChange*: small cameras that can produce real-time videos.

This is important for transparency because this is connected with some very interesting elements also regarding transparency towards oneself and in interpersonal relationships. First of all Mae's experience. She becomes transparent bringing a portable camera 24 hours a day. This device shows to the people who is watching it everything she does (except for nights and three minutes at the toilet). Mae declares that she wants to make herself totally transparent and, at the end, this intention turns her parents' lives upside down because they refuse to share their private life with other people. There is also the example of Stewart, called "the Transparent Man", who in the past had performed a similar experiment, using a small camera too: "a man who's willing to open up his life now for five years, and it's been an invaluable asset to the Circle, and soon, I bet, to all of humankind" (Eggers 2013, 205).

Gradually Mae becomes increasingly involved in *The Circle*, with consequences for her personal, familiar and social life. The pressure on transparency seems to be an imperative only for people that have a Circle account, but gradually tends to expand itself and also involve people outside. The company becomes more and more intrusive.

In this novel transparency is linked to a very precise normative model, according to this belief: truth is knowledge and total knowledge is a vehicle of progress for humanity. Mae says:

> For example, if there's a locked door, I start to make up all kinds of stories about what might be behind it. I feel like it's some kind of secret, and it leads to me making up lies. But if all the doors are open, physically and metaphorically, there's only the one truth (Eggers 2013, 297).

The truth is reduced to the only possible truth: that inside "the circle", that everyone can see and share. This condition brings to peace of mind: "As we all know here at the Circle, transparency leads to peace of mind" (Eggers 2013, 68). This is also the basis for an ideal democracy (see paragraph 3).

Eamon Bailey, one of the founders of *The Circle*, says: "And everything we do here is about knowing the previously unknown, right? " (Eggers 2013, 63). The slogans used within the company summarize this social model: "ALL THAT HAPPENS MUST BE KNOWN" (p. 67); "PRIVACY IS THEFT / [...] / SECRETS ARE LIES / SHARING IS CARING / PRIVACY IS THEFT" (Eggers 2013, 303). The regulative ideal is "the ultimate transparency": "No filter. See everything. Always" (Eggers 2013, 69); "We will become all-seeing, all-knowing" (Eggers 2013, 70). And again:

> "[...] But I'm a believer in the perfectibility of human beings. I think we can be better. I think we can be perfect or near to it. And when we become our best selves, the possibilities are endless. We can solve any problem. We can cure any disease, end hunger, everything, because we won't be dragged down by all our weaknesses, our petty secrets, our hoarding of information and knowledge. We will finally realize our potential" (Eggers 2013, 291-92).

I'd like to focus on two main points. First of all, citizens' control of politicians. The device used to make this control real is a micro-camera that shows and shares the entire political politician's activity, which is so totally "open" to those who intend to watch it. This is what Mrs Santos, a congresswoman, does and says:

> So I intend to follow Stewart on his path of illumination. And along the way, I intend to show how democracy can and should be: entirely open, entirely

transparent. Starting today, I will be wearing the same device that Stewart wears. My every meeting, movement, my every word, will be available to all my constituents and to the world (Eggers 2013, 208).

The first issue to be considered is certainly the impact that the application of this principle has on privacy right and the balance that needs to be established between the right for access, the visibility of politicians' actions and privacy right. In the dystopian world of *The Circle* this balance should not actually be found, because the central idea of all the activities of this company is that privacy is a theft. So there is no privacy right.

The relationship between transparency, the right to privacy and, in this context, the limitation of personal freedom, is a widespread theme in the literature on transparency[6]. The focus on the dystopian aspects that an absolutization of transparency brings with it alerts us about possible degenerations related to the application of this principle.

There is another question, closely linked to the first. Is transparency really useful, if only one representative of the institutions submits to the "moral" obligation of transparency? This process seems to work only with the actions and issues dealt with by a transparent individual. Transparency would be good only if everyone (or at least many) becomes transparent. In *The Circle* transparency seems to be an either-or choice, so a situation in between does not seem possible. This means that either you are transparent or you are not. But this means that the transparency system must be accepted by everyone in order to work properly:

> "And what if those who want to meet with you don't want a given meeting to be braodcast?"
> "Well, then they will not meet me," she [Santos] said. "You're either transparent or you're not. You're either accountable or you're not. What would anyone have to say to me that couldn't be said in public? What part of representing the people should be not be known by the very people I'm representing? (Eggers 2013, 209).

---

[6] See, for example, Carloni 2022, p. 197 ss.; Carloni 2014 (chap. 9); Pozen 2017; Timiani 2016.

Certainly transparency is a positive principle when it is considered related to the openness of political power in its institutional form towards citizens (see, for example, the interesting studies on administrative transparency[7]). In the dystopian versions of transparency, the focus is on the negative aspects linked to a pervasive and total translation of transparency itself[8].

Finally, the third issue concerns the fact that the obligation of transparency for political representatives, which should be a precondition for the mechanism to work, is either associated with an equally stringent obligation for citizens to look or, again, it wouldn't work.

Norberto Bobbio wrote:

> The definitions of democracy, as everyone knows, are many. Of all of them I prefer the one that presents it as "power in public". I use this synthetic expression to indicate all those institutional expedients that force the rulers to make their decisions in the light of the sun and allow the governed to "see" how and where they affect them (Bobbio 1999, 339).

But we could say that:

> there is audience and audience. Following Hegel's contemptuous assertion that the people do not know what they want, one could say that citizens that democracy needs are those who know what they want" (Bobbio 1999, 352)[9].

In *The Circle* the system seems to solve the problem related to the fact that in a democracy there must be an audience that wants and is able to "see", that is to say to know consciously (and often there isn't this kind of audience). In fact the private company involves workers and users all the day and forces them to transparency. In the next and final paragraph, I shall deal more specifically with this point relating to democracy and political participation.

---

[7] Some aspects of the questions related to administrative transparency are presented in Ponti 2022.
[8] The considerations of the philosopher Byung-Chul Han about transparency are well known. In *Transparenzgesellschafts* (2012), he critics the "society of positivity" [my translation] which has the traits of control, surveillance and which totalize the experience of human beings. I believe that this kind of reflections are important and interesting, but they should be read as considerations on the consequences of an absolutization of transparency, its dystopian version.
[9] My translation.

Transparency and the Idea of Democracy

Another element I would like to stress is related to the fact that in *The Circle* there is also an extra step proposed by Mae, that should lead to total transparency, the ultimate one. It concerns the obligation to transparency, to vote and to express and share one's opinions. This democatic model is named "Demoxie". It is a voting system, which requires every citizen to publish their vote through a Circle account. Thanks to this account, it will be possible for citizens to carry out some actions that concern the private sphere (for example, checking their emails) and other actions that concern both the private and the public sphere (another example, paying taxes). But this hypothetical model — imagined as desirable in the future — will also invade the framework of one of the cornerstones of democracy as a representative system: voting. Mae says: "You use your Circle account to pay taxes, to register to vote, to pay your parking tickets, to do anything. I mean, we would save each user hundreds of hours of inconvenience, and collectively, the country would save billions" (Eggers 2013, 390). It is no coincidence that this idea is also presented as a way of fight abstentionism.

About demoxie, we could say that it is "a form of direct, aggregative democracy, with no time for deliberation and no need for representatives" (Maurer, Rostbøll 2020). In fact, it is not just a matter of connecting the idea of democracy with the technological development of media. Of course we can consider what kind of influence this development could have on governmental procedures. But in this case an alternative model of democracy emerges, the "own Internet-based Democracy" (see again Maurer, Rostbøll 2020).

About this I would like to consider some final topics. The first concerns the fact that this model of democracy can be developed in reality only from a very high technological level, which, in the case described by Eggers, is in the hands of a private company. There is certainly a problem of overlap between private and public space, or rather the appropriation of public space by a private.

This is what Ty, one of the three founders of *The Circle*, admits. In fact, he doesn't agree with the increasingly pervasive choices of the other two partners. He tries to convince Mae of the distortions of reality that she is living and wants to push her into a sort of rebellion against the System.

> This idea of Completion, it's far beyond what I had in mind when I started all this, and it's far beyond what's right. It has to be brought back into some kind of balance. […] I didn't picture a world where Circle membership was mandatory, where all government and all life was channeled through one network (Eggers 2013, 480)[10].

This is exactly the point that Margaret Atwood emphasizes:

> The outpouring of ideas is central to *The Circle*, as it is in part a novel of ideas. What sort of ideas? Ideas about the social construction and deconstruction of privacy, and about the increasing corporate ownership of privacy, and about the effects such ownership may have on the nature of Western democracy (Atwood 2013)[11].

The second topic concerns the fact that this completely open and transparent democracy leads to the end of representative democracy. The most dystopic scenario is the final outcome of this widening of the space of transparency (through the Circle):

> "It would eliminate the guesswork," Stenton said, now standing at the head of the table. "Eliminate lobbyists. Eliminate polls. It might even eliminate congress. If we can know the will of the people at any time, without filter, without misinterpretation or bastardization, wouldn't it eliminate much of Washington?" (Eggers 2013, 391-92).

With "demoxie" we would have a direct democracy thanks to the technological mediation of *The Circle*. This is the dream of cyberdemocracy, as it was designed, for example, by Pierre Lévy. He imagined as next a society based on the progressive and necessarily

---

[10] "In short, the warning of the novel is not so much against Internet technology complementing democracy, but rather of one Internet company absorbing and dominating all private and political activity. Or put differently, the dangerous turning point is the point at which the Web not only supplements democratic institutions but becomes the only institution in society—knowing, organizing, and administering everything" (Maurer, Rostbøll 2020).

[11] Atwood doesn't consider Eggers' novel a dystopia: "Instead we are in the green and pleasant land of a satirical utopia for our times, where recycling and organics abound, people keep saying how much they like each another, and the brave new world of virtual sharing and caring breeds monsters" (Atwood 2013).

positive collaboration between democracy and cyberspace (see Lévy 2002).

We could call "demoxie" an instant democracy[12], which transforms transparency into something that makes the relationship between the level of institutional political power and that of the citizens immediately usable and, at the end, possible. However, in this new kind of democracy public space is temporally crushed. It is bigger, but empty, not creating the possibility of any exchange or interaction between the two levels.

Last but not least, it seems that this democracy is based on a model of domination that does not include positions against to transparency itself: "The point at which demoxie turns totalitarian is the point at which the Circle encompasses everything. When the Circle closes, there are no alternative sources of information, no other places to organize, no option of opting out, no hiding places" (Maurer, Rostbøll 2020). So we would have a direct and inclusive democracy, but based on a system that, at the end, suppresses pluralism. And this is my real final consideration. When transparency becomes more pervasive, the possibility of its erosion becomes more concrete, bringing out its extreme fragility. Taken to its extreme transparency seems to become something different: from a right principle of organization of personal, social and political relationships to a device that could limit and damage the freedom of individuals.

In the dystopias taken into consideration, all those problems — that emerge reflecting on the principle of transparency, its potential and its limits — are taken to their extremes. Transparency is a principle that, in order to maintain its positive charge of desirable value, must be continually subjected to criticism and its structurally dark sides must be highlighted.

---

[12] "Transparency of the sort created by the SeeChange cameras or surveillance technology might create a type of instant accountability, but it does not create the space and time required for reflective accountability" (Maurer, Rostbøll 2020).

References

Attimonelli, Claudia. 2020. "Body." In *I riflessi di Black Mirror. Glossario su immaginari, culture e media della società digitale*, edited by Mario Tirino and Antonio Tramontana, 961-1183. Roma: Rogas Edizioni. Kindle.

Atwood, Margaret. 2013. "When Privacy Is Theft." Review of *The Circle*, by Dave Eggers. *The New York Review*, November 21, 2013. https://www.nybooks.com/articles/2013/11/21/eggers-circle-when-priva cy-is-theft/?lp_txn_id=1437478.

Bennato, Davide, ed. 2020. *Black Mirror. Distopia e antropologia digitale* (2018). Catania: Villaggio Maori Edizioni. Kindle.

Bentham, Jeremy. 1843. *The Works of Jeremy Bentham*, vol. 4. London: William Tait. https://oll.libertyfund.org/title/bowring-the-works-of-jeremy-bentham-vol-4#lf0872-04_head_010.

Bobbio, Norberto. 1999. *Teoria generale della politica*. Torino: Einaudi.

Carloni, Enrico. 2014. *L'amministrazione aperta. Regole strumenti limiti dell'open government*. Santarcangelo di Romagna: Maggioli Editore.

Carloni, Enrico. 2022. *Il paradigma trasparenza. Amministrazioni, informazione, democrazia*. Bologna: il Mulino.

Eggers, Dave. 2013. *The Circle*. London: Penguin Books.

Foucault, Michel. 1975. *Surveiller et punir. Naissance de la prison*. Paris: Éditions Gallimard.

Garofalo, Damiano. 2017. *Black Mirror. Memorie dal futuro*. Roma: Edizioni Estemporanee – Azulee srl.

Garofalo, Damiano. 2020. "Memory." In Tirino, Tramontana 2020, 1735-845. Kindle.

Han, Byung-Chul. 2014. *Transparenzgesellschafts* (2012). Translated by Federica Buongiorno. *La società della trasparenza*, Milano: Nottetempo.

Koivisto, Ida. 2016. *The Anatomy of Transparency: The Concept and its Multifarious Implications*. San Domenico di Fiesole (FI): European University Institute.

Maurer, Kathrin, and Christian F. Rostbøll. 2020. "Demoxie: Reflections on Digital Democracy in Dave Eggers' Novel The Circle." *First Monday* 25 (5). https://firstmonday.org/ojs/index.php/fm/article/download/10650/9425 https://doi.org/10.5210/fm.v25i5.10650.

Lammoglia, Fausto and Selena Pastorino. 2019. *Black Mirror. Narrazioni filosofiche*. Sesto San Giovanni (MI): Mimesis.

Lévy, Pierre. 2002. *Cyberdemocratie*. Paris: Editions Odile Jacob.

Merloni, Francesco and Alberto Pirni. 2021. *Etica per le istituzioni. Un lessico*. Roma: Donzelli.

Ponti, Benedetto, ed. 2022. "Transparency in tension: between accountability and legitimacy." *Etica pubblica. Studi su legalità e partecipazione*. Special issue, 2.

Pozen, David E. 2017. "Freedom of Information Beyond the Freedom of Information Act." *University of Pennsylvania Law Review*, 165: 1097-158.

Orwell, George. 2012. *Nineteen Eighty-Four* (1949). Faded Page ebook #20120511.

Timiani, Matteo. 2016. "La trasparenza di cosa? L'evoluzione dell'ambito oggettivo." *Giornale di storia costituzionale* 31, I: 141-54.

Zamjatin, Evgenij. 1954. *Мы* (1924). Translated and with a Foreword by Gregory Zilboorg. *We*, New York: E. P. Dutton.

Filmography

Welsh, Brian, director. "The Entire History of you," *Black Mirror*. Produced by Annabel Jones and Charlie Brooker. Series 1, episode 4. Channel 4, 2011.

Hillcoat, Joan, director. "Crocodile," *Black Mirror*. Produced by Annabel Jones and Charlie Brooker. Series 4, episode 3. Netflix, 2017.

A Dystopian Reality: Social Inequality and Dystopian Narratives in Korea's Contemporary Cultural Production

Marco Milani

Introduction

The connection existing between dystopian narratives and social commentary is widespread and easily recognizable. Often times the use of these narratives, in audiovisual production and literature, is used by authors to describe, represent, interpret social reality and to critically address important issues that affect people's lives. The so-called "critical dystopia" (Moylan 2000) has become increasingly popular in cultural production, not only to criticize the existing reality but often to propose a sort of utopian impetus and an aspiration desire for social reform.

South Korea's reality and cultural production has also followed this trend. In recent years, dystopian narratives have become a key feature for the country's audiovisual production and in many cases these products have obtained a widespread success, not only in Korea but also at the international level. One important characteristic that most of these products share is that they are deeply rooted in the social and economic context of contemporary Korea and offer harsh criticism of social issues and problems, especially socio-economic inequalities. The most relevant case of this trend is represented by the TV series *Squid Game*, released and distributed by Netflix, that has become the most-watched Netflix show of all time. The success of *Squid Game* has certainly put a new light on these productions — and on Korean TV shows in general — but it is important to notice that it was not an isolated case and it did not come out of nowhere. In the last decades there has been, in Korea, a sharp increase in the attention that authors have reserved to the representation and interpretation of social issues; and in this perspective dystopian narratives, while neglected at the beginning, have achieved an increasingly important role. It is thus worth asking why there has been such an increase in the representation of social tension and conflicts and also how their representation has evolved over time, until achieving such significant results.

This chapter aims at analyzing the historical, political and economic roots of the rising social tension and inequality in South Korea and how cultural products have started to represent them. In order to achieve this goal, the chapter starts from describing the characteristics of the socio-political and economic model of development in South Korea in the early stages of its remarkable economic growth, focusing on the levels of inequality and social mobility. Subsequently, the chapter analyzes a key turning point represented by the 1997 economic crisis, that led to a substantial transformation of the economic and social structure and to the emergence of new forms of social inequality during the 2000s. The second part of the chapter focuses specifically on how these inequalities have been represented in audiovisual production, both in its first stages and also after the explosion of the *Korean Wave* phenomenon that brought these products to a global audience. The goal is to understand where the conflicts and tension of contemporary Korean society come from, why they have influenced cultural production so much and how their representation on screen has evolved over the years.

Key Characteristics of South Korea's Socio-Political and Economic Model

From an historical perspective, economic development has represented a key aspect of the socio-political development of South Korea. In the last sixty years, the country has undergone a series of crucial transformations that allowed it to pass from being one of the poorest countries in the world in the 1950s to become one of the so-called 'Asian tigers'[1] starting from the 1970s. The process of

---

[1] The term 'Asian Tigers' has been used starting from the 1970s to designate four East Asian economies that underwent a rapid process of industrialization and economic growth starting from the 1960s. These economies were those of South Korea, Taiwan, Singapore and Hong Kong.

economic development achieved its final stage in the 1990s, epitomized by the access of South Korea in 1996 to the Organization for Economic Co-operation and Development (OECD), an intergovernmental organization composed of the richest and most developed countries at the global level.

The historical and political vicissitudes that have characterized South Korea over the course of the decades have thus strongly influenced its economic development. After the tragic events of the division of the peninsula in 1945 and the following Korean War (1950-1953), the authoritarian governments that dominated South Korea prioritized economic reconstruction as the main goal. The first authoritarian government, led by Yi Sungman from 1948 to 1960, was not able to achieve relevant results in economic terms. After Yi was ousted by popular protests in 1960, the political power was quickly seized by a member of the military, general Park Chung-hee, who inaugurated a long period of authoritarian rule that lasted until his death in 1979 (Buzo 2007, 97-111). Park Chung-hee's regime immediately launched a process of economic development and modernization that was able to achieve very important results in a short period of time, to the point that the country's economic development was later defined as the 'Miracle on the Han River'.[2] The strategy implemented by Park's government was in line with what would be later defined as the 'Developmental State' model,[3] in which State intervention represented a key aspect, together with a strong focus on exports, protection of domestic industries, coordination between different political and economic actors and very limited political contestation. South Korea proved to be

---

[2] The term 'Miracle on the Han river' started to be used in the 1960s in relation to South Korea's economic growth with a reference to West Germany postwar surprising economic growth that was called the 'Miracle on the Rhein'. The Han river is the main river that flows through Seoul, South Korea's capital.

[3] The 'Developmental State' is a term used in economics to define a model of development which characterized some East Asian countries in the second half of the XX century, that achieved impressive economic growth with a very important role of the State in planning and implementing macro-economic policies. The model was first conceptualized by Chalmers Johnson in his book *MITI and the Japanese Miracle* (Stanford: Stanford University Press, 1982), based on the case of Japan, and was later expanded to include other economies such as South Korea, Taiwan, Singapore and several Southeast Asian countries.

one of the most successful examples of this economic approach — together with Japan and Taiwan — achieving impressive results in terms of economic growth in a relatively short period of time (Amsden 1989, 55-113). In the Korean case, this strategy led also to the consolidation of large family-owned industrial conglomerates (*chaebol*) that benefited from their proximity to the State and to financial actors, and that quickly evolved to dominate the country's economic development (Kim and Park 2011, 265-294).

The effects of this fast process of recovery and reconstruction were strongly felt within South Korea's society. Economic growth led to a substantial increase in the economic power of families and individuals and a significant increase in people's livelihood and quality of life. The country passed from being considered one of the poorest in the world in the 1950s, to become a middle-income country with a growing middle class in the mid-1970s (Lee 1994, 79-86). A further significant aspect of this development was that the level of socio-economic inequality decreased significantly and remained relatively low in the following years. Poverty still characterized some parts of the country, especially in rural areas that did not benefit from the industrial boom; however, overall the population experienced a general increase of the economic level and a decrease of inequality (Kang 2001, 7-8). A key aspect in this perspective was represented by the role of education. From the very beginning, the State strategy for economic development involved the creation of a strong system of primary, secondary and higher education: schools and universities became one of the most important instruments for upward social mobility, especially starting from the 1970s (Kang 2001, 12). The government policies on education also reflected the changing situation of the labor market over the years: on a first phase, in the late 1960s and 1970s, the focus was on secondary education with the goal of training workers for the manufacturing industries; while in the 1980s, when the economy evolved and became more mature — with higher skills required for production and an expansion of the service sector — the emphasis shifted towards university and higher education (Kang 2001, 12-13). Education was thus a key aspect in order to provide more balanced and widespread growth across large sectors of the population.

In this context, it is important to notice that economic growth and the increase in the living conditions of the population came together with a strong authoritarian approach by the government — both during the Park Chung-hee (1961-1979) and the following Chun Doo-hwan regimes (1980-1987) — that severely restricted the civil liberties and basic rights of the South Korean people, resorted to an extensive use of violence against any kind of social and political opposition and systematically repressed workers' protests and demands.

The 1997 (IMF) Crisis as a Turning Point

The socio-political situation in South Korea dramatically changed in 1987. During this key year the pressure on the authoritarian regime from the social and political opposition, became unsustainable and unmanageable through the use of violence. This situation of instability, together with an increased international attention toward South Korea on the eve of the organization of the Olympic Games scheduled for 1988, led to the collapse of Chun Doo-hwan's authoritarian regime and to a democratic constitutional reform that brought the first truly democratic presidential elections in December of the same year (Buzo 2007, 148-151).

For the South Korean population, democratization meant not only the opportunity to freely elect their political leaders, but also the abolition of most of the laws that previously limited civil and personal liberties and the elimination of the use of violence by State authorities. Civil society movements flourished and broadened their scope and goals (Kim 2000, 105-136).

In terms of economic growth, the early 1990s were a very positive moment for South Korea. The model that had been created in the previous decades remained mostly in place, with a strong export-driven industrial production and a growing domestic market that followed the improvements in the living conditions of the population and the expansion of the middle class. The South Korean government fully embraced the process of globalization that was permeating the world economy after the end of the Cold War. For South Korea, the growth of economic and trade exchanges, thanks to technological advancements and to the emergence of new key actors such as China, represented a very important opportunity to advance and promote economic development. In addition, South Korea had diversified the type of products and increased their quality in the 1980s and early 1990s, starting to become a real powerhouse also in electric and electronics and other advanced consumer goods. In this period, for the first time, also cultural products and cultural industries started to be considered as a possible source of economic income for the country (Kwon and Kim 2014, 425-428).

During the same period, another trend that further propelled economic growth emerged. Starting from the early 1990s, thanks to a series of financial liberalization put in place by the government, Korean banks and corporations began to borrow heavily on international markets with a large increase of foreign capitals in the country. This situation left the country vulnerable to dramatic consequences in case of capital flight or a sharp devaluation. In addition, South Korea's financial system was not well-equipped to manage the large inflows of foreign capital and these liberalizations, with a lack of proper regulations and supervision (Chopra et al. 2001, 4-14).

Under these risky and dangerous conditions, the perfect storm gathered in 1997. First, early in the year, some large corporations started to go bankrupt because of a series of negative external market conditions that led to a decrease in their revenues and to the inability to repay short-term borrowings. The series of failures had the consequence of putting more pressure on financial institutions increasingly burdened by a high number of bad loans. This situation immediately affected the credibility of the entire Korean financial system, with a sharp decline of stock prices, multiple downgrading by the credit ratings agencies and a strong devaluation of the currency (Yoo and Moon 1999, 272-273). By September 1997, South Korea's economy was in a very dangerous situation and in that moment a further external shock gave the final blow: the collapse of the Thai currency led to a rapid and unexpected capital flight from several countries in Southeast Asia, and eventually the contagious spread also to South Korea. The banking system was burdened by a huge amount of non-performing loans, many industrial conglomerates had to file for bankruptcy or were rescued by the State, and the access to international credit became unavailable. In this situation the government was forced to intervene to prevent a full collapse of the entire economy, and in order to get access to the necessary funds to stabilize the situation it managed to negotiate a deal with the International Monetary Fund (IMF). Before the end of the year, the IMF intervened with a rescue package of almost US$ 60 billion (Buzo 2007, 172-174). This intervention gave to the Korean version of the 1997 Asian Financial Crisis its new definition of the 'IMF crisis'.

The multi-billion rescue package, however, was not unconditional. In order to get access to the credit line, the South Korean government had to pass a series of laws aimed at liberalizing domestic economy, with a strong emphasis on the 'neoliberal' approach. First, the country had to stabilize its macroeconomic aspects and restructure the financial system; secondly, it had to promote a full trade, exchange and capital liberalization and reform the labor market with an increase of 'flexibility', that led to a sharp increase of precarious jobs.

The IMF recipe made possible for South Korea to return to economic growth faster than expected and also to repay its loan three years ahead of schedule in 2001 (Gluck 2001). However, the crisis structurally changed the economic and social fabric of the country, leaving consequences that lasted far longer than the relatively short IMF intervention. The 1997 crisis was a transformative event for South Korea. In the immediate aftermath of the crisis, the series of failures of banks and corporations negatively affected both the unemployment rate and the private savings invested in the country's stock market. However, when the worst of the crisis passed, the reforms that had been implemented by the government led to structural changes that remained also after the end of the IMF intervention. The 'Developmental State' model was largely abandoned, in favor of a neoliberal model, with a substantially reduced role of the State in the economy. Concurrently, the reform of the labor market led to an increase in the precarization of work conditions, with more flexible job contracts and non-regular workers, with the effect of increasing inequality within the society (Shin 2011, 17-23).

From the perspective of income and inequality, the new situation was characterized by a higher level of differentiation among the sectors of society. According to the Gini coefficient, one of the main indexes to measure income, wealth and consumption inequality, there was a sharp increase immediately after the 1997 crisis — from the levels of the early 1990s around 0.27-0.28 to 0.32 in 1998 (Kang 2001) — but also a following trend that remained at the same levels and even increased in the following years (Lee, Kim and Cin 2013, 95-99). This meant that the crisis not only increased economic inequality in its aftermath, but it also led to structural changes that maintained inequality at higher levels in the long term.

In addition, precarious employment hit especially hard younger generations that started to be unable to find permanent well-paid jobs in large corporations after completing higher education cycles. Schools and, even more, universities, considered as the main instrument for upward social mobility in the pre-crisis phase, lost their power to push people towards higher living standards. The social contract based on the idea that through hard work — and hard study — it was always possible to climb the socio-economic ladder started to falter, with the resulting effect of undermining social cohesion. Starting from the mid-2000s, this situation led to the emergence of the so-called 'Spoon theory',[4] to epitomize the disillusionment, especially of younger generations, towards their possibility to achieve economic stability and fulfillment (Kim 2017, 843-847).

The neoliberal turn after the 1997 crisis, and the social consequences it caused, changed the very fabric of South Korea's society. Inevitably, these changes almost immediately started to be represented and interpreted in audiovisual — and more in general cultural — production, with different narratives, styles and languages

---

[4] The term 'Spoon theory' emerged starting from 2015 to categorize individuals in Korea, especially young people, according to the socio-economic conditions of their families: 'gold spoon' are those who come from upper class families with large amounts of wealth and social influence, while the rest of the population was defined as 'dirt spoon'. This division emerged mostly on social media and became widespread in the following years. The emphasis was on the characteristics of wealth as inherited, and thus also on inequality as inherited.

that evolved over the years. Among these, dystopian narratives came to play a paramount role, representing and narrating a socio-economic reality that started to increasingly resemble a real-life dystopia.

The Evolving Representation of Social Inequalities in Audiovisual Production

Representations of social inequality has been a recurrent feature of Korean film and audiovisual production, in particular starting from the late 1980s-early 1990s, and has become one of the most recognizable characteristics of this production also outside of the country. For several years, films, and cultural production more in general, were not allowed to represent, narrate or interpret issues that could negatively refer to the social, economic or political situation of the country. Under the long authoritarian period, that lasted from the late 1940s to the late 1980s, cultural production was mostly considered as a means to strengthen the grip on power of the regime or to produce entertainment for the population. For this reason, most of the products, with very few exceptions,[5] tended to avoid socio-political, or even historical, issues, and when they did represent them it was only through nationalistic narratives that celebrated the regime.

After 1987, democratization led to the flourishing of a new wave of Korean directors, writers and producers—that were aptly called the Korean *New Wave*—that immediately started to represent on screen all those themes, issues and problems that for decades were not allowed to represent. Social protests, economic inequality, industrial unrests, family problems became some of the most represented issues, together with a reinterpretation of key historical events of modern Korean history, and a new and less ideological approach to the North/South division and North Korea in general

---

[5] One notable exception was the film *Obaltan* by Yu Hyun-mok; released in 1960 during the short window of freedom between two authoritarian regimes and strongly influenced by Italian neorealism, the film describes in details the very difficult socio-economic situation of the Korean population in the aftermath of the Korean War.

(Standish 1994, 77). The Korean *New Wave* can be seen as the first true movement of protest cinema since the colonization (Kim 2022, 36). Directors like Park Kwang-su, Chun Ji-young, Jang Kil-soo, Jang Sun-woo, and producer Shin Chul were all part of this movement and produced some of most important movies between the late 1980s and early 1990s. Despite the differences in their styles, one common feature was the emphasis on social and political issues and the idea that realism was not only the more appropriate aesthetic through which representing these themes, but also a political ideal to which aspire. After decades of censorship there was in these authors, strongly influenced by European films, a real need to create a realistic and politically informed cinema with the working class at the center (Paquet 2008, 21-22). This was the key moment in which social inequalities and their representation acquired a prominent role in the country's cultural production, after being neglected for decades. However, they were interpreted and described mostly through realism and realistic narratives; dystopian narratives were not there yet.

The 1997 crisis, as we have previously explained, substantially changed the socio-economic dynamics of the country, with an increase in socio-economic inequalities. This transformation, that started in the early 2000s, was further deepened by the following global financial crisis of 2008, that for South Korea was certainly much less consequential than the one in 1997, and by the election in 2007 of a conservative president, Lee Myung-bak, who had a strong neoliberal agenda.

The rapid neoliberal turn of this phase can be seen as a further step in the process of 'compressed modernity' that has been applied to South Korea's post-World War II history and that so strongly influenced the country's socio-cultural development and identity. As Chang Kyung-sup noted "South Koreans have experienced Westerners historical development of two or three centuries over merely three or four decades." (Chang 1999, 48) The experience of modernity through the expansion of capitalism and the strong influence of the United States was compressed in a relatively short period of time, creating a series of socio-economic and cultural tension that were kept under control by the strong authoritarian rule. The 1997

IMF crisis represented a new stage in this process of 'modernization', and it also happened at a very fast, compressed pace, with the redefinition of key economic rules and relations that took place in a very short period of time, with basically no time for the population to adjust to the new situation. This transformation led to the emergence of new socio-economic tensions over the following years that further reinforced the need to be represented, interpreted and narrated in the country's cultural production.

Compared to the tension and demands of the authoritarian era, basically revolving around the issues of democratization and the improvement in working conditions, in this new phase social inequality became of paramount importance. After the post-1997 reforms, not only the indexes of inequality registered an increase and remained higher than before, but even more importantly upward social mobility stalled, youth unemployment grew, together with the growth of non-regular jobs, while social competition continued to remain fierce starting from a very young age. The influence of rich and powerful families became the key factor for success in life, upward socio-economic mobility was reduced while competition became even more extreme.

This transformation of the socio-economic landscape was accompanied by a transformation in the way these issues were narrated and represented on screen. The strong emphasis on realism, that had characterized the late 1980s-1990s period, began to give way in the early 2000s to new narratives, including dystopian narratives.

Dystopian themes in South Korea's films and literature were not completely new, but they had remained for many years at the margins of cultural production. These narratives had emerged as a sub-branch of science fiction in the 1970s and 1980s as a critical and subversive way "to make a countercultural statement against the malaise of living under dictatorial conditions in a modern industrialized society." (Park 2018, 353) Critical dystopian fiction became a new use of science fiction to criticize the authoritarian regime on one side, but also the socio-economic transformations in a 'compressed modernity' situation. These narratives remained mostly in literature, because at the time the film industry was heavily regulated and controlled by the regime.[6]

With the 1997 crisis, science fiction came back as an important instrument to interrogate the direction of South Korea's modernity (Park 2018, 358) and propose a critical interpretation of the tensions that increasingly began to agitate society. Compared with the previous phase, however, this time there were significant differences that led to a much more widespread success of these products. First, the South Korean film and audiovisual industry had transformed and evolved in the last part of the 1990s: after the first reforms of the film industry in the 1980s, the opening of the market towards major international players and the massive influx of foreign movies, especially from the US, the industry had modernized and was able to produce movies with a much higher budget and to compete within and outside the country with major foreign production, as demonstrated by the great success of the first Korean blockbuster, *Shiri* (*Swiri*) by Kang Je-kyu, in 1999 (Choi 2010, 31-59). Similarly, also the TV industry was in the first phase of its success, especially in East Asia, with the emergence of the K-Drama model, benefiting from a substantial expansion of investments and keen on experimenting with different genres (Jin 2023, 101-107). This development created favorable conditions for the creation of new audiovisual products with different narratives and styles which included also science fiction and dystopian narratives. A second key factor was related to the emergence of a new generation of directors, writers and producers that were not committed to realism and realistic narratives, as the ones in the Korean *New Wave*, and were not as connected, emotionally and artistically, to the democratization movement of the authoritarian years. These authors were also much more influenced by Western and Japanese products, that started to flow in the country from the mid-1990s thanks to the market liberalization of those years, which included cultural industries (Kwon and Kim 2014, 427-428). Some of these new authors started to gain almost immediate national and international recognition, such as

---

[6] One notable exception from this era is the film *Killer Butterfly* (*Salinnabireul jjotneun yeoja*) by Kim Ki-young, 1978.

Park Chan-wook, Bong Joon-ho, Kim Jee-woon, and already in their first movies they started to infuse characteristics from science fiction, horror and dystopian narratives, as in the cases of *Old Boy* (*Oldeuboi*, 2003) by Park, *A tale of two sisters* (*Janghwa, Hongryeon*, 2003) by Kim and *The Host* (*Gwoemul*, 2006) by Bong.

By the mid-2000s, the elements that led to the following spread of dystopian narratives in Korean cultural products, especially films and TV series, and that made them one key feature of this production were all in place.

Social Inequalities and Dystopian Narratives in the Age of the *Korean Wave*

The increase and spread of films and TV series representing and interpreting Korea's social and economic inequalities through the use of dystopian narratives was strongly influenced also by another process that emerged in the late 1990s and exploded at the global level in the early 2010s: the *Korean Wave*. South Korean cultural production became an international phenomenon gaining success and audiences first in East Asia and then at the global level. Pop music—the so-called K-Pop—and TV shows—called K-Drama—were the first driver of this transformation in the region; however, with the global diffusion of new technological instruments, such as digital platforms and social media, this phenomenon became global and all the sectors of Korean cultural production started to benefit from a strong interest and attention almost everywhere in the world (Song 2020). This development massively impacted on audiovisual production, both for what concerned TV shows, that were a key component of the Korean Wave from the very beginning, and also for films, that benefited from the success of the brand 'Korea' at a later stage.

In this new environment, the dystopian representation of social inequalities started to play an increasingly important role as a recurring theme in several productions. As outlined in the previous section, the socio-economic situation of Korea in this phase was characterized by a higher degree of inequality, compared with previous stages of the country's development, and social mobility was significantly reduced, with a fragmentation of society into almost impermeable social 'classes', where the privilege to be born in a 'high-ranking' family became the main determining factor for individual success, to the detriment of merit and fair competition. This situation of disillusionment was felt particularly strongly by younger generations, as epitomized by the 'spoon theory' paradigm mentioned before.

With all the possibilities granted by a well-developed and successful audiovisual industry, inequalities have been increasingly narrated and interpreted through the allegories of dystopian narratives. Two of the most successful and clearest examples of how these narratives are intertwined with social issues are represented by the movies *Snowpiercer* (*Seolgungnyeolcha*, 2013) by Bong Joon-ho and *Train to Busan* (*Busanhaeng*, 2016) by Yeon Sang-ho. Both films present a dystopian future, although with very different characteristics: *Snowpiercer* takes place in a post-apocalyptic world in which humanity has been decimated by a new ice age and a running train has remained as the only livable place on Earth; *Train to Busan* presents a zombie apocalypse that suddenly breaks out in the country, threatening the passengers of a train while trying to reach the city of Busan hoping to find a safe haven. In both cases, the train appears as the main means of survival, but at the same time as the plastic manifestation of a rigid division in social classes, represented by the different cars of the train. In the case of *Snowpiercer*, this discrimination is clearly illustrated by the abysmal difference in the living conditions of the passengers in the tail and in the front of the train, a division based only on the amount of money paid by the passengers. But also in *Train to Busan* the role of social 'classes' is of paramount importance, as demonstrated by the characterization of the protagonists and by the actions they take in order to survive. Both movies achieved important results both in South Korea and abroad, demonstrating not only the appeal of Korean productions on the international audience, but also the interest towards representations of social issues through dystopian narratives.

Global success attracted more investments for the Korean creative industries, which, combined with increased technical know-how, gave Korean directors the opportunity to take to the screen even more ambitious visions. In addition, the success enjoyed by Korean contents worldwide led the main digital platforms to invest more in the industry and bring an increasing number of products to a global audience. The results can be seen in the success of the Netflix TV show *Squid Game* (*Ojingeo Geim*) by director Hwang Dong-hyuk, released in 2021. The show achieved an unexpected global success unlike any other Korean TV series and became Netflix's most watched show of all time (Kim 2023, 108-110). *Squid Game* is the quintessential example of the global appeal of Korean dystopian narratives that portrays social inequalities, since this theme serves as the main foundation for the entire plot, based on popular children's games that become death games in which Koreans in economic difficulties fight to survive and receive money for the amusement of members of the economic and social elite. In the perspective of the previous analysis of socio-economic inequalities in Korea and of their representation, it becomes clear how this show came into being as a sort of point of arrival of a long path that had started years before with the sweeping changes brought to South Korean society by the 1997 financial crisis and also by the transformation and success of the audiovisual industry in the country. *Squid Game* is on one side fully 'internationalized', created by a global platform with a global audience in mind, but at the same time it is also deeply rooted in the specific socio-economic reality of South Korea.

The astonishing success of *Squid Game* created a sort of momentum for Korean TV series distributed through digital platforms. One of the first TV show that achieved relevant results after *Squid Game* was also based on a dystopian narrative representing social tension and inequalities in South Korea. *All of us are dead* (*Jigeum uri hakgyoneun*), distributed by Netflix in 2022 and based on a very successful webtoon published between 2009 and 2011, is a zombie apocalypse horror show that takes place inside a high school. The series revolve mostly around the efforts of a group of students to survive in the midst of the zombie outbreak, but it also critically depicts several elements of contemporary South Korean society. The frustration and disillusionment of teenagers certainly represent the main theme of the show, together with social issues such as bullying, sexual assault, suicide, and the ubiquitous, and in some cases nefarious role, of social networks (Conran 2022). However, as the director and creator Lee Jae-kyoo stated in an interview, it is not only a story of school bullying, but also a representation of the society at large (Lee 2022). Social inequality enters the show through the strict social class hierarchy inside the school, where socio-economic status and seniority are crucial for the characters. This divide remains to a certain extent also after the outbreak starts, influencing the dynamics within the group that tries to survive. In addition, the show depicts very critically the role of public authorities and adults: the school administration, police officers, and soldiers, that first fail to prevent the outbreak and then are unable to rescue the students (Later 2022). The adults who really try to help them act outside procedures and chains of command. This further aspect highlights even more the disillusionment and lack of trust of younger generations towards the socio-political system in place.

These examples shows that the use of dystopian narratives to represent social issues, and in particular social inequalities, has reached notable results in terms of success, both in Korea and abroad. The *Korean Wave* phenomenon has certainly played an enabling role for this, especially in terms of increasing the international attention towards South Korean productions, but also in making these products more familiar for a global and diversified audience. This development, that comes from a fairly long history of audiovisual products that represent social criticism, points in the direction of a further increase in the number of productions which will include these themes and narratives.

Conclusions

The success of some of the most relevant Korean cultural products emerged in the last few years share their use of dystopian narratives to critically represent social tensions and conflict, and in particular socio-economic inequalities. This has been the case of the most successful of this product, *Squid Game*, but, as we have seen in the chapter, there are several other important examples, such as in the case of the movies *Snowpiercer* and *Train to Busan* and the TV series *All of us are dead*.

This trend has its roots in a series of structural transformation of the socio-economic conditions in South Korea that can be traced back to the 1997 crisis and more specifically to the post-crisis reforms, that on one hand allowed a fast recovery of economic growth, but on the other hand led to an increase of social inequality and to a reduction of upward social mobility that remained after the immediate effects of the crisis had dissipated. When the transformation became structural it started to be represented and interpreted also in the cultural industry and dystopian narratives quickly became widely used for this purpose. Starting from the 2000s, the maturity of a well-developed audiovisual industry, the growing influence of foreign products and the emergence of a new generation of directors and authors, keen on experimenting with different genres and solutions, paved the way for a differentiation of the traditional realist narratives that had dominated socially engaged cultural products up to that moment. The following global spread of the *Korean Wave* was the last piece for the international success of these products. Precisely because of this success, lately we are seeing a further proliferation of Korean films and TV shows that points in this direction, with titles such as Netflix's TV series *Hellbound* (*Jiok*) and movie *Jung_E* (*Jeongi*), both by director Yeon Sang-ho, TV shows *Sweet Home* (*Seuwiteuhom*), *Black Knight* (*Taekbaegisa*), *Bargain* (*Momgap*), and movie *Space Sweepers* (*Seungriho*).

At the same time, the social tensions that have emerged in the last two decades are still strongly felt by large parts of the population, especially the younger generation, and have been able to transcend political, cultural, linguistic borders and become transnational issues felt among very different and diverse audiences around the world. The combination of these factors leads us in the direction of a possible future reinforcement of this existing trend that has its roots in the historical socio-economic and political development of a country but that also opens up important scenarios for the future.

References

Amsden, Alice H. 1989. *Asia's Next Giant: South Korea and late industrialization*. Oxford: Oxford University Press.

Buzo, Adrian. 2007. *The Making of Modern Korea*. Abingdon: Routledge.

Chang, Kyung-Sup. 1999. "Compressed modernity and its discontents: South Korean society in transition". *Economy and Society* 28, No. 1: 30-55.

Choi, Jinhee. 2010. *The South Korean film renaissance: Local hitmakers, global provocateurs*. Middletown: Wesleyan University Press.

Chopra, Ajai, Kenneth Kang, Meral Karasulu, Hong Liang, Henry Ma, and Anthony Richards. 2001. "From Crisis to Recovery in Korea: Strategy, Achievements, and Lessons". *IMF Working Paper WP/01/154*. October 2001.

Conran, Pierce. 2022. "The Enduring Appeal of Korean Dystopias". *Korean Film Council KO-Pick*, February 22, 2022. https://www.koreanfilm.or.kr/eng/news/features.jsp?blbdComCd=601013&seq=556&mode=FEATURES_VIEW.

Gluck, Caroline. 2001. "Seoul pays off its IMF debts". *BBC News*, August 23, 2001. http://news.bbc.co.uk/2/hi/business/1505131.stm.

Jin, Dal Yong. 2023. *Understanding the Korean Wave: Transnational Korean Pop Culture and Digital Technologies*. Abingdon: Routledge.

Johnson, Chalmers. 1982. *MITI and the Japanese Miracle: The growth of industrial policy, 1925-1975*. Stanford: Stanford University Press.

Kang, Seoghoon. 2001. "Globalization and Income Inequality in Korea: An Overview". *FDI, Human Capital and Education in Developing Countries FDI, Human Capital and Education in Developing Countries: Technical Meeting*. OECD Development Centre. December 2001.

Kim, Eun Mee and Gil-Sung Park. 2011. "The *Chaebol*". In *The Park Chung-Hee Era: The transformation of South Korea*, edited by Byung-Kook Kim and Ezra F. Vogel, 265-294. Cambridge: Harvard University Press.

Kim, Hyejin. 2017. "'Spoon Theory' and the Fall of a Populist Princess in Seoul". *Journal of Asian Studies* 76, No. 4 (November): 839-849.

Kim, Kyung Hyun. 2002. "Korean Cinema and Im Kwon-Taek". In *Im Kwon-Taek: The making of a Korean National Cinema*, edited by David James and Kyung Hyun Kim, 19-46. Detroit: Wayne State University Press.

Kim, Sunhyuk. 2000. *Democratization in Korea: The Role of Civil Society*. Pittsburgh: University of Pittsburgh Press.

Kim, Youna. 2023. "The Korean Wave Television: From Winter Sonata to Squid Game". In *Introducing Korean Popular Culture*, edited by Youna Kim, 103-117. Abingdon: Routledge.

Kwon, Seung-Ho and Joseph Kim. 2014. "The cultural industry policies of the Korean government and the Korean Wave". *International Journal of Cultural Policy* 20, No. 4: 422-439.

Later, Naja. 2022. "Zombies continue to be the 'little black dress' of social allegory in Netflix's All Of Us Are Dead". *The Conversation*, March 13, 2022. https://theconversation.com/zombies-continue-to-be-the-little-black-dress-of-social-allegory-in-netflixs-all-of-us-are-dead-177625#:~:text=Anti%2Dauthoritarianism,them%20make%20it%20out%20unscathed.

Lee, Gyu-lee. 2022. "Director depicts school as microcosm of society in 'All of Us Are Dead'". *The Korea Times*, February 8, 2022. https://www.koreatimes.co.kr/www/art/2022/02/688_323467.html.

Lee, Hae-young, Jongsung Kim and Beom Cheol Cin. 2013. "Empirical Analysis on the Determinants of Income Inequality in Korea". *International Journal of Advanced Science and Technology* 53 (April): 95-109.

Lee, Jung-Whan. 1994. "Industrialization and the Formation of the New Middle Class in Korea". *Korea Journal of Population and Development* 23, No. 1 (July): 77-96.

Moylan, Tom. 2000. *Scraps of the Untainted Sky: Science fiction, utopia, dystopia*. Boulder: Westview Press.

Paquet, Darcy. 2009. *New Korean Cinema: Breaking the Waves*. New York: Columbia University Press.

Park, Sunyoung. 2018. "Between Science and Politics: Science Fiction as a Critical Discourse in South Korea, 1960s-1990s". *Journal of Korean Studies* 23, No. 2 (October): 347-367.

Shin, Kwang-Yeong. 2011. "Globalization and social inequality in South Korea". In *New Millennium South Korea: Neoliberal capitalism and transnational movements*, edited by Jesook Song, 11-28. Abingdon: Routledge.

Song, Sooho. 2020. "The Evolution of the Korean Wave: How is the third generation different from the previous ones?". *Korea Observer* 51, No. 1 (Spring): 125-150.

Standish, Isolde. 1994. "Korean Cinema and the New Realism: Text and Context". In *Colonialism and Nationalism in Asian Cinema*, edited by Wimal Dissanayake, 65-89. Bloomington: Indiana University Press.

Yoo, Jang-hee and Chul Woo Moon. 1999. "Korean financial crisis during 1997-1998: Causes and challenges". *Journal of Asian Economics* 10: 263-277.

Part 2:
De-Humanized Worlds and Contaminations

La terra dei figli.
From the Graphic Novel to the Movie. Dehumanization and Reconfiguration of Imaginaries and Identities through Landscapes

Ivana Mette

Introduction

This essay focuses on Claudio Cupellini's *The Land of the Sons*, a 2021 film based on the graphic novel of the same name by Gipi. As we know, for some time now the dystopian-apocalyptic genre has been imposing itself in the media imagination at an international level, but few Italian productions have dedicated themselves to the genre. One is the one in question.

We are inhabiting a dystopian cultural milieu, observes Tom Moylan in one of his most recent essays (2020, 190). We are enveloped in a dystopian mood that has exceeded the boundaries of fiction and has seeped into the daily news and the collective perception of reality. We seem, most importantly, to have stopped looking at the future with optimism, replacing it with resignation and despair. Dystopia put in place hellish scenarios in which our society has succumbed, leaving behind the ruins of our civilization.

Few other times in history has dystopian fiction been more relevant: we are living through its "Golden Age," as Jill Lepore called it in a 2017 article for *The New Yorker* (Lepore 2017). Indeed, dystopias are rather ubiquitous of late: they have invaded the literary market, the film and video game industries, and even the theatre.

It has always been clear that dystopias, despite their future setting, are a direct critique of the present (Atwood 2011; Pagetti 2012; Moylan 2014; Wegner 2014). Hence, they acquire particular relevance in times of crisis: the link between the current society and those portrayed in dystopian fiction becomes more evident, more explicit.

Dystopia, as a branch of science fiction, has often been classified as mere entertainment without presumptions of artistic quality. I strongly reject this reductive view of the genre and I prefer to focus on the multiple qualities that makes them worthy of attention.

Representing Dystopian Landscapes

It will become evident that dystopian fiction expresses both a warning for our real society and one of its fundamental features: in depicting worst-case scenarios, it alerts us to the consequences of our present choices and actions, while articulating the intrinsic human yearning for change, fostered by hope. This is especially true for the so-called *critical dystopias*. But it's also true for my case study. The land of children can be considered more of an ecological dystopian. We do not know anything about what brought the end, we only know that the world, as we know it, no longer exists because of the poisons. The incipit itself contains a reference to the ecological crisis we are facing, particularly in the last 20 years. Crisis that also brings with it a humanitarian crisis that is not only natural or ecological. Social structures collapse and the education of children, keepers of the memory and knowledge of their fathers, is concentrated only on survival, depriving them of what is a specific and unique characteristic of human beings: feelings.

The movie proposes a dystopian representation of Italy in the near future, but temporally not well defined, in which the wandering becomes a key element in the search for the self and the definition of one's own identity. The dehumanization of humanity is carried out by man himself as a function of a reconfiguration of imaginaries and social fragility through the landscape, barren and swampy, where there's a daily struggle for survival. A place where social practices and interpersonal relationships are rewritten and remedied according to the new world in which they have been placed, bringing with it a perennial echo of the past that influences the definition of the present and of individuals. The one of *La Terra dei figli* is an environment dominated by Augè's *non-places*, which relays us spectators to invisible beings, hurled against a muffled world that awakens our innermost anxieties of loss, emptiness and death and to which we can annex, albeit by mere helpless spectators, without cluttering up any visual space. Marc Augé defines non-places as those environments in which any connotation of identity ceases and which therefore become places of anonymity. They are the elements at the base of what Augé defines surmodernity that comes to be placed as the reverse side of the coin, the side and the positive meaning, of postmodernity and its negative and oppositional matrix from which thinkers have nourished it, especially those who deviate from Augé and its triple access to postmodernity, made up of three elements: time, space and the ego.

Yet, in this experiential classism the value of the man-environment relationship is never eclipsed. Relying on what Sandro Bernardi stated, in this specific case study, the landscape becomes, a real character, an interlocutor, often a ruthless antagonist towards the characters; it's no longer a mirror of the soul, it's no longer a space for action but, on the contrary, it often becomes a vast, opaque place in which the action and sometimes even the characters risk getting lost.

Bernardi, believes that:

> In cinema, landscape means not only the relationship between character and space, between man and the world, but also the relationship between different levels of gaze; there is the observer, who is a character, and the camera, which observes the observer. A more complex game of points of view is therefore articulated, and when this relationship is proposed as a comparison between two gazes, between two points of view, the cinematographic landscape becomes the starting point for a reflection not only on cinema, but implicitly also on the act of looking understood as a cognitive act (Bernardi 2004, 16)

The cognitive act, in the case of *La terra dei figli*, is linked to the awareness of an existence threatened by the inevitability of the real contextualized in the film, within which the missing element is the man subjected to a world that is direct consequence of our actions and bound, at the same time, to analyze and rediscover our identity in society and in history. Leaden photography becomes the very material of the architecture of those places. The landscape becomes an expression of the protagonist's ego, who, like it, finds himself emptied and poisoned by man's need to survive at any cost, basing his work on cruelty, justified by desperation.

So a strong element of analysis is to be considered *the landscape*. A landscape that arouses in us a call to a primordial state of existence, where everything was in the hands of forces to which we humans can only submit. Landscape where the binomial between the subjectivity of the individual and the objectivity of the places is evident, which in a certain way become the real protagonists of the story. They are there, enveloping the experience of the characters and dominating it. They impose their laws and influence on them, and as a result, they can themselves be seen as a new form and self-imposed political force in a seemingly anarchic reality. Thus, Michel Foucault's concept of heterotopia—integrated into Marc Augé's most recent theory—yields, in an agony without emotions, to the bleak and fatalistic image of the non-place.

In the logic of Foucault's flows, the task of places is to make spaces and consequently non-places communicate with each other, places of absence, in which we see where we are not, an unreal space, but virtually real, connected to the environment that surrounds us and its meanings. In the reasoning of the French philosopher, there is a space that is configured as a meeting point between what he defines utopias, that is, spaces without a real place and enterotropies, that is real spaces that Foucault also defines counter-places, a sort of utopias in fact localized and realized. This space is that of the mirror. The mirror is a utopia, a place in which the subject sees himself exactly where he is not, in a movement of presence-absence. The reflection is configured as a virtual, illusory space that cannot be actually touched by hand. But this place is also placed among the heterotopias, to the extent that the mirror really exists and the world opens up in its reflection, developing in the subject a disturbing dynamic, in which one perceives himself as present and absent at the same time (Foucault 2006).

Ursula Le Guin, excellent anthropologist, offered an admirable definition of the concept of "dystopias", as "subjectivized" universes, which do not just embody our desires or fears, but explain them (Cois 2019). In the potential and further worlds, in the deviated realities of dystopias, there is sufficient sidereal distance to reread one's existential context, individual and collective, with the aid of a simple device: asking oneself a question. What would happen if what we believe to be a cornerstone of our Real, in which we have been so intensely immerse as to seem "obvious" or even "natural" to us, changes and is replaced with its Absence or with its Opposite? What does it mean to become Aliens in hypothetical worlds, which are feared and fascinated, and distant cousins of ours?

From the Graphic Novel to the Movie

An important difference between Gipi's graphic novel and Cupellini's film is the latter's choice to focus the entire narrative on the existence of an only child, as opposed to the story of Gipi which features two brothers, incarnating two different, but complementary and significant characters in the evolution of the events dealt with. Cupellini's choice seems to be aimed at the desire to underline the sense of alienation and loneliness in which the human being finds himself. His individuality is laid bare, the son becomes an individual even more marginalized and left alone, abandoned to a hostile world, without a guide and in which social rules are rewritten in favor of a return to a dominated barbaric and primordial past. This can be seen as a metaphor of the disorientation of the postmodern condition, altered in the image of the characters that wonder without destination in a land hostile to human presence: the so-called wasteland.

The wasteland is a space shaped (involuntarily) by man but at the same time radically hostile to the human presence, a place animated only by impulses, traumas and fears of a humanity with no more point of reference. The lack of specific points articulates, on the spatial level, that lack of orientation which, for Jameson, corresponds to the fragmentation and dissipation of the subject, typical of the postmodern condition (Jameson 1998). The post-apocalyptic translates into a metaphor the impossibility of orienting among the complexities of the contemporary by elevating the lost man in space and time, without points of reference, to the protagonist.

Although in this scenario, it is not really the world, understood in an ecological sense, that is hostile, but it is man himself who, due to the continuous struggle for survival, returns undeterred to being hostile to his own species.

Yet in this so calm and leaden world, in which horrors lurk, a small state form is generated. We meet, in the second part of the narration, a group of men, governed by "The Boss", who present a very organized form of society, more of a totalitarian one.

Claire Curtis in *Postapocalyptic fiction and the social contract* (2010) says that the post-apocalyptic narrative represents the condition of humanity regressed to the state of nature, generally showing a transition (or at least a tension) towards some form of new social contract. Deleting all hierarchies, laws and organizations causes a generalized climate of violence, but it also opens up the possibility of re-discussing ways of political organization, gender norms and social practices.

The characters painted by Cupellini become the social actors mentioned by the Norwegian Marxist sociologist and philosopher Jon Elster, in his *The cement of society*. Elster argues that social actors decide how to act and interact following mainly three indications or modes of orientation: their desires and preferences (what they want to do), the constraints and opportunities that lie ahead (what they can do), beliefs and expectations. they feed (what they think they can do) (Elster 1989).

The collapse of society has led to violence and loneliness in a perennial search for survival, in which the wandering of bodies, turns out to be a rhythmic journey accompanied by the protagonist's desire to know his past and find his own identity through the reading of the notebook of the father. In relation to the figure of the father, we could mention Gregory Claeys who, in his 2017 *Dystopia: A Natural History*, analyses what he defines as prototypical dystopian societies through the theories of group and crowd psychology, states that the figure of the father may be considered as the Great Dictator personified. In fact, what "the father" in the film does is to impose his laws and his authority in a totalitarian way, hiding behind the need to educate his son for survival, but keeping him subject to his will, depriving him of any form of memory and nostalgia for the past, even though it has never known it, having been born "after poisons".

Dystopia, always connected to the ills of society, is now alerting us that we are producing a 'literature of (social) exhaustion,' to displace and adjust Barth's expression. At the end of an era, when social issues have acquired global dimensions and seem increasingly unsolvable, these tales, like this movie or the graphic novel, narrate of despair, but not resignation. Yet, they do not limit themselves to the blunt reproduction of thwarted hopes.

To quote Roberto De Gaetano, what we see with *The land of children* "is a synchronic image of the history of the world and of humanity, where layers of past time emerge and coexist in the present" (De Gaetano and Maiello 2020, 11).

These "places of absence" staged by the film accompany a narrative that puts the viewer "face to face with the naked and raw fact", making sure that events and circumstances speak for themselves, thus offering an aseptic gaze, as well as the world that is placed before us. A look that accompanies a subject in the perennial search for the self.

An interesting point of contrast between Gipi's work and the great dystopian literature is undoubtedly a discourse on language. The graphic novel features an impoverished language that has lost its basic grammatical and terminological structures. Linguistic impoverishment that mirrors the human and ecological pauperization brought about by history and which, however, is lost in the cinematographic transposition. Even though what Cupellini does is replace the use of the spoken language with a large use of silences, which is quite rare in our contemporary cinema.

Conclusions

Looking at some of the most well-known dystopias of the twentieth century, it is easy to see how much the theme of language and its manipulation played in them. Both the texts that gave shape to the 'canon' of dystopian literature in the early decades of the twentieth century (*Noi, Il mondo nuovo*, 1984) and the stories that were inserted into that canon, renewing it, all have, each in its own way, established a fundamental link between dystopia and language.

The centrality of the logos is a trait that dystopia has, so to speak, inherited from utopia. Thomas More himself baptized it, inventing a non-existent word that, by virtue of its enigmatic status, simultaneously refers to the non-place and the happy place.

Find the utopia again it's not a new idea and finds its roots in the biblical tradition of the final judgement. The forms through which those hopes of rebirth are represented, however, depend on the socio-cultural context: if until the 70s the post-apocalyptic utopia was actualized in a rejection of modernity in favor of a return of those heavenly rural landscapes. In the contemporary cinema nowadays, we can identify the potential of rebirth from the same ruins of the old world.

In the works in question, it must be said that the function of language, with respect to literature and dystopias, historical or cinematographic, is not to subjugate or control the masses, but to strengthen the degradation of the society built and destroyed by the fathers and left as a last legacy to the children.

As a direct consequence of the occurrence of an apocalyptic event, people are led to the direct consequence of rediscovering the sense of community, thinking in this way in a collective and not an individual way.

This perspective does not occur in the world of *La terra dei figli*, but what emerges is the need to recover the lost values, those of another era that defined their present.

Products like this one by Cupellini manage to establish themselves as a forge of experimentation and places of memory, the memory of a possible future or a warning for a possible future. And they, without any doubt, represent the possibility of being able to create interesting genre products also in our cinematography.

References

Augé, Marc. 2009. *Nonluoghi. Introduzione a una antropologia della surmodernità*, Elèutera, Milano.

Bernardi, Sandro. 2004. *Il paesaggio nel cinema italiano*, Marsilio, Venezia.

Canova, Gianni and Farinotti, Luisella. 2011. *Atlante del cinema italiano. Corpi, paesaggi, figure del contemporaneo*, Garzanti.

Ceretta, Manuela. 2014. *Il linguaggio nella distopia, i linguaggi della distopia*, "Azimuth. Philosophical Coordinates in Modern and Contemporary Age", II, n. 1, 139-153.

G. Claeys, Gregory. 2017. *Dystopia: A Natural History*, Oxford University Press, Oxford.

Cois, Ester. 2019. *Uni-Versi: L'Altro, il Quasi e le Distopie*, "Medea", V. 1, DOI: http://dx.doi.org/10.13125/Medea-3961.

Colombo, Arrigo (a cura di). 1993.*Utopia e Distopia*, Bari, Dedalo Edizioni.

Curtis, Claire P. 2010. *Postapocalyptic Fiction and the Social Contract: We'll Not Go Home Again*, Lexington Books, Lanham.

De Gaetano, Roberto and Maiello, Angela. 2020. *Virale. Il presente al tempo dell'epidemia*, Luigi Pellegrini Editore, Cosenza.

Elster, Jon. 1989. *The cement of society*, Cambridge University Press, Cambridge, 1989.

Foucault, Michel. 2006. *Utopie. Eterotopie*, Cronocopio Edizioni, Napoli.

Guerrini, Riccardo, Tagliani, Giacomo, and Zucconi Francesco. 2009., *Lo spazio del reale nel cinema italiano contemporaneo*, Le Mani, Lecce.

Jameson, Fredric. 2017. *The cultural turn: selected ritings of the Postmodern: 1983-1998*, Verso, London-NewYork.

Lepore, Jill. 2017. *A Golden Age for Dystopian Fiction. What to make of our new literature of radical pessimism*, The New Yorke, May 29, 2017, https://www.newyorker.com/magazine/2017/06/05/a-golden-age-for-dystopian-fiction.

Malavasi, Luca. 2017. *Post moderno e cinema. Nuove prospettive di analisi*, Carocci, Roma.

Moylan, Tom. 2020. *"The Necessity of Hope in Dystopian Times: A Critical Reflection."* Utopian Studies, vol. 31, no. 1, pp. 164-193. https://doi.org/10.5325/utopianstudies.31.1.0164.

Zagarrio, Vito. 2022. *La Nouvelle Vague Italiana. Il cinema del nuovo millennio*, Marsilio, Venezia.

Hybridizations and Interspecies Relations: Turning Dystopias into Potential Assets

Matteo Quinto

This article aims to show how the philosophical and aesthetic approach of contemporary posthumanism (Haraway 1992; 2016; Braidotti 2013; Tsing 2015; Tsing, Swanson, Gan, and Bubandt 2017; Ferrando 2019) and ecocriticism (Barad 2007; Iovino 2008; Morton 2009; 2013; Alaimo 2010; Garrard 2010; Danowski and Viveiros de Castro 2014) can enhance the deconstructive function of dystopias concerning relations and hybridizations between human and non-human beings. As well as serving as a critique of the present and as a warning about the future, many of these narratives also encourage us to analyze and question the very categories and values that cause the represented scenarios to be judged negatively. In this way, what was only perceived as a threat may instead prove to be a positive possibility, however complex or risky.

The first section presents some frequent narrative patterns in dystopias concerning the connections between human and biological non-human, including those of *invasion, contamination or infection* and outright *hybridization*. The second paragraph focuses on the structures of the narrative revolving around the relationship between human and cybernetic non-human, from those of the *AI takeover* and *technocratic dystopia* to those of *hybridization*, in this case human-machine. To conclude, the third section begins with a reflection around the typical functions of dystopia, including those of providing a "critique of contemporary life by exaggerating certain elements already existing" and of generating a sense of "alarm and warning" (Napier 1997, 183) about the future; then, we will add to these functions the posthumanist deconstruction of the categories underlying the negative judgement on hybridization and on the relations between human and non-human.

The examples that will be analyzed are drawn from *Love, Death + Robots* (2019-), an animated sci-fi anthology series produced by Netflix. Each episode is narratively disconnected from the others, it is set in a different universe and features different themes. Directors and scriptwriters are also different, as are the drawing and animation styles. Thus, the series offers a wide range of sensibilities, contexts and narrative situations.

Relations and Hybridizations between Human and Biological Non-Human

Most episodes of the series are dominated by sharp dichotomous divisions between human and non-human and focus their dystopian narrative on the threats the latter poses to the dominance of the former. The ontological, technical and cultural superiority of humanity is perceived as natural and just, and even the ethical and moral superiority is taken for granted. The paradigm of human exceptionalism, therefore, legitimizes that humankind disposes of the environment and the non-human at its own will and advantage. For this reason, the agency (Barad 2007; Alaimo 2010; Bennet 2010; Croce 2020) of other species and machines is perceived as uncanny (Freud 2003) and lays the basis for a dystopian imagery.

Several recurring narrative patterns regarding the relationship between human and biological non-human can be identified in *Love, Death + Robots* and in science fiction and dystopian narratives more generally. The first one is that of the *invasion*. It is present, for instance, in the episode *Suits* (season 1), in which the world is depicted as distinctly reminiscent of the rural United States in which, however, humans have to fight a race of alien insectoids with the help of armed mechanized exoskeletons.[1] This is a classic reception of the myth of the American pioneers fighting the wilderness with a sharp dichotomy between Nature and humanity. On one side an idyllic anthropized rural environment, inhabited by human beings, heroic as individuals and united in a supportive community; on the other side the invading aliens, feral, monstrous in

---

[1] Next to the title of the episodes I only indicate the number of the season since the order of the episodes within each has been changed, so the reference would therefore risk being inconsistent or cause confusion. The belonging of the episodes to the seasons, on the other hand, has been unambiguous and constant.

appearance and with no other purpose than to destroy and devour. In this narrative model, approached with this rhetoric, it is difficult to imagine positive interspecies relations; the survival of human beings and their community appears as such a pressing imperative as to cancel out any other reflection, value or moral nuance.

A second pattern, often more interesting and varied than the previous one, is that of *contamination or infection*, i.e. the invasion not only of the anthropic environment, but also of the body, and thus the identity, of humanity. An example, among many in the series, is the episode *In Vaulted Halls Entombed* (season 3), in which a military unit chases a group of enemies into a crypt where they find a creature in chains, a reference to H.P. Lovecraft's *Cthulhu*. The creature's powers and presence are indeed so perturbing, alien and unsettling that they drive human beings to madness, or enslave them imposing telepathically commands on them. A peculiar contagion is thus represented, not so much a biological contagion, but rather a gnoseological and psychic one. The creature does not infect the body of human beings through viruses, bacteria or spores, but invades their minds through their thoughts. Physical proximity, eye contact, even mere theoretical or imaginary knowledge of the creature cause a deleterious bond that degrades humanity from their position of dominance by depriving them of the most fundamental element of their essence: free will and rationality. Only one character, after having gouged out her eyes to escape the creature's influence, manages to re-emerge alive from the crypt, although her mental condition is not clarified to the viewer. Even in this narrative configuration, in which the purity of the human being is often the value to be defended and contaminations appear only as a danger to survival, it is difficult to imagine any other perspective than that of a future to be avoided.

Another narrative pattern that can be traced is that of outright *hybridization*, i.e. where the contamination between human and non-human is so extensive, intense and irreversible that it leads to the crossing of species boundaries and the generation of a new being, different from the previous two. One of the most complex and interesting examples of this is the episode *Swarm* (season 3), in which two scientists, a man and a woman, study an alien race that collectively calls itself 'Swarm'. They do not possess individual personalities, individualities or self-awareness, but function as one collective mind communicating with each other by means of biochemical messages.[2] While the female scientist only wants to study this species, her male colleague plans to learn how they communicate bio-chemically and he aims at stealing their eggs to breed an entire Swarm to serve humanity as slaves. He argues the amorality of his intentions on the basis that, since this species has no individual free will and self-awareness, there would be no distinction for them between serving their collective mind or humanity. What emerges quite clearly is the human tendency to impose its dominance over other species through technical knowledge. The plan seems to work, but the Swarm generates a creature that hybridizes with the female scientist and becomes capable of personal individuation. The tale of this creature delineates a clear and symmetrical opposition between the two species: on one side is humankind, whose supreme values are those of Humanism (such as free will, creativity, individual responsibility, self-determination, independence and purity), and on the other side is the Swarm, which bases its existence on the collectivity of thought and purpose based on contaminations and hybridizations. The creature explains to the scientist that the Swarm has spent millennia combining generically with other races, assimilating their advantageous traits and annihilating their differentiation and autonomy. The Swarm, therefore, is at the other extreme of humanity also in terms of how it relates to other species: it does not pursue purity and supremacy by subjugating other species with technology but obliterates all differences with

---

[2] The idea of species characterized by a collective self-awareness (usually referred to as 'hive mind' or 'group mind') has a long and widespread tradition in science-fiction narratives ranging from the novels of the early decades of the 20th century to the transmedia game universes of *Warhammer 40.000* and *StarCraft* (in particular, the appearance of the episode's hybrid creature recalls that of *StarCraft*'s protagonist, Sarah Kerrigan, just as 'the Swarm' is also the name by which the Zergs of this video game define themselves). This tradition builds its imagery in relation to ethological studies on the behavior of certain social insects (such as ants, bees and termites) and studies on swarm intelligence (SI) that characterizes natural or artificial self-organizing systems (SOS), particularly in the field of robotics.

respect to and between them through genetic hybridization. Even in this narrative scheme, starting from a dichotomous contraposition characterized by attitudes of overpowering and domination, relations and hybridizations cannot be anything but repulsive, uncanny, dangerous and undesirable.

Relations and hybridizations between human and cybernetic non-human

The relationships and hybridizations between humans and machines have also been, and are, a very fertile ground for the development of dystopias. These dystopias often begin by depicting technology as a product of human creativity placed under the control of human will. Just as often, however, machines also come to display their own menacing otherness. If they remain an inert, passive tool, devoid of their own will and any form of agency, they reinforce the idea of human exceptionalism and its grip on reality, the environment and the non-human. They become an extension, not indispensable but valuable, to amplify anthropic action and to gratify the ego and the desires of humanity. The very proximity of technology to human beings and its daily presence as a familiar and instrumental inert element, however, are also what grants its efficacy as a disturbing element. Indeed, as Freud (2003) pointed out, the ability of inanimate, everyday objects to manifest intentionality is one of the phenomena that is most successful in generating uncanny feelings in human beings. Adding to this a representation of technology as a necessary support for humanity, without which the latter would lose not only control of the world, but also its own possibilities of action and survival, relations with it are charged with even greater perturbing and dystopian potential.

It is also possible to identify certain recurring narrative situations with regard to the relations between human and cybernetic non-human, including that of the *AI takeover*, which has at its center precisely the emergence of the agency of mechanical beings. Developing cognitive capacities such as to achieve self-awareness and free will, mechanical beings thus manage to undermine human exceptionalism and challenge its supremacy, and even its very survival. An example of this model is the episode *Automated Customer Service* (season 2), in which a lady, living in a hyper-mechanized village for the elderly, tragicomically tries to get in touch with the customer service of the company that provided her with a domestic robot that decided to kill her. The episode has several comic traits, in which risk and tension are mixed with a grotesque normalization of what is happening. Once again, therefore, the relationship between human and non-human cannot but result in a technophobic dystopia, if they are based on dichotomous categorizations or on the reduction of the other to a tool and on the fear that such a relationship may break down.

A second recurring narrative situation is that of the *technocratic dystopia*. The association between authoritarian or totalitarian dystopia and technological development (be it cybernetic, chemical or in the field of bioengineering), in fact, is not casual. Any new technology — not only those with a direct and immediate application in the military or surveillance sphere, but all of them — creates an imbalance of power that is proportionately greater the more relevant the innovation it brings. The root that links political and social dystopias to technological development is that progress divides between those who have access to the innovation and those who do not. So any new technology can be monopolized and exploited by a social, political or economic group that gains a position of absolute pre-eminence in doing so. As Susan Napier points out, "this contemporary concept of dystopia usually expresses itself in two reinforcing visions — technology run amok and a repressive totalitarian government able to exploit that technology" (Napier 1996, 185). The examples of this narrative framework in the series under examination are not many, not only in comparison with other series of the same genre — for instance, *Black Mirror* (2011-) or *Philip K. Dick's Electric Dreams* (2017-) —, but also in comparison with much science fiction in general, which has made it a pivotal feature since the beginning of the 20th century and even more so throughout the second half of the century. The most significant example in this sense is the episode *Pop Squad* (season 2), which depicts a humanity for which they have developed pharmaceutical technologies that can extend life forever. To avoid overpopulation, however, reproduction has been strictly forbidden and unregistered children are killed immediately by the police. This example shows how the relations between human and non-human are usually not the focus of these dystopias, as change in the technological sphere is mainly considered for how it modifies social relations within the human sphere. In *Pop Squad*, for instance, the reflection revolves around the life-extending technology much less than it focuses on the effects of mankind's loss of mortality, the kind of values and life this immortal humanity leads, the meaning of having sons and daughters, and the psychology of the protagonist (an agent assigned to search for and kill unregistered children). In this framework, therefore, the non-human often plays an instrumental role in the hands of the human or merely has an adverse influence on it.

The third narrative scheme, that of the *hybridization* between human and non-human, on the other hand, centers around the relationships and contaminations between the two. The focus is often the disturbance that anthropomorphic machines or artificial humans can generate. As theorized by Mori Masahiro in 1970 (Mori, Macdorman and Kageki 2012), the empathy that humans feel towards machines increases with their increasing anthropomorphisation up to a critical point where it becomes fear and revulsion (the point on the curve to which Mori gives the name "Uncanny Valley"). This occurs when the resemblance between human beings is such that the demarcation line between the two categories is challenged. This feeling is linked to the fear that machines might acquire the prerogatives that humans consider exclusive to their own species and surpass them in the faculties by which they justify their dominance. Again, however, the examples in *Love, Death + Robots* are fewer than one might expect given the prevalence and constant popularity of the theme in science fiction novels, films and series. Among the episodes in which cyborgs, replicants or anthropomorphic machines appear, one of the most interesting is the episode *Good Hunting* (season 1), set in a steampunk Victorian Hong Kong. Among the various themes explored in the episode (the relationship with the preternatural in traditional rural societies, modernization, colonialism, gender difference) is the transformation of the female protagonist—fox spirit stuck in her human form due to the disappearance of magic caused by the modernization of her country — into a cyborg. Placed in a position of subordination by modernization, colonization, gender and by the loss of her animal part, she comes to suffer the replacement of her biological body by mechanical parts through deception and force. She decides, therefore, to complete the transformation into a machine by becoming a cyborg capable of taking human and feral form in order to hunt down powerful men who commit violence against women. Although the episode is interesting for its complexity (e.g. in the way the male protagonist deals with modernization and the advent of automatons or in a post-colonial perspective), the transformation of the protagonist sinks into the Uncanny Valley. Her hybridization is portrayed as the terrible concretization of a fetishism (made possible by colonialism and gender violence) and then as an ambiguous devotion to revenge.

What Purpose Can Dystopias Serve?

The aims of a dystopian narrative can be several, and a single narrative can strive to achieve a number of them. Among the many identifiable is certainly that of investigating the present, "exaggerating certain elements already existing" (Napier 1997, 183). In fact, by intensifying what exists in its dawn, one can better understand its foundations and possible or probable development. A dystopia, moreover, can become a valuable tool for investigating removed fears and anxieties of a society. Indeed, what consciously worries a human community finds a place in political debate and social confrontation. On the contrary, what is not perceived as an ongoing problem, but as an anxiety about the future, or what is perceived as a risk only by some, but it is rejected by the collective debate, hardly finds a form for expression. Dystopia precisely ponders what has no place in the "social frames of memory" (Halbwachs 1925; 1950) of the past, as well as in the representation of the present. The things of a society that are not "visible" (Sorlin 1994), i.e. communicable and widely interpretable, can therefore encompass fears and anxieties that only dystopias can represent and make intelligible and conscious to the whole community.

Another fundamental purpose of these narratives is to project into the future, not to investigate the present, but to guide the coming action by avoiding drifts or dangers on the horizon. Undoubtedly, this is also one of the goals of politics, scientific investigation and journalism. Intellectuals and politicians, for example, have always spoken about the risks for the future in the cultural, social and political spheres within the horizon of the "topic of denunciation" (Boltanski 1999), just as economists and climatologists have done in the economic and environmental spheres. These kinds of talk find their strength in a realist narrative, a logical argumentative structure, factual data, documents and the rhetoric of objectivity and testimony. Dystopias, on the other hand, being fictional narratives, have access to very different tools. These include the identification with the characters, the search for emotional effects, the use of an "aesthetic topic" (Boltanski 1999) that exploits the metaphorical and analogical power of the imaginary and artistic language (Meschiari 2020). Although with different tools and mechanisms than other narratives, dystopias too contribute to the formation of an ethical disposition towards the present, to the creation of a sensitivity towards the risks of the future and to a taking of responsibility towards the generations to come. This aim of dystopia is particularly evident both in socio-political dystopias and, more recently, in climate fiction.

Alongside complex aims, dystopias may also have simpler goals, which do not always succeed in triggering critical reflection and having an ethical relevance. They may focus, for instance, on the very spectacularity of the apocalyptic catastrophes much more than on the analysis of their causes and the responsibilities involved. Or they may exploit the "topic of suffering" (Boltanski 1999) by aiming for easy commotion. Even the cathartic effect they may have can be either critically effective or merely a rather unnecessary and elementary means of emotional involvement. The relief of finding hope even in the most terrible horizon, or simply of discovering oneself outside of this narrative, can be seen, in fact, either as a moment of escapism from reality without any consequence, or as a moment of awareness that follows a profound elaboration.

The Deconstruction of Dystopia as a Horizon of Hope

In the landscape of contemporary posthumanism and ecocriticism, however, dystopias can also stimulate critical reflection in another way, namely by attempting to deconstruct the reasons why the scenarios depicted are judged negatively. These narratives, in fact, stage the subversion of the values of a society to reveal fears and risks perceived and to analyze them trying to prevent them. Thus, for instance, if personal freedom is a shared value, a totalitarian dystopia will aim to criticize or avoid the phenomena that endanger it. There are dystopias, on the other hand, that intend to question, by deconstructing them, the very values that make what they represent undesirable. In this way, they show as a horizon of hope not the avoidance of the scenarios they represent, but a revision of shared values (however problematic) and an acceptance of previously feared eventualities (albeit partial, conditional and risky). The outcome is double: first, getting rid of certain inherited values now unsuited to the context and making new values emerge, on the basis of which the future is less frightening. Indeed, fantastic representations (even if connected or close to reality or not) are not necessarily limited to escapism but can also be fundamental in imagining alternatives to the existing. It is a faculty without which it would not even be possible to consider that other possibilities exist, and without which reality becomes the necessary (Jackson 2014; Meschiari 2019; 2020).

The goal then is no longer to prevent or solve the identified problem, but to stay "with the trouble" (Haraway 2016), i.e. to live with it, to accept some parts of it as negative but unavoidable and others even as positive, once we have adapted ourselves and our shared values to changes in society and the world. In the environmental sphere, for example, the point is no more about preventing the final Apocalypse through anthropophobic conservation, but about finding ways to accept changes, perhaps even by limiting, conditioning and slowing them down, with the aim of finding ways to live "on a damaged planet" (cf. Tsing, Swanson, Gan 2017). In this horizon, therefore, the dichotomy between human and non-human must be deconstructed and relationships and hybridizations between them can thus also become positive.

An example of this in *Love, Death + Robots* is the episode *Mason's Rats* (season 3), in which a farmer calls in a pest control company to exterminate the rats infesting his barn. The company resorts to more and more extreme means until they get a robot that kills the animals mercilessly. It does so in a truculent, icy and methodical manner, to the extent that the viewer perceives a certain sadism in the killing. In contrast, the rats are depicted in a photorealistic style that balances verisimilitude and anthropomorphisation. The issue of depicting animals (Baker 2001), especially in animation, is much debated because, on the one hand, anthropomorphisation increases empathy towards them, while on the other hand it reduces their otherness, adherence to reality and autonomy. In this case, the balance between anthropomorphic expressive abilities and realism is highly effective in balancing the empathy they create and the otherness they conserve. Moreover, these rats use clothes and tools, as well as manifesting social bonds such as helping each other, rescuing the wounded, sacrificing themselves and asking the robot to be spared. In this episode, therefore, certain values that are now inadequate to meet the challenges of the present and the future are deconstructed in a fantastic way. For example, the dichotomous division between humans and animals, the right of human beings to dispose of other living beings on the basis of his exceptionalism, and the instrumental value of non-human lives have been overcome. At their opposite, positive interspecies reactions, sympoiesis, becoming-together (cf. Haraway 2016) and interspecies solidarity are presented as values. The "creaturality" that Erich Auerbach (2003) discusses as a value of Christianity—i.e. the dignity that every human being has as such, independently of any other characteristic or subdivision—is also extended to non-human beings in a secular prospective. Of course, the episode also has very strong limitations, as this extension is much more based on the anthropomorphisation of the animal than on the acceptance of its otherness or co-determination, and because it isolates the cybernetic being with a strongly negative characterization. Its deconstructive intent and its depiction of interspecies solidarity, however, differentiate it from others in which interspecies relations and hybridizations have a merely dystopian connotation and outcome.

Even the fear of hybridization with technology can be deconstructed, as happens for instance in the episode *Zima Blue* (season 1), in which a human artist during his existential and creative quest has his body replaced with mechanical components until he becomes completely cybernetic. He does this in order to experience sensations that would be impossible to bare for a human body, such as contact with lava or the most intense cold. During the episode, he organizes a performance in which he reveals that he was not just a man who had become a machine, but that he was born as an automatic pool-cleaning machine, and then became more and more complex in hardware and software until he achieved self-awareness. He must then have found a way to obtain a biological body, which was later replaced with the cybernetic one. What is most interesting beyond the surprise effect, however, is that this revelation changes very little of the spectator's perception of him. The perspective of hybridization, although extreme, is no longer exclusively dystopian, but rather becomes a possibility of artistic, existential and experiential research. In this narration the dichotomous division softens, the material that makes up a body becomes less relevant than the choices the individual makes, and the relationship opens up to hybridization as a resource and not as a nightmare. In this way humans and non-humans can share similar characteristics without purity and exceptionalism being implicated or endangered, because they no longer appear to be a value in the face of the vastness of Zima's aesthetic quest, no matter how senseless, extreme or even parodist one might find it.

In this way, then, a dystopia that embraces a posthumanist and ecocritical sensibility can manage to deconstruct the values and assumptions that generate the dystopian imaginaries themselves. The hope they aim for, therefore, is not only embedded in avoiding negative future scenarios, but in questioning whether there is anything positive in them. Through the representation of interspecies relations and hybridizations, first presented as disturbing and then deconstructed and accepted as positive, they generate a "rich ethical sense of kinship between the human and other animals [*or machines*] or, at very least, deny us the mental or spiritual exceptionalism that underwrites the untrammelled use of the rest of the world" (Alaimo 2010, 151). In doing so, deconstructed dystopian narratives can turn risk into possibility, horror into curiosity and dystopia into a horizon of hope, at least in part.

References

Alaimo, Stacy. 2010. *Bodily Natures: Science, Environment, and the Material Self*. Bloomington: Indiana University Press.

Auerbach, Erich. 2003 [1946]. *Mimesis: The Representation of Reality in Western Literature*. Translated by Willard R. Trask. Princeton: Princeton University Press.

Baker, Steve. 2001 [1993]. *Picturing the Beast: Animals, Identity and Representation*. Urbana: University of Illinois Press.

Barad, Karen. 2007. *Meeting the Universe Halfway: Quantum Physics and the Entanglement of Matter and Meaning*. Durham: Duke University Press.

Bennett, Jane. 2010. *Vibrant Matter: A Political Ecology of Things*. Durham: Duke University Press.

Boltanski, Luc. 1999. *Distant Suffering: Morality, Media and Politics*. Translated by Graham D. Burchell. Cambridge: Cambridge University Press.

Braidotti, Rosi. 2013. *The posthuman*. Cambridge: Polity Press.

Croce, Mariano. 2020. *Bruno Latour. Irriduzionismo. Attante. Piattezza. Ibridi. Gaia*. Roma: DeriveApprodi.

Danowski, Déborah and Eduardo Viveiros de Castro. 2017. *The ends of the world*. Translated by Rodrigo Nunes. Cambridge: Polity.

Ferrando, Francesca. 2019. *Philosophical Posthumanism: A Critical Appraisal*. London: Bloomsbury Academic.

Freud, Sigmund. 2003 [1919]. *The Uncanny*. Translated by David McLintock. New York: Penguin Books.

Garrard, Greg. 2010 [2004]. *Ecocriticism*. London: Routledge.

Halbwachs, Maurice. 1925. *Les cadres sociaux de la mémoire*. Paris: Librairie Félix Alcan.

Halbwachs, Maurice. 1950. *La mémoire collective*. Paris: Les Presses Universitaires de France.

Haraway, Donna. 1992. *The Promises of Monsters: A Regenerative Politics for Inappropriate/d Others*. New York: Routledge.

Haraway, Donna. 2016. *Staying with the Trouble: Making Kin in the Chthulucene*. Durham: Duke University Press.

Iovino, Serenella. 2008 [2004]. *Filosofie dell'ambiente. Natura, etica, società*. Roma: Carocci.

Jackson, Rosemary. 2014 [1981]. *Fantasy: The Literature of Subversion*. London: Routledge.

Meschiari, Matteo. 2019. *La grande estinzione. Immaginare ai tempi del collasso*. Roma: Armillaria.

Meschiari, Matteo. 2020. *Antropocene fantastico. Scrivere un altro mondo*. Roma: Armillaria.

Mori, Masahiro, and Karl F. MacDorman, and Norri Kageki. 2012 [1970]. "The Uncanny Valley". *IEEE Robotics & Automation Magazine* 19 (2): 98-100.

Morton, Timothy. 2009. *Ecology Without Nature: Rethinking Environmental Aesthetics*. Cambridge-London: Harvard University Press.

Morton, Timothy. 2013. *Hyperobjects: Philosophy and Ecology after the End of the World*. Minneapolis: University of Minnesota Press.

Napier, Susan. 1996. *The Fantastic in Modern Japanese Literature: The Subversion of Modernity*. London: Routledge.

Sorlin, Pierre. 1994. "Il visibile". In *La storia al cinema. Ricostruzione del passato, interpretazione del presente*, edited by Gianfranco Miro Gori, 277-83. Roma: Bulzoni.

Tsing, Anna Lowenhaupt. 2015. *The Mushroom at the End of the World: On the Possibility of Life in Capitalist Ruins*. Princeton: Princeton University Press.

Tsing, Anna Lowenhaupt, and Heather Swanson, and Elaine Gan, and Nils Bubandt (ed. by). 2017. *Arts of Living on a Damaged Planet: Ghosts and Monsters of the Anthropocene*. Minneapolis: University of Minnesota Press.

To Dystopia and Beyond.
Escape from the Techno-Economic Paradigm with *Wall•E*

Raffaele Chiarulli

I Am a Legend.
The Ideal Citizen for Our Post-ideological Era.

Years since its release in theaters, *Wall•E* (2008), like the great classics of dystopian science fiction, still distinguishes itself as a film that sheds light on the most disturbing aspects of our reality. The ninth feature film by Pixar Animation Studios can be defined as a successful and uncommon experiment in applying the philosophical themes of sci-fi to a mainstream animated film, a film geared towards a wide audience, including families.

That *Wall•E* has entered the collective imagination is evidenced by the number of times it has been referenced in public debate subsequent to its release in theaters, well outside the realm of film criticism. Philosophers, sociologists, political scientists, and bioethicists have added the film to their arsenal, each unpacking its wisdom according to their own vision (see Mattie 2014; Zaccuri 2016; Herhuth 2017; Munk Rosing 2017; Uva 2017; Ferrando 2019; Tynan 2020). As a work of dystopian fiction, *Wall•E* fulfills its function, meditating over primal questions and conversing allegorically on the topic of the identity, purpose, and destiny of humankind through the ages[1].

In July 2008, in the midst of the turmoil of the presidential elections in the United States, an op-ed in *The New York Times* identified the robot Wall•E as the most suitable candidate for the White House because he was far more attentive to the needs of the people than the real-life contenders for the presidency. Essayist Frank Rich

---

[1] This theme has already been touched upon in Chiarulli (2019). I would like to thank Avigayil Kelman for the revision of the English text.

suggested that John McCain watch *Wall•E* to realize just how askew his proposals for tax reform were considering America's exigencies, and that Barack Obama "should see it to be reminded of just how bold his vision of change had been before he settled into frontrunner complacency" (Rich 2008). What the article admitted, after establishing the film as a historical and political allegory of the United States, was that *Wall•E's* message transcended national borders. In Rich's words, "What [the kids in the audience] applauded was not some banal cartoonish triumph of good over evil but a gentle, if unmistakable, summons to remake the world before time runs out" (Rich 2008). With the claim that "a cartoon robot evokes America's patriotic ideals with more conviction than either of the men who would be president," Rich underlines the point that *Wall•E* may be offering us a role model for our time, or to put it politically (in line with the aims of Rich's article), a model for the ideal citizen, not defined by his partisan vision but by higher virtues altogether, virtues for our post-ideological era.

As a work of sci-fi, the screenplay is tasked with divining the future state of the world, and the human role in it, specifically, seven hundred years into the future. Lilian Munk Rösing describes *Wall•E* as "a poetic vision of earth as a post-apocalyptic wasteland, and a dystopian vision of the ultimate consumers' society as a totalitarian state" (Munk Rösing 2017, 129). The film reveals that at the start of the 22nd century, the pollution level of planet Earth was such that the Buy'n'Large Corporation (BnL), "a control body with Orwellian pervasive power" (Uva 2017, 111), organized a temporary evacuation of the vast majority of humanity via a luxurious spacecraft. Meanwhile, hordes of robots with the "Wall•E" logo — an acronym for "Waste Allocation Load Lifter Earth-Class" — worked to compact and dispose of the waste, which had invaded the entirety of the Earth's surface. Originally, the space cruise was supposed to last only a few years, but the situation on the planet, far from improving, gets out of hand. Its "preservers" decided to abandon it definitively and reach the rest of humanity in space. Centuries passed, and the robots tasked with waste compaction were deactivated, all save one, the titular Wall•E, who has devised a way to recharge his batteries and continue to function perpetually. This backstory is given to the audience through advertisements and official BnL communications that are automatically broadcast by surviving media or as character flashbacks during the film. The actual events take place seven hundred years later: humanity has now forgotten the existence of its home planet, where piles of garbage are so high that they tower over the tallest skyscrapers. In perfect solitude, Wall•E has continued meticulously to carry out the work for which he was designed.

Meanwhile, on the spaceship, the control body (now led by autonomous artificial intelligence) oversees and manipulates the lives of humans—who are reduced to the larval state of pure consumers— and even hides from them the possibility of returning to Earth. "The first time the audience views humans in *Wall•E* is on the spaceship where passengers passively cruise the ship in hoverchairs with malformed bodies from no physical use while paying rapt attention to screen media. In contrast to this parodic presentation of the humans, the robots in *Wall•E* are presented with vivid personalities, hopes, dreams, and, paradoxically, a love for life" (Van Oosterwijk and McCarthy 2022, 14).

When the hero, Wall•E, pursues a robot probe that descended to Earth in search of life forms, he sets off a chain-reaction—triggered by a live plant brought aboard the human spaceship—that will free humanity from its gilded cage and finally restore it to its home planet.

Last Axiom Hero. Is Globalization a Dystopia?

From the first few minutes of the movie, the key feature that emerges is the omnipresence and omnipotence—especially through the media—of a multinational corporation that governs the world, in place of traditional political forces. It represents the complete realization of a globalist utopia founded on the market (which in the film takes on the traits of a dystopia), the dynamics of which modern philosophy and sociology have already explored from every angle. The film presents us with Lunt and Livingstone's (1992) outline of consumer culture "with consumption not just being an economic practice but also the construction of people's identities and socio-cultural environment" (Van Oosterwijk and McCarthy 2022, 19).

Arjun Appadurai (1996) noted how the informatization and globalization of the economy has prompted the birth of new transnational corporations, ultimately accelerating the death of the very concept of the nation-state. With the demise of nation-states, the world depicted in *Wall•E* emerges "as a single unit of interconnected activity unobstructed by local borders" (Hobsbawn 2007, 11; see also Bauman 1997; Bauman 1999), a scenario that echoes the now-classic end-of-the-millennium nightmare, *The Matrix* (1999) and resonates even more deeply with *Blade Runner* (1982), from which it borrows some major themes: the aforementioned substitution of political power with economic power; the emphasis on the paradox of the "fetishism of commodities" (see Menarini 2000; Munk Rösing 2017) identified by Marx (according to the well-known formula) in the dialectic between the "personification of things and the reification of people"; the role of memory in the construction of identity as a distinctively human trait.

In *Wall•E*, the control agency programmed by BnL to preserve the human race has become, effectively, a government agency, to which even its programmers (or rather their successors) are now subject without remembering anything of the process, a process that we can hypothesize began with the "artificialization of experience" (Eugeni 2005), a typical feature of modern consumer society. "To BnL, humanity's problem of how to live on Earth is a technical, not a moral or civil, matter. Despite the global crisis, there is no need for human beings to form a political community, to identify or cultivate excellence, or to deliberate and decide on how best to use common but limited resources. BnL proceeds on Bacon's maxim that technological inventions transcend and obviate political reform" (Mattie 2014, 14). A year before *Wall•E*, Jürgen Habermas gave this famous definition:

> By globalization is meant the cumulative process of a worldwide expansion of trade and production, commodity and financial markets, fashions, the media and computer programs, news and communications networks, transportation systems and flows of migration, the risk generated by large scale technology, environmental damage and epidemics, as well as organized

crime and terrorism. These processes enmesh nation-states in the dependencies of an increasingly interconnected world society whose functional differentiation effortlessly bypasses territorial boundaries (Habermas 2006, 175).

It is truly incredible to watch the sequences of *Wall•E* containing doses of social criticism and compare it with the discussion of philosophers from the preceding or succeeding decade. Byung-Chul Han (2017) writes that concepts like class struggle, exploitation, and alienation have become outdated in theory and practice, since technological progress, along with an archaic concept of personal freedom, has confused or even canceled the distinction between exploiters and exploited, generating a world where everyone, in the illusion of being free, only exploits themselves to the advantage of an entity that develops its own needs that we mistakenly perceive as ours. Fabrice Hadjadj (2017) observes instead how individualism is the result of a social construction that disintegrates natural communities to invent a "society of competition and innovation" and paradoxically leads to the disintegration of the individual, who is separated from their own family and body, as well as from their own inheritance and history: at the very moment when the individual claims themselves as autonomous, they become a slave of the techno-liberal world, which has also recently been called the "techno-economic paradigm" in Catholic teaching (Francis 2015).

The plot of the film repeatedly links the inadvertent imprisonment of human beings with the weakening of relationships, mediated by social networks—the place where the "I", as an entrepreneur of the self, produces oneself, performs oneself, and offers oneself as a commodity, where authenticity is a factor in increasing sales (Han 2017). Upon the spaceship, whose name is symbolically *Axiom*,

> rule is provision, a technical matter that the ship has mastered. Thus, technology seems to have liberated humanity from the necessity of work but also of politics—of the need to rule and be ruled in a community. However, easy living on the *Axiom* only shifts, obscures, and increases the power of the real rulers. Though not visible among the homogenous mass of human passengers, the political order on the *Axiom* lies in the classes of robots (Mattie 2014, 16).

This is a dystopian scenario is far from unrealistic, and is feared by scholars who have observed how technology no longer develops based on the goals to be achieved, but according to its own internal logic, according to its possibilities for growth: "From a logical point of view [...] we are used to believing that we start by posing problems before arriving at solutions. [...] In technical reality, the order must be reversed: the interdependence of technical elements makes possible a great number of "solutions" for which there is no problem" (Ellul 2004, 281). Hadjadj (2019) also noted that the task of the 21st century man will therefore be to rediscover the "spirit of matter", which would free him from the problem of having reduced the "data" of nature to elements to be reconfigured to one's liking: matter deconstructed into atoms, the living deconstructed into genes, intelligence deconstructed into neurons, society deconstructed into individuals, individuals deconstructed into a sum of functions. The consequence being that, as soon as the elements prevail over the natural form in contemporary man's line of vision, it will be impossible to generate anything but an artificial form made up of a new configuration of those same elements[2].

What is Natural and What is Not. Rediscovering the Spirit of Matter.

Wall•E points to a perfect crime, already quite complete, but it leaves us with more than a glimmer of hope. Together with the film's protagonist, as he clings to the rocket that will take him to the spaceship, we, the viewers, are urged to break through the shell of garbage that surrounds planet Earth and "go out to see the stars" again. The fact that Wall•E is a comedy is a new angle in and of itself. It playfully reimagines the common science fiction trope of man's disappearance from Earth, a theme that was especially prevalent during the first decade of the new millenium. The same decade saw the release of films such as I Am Legend (2007) and The Road

---

[2] Hadjadj's proposal for breaking free from this paradigm and its consequences consists of a return to the model of natural communities: the family, as the foundation for rebuilding the political dimension; the community with nature; and that of man with God.

(2009). The latter was an adaptation of Cormac McCarthy's masterpiece of the same name (2006), published a year after Michel Houellebecq's novel, *The Possibility of an Island* (2005), in which the French writer likewise pondered the future of humanity (see Zaccuri 2016, 140). The year before Wall•E, Weisman's non-fiction bestseller, *The World Without Us* (2007), which considered what planet Earth might look like after the disappearance of humans, caused an enormous stir.

According to Pixar, however, the last sentient being remaining is not a tormented scientist, nor a rugged action hero. It is instead a faithful and meticulous custodian. Life is a game for him, the way that it is for a child; it is pure curiousity, adventure in action, delight in novelty, the search for beauty, and the accumulation of meaning. It is symbolic that he is the ultimate "collector" of the worthless — "trash" — which he imbues with the significance of treasure. Of course, he is artificial intelligence, yet he is the trace, the blueprint, for a human way of doing things that is still somehow anchored to the earth and its raw realities. He is an artificial intelligence that remains the only guarantor of humanity itself, the only one capable of perpetuating its knowledge, memory, and affections. As a garbage collector, he is also a law enforcement agent called upon through his work to foster the conditions for "livability" (Bauman 2007; Cuozzo 2013).

During his cleaning duties, the robot does not just compact waste but begins to select it, keeping for himself all the objects he deems interesting and worthy of being saved, everything he considers deserving, not because it is objectively so but because it matches his tastes, his own personal criteria of beauty or usefulness. Wall•E preserves all these objects saved from the debris in the trailer of a truck, which he has set up as his home and as a sort of museum of human creativity, which he loves to surround himself with when not at work. "One of the many delightful ironies of Wall•E is that, as a mass-produced model of technology, he is quite an individual [...]. Only he operates, but that is because, as he carries out his directive, Wall•E attends to his own good, recognizing the provisions that nature — his own and that of his surroundings — has made available for use" (Mattie 2014, 14). If Pixar characters have always "expressed an ontological crisis that requires the reconfiguration of what is natural and what is not" (Herhuth 2014, 74) (i.e. *Toy Story, Monsters Inc., The Incredibles*), *Wall•E*, in particular, raises a direct question about what is specific to human nature. For example, our protagonist shows a desire for companionship, for someone to share his discoveries and inventions with. "The dancing and especially the courtship scenes in *Hello, Dolly!* (the film that Wall•E watches from a "prehistoric" surviving videotape) make him yearn for 'all that love's about'." (Mattie 2014, 15).

In a brief scene, the protagonist takes the time (before returning home to escape the daily sandstorm) to contemplate the night sky. The stars appear through a crack in the smoggy clouds and the small waste compactor emits a sigh of consolation. Directing his robotic and binocular gaze at the heavens, Wall•E seems to be reaching out to receive a calling, a sign, a notion of the paternity of the beautiful constellations which he has been studying and tracing for centuries. "Gazing into the vast night sky, he ponders his incompleteness on Earth and what wholeness might lie beyond" (Mattie 2014, 15).

Based on the interpretations of symbolic anthropology, it can be said that Wall•E intuits a hypothesis of the sacred:

> Homo erectus is a homo symbolicus, an artisan who becomes a creator of culture [...]. The contemplation of the celestial vault brought the symbolic capacity of man into play, and he discovered, according to Mircea Eliade's expression, a primordial symbolism: Transcendence, Force, and Sacredness [...]. It is from this discovery of the religious significance of the celestial vault that the archaic man had his first religious experience. Man became aware of his situation and his position in the Universe [...]. Therefore, in the history of humanity, the religious man is the normal man (Ries 2007, 322).

In line with this approach, we better understand how the movie supports the cause of environmental protection, but only because of the wider question it asks about what the "good life" is, and what virtues must be cultivated for a human being to prosper in every aspect.

The transformation of the occupants of the spaceship can be interpeted through the lens of "spiritual waste". Humanity is atrophied and now bows before the altar of "consumption": its inhabitants have no remaining sense of objectivity because they quickly obtain any "material good" even before manifesting the need for it. The good is replaced with ease, happiness with comfort. Humans are all corpulent because they no longer need to move, "served" by dictatorial robots that "free" them from the problem of making decisions.

Certainly, the technological regime and its patterns of endless motion divert everyone's attention away from contemplating oneself, from pondering (like Wall•E) a greater order, higher fulfillment, or final cause for one's existence. Instead, the *Axiom* and its passengers seem to affirm Bacon's proposition that the final cause or center of the whole world is man (i.e. human power or relief). Living on the *Axiom* has become an end in itself (Mattie 2014, 16).

With the Feet on the Ground and the Gaze to the Sky. Conclusions.

In the film, humans have become products of consumption, slaves to the system they have created. *Wall•E* becomes their liberator when he allows two passengers, who like everyone else only relate through a virtual interface, to touch and look at each other in the eyes, generating a sense of longing for a more authentic and real relationship with each other: a human relationship.[3]

The plot reaches its climax when the captain of the spaceship (the only human being who holds a position of responsibility aboard the luxurious trap) deliberately disobeys the "directives" of the onboard computer and brings humanity back to Earth, driven by nostalgia for a condition that includes, among other things, the upright position, in other words, *standing on two legs*. "He begins to distinguish nature from artifice and to understand that provision on Earth is distinct from that on the *Axiom*: It is potential and conditional on human attention and labor. In learning about Earth, the

---

3   Speaking about *Wall•E* in 2008, Andrew Stanton said: "It was always the robot love story, first, second and third. Wall•E cared more about what living is truly about, more than the humans, which they'd forgotten. He was man-made, yet had something real about him; humans were real, yet they'd lost the point of living, to love one another. I loved the poetry of that" (see Verini 2010, 46).

Captain discovers that work is necessary, not only to revive the planet but also to fulfill human nature" (Mattie 2014, 18).

Wall•E opens with a terrifying vision of its human characters, tasked with staying in space and doing nothing. The epilogue of the adventure overturns the hierarchy between machine and man, and restores humanity to earth, and obliges it to rediscover its primitive relationship with the planet, a relationship based on fertility, that is first and foremost, personal and reciprocal.

Like the biblical Adam, Wall•E is called on to take care of the habitability of the "paradise on earth," performing the biblical dictate, "God took man and placed him in the garden of Eden to cultivate it and keep it" (Gen 2:15). Literally, Wall•E "cultivates" when he saves the plant that allows humanity to return home. He "keeps" (safegaurds) when he collects the leftover artifacts of humankind. Above all, however, he "cultivates" and "safeguards" the inner lives of human beings, revealing to them their own joy in reciprocity and giving them a taste of existence as generative and reproductive creatures.

Man, unlike any other living being, not only uses life (of other living beings) in order to live, but he is also called on to take care of every other living being, and therefore all life [...] existence and life must be guarded, they must be safeguarded, as they are "other," they emerge and impose themselves as "other," as manifestations of an "irreducible otherness." In other words: one can only take care of the other, the otherness of the other, or also: where there is care, there is always otherness — if there must be care, it is because there has always been otherness. In this sense, the terms "care" and "custody" are imposed by the expansion of that horizon of otherness that coincides with the very dawn of the human scene (Petrosino 2011, 14-15).

The little plant that is contested in the fight between those who wish for Earth to once again host humanity and those who do not is strongly symbolic of this otherness. Ultimately, an answer for humanity can be found on the third day of creation, when, after the creation of materials (the sky, the earth, the sea), life appears. The Bible reads: "And God said, Let the earth bring forth grass, the herb yielding seed, and the fruit tree yielding fruit after his kind, whose seed is in itself, upon the earth: and it was so" (Gen 1:11). In the creation of the plant world, according to an exegetical hypothesis, God creates a sort of creation within creation, and with it the premise of fertility: the sprout produces the fruit tree, and the fruit contains the seed that will produce new fertile fruit trees. This motif passes on to humans: "from the sixth day, the first word and the first task that God gives them, creating them in His image and likeness: [...] 'Be fruitful and multiply, fill the earth' (Gen 1:27-28)" (Lepori 2006, 29; see also Hadjadj 2019).

Disrupting the techno-economic paradigm — too well articulated in *Wall•E* — in which humans have become entangled, losing their naturalness, Wall•E the robot, like a new, more purposeful Adam, decides to restore to humans their sense, horizon, and direction. How does he do this? By cultivating their desire and guarding their hearts.

References

Appadurai, Arjun. 1996. *Modernity at Large. Cultural Dimensions of Globalization*. Minneapolis: University of Minnesota Press.

Bauman, Zygmunt. 1997. *Postmodernity and its Discontents*. Cambridge: Polity Press.

Bauman, Zygmunt. 1999. *In Search of Politics*. Cambridge: Polity Press.

Bauman, Zygmunt. 2004. *Wasted Lives. Modernity and its Outcasts*. Cambridge: Polity Press.

Chiarulli, Raffaele. 2019. "*Wall•E*. Quel che resta dell'uomo" [Wall•E. What remains of man]. *Fata Morgana* 13, no. 37 (Jnuary-April): 189-197.

Cuozzo, Gianluca. 2013. *Filosofia delle cose ultime. Da Walter Benjamin a Wall-E* [Philosophy of ultimate things. From Walter Benjamin to *Wall-E*]. Bergamo: Moretti&Vitali.

Ellul, Jacques. 2004. *Le Système technicien* Paris: Le cherche midi (2018. *The Technological System*. Translated by Lisa Richmond. Eugene, Oregon: Wipf & Stock).

Eugeni, Ruggero. 2005. "Il film ideale in relazione alla comunità" [The ideal film in relation to the community]. In *Pio XII e il cinema*, edited by Dario Edoardo Viganò, 91-101. Roma: Fondazione Ente dello Spettacolo.

Ferrando, Francesca. 2019. *Philosophical Posthumanism*. New York: Bloomsbury.

Francis. 2015. Laudato si'. *Encyclical Letter of the Holy Father Francis on Care for Our Common Home*, May 24, 2015.

Habermas, Jürgen. 2006. *The Divided West*. Translated by Ciaran Cronin. Cambridge: Polity Press.

Hadjadj, Fabrice. 2017. "Individualismo e disgregazione sociale. Il paradigma tecno-economico" [Individualism and social disintegration. The techno-economic paradigm]. *Studi Cattolici* 61, no. 671 (January): 4-7.

Hadjadj, Fabrice. 2019. "Lo spirito della materia. Crisi e cultura" [The spirit of matter. Crisis and culture]. *Studi Cattolici* 63, no. 699 (May): 324-330.

Han, Byung-Chul. 2017. *Psychopolitics. Neoliberalism and New Technologies of Power*. Translated by Erik Butler. London — New York: Verso.

Herhuth, Eric. 2014. "Life, Love, and Programming: The Culture and Politics of Wall-E and Pixar Computer Animation". *Cinema Journal* 53, no. 4 (Summer): 53-75. Project MUSE.

Herhuth, Eric. 2014. *Pixar and the Aesthetic Imagination*. Oakland: University of California Press.

Hobsbawn, Eric. 2007. *La fine dello stato* [The End of the Nation State]. Translated by Daniele Didero. Milano: Rizzoli.

Houellebecq, Michel. 2005. *The Possibility of an Island*. Translated by Gavin Bowd. New York: Alfred A. Knopf.

Lepori, Mauro Giuseppe. 2006. *Fu invitato anche Gesù. Conversazioni sulla vocazione familiare*. [And Jesus was called. Conversations on the family vocation]. Siena: Cantagalli.

Lunt, Peter Kenneth and Livingstone, Sonia. 1992. *Mass Consumption and Identity: Everyday Economic Experience*. Buckingham: Open University Press.

Mattie, Sean. 2014. "Wall•E on the problem of Technology." *Perspectives on Political Science* 43, no. 1 (Winter):12-20. https://doi.org/10.1080/10457097.2013.784576

McCarthy, Cormac. 2006. *The Road*. New York: Alfred A. Knopf.

Menarini, Roy. 2000. *Blade Runner*. Torino: Lindau.

Munk Rösing, Lilian. 2011. *Pixar with Lacan. The Hysteric's Guide to Animation*. New York: Bloomsbury.

Petrosino, Silvano. 2011. *Abitare l'arte. Heidegger, la Bibbia, Rothko* [Inhabiting art. Heidegger, the Bible, Rothko]. Novara: Interlinea.

Rich, Frank. 2008. "Wall•E for President." *New York Times*, July 6, 2008.

Ries, Julian. 2007. *L'uomo e il sacro nella storia dell'umanità* [Man and the sacred in human history]. Translated by Riccardo Nanini. Milano: Jaca Book.

Tynan, Aidan. 2020. *Desert in Modern Literature and Philosophy. Wasteland Aesthetics*. Edinburgh: Edinburgh University Press.

Uva, Christian. 2017. *Il sistema Pixar* [The Pixar System]. Bologna: Il Mulino.

Van Oosterwijk, Iris and McCarthy, William. 2022. "Once upon a Dystopian Time... the Portrayal and Perception of Environmentalism in Pixar's Finding Nemo and WALL-E", *Quarterly Review of Film and Video*, published online, March 17, 2022: 1-26. https://doi.org/10.1080/10509208.2022.2049181

Verini, Bob. 2010. "The Top 10 Screenwriters of the Decade". *Script Magazine* 16, no. 6 (November-Dicember): 43-47.

Weisman, Alan. 2007. *The World Without Us*. New York: St. Martin's Press.

Zaccuri, Alessandro. 2016. *Non è tutto da buttare. Arte e racconto della spazzatura* [It's not all rubbish. Rubbish art and storytelling]. Brescia: La Scuola.

The Coming of Machines: Dystopian Visions of Society in Samuel Butler and George Dyson

Alessandro Dividus

Introduction

One of Butler's sentences from his *Erewhon Revisited* (1901) — the belated sequel of his most famous work *Erewhon* (1872) — perfectly reveals and summarises his opinion about the work of the historian. Through the words of the narrator John, the son of the novel's protagonist, Butler states: "It has been said that though God cannot alter the past, historians can; it is perhaps because they can be useful to Him in this respect that He tolerates their existence" (Butler 1925, 132; see Nikolajeva 2009).

This passage points out two fundamental characteristics of Butler's general approach to society and life. On the one hand, his continuous opposition to any kind of Church, be it religious or scientific (Butler 1879; 1909; see Grendon 1918), on the other, instead, his continuous hostility to the dogmatism of the past and present and his focus on the future. For him, Victorian Britain is a cage of customs, dogmatism of all kinds and moral hypocrisy (see Butler 1916; Jones and Bartholomew 1923), and it is no coincidence that a soul like Butler escapes, both spiritually and physically, to places far from conventional. In 1859, after graduating from St John's College in Cambridge[1], Butler leaves the shores of England, his father's dreams of him becoming a clergyman and even his faith to reach the lands of New Zealand (see Streatfeild 1914). Here, Butler publishes a series of articles for the local newspaper, *The Press*, including the letter 'Darwin among the Machines', which will be later

---

[1] The same one that welcomed personalities such as T. Hobbes, W. Wilberforce, W. Wordsworth, Lord Palmerston, P. Dirac, R. Penrose and many other politicians, philosophers and Nobel Prize winners.

incorporated in 'The Book of the Machines' (Cole 1948, 14). The ideas developed in these works constitute the intellectual framework of his most famous *Erewhon*, a satire against Victorian society and the Industrial Revolution and an analysis of the concept of artificial intelligence.

However, his breaking out of the fiction of reality towards the reality of his fiction comes at a high price. The religious father, Rev. Thomas Butler, and society alienate him because they do not accept the directness of his positions towards the present (see Silver 1962). As Butler notes: "I attacked people who were at once unscrupulous and powerful, […] and preferred addressing myself to posterity rather than to any except a very few of my own contemporaries. […] Posterity will give a man a fair hearing; his own times will not do so if he is attacking vested interests, and I have attacked two powerful sets of vested interests at once. [The Church and Science]" (Harris 1916, 19).

It is interesting to note that Butler's personal experiences – his relationship with his father and society in particular – are somewhat similar to those of George Dyson, the historian and novelist who was so inspired by the work that he published, in 1997, the novel *Darwin among the Machines: The Evolution of Global Intelligence*. Whereas Butler's father belonged to the Church of religion, Dyson's father belonged to the Church of science. His father was the famous English physician Freeman Dyson and his grandfather was the popular musician and composer Sir George Dyson. Although more than a century separates the lives of these two characters, both feel oppressed by their society and the ideas that dominate it. Butler directly experienced the materialistic reduction of man and the mechanisation of his social and productive functions. Dyson, in turn, experienced not only the destructive force of machines[2] but also the project of one day witnessing a world in which man is completely replaced by them. He developed the narrative ideas of his novels not based on imaginary flights of fancy but on the concrete hopes

---

[2] His father's research were oriented towards the study of nuclear energy and, furthermore, the Cold War period and the war in Vietnam deeply influenced young George's personality.

for the future expressed by his father. In a 1972 lecture at Birkbeck College in London called 'The World, the Flesh, and the Devil' F. Dyson, in honour of his friend and colleague J. D. Bernal, remembers and shares his ideas stating that:

> Man would defeat the Flesh, its various diseases and infirmities, with the aid of bionic organs, biological engineering, and self-reproducing machinery. Man would defeat the Devil—the irrational in his nature—by reorganizing society along scientific lines and by learning intellectual control over his emotions. Bernal understood that his proposals for the remaking of man and society flew in the teeth of deeply entrenched human instincts. He did not on that account weaken or compromise his statement. He believed that a rational soul would ultimately come to accept his vision of the future as reasonable, and that for him was enough. He foresaw that mankind might split into two species, one following the technological path which he described, the other holding on as best it could to the ancient folkways of natural living. And he recognized that the dispersion of mankind into the vastness of space is precisely what is required for such a split of the species to occur without intolerable strife and social disruption (Brower 1978, 33).

Like Butler, Dyson chose not to come to terms with the ideas of his father and American society, especially the Princeton elite in which he grew up. Instead of New Zealand, Dyson, at the age of sixteen, left his home to move to British Columbia living in a tree house and dedicating himself to his passion for kayaking, a completely different technology from that praised by his father.

Shall We Be Afraid of Machines? The Replication Mechanism

Butler was never an admirer of Charles Darwin for two reasons in particular. Firstly, Darwin never gave adequate credit to the evolutionary ideas of his predecessors—such as G. Buffon, J. B. Lamarck, P. Matthew, R. Chambers and E. Darwin—from whom he borrowed many of the ideas underlying his theory. Secondly, and most importantly, Butler never accepted the idea that the universe was devoid of intelligence (Jones 1920, 300; see Butler 1877; 1879). For him, intelligence is both the cause and the result of evolution (see Butler 1887) and this is why Butler's positions are much closer to those of Darwin's grandfather, especially to his idea of 'the first great cause' developed in his 1794 work *Zoonomia* (Darwin 1794, 505)[3]. From Erasmus, he also borrows another distinctive interest, that of machines (Darwin 1887; Schofield 1963) and the relations between mind and mechanism. In his work *Luck, or Cunning?* (1887), Butler, merging the theories of evolutionism with those of mechanism, formulates the hypothesis that machines can possess consciousness as well as sentient animals. As he states: "I may say the theory that living beings are conscious machines, can be fought just as much and just as little as the theory that machines are unconscious living beings" (Butler 1887, 120; see Huxley 1893). This hypothesis, however, carries with it an unavoidable consequence. Given that evolution, according to Butler, is linked to consciousness, then sentient machines can also follow its laws.

If these assumptions are valid — and for Butler they are — then it is reasonable to ask "what the end of this mighty movement is to be. In what direction is it tending? What will be its upshot?" (Streatfeild 1914, 180). The history of the natural world revealed how living beings diversify in the course of their evolution, creating a mosaic of genera, sub-genera, species, varieties and sub-varieties and if we look at the history of machine evolution, Butler argues, we may observe the same process going on. As he states:

> Take the watch for instance. Examine the beautiful structure of the little animal, watch the intelligent play of the minute members which compose it; yet this little creature is but a development of the cumbrous clocks of the thirteenth century — it is no deterioration from them. The day may come when clocks, which certainly at the present day are not diminishing in bulk, may be entirely superseded by the universal use of watches, in which case clocks will become extinct like the earlier saurian, while the watch (whose tendency has for some years been rather to decrease in size than the contrary) will remain the only existing type of an extinct race (ivi, 181-82).

---

[3] "Would it be too bold to imagine, that in the great length of time, since the earth began to exist, perhaps millions of ages before the commencement of the history of mankind, would it be too bold to imagine, that all warm-blooded animals have arisen from one living filament, which the great first cause endued with animality, with the power of acquiring new parts, attended with new propensities, directed by irritations, sensations, volitions, and associations; and thus possessing the faculty of continuing to improve by its own inherent activity, and of delivering down those improvements by generations to its posterity, world without end! ".

Machines can evolve just as living beings but there are at least two elements that distinguish their way of evolution. First of all, machines need human intervention to progress and this would create a kind of balance between humans and machines (Parrinder 2005), since, as Butler states in the 'The Book of the Machines', "A 'machine' in only a 'device'" (Butler 1872, 192). However, Butler accepts the possibility that this element may disappear in the future since humans "are daily adding to the beauty and delicacy of their physical organisation; [...] giving them greater power which will be to them what intellect has been to the human race" (Streatfeild 1914, 182; see MacDonald 1926-27). If this were to happen then the second distinctive element would occur, which is directly related to the first and potentially dangerous for the very survival of the human race. This second element is the time factor.

It is undeniable that the evolution of machines is exponentially faster than that of organic matter. If things continue in this direction, there will only be two possible scenarios for mankind: enslavement or extinction. Butler seems to be more inclined towards the former. As he states:

> We are ourselves creating our own successors; [...] In the course of ages we shall find ourselves the inferior race. Inferior in power, inferior in that moral quality of self-control, we shall look up to them as the acme of all that the best and wisest man can ever dare to aim at. No evil passions, no jealousy, no avarice, no impure desire will disturb the serene might of those glorious creatures. Sin, shame, and sorrow will have no place among them. Their minds will be in a state of perpetual calm [...] man will have become to the machine what the horse and the dog are to man. He will continue to exist, nay even to improve, and will be probably better off in his state of domestication under the beneficent rule of the machines than he is in his present wild state. [...] it is reasonable to suppose that the machines will treat us kindly, for their existence is as dependent upon ours as ours is upon the lower animals (Streatfeild 1914, 182-83).

Butler reflects this vision of a dystopian future in his novel *Erewhon*. The protagonist of the story, Higgs, the narrator who informs the reader about the nature of Erewhonian society, if at first believed he landed in a utopian world, he is later forced to change his mind after learning about what happened five hundred years before his arrival. Reading the pages of a book given to him by one of the country's most famous antiquaries, who was particularly interested in the technology of his watch, Higgs makes a terrible discovery. A bloody civil war took place among the Erewhonians that decimated half the population and led to the destruction of all machines (Butler 1872, 187). The civil war took place between two factions – the machinists and the anti-machinists – and it ended with the victory of the latter.

It is particularly interesting to note how both Butler's evolutionary assumptions and the fiction of his novel anticipate many aspects of contemporary reality. As G. Dyson claims: "Butler's own evolutionary theories [...] anticipated questions that gnawing at the pillars of Darwinism today" (Dyson 1997, 43). Regarding his idea of evolution guided by an intelligence that is both cause and result of evolution itself, which in Butler's mind means substantial identity between heredity and memory – the reintroduction of design into organic development –, it is Dyson's father who takes up and scientifically supports this hypothesis. Indeed, in *Origins of Life* (1985), F. Dyson argues in favour of a twofold beginning of life based on the distinction between reproduction and replication (see Dyson 1987) which, without going too much into technicalities, is theoretically similar to that advanced by Butler.

But apart from the theses of evolutionism, which would require further study beyond the purpose of this work, it is impressive to note how F. Dyson's statements go far beyond the fictional narrative of the inhabitants of *Erewhon*. In his 1997 work, *Imagined Worlds*, F. Dyson puts forward his theories in favour of technology and his ideas on the future of human civilisation. According to him: "genetic engineering and ectogenesis are destined to give us rude jolts in one way or another. [...] Both innovations are likely to sharpen the social conflicts between liberal and conservative, between believer and unbeliever, between rich and poor. [...] in the long run both innovations are likely to prevail over the opposing forces" (Dyson 1997, 188-90). In what is remarkably reminiscent of a clash of religions, F. Dyson considers technology as a solution to human misery. Physical, economic, political and social problems can be overcome if only technology were made accessible to all (ivi, 150-1).

Thanks to technology, it will be possible—and this is what F. Dyson wishes—to change the qualities of men and create through a kind of radio-telepathy what he calls a 'collective memory', or 'collective consciousness' (ivi, 157). In the end, he prophesies that:

> The most serious conflicts of the next thousand years will probably be biological battles, fought between different conceptions of what a human being ought to be. Societies of collective mind will be battling against societies of old-fashioned individuals. Big brains will be battling against little brains. Devotees of artificial intelligence will be battling against devotees of natural wisdom. Such battles may lead to wars of genocide. [...] Societies that disagree fundamentally concerning the meaning and purpose of life may agree to keep out of each other's way by migrating to opposite ends of the solar system (ivi, 158).

The similarities with the Erewhonians society are extraordinary and G. Dyson is completely right when he states that: "Butler's crusade was not *against* Darwin but *beyond* Darwin" (Dyson 2020, 194). But whereas Butler could only imagine such a dystopian future by seeing it through the filters of his imagination, G. Dyson, instead, touches it with his own hands. According to him: "Samuel Butler foresaw the evolution, perhaps not so far off as he imagined, of that phenomenon, somewhere between mechanism and organism, now manifested as the World Wide Web" (Dyson 1997, 50).

From Analog to Digital Era and Back

In 2005, on the occasion of the 60th anniversary of John von Neumann's digital computer proposal, Google engineers invited G. Dyson to visit their company. After his visit, Dyson wrote an essay entitled 'Turing's Cathedral' — which would be later developed in the 2012 homonymous book *Turing's Cathedral: The Origins of the Digital Universe—*, in which the author warns about the plans Google has in store for the world (Dyson 2019, 54).

"Computer science", Dyson states, "has a long history of implementing neural networks, but for the most part these have been simulations of neural networks by digital computers, not neural networks as evolved in the wild by nature herself. This is starting to change" (ivi, 57). What concerns Dyson most is the possibility—

no longer remote after the emergence of the Internet—, that artificial intelligence may not only implement itself through the instructions provided by developers but rather take control over them. This qualitative leap is due, according to Dyson, to the return of analog technology combined with developments in digital one. His *Turing's Cathedral* is a thorough analysis of the historical evolution of the first computational models up to their current development. This evolution, Dyson argues, can be traced back to the works on logic by Hobbes and Leibniz—what he calls 'the Old Testament of computing'—up to the prophets of 'the New Testament', John von Neumann and Alan Turing (Dyson 2012, 297). What Dyson finds most unsettling about the appearance of technology with both analog and digital characteristics is the extreme similarity of its structure to that of nature. Indeed, many biological systems operate across both analog and digital regimes. "A tree", as he states, "integrates a wide range of inputs as continuous functions, but if you cut down that tree, you find that is has been counting the years digitally all along" (Dyson 2019, 56). Its roots function in an analog manner by expanding into the surrounding soil and using the topology as a connection network. Its internal structure, instead, i.e. its genetic code, works digitally by using systems of storage, replication and recombination of sequences of nucleotides. The combination of analog and digital systems—which is nothing more than a connection between temporal and space factors—is reproduced in the same way by modern computers. As Dyson claims:

> Digital computers execute transformations between two species of bits: bits representing differences in space and bits representing differences in time. The transformations between these two forms of information, sequence and structure, are governed by the computer's programming, and as long as computers require human programmers, we retain control. Analog computers also mediate transformations between two forms of information: structure in space and behaviour in time. There is no code and no programming. Somehow—and we don't fully understand how—nature evolved analog computers known as nervous systems, which embody information absorbed from the world. They learn. One of the things they learn is control. They learn control their own behaviour, and they learn to control their environment to the extent that they can (ivi, 57).

Dyson's father, while admitting he might be wrong, believed that thinking machines could not exist (Dyson 2015, 85). George Dyson agrees with him by stating that machines can not think in the same way as humans do given that the peculiarity of human beings lies in their creative intuitive thinking, which requires nondeterministic machines that sometimes work without logic. Nevertheless, by mentioning what Butler once said about the difference between organic and inorganic life, i.e. the arbitrary nature of this distinction (Dyson 2007, 69), Dyson points out the subtle and important difference when dealing with nondeterministic networks of deterministic machines (Dyson, 2019, 231-32). Indeed, a nondeterministic machine—as the already existing nondeterministic Turing machine (NTM)—is a computing machine which computes with continuous functions rather than discrete strings of code. There is no digital code but a relative frequency which, as von Neumann believed, was how the human brain does its computing (Dyson 2022).

A nondeterministic machine, in principle, is analogous to a living organism and just as there is no limit to man's continuous evolution then there is no limit to the evolution of machines either and it is here that Dyson puts forward a hypothesis for the future of a society that is both fascinating and alarming. During the von Neumann centennial in 2003, as Dyson reminds, the Templeton Foundation held a series of meetings in honour of von Neumann. One of the topics of these meetings was game theory, a research field in which von Neumann made particular and important contributions. One of the speakers, a Scottish mathematician, presented the results of a research which combined game theory with an attempt to prove the existence of God. The result of his research did not give proof of the existence of God but proved that if there was a God, no matter what value function you choose, the payoff is higher if God does not reveal herself. The fascinating demonstration provided by this mathematician is the foundation of Dyson's prophecy. As he states: "The message to take home is that faith is better than proof. You don't want proof. [...] To me the Turing test is wrong. Actually, it's the opposite. The test of an intelligent machine is whether it's intelligent enough *not* to reveal its intelligence.

[...] I believe it exists, but we don't want proof of it. It's a game of faith" (*Ibidem*).

Dyson's prophecy implies two worrying assumptions for the future of human society. Firstly, machines built with analog and digital systems may be able to follow the same natural laws of evolution that characterise biological organisms. Shortly, the distinction between man and machine might become so blurred as to make them indistinguishable. If this assumption were true and so was Butler's time hypothesis, i.e. the extreme acceleration at which machines evolve compared to the normal course of evolution, then it is just a matter of time before machines overtake humans. By overtaking them, and this is the second assumption, machines might become so sophisticated as to be similar to God not revealing himself as the God of religions. Through the continuous search for God, man may have already created him and not even be aware of it.

These two assumptions lead to a conclusion similar to the one that Butler's Erewhonians faced which would depend solely on the will of God. Thus, humanity could face either enslavement—completely unconscious enslavement in this case—or extinction.

Conclusions

The purpose of this work, apart from tracing a line of continuity between the ideas of two authors so distant in space and time, was to highlight the thin line between dystopian visions of the future and reality. What Butler saw with the eyes of imagination is what Dyson touches concretely. Their ideas, hypotheses and conclusions intertwine and show how the vision of society they describe probably has a more realistic basis than it might seem. Whatever the future may look like, the direction in which it is moving seems to be the one described by both Butler and Dyson. Given these premises, it is only up to mankind to decide whether to follow them or not.

References

Brockman, John (ed.). 2015. *Possible Minds: 25 Ways of Looking at AI*. New York: Penguin Press;

Brockman, John. (ed.). 2007. *What Is Your Dangerous Idea?*. New York: Harper Perennial;

Brockman, John. (ed.). 2015. *What to Think About Machines That Think*. New York: Harper Perennial;

Brower, Kenneth. 1978. *The Starship and the Canoe*. New York: Perennial Library;

Butler, Samuel. 1872. *Erewhon or Over the Range*. London: Trübner & Co.;

Butler, Samuel. 1925. *Erewhon Revisited*. London: Jonathan Cape;

Butler, Samuel. 1879. *Evolution, Old and New*. London: Hardwicke and Bogue;

Butler, Samuel. 1909. *God the Known and God the Unknown*. London: A. C. Fifield;

Butler, Samuel. 1877. *Life and Habit*. London; Trübner & Co;

Butler, Samuel. 1887. *Luck, or Cunning?*. London: Jonathan Cape;

Butler, Samuel. 1916. *The Way of All Flesh*. New York: E. P. Dutton & Co;

Cole, George Douglas Howard. 1948. *Samuel Butler*. London and Edinburgh: Morrison and Gibb.;

Darwin, Erasmus. 1794. *Zoonomia; or, the Laws of Organic Life*. Vol. I. London: J. Johnson;

Dyson, Freeman. 1997. *Imagined Worlds*. Cambridge: Harvard University Press;

Dyson, George. 2022. "AI That Evolves in the Wilds", A Talk By George Dyson, 14th August 1919. Accessed July 2022. https://www.edge.org/conversation/george_dyson-ai-that-evolves-in-the-wild;

Dyson, George. 2020. *Analogia. The Emergence of Technology Beyond Programmable Control*. US: Macmillan;

Dyson, George. 1997. *Darwin among the Machines: the Evolution of Global Intelligence*. New York: Basic Books;

Dyson, George. 1987. *Origins of Life*. Cambridge: Cambridge University Press;

Dyson, George. 2012. *Turing's Cathedral: the Origins of the Digital Universe*. New York: Pantheon Books;

Grendon, Felix. 1918. "Samuel Butler's God." *The North American Review* 208, no. 753: 277-286;

Harris, John Francis. 1916. *Samuel Butler. Author of Erewhon: The Man and His Work*. London: Grant Richards;

Huxley, Thomas. 1893. *Method and Results*. London: Macmillan and Co.;

Jones, Henry Festing. 1920. *Samuel Butler: A Memoir*. Vol. 1. London: Macmillan and Co.;

Jones, Henry Festing, and Bartholomew, Augustus Theodore. 1923. *The Shrewsbury Edition of the Works of Samuel Butler*. London: Jonathan Cape;

MacDonald. W. L. 1926-27. "Samuel Butler and Evolution." *The North American Review* 223, no. 883: 626-637;

Nikolajeva, Maria. 2009. "Time and Totalitarianism." *Journal of the Fantastic in the Arts* 20, no. 6: 184-192;

Parrinder, Patrick. 2005. "Entering Dystopia, Entering "Erewhon"." *Critical Survey* 17, no. 1: 6-21;

Schofield, Robert. 1963. *The Lunar Society of Birmingham*. Oxford: Clarendon Press;

Silver, Arnold. 1962. *The Family Letters of Samuel Butler 1841 – 1886*. London: Jonathan Cape;

Streatfeild, Richard Alexander. 1914. *A First Year in Canterbury Settlement With Other Early Essays*. London: A. C. Fifield.

The Retrotopia Science Fiction, Cacotopy, and Not Only Distopy: Scattered Notes on the "cold science fiction of the 21st century"

Ivo Stefano Germano and Massimiliano Panarari[1]

The 19th Century of positivism and "magnificent and progressive fortunes" — which united the historical ideologies of the time, from liberalism to socialism — generated a science fiction literature that reinforced and expanded the category of utopia (Altini 2012), which, on the other hand, according to some scholars, must necessarily be considered as a sub-genre of science fiction literature (Suvin 1985). The Nineteenth Century turned the idea of utopia into a cultural product intended for a much wider audience than intellectual circles, in the name of the value of progress generally shared by political cultures. The "Short Twentieth Century" and the "Age of Extremes" (Hobsbawm 1994), marked by the catastrophes of world wars and totalitarianism and from the terror of the atomic bomb, built the material and conceptual context for the conversion of utopia into the notion of dystopia. Under the banner of a radical paradigm shift — or, rather, an outright reversal — for which the very victory of a certain kind of progress generates dystopian societies and regimes. In essence, it is no longer the sleep of reason that breeds monsters, but its hyperactivism in a "technocratic" version.

Writers such as Herbert G. Wells (*A Modern Utopia*, 1905; *When the Sleeper Wakes*, 1910; *The New World Order*, 1940), Aldous Huxley (*Brave New World*, 1932), George Orwell (*1984*, 1948), Ray Bradbury (*Fahrenheit 451*, 1953) and Philip K. Dick (*The Man in the High Castle*, 1962) create fictional universes where the existence of humankind is rigidly programmed by political authorities (usually for the

---

[1] The essay has been conceived jointly by the authors. More specifically, Massimiliano Panarari wrote the introduction and paragraphs 1 and 2, while Ivo Stefano Germano wrote paragraphs 3, 4 and 5.

fulfillment of a series of biological or labor purposes useful to the "System"), and the individual, deprived of many of his (or her) individual freedoms, is enslaved to a collective dimension. And constantly surveilled by a "Big Brother" State and by a mass media apparatus that pushes him to the approval and conformity desired by the power.

In this way, these first great Twentieth-Century examples of dystopian science fiction revealed the profoundly ambiguous nature of utopia, as well as its structurally political character (Jameson, 2007). The ultimate foundation of utopia is social constructivism, the realization of a project of a perfect society, which cannot be further improved, through the tools of rationality, which, at least hypothetically, are understandable by all mankind. And, if not, that they still have to accept for their highest good. When utopia ceases to be a critical contestation, and comes to power, the rationality that directs it cannot be contested, and it is legitimate to resort to any means to create "heaven on Earth". Thus, utopia takes on the face of dystopia, as science fiction highlights through uchronies, parallel universes or projections into the future.

The Viral and Catastrophic Imagery of Postmodernism

In the postmodern world of distopic science fiction different trends are stirring, and one of the most "fortunate" of them is that of the apocalypse, which television seriality, as Aldo Grasso highlighted, has been able to root in the visions of the public through the iterativity that identifies one of its structural features (Grasso 2011). And which provides a kind of "viral imagery" for its aptitude for propagation in the transmedia and convergent universe of the postmodern landscape of mass communications and pop culture. The catastrophe has for some time now coincided with a rather precise subgenre of the end of times: the so-called "zombie apocalypse". A subversion of civilization that is invariably triggered by an epidemic, which sees the population decimated and determines the simultaneous multiplication of the "living dead". The zombie—which turns out to be attributable to the notion of the "uncanny/perturbing"—according to Sigmund Freud (Palano 2020)—is one of the most polysemic and reshaping products of the twentieth-century imagination according to the creative purposes of the different authors who use it. The zombies are also an anticipation of a further theme that is going through, from different perspectives, the painful reflection of the era of Covid-19: the category of the posthuman, declined under the pandemic regime. The "zombie-politik" is largely attributable — naturally on a fantastic level — to a general climate of biopolitical opinion such as that in which humanity was thrown by the coronavirus health crisis. And, in fact, the living dead is attributable precisely to the category of the posthuman, which from the pandemic emergency will very likely receive a series of further redefinitions inside the cultural debate. Thus, posthuman is not only the cyborg celebrated by the cyberpunk vein, but also the virus, in many ways, on which rivers of ink have been poured (and will happen again in the near future) in the name of a very curious — and deviant — process of "subjectivization". And that, in its most irrationalistic version and imbued with new age suggestions, practically identifies Covid-19 with a sort of "ambassador of doom" sent by "Gaia", the suffering Earth that would send its punisher (another figure that constellates the comic imagery and TV series) to take revenge for the excessive human footprint on its soil and for the pollution of ecosystems. All manifestations and expressions of a postmodernism in which the visions of the apocalypse are one of the fundamental ingredients, and which has also seen the genesis and diffusion in these last three decades (especially in French-speaking circles) of the knowledge of "disastrology", which found its standard bearer in the philosopher Paul Virilio (1932-2018). His thinking has constantly measured itself against what is probably the question par excellence around which postmodernism revolves in its various forms: the technique.

It identified the profound thread that ran from its analyses of the impact of speed in redefining society to its reflections on disasters as a sign of the times and the category of "stereoreality" (the "augmented reality" resulting from the split between the real and the media experience).

An elaboration always under the banner of a strongly critical vocation that led him to express very worried judgements about the age of dromocracy and turbo-capitalism, summed up in the formulas of the disappearance of art, the "epidemic of the imaginary" and the museification of the world as an effect of the disappearance of reality. So many visions of a desolate and dematerialised Earth in line with the crucial theme of catastrophe, which stemmed from his being the theorist of the accident—from the Chernobyl reactor explosion to the stock market crash—as an inevitable and ineluctable outcome of technological advancement (and the failure of technical rationality). In his thinking, the "computer bomb" (the use of the Net in a logic of war) leads to homologation and cultural colonisation with no way back, as well as to the new cyberwar.

The "futurism of the instant", disseminated everywhere by urban screens, abolished the depth of time and imposed a social culture dominated by absolute presentism.

That is, the signs of what Virilio identified as contemporary catastrophe, which feed into works of cultural theory inspired by him that analyse through his conceptual grids symbolic cultural products of the postmodern imagination, such as Don DeLillo's *Cosmopolis* (Bagherzadeh Samani, Pirnajmuddin and Akhavan, 2018) and *Mao II*. Although, in confirmation of his originality, several scholars now agree on the inappropriate nature of a judgement qualifying Virilio as a postmodernist or a poststructuralist (Armitage 1999). In fact, the heterodox scholar conceived the present age as a form of hypermodernity, somewhat distant from the "classical" and historicised modernity that had started with the Enlightenment, but still located within its conceptual perimeter.

A humanist, in some ways, who does not condemn modernity tout court and adopts a "catastrophic", but not "catastrophist" perception of technology, just as critical, but by no means antithetical, was his view of the legacy of the modern Enlightenment project.

This had been precisely the final landing place of his meditation, which had moved towards the shores of "disasterology" as a "neo-discipline" that derived in a necessary way from "dromology", the science of speed, the quintessential expression of the earlier phases of modernity and late-modernity that continued precisely to offer the frame of reference in which reflection on that hypermodernity, that was not postmodernity, was placed.

A conception that has found fertile ground in the cultural and economic debate of a certain left-wing, especially French-speaking, and which also underlies "collapseology", another strand that proves to be in tune with today's anxious times and is invested with the ambition to think of a "post-collapse" future. The catastrophe is that of thermo-industrial civilization, which, according to the intellectuals who elaborate these doctrines, would already be largely in action.

In a 2018 book (*Une autre fin du monde est possible*), three of the leading exponents of this strand — writer Pablo Servigne, social-ecological systems resilience specialist Raphaël Stevens, and agronomic engineer (and advisor to the Institut Royal des sciences naturelles de Belgique) Gauthier Chapelle — outline a cultural manifesto of collassology (or, as they prefer to put it, a "treatise on collassosophy"). It is a radically anti-industrialist text, which also stems from anarchist inspiration — a political, or perhaps even impolitic orientation (in the meaning evoked by the philosopher Roberto Esposito) structurally underpinning its authors — and which also aims to prepare people to live with the consequences of the collapse of the western production model. Global warming, the extinction of various "non-human populations" (fauna, flora, fungi and micro-organisms) and, conversely, human overpopulation and repeated economic crises make, in their view, collapse no longer a prediction, but the fate — and, in many ways, already the present — inexorable of the Anthropocene. A vision that, under various aspects, is placed at the antithesis of that of the optimistic Californian Ideology, the "latest ideology" (Balbi 2022). Nonetheless, disastrology — which in French culture has fueled the most recent cultural strand of "collassologie" — is not entirely attributable to an apocalyptic gaze. Collapsology is part of the idea that man alters his environment permanently, and propagates the concept of ecological emergency, linked in particular to global warming and the collapse of biodiversity. Collapsologists believe, however, that the collapse of industrial civilization could come from the conjunction of different crises: environmental crisis, but also energy, economic, geopolitical, democratic. Not social construction of reality, but natural distruction of it, in the Anthropocene Era. The three "collaxologists" adopt, not by chance, a multidisciplinary approach, including in their elaborations references to science fiction and the evocation of the zombie apocalypse, and putting a lot of psychoanalysis into the text, in the name of a reflection where a certain collective imagery marked by pop culture and the cultural industry after the 1990s (those of the proclaimed end of the Short Twentieth Century) turns out to be central.

The New Age of Anxiety and "retrotopia science fiction"

Then, the era of Covid-19 has, curiously (but not too much), a component of *déjà vu*. Or, better, a component of already imagined. And the West, in particular, seems to be experiencing the "perfect storm" of this new "Age of anxiety" — which is significantly devastating its social, economic as well as political structure (putting the paradigm of liberal democracy under awful stress) — according to some behavioral and visual models. Or, better said, according to some formats (also in the "philological" sense of media products), which have in fact been built over time as substantial contemporary archetypes. For example, a well-known science fiction comic, *L'Eternauta* by Héctor Germán Oesterheld and Francisco Solano Lopez, published in 1957 in Argentina, told of an alien invasion that began with a snowfall that carried a lethal virus; an allegory of the unstable political situation in Latin America battered by frequent coups d'Etat. And its authors directly experienced the tragic consequences. What could be called the predictive capacity of science fiction has largely assumed, from the fiction of Philip K. Dick onwards, the connotation of dystopia. The category of "retrotopia", as is well known, derives from Bauman's neologism and reflection on liquidity. The sociologist has noticed that we no longer look to the future with any kind of optimism. Mostly, we look to it with fear. For reassurance, we look fondly backward, to some imaginary time when everything was great, especially the future. A category in which one can also include the "nostalgia of the present", understood as the past of a dystopian or apocalyptic future, that Fredric

Jameson used to analyse Philip Dick's literary corpus (Jameson, 2007).

In its homonym book *Retrotopia* Bauman cites hundreds of speeches, papers and books to show western society is crumbling. Nationalism, globalization, automation, safety net removal, lack of community, loneliness, inequality are destroying all hope for the future in Western societies. The retrotopia, in fact, is the riversal of utopia, a utopia turned backwards. It is our recent attitude to place in the past—and no longer in the future or in a legendary place— the imagination of a better society. The change, therefore, as a step backwards, towards a known, reassuring time and, above all, with extraordinary unexpressed or denied potential. Even if this is not his belief. In fact, some products of the most contemporary science fiction can be considered as manifestations of this "retrotopia science fiction", which is mainly a narrative and also ideological mirror of the fears (individual and collective, economic and political ones) of our renewed, contemporary age of anxiety. Bauman concentrated his research on "societal" dimension. However, at the heart of collective agenda and fears (above all those of new generations) we find now the destruction of the ecosphere, the climate change, the eco-anxiety caused by the perspective of an inhospitable planet. Therefore in "retrotopia science fiction", as film remakes realized by director Denis Villeneuve (firstly *Blade Runner 2049* and *Dune*), we can find the thematization of the environmental crisis and the decomposition of urban space. *Dune*, the masterpiece of Frank Herbert (originally published in 1965), was to some extent the progenitor novel of the environmentalist science-fiction, imbued with the rising postmaterialist sensibility of the Sixties and Seventies. And, effectively, Villeneuve's film adaption—after the failure of the attempt by Alejandro Jodorowsky and the controversial and too dreamlike movie by David Lynch—constitutes a retrotopic (and faithful to the original *green* inspiration) version. In 1995, the movie *Waterworld*, directed by Kevin Reynolds, the retrotopic vision of the Earth "submerged but unsaved"—we could say—anticipates concerns about global warming. And the environmentalist footprint is also very marked in *Foundation*, the series taken from the famous Isaac Asimov's cycle.

The decomposition of urban space (understood as the sphere of politics and civil society), and the dehumanized society proposed by these movies, therefore, could be interpreted in a perspective that is not exclusively apocalyptic. Ultimately, retrotopia science fiction poses a desperate question of the future; and it is opposed — sure, without the "principle of hope" typical of the Age of the Extremes — to dystopia. A look to the past to decipher and identify the signs of the mistakes made. One last call, basically.

Cacotopy: A World in Evolution

This essay aims to attempt a possible analysis of the continuities and discontinuities of the social, political and cultural role of the word dystopia. In particular, the fundamental questions that will be asked will concern, in order, what are the historical characteristics of the dystopia? How have they changed over time and how have they adapted to new digital technologies? How have these works progressively gone beyond the context of their original production, to become keys to understanding better the symbolic and imaginary connections of contemporary society? Making the theme of dystopia has become increasingly evident, from an interdisciplinary point of view.

One of the most important cultural responses concerned the production of "counter-utopian" texts, i.e. aimed at emphasizing the inhumanity, alienation, coldness of a literally "nightmarish" social structure (Guardamagna 1980). Literature, art, cinema, television, advertising have focused on the Weltanschauung of dystonia, both as a contemporary declination of themes typical of critical sociology, such as alienation, reification, social control, and as a specific object of public debate, above all, as a result of the pandemic health emergency.

The electronic media have contributed to the liquefaction of social ties, it is true that writing this essay in the midst of the profound health crisis of the Coronavirus leads to new reflections, if not second thoughts. The "social distancing" mantra of the months of quarantine imposed by government decrees has confronted us with the fact that technological "black magic" [...] has allowed hundreds of millions of people to maintain relationships. Video calls, chats, social media: everything has gone through divided existences giving the (necessary) illusion of a possible recomposition. Grandparents and grandchildren, teachers and pupils, distant parents and children, the sexting of distant lovers, multiple video chats for an aperitif with friends constitute an articulated social phenomenology that seems to have given a new and more concrete relational meaning to the technologies of the domain. Pages of affections in our dystopian novel (Carboni 2020, 48). Dystopia, in some ways, has been considered, like the preview of the completion of the technologized age, in a continuous dance of masking and dissimulation. In fact, amplified by the information overload, in itself, a source of contradiction and abuse of attention. In the light of what has been examined, the need to historicize the concept again, in the name and on behalf of greater theoretical and methodological clarity, has been demonstrated.

The invention of the term cacotopy has been attributed to the English philosopher John Stuart Mill, as emerged from a speech held in the House of Commons on March 12, 1868.

Perhaps it is an excessive compliment to call them utopians, rather we should call them dystopians or cacotopists. What we commonly call utopian is something too beautiful to achieve; but what they support is too bad to think of realizing it. (speech given in the House of Commons). Understanding cacotopy means a historical overview about the birth of a word or a term used by John Stuart Mill, about a reflection to the theme of happiness in Jeremy Bentham. Cacotopy is the overturning of the machinery:

> from the terror aroused by the possibilities of machinery, sciences and techniques; from the extension of a soulless materialism that questions the meaning of a civilization built at the expense of the human, and that obtains happiness with recklessness and with the mechanization of behaviors (Di Minico, 2018, 38).

Technological development, above all, from the point of view of "mechanism", if correlated to the consolidation of scientific explanation of a positivist matrix, based on the formulation of general laws capable, in fact, of explaining society, give back a general idea of autonomy and strength of industrial apparatus on humans. Cacotopia as a sign of unhappiness and increasingly mechanized social behaviors, largely unaware, all in all, meaningless. More clearly, cacotopia is not synonymous with fear, but rather with desperation and alienation which, throughout the 19th century, was denoted, in literary and philosophical thought, starting from the topos, like the place/place of a future collapse of civilization. In clear contrast to the idea present in certain modern political thought of the concrete realization of utopia, as a real socio-political and ideological alternative to the Industrial Revolution. Technology and science, ceasing to arouse enthusiasm, tended to become a source of slavery, the main consequence of which concerned the reversal of plans between social and cultural progress and a cybernetic approach.The landscape of a society that no longer thinks about the future, but takes refuge in invention, a reconstruction of a past that offers a comfortable oblivion, appears full of contradictions, contortions, paradoxes that are transformed into media and literary speeches and narratives. This is not a novelty, but a precise form of cultural production that has developed in the last two decades around the multidisciplinary and multidimensional issues of a smug delight in contemplating catastrophe. A fading world that is not replaced by others, whether complementary or antithetical, but which stops at an explicit acknowledgment in digital nihilism. The cultural and communicative codification, both in terms of criticism and of mere description of the "miseries of social life at the time of dystonia" has oscillated between surreality and hyperreality, for which, on the one hand, the science fiction story has registered the betrayal of the future in what a promise, on the other hand, thanks to a profound contamination of genres, he focused on the fulfillment of what seemed impossible, unthinkable, unwatchable, unimaginable. A "society of the spectacle" without spectacle, a "society of simulacra", without simulacra, such as to eclipse any possibility of a future in a globalized context.

Cacotopy: The Era of Aphasic Science Fiction

From the earliest days of the dystopian pandemic it was at home, whether language is still someone's or something's home. More and more than resilience, new normality, sustainability, social distancing, the adjective dystopian inundated the symbolic, within a more complex process of transformation of the hybrid imaginary of a virus seen as "black swan" or irreversible destiny of the global technocapitalist system marching towards the "great transformation". The death of every future, at the hands of a modernizing nihilism that has removed every symbolic ritual.

The social imagination is no longer able to redeem reality. The apology can be read in the recent film adaptation of *Dune*, directed by Denis Villeneuve in 2021. The third attempt after the preliminary draft by Alejandro Jodorowsky in the seventies and the historical precedent directed by David Lynch in 1984. The last *Dune* absorbs in full the simulacral vacuum of every mythopoiesis of and about the future, that subtle omnipresent tension in fights against aliens who wanted to subdue the earth until the transposition of rites of passage to become Jedi, as in the grueling epic of Star Wars, in the name of a marketing Disney's infinity no longer flows into the being or becoming of a cosmos or parallel universes.

The current architrave is fear, or better, the many daily phobias that tend to turn into small deaths of desire, of dreams, of possibility.

Ultimately, the question to start with is the following: "Is the future that has become nostalgic", vice versa, "is it the pandemic that has produced a piercing nostalgia for the future"?

The vast repertoire of fiction, comics, science fiction cinema, long television series that revolves around a phase characterized by a strong aphasia on the future and a parallel sociopolitical allegory of the return to an unreal and paradoxical past tries to answer many questions. The main consequence concerned the oscillation between an aphasic stage, that is, a suspension of the story and a painful and unproductive stiff neck of ideas and imaginaries. To say the least, paralyzing and, in all evidence, static.

It seems evident that the preliminary question to be asked has as its object the sociological relevance of science fiction, that is, whether it can constitute, from a theoretical and methodological point of view, a significant field of study. Within and beyond the whirlwind of definitions, a corpus of volumes, essays, research is outlined which, in manifest or latent form, have modulated multiple and articulated scans of sociological reasoning on actors, contexts, processes, ideologies, representations of the relationship between science fiction and social.

Fleeing from the Future, No Longer Near, Let Alone the Future

Contemporary science fiction is nostalgically declined, from the fashion system to fiction, from streaming on platforms to social media. It is not a recursive mechanism, but a sheltered refuge from all that is outside, beyond, beyond. The past as hyper-connected, digital, instant Arcadia you can count on. Perhaps, the only possible foothold, as long as you have not experienced it directly or concretely. In recent years, science fiction has subsumed, structured and de-structured an excruciating fear of tomorrow, at the same time, a stubborn rejection of the future. From a pop-culture perspective, all this has translated into an incurable nostalgia for the future, at the base of which there seems to be a precise cultural datum: ours is a society unable to psychologically and socially withstand tomorrow and prefers to hole up in the kennel, comfortable and reassuring, of the past.

Bittersweet, self-referential, digitized. If we will never be again, then, all that remains is to share memories, memories, fragments of the past, ad libitum. An aura of the sublime, to put it in Benjamin's style, steeped in splinters of the past of which to make the most of the hype, the engagement, where the time of memory, that is, something capable of fixing the instant, has prevailed over the time of memory collective that, beyond any semantic short-circuit, instead, possesses in itself the sense of duration. The sociological study on the "current vocation" of science fiction (Bennato 2018) revolves around the awareness of escaping from the simple link between aesthetics and ethics, commitment and historical and existential attitude. It is a question of engaging in an interpretation that takes into account claustrophobia, impediments, denials, blocks, drifts, conjectures, in some ways, at the end of the race. Science fiction is no longer just a social show, albeit, at least initially niche, but one of the most advanced forms of surrender, almost total, to the laws of the present, that's how things go, that's how they must go. The oxymoron is constitutive of the "present state of science fiction" which, according to this type of sociological analysis, would seem to renounce the future as an explicit temporal practice. More or less paradoxically, by taking to extremes, within an increasingly platformized society, the tendency to feel nostalgia for the future, but also for the past. No longer relegated to a dimension of "inner exile", rather, in a value dimension focused on becoming technical and technological, hyper-connected and vertiginous, in most cases, of a syndromic nature.

A multitematic and multidisciplinary framework, from literature to television series, from the cinematographic medium to neuroscience, has been increasingly intertwined with a certain idea of consciously living real dystopias.

More specifically, the science fiction of the 21st century seems to oscillate between a real, increasingly dictated by apocalyptic forms and ways, and an almost certainty that a despotic real is dizzyingly in the process of being realized. This is a far from unprecedented plan, to the extent that it refers, as inspiration and overall modality, to what would once be called "social science fiction": a mix of scenarios, revelations, "hidden truths", profound references.

Cold Fiction: Between McLuhan and Baudrillard

In the previous pages, the cacotopy serves as a perspective to put the new contents of science fiction as a theme, no longer a pure atmosphere and / or an apologue on the existing:

> a materialization of the processes of conventionalization in which the synthetic icon is inspired in order to come into existence (Baudrillard 1988, 19).

On a more detailed reading, it becomes possible to recover some historically relevant strands. For example, regarding the fear of the atomic bomb, *The Day After*, a television documentary film, written by Edward Hume and directed, in 1983, by Nicholas Meyer, aired on November 20 on ABC. Shortly thereafter, the ecological catastrophe became a genre, rather than a reality, aestheticized as part of the "Cold War", within which the mental and social framework perceived the start of a gigantic and pervasive countdown. The day after represented the construction of social alarm and fear of the end, due to, here the spectrum is very broad, a meteorite, a comet, a rain of frogs, as in the finale of *Magnolia* by Paul Thomas Anderson (1999). The metaphorical posture of science fiction, from the Eighties onwards, tends to merge with cultural typologies well defined by nihilistic prophecy, by the pessimism of the so-called "professionals of the apocalypse" in the near future. In the face of experiences such as Koyanisquatsi, with the music of Philip Glass, Powaquatsi and Nakoysquatsi, filmic paraphrases of a social unbalanced and desertified, completely devoid of a vision of elsewhere.

Even more cacotopic, *Rollerball* (1975) directed by Norman Jewison, which tells of Jonathan's fight. The poster appears very topical: "in the near future, there will be no more wars, but rollerball, something you have never seen, but you will be able to see". Based on a short story by William Harrison published in *Esquire Magazine*, who participated in the screenplay of the film. It is a very serious game capable of deciphering the signs of an imaginary passage, in the midst of the US-USSR cold war that seemed to lock the world up. A society that has become unbearable that of 2018, gloomy, bored, with no more nations, governed by a directory that, to better control aggressive impulses and violent raptus, devises the *Rollerball*. Nations and wars have disappeared and everything is a generalized luxury, since "man must no longer have desires because he already has everything he wants". Beautiful world which has as its counterpart a battle, practiced by each Corporation, through its own team with a collective anthem, for skaters who beat each other to death, in technologically advanced arenas.

It is a cinematically beaten theme in the 70s (Cossi 2012) by *THX 1138, The Man Who Escaped from the Future, Logan's Escape*.

More direct than Ridley Scott's *Blade Runner* (1982), *Rollerball* really tells the future and the removal of all grounding and memory. At a certain point, in fact, Jonathan will challenge the interdict, on books and documents, swallowed by Zero a liquid brain, programmed to put into practice the chilling outcome of Ray Bradbury's *Fahrenheit 451* (1953).

The "depth psychology" joins George Orwell's negative utopia prophecy in *1984*.

On the basis of the examples used, it is possible to reason on the gradual detachment from the narrative perspective on social transformations, in the form of future promises (Spanu 2001), typical of a genre that has been affirming itself in the second half of the nineteenth century, driven by a strong vitality society and a deep faith in scientific and technological progress:

When new technologies impose themselves on societies long accustomed to older technologies, all kinds of anxieties arise. Our electronic world now needs a unified field of global awareness; the private conscience, suited to the man of the press age, can be considered as an unbearable loophole compared to the collective conscience required by the electronic flow of information. In this impasse, the only adequate response would seem to be the suspension of all conditioned reflexes (McLuhan 1963, p.19).

Science fiction has become cold, distant, remote, prey to a carousel of special childish effects, or to endless dialogues on the "meaning of life". In both cases: cold fiction. Between Marshall McLuhan and Jean Baudrillard.

References

Altini, C. 2012. *Introduzione. Appunti di storia e teoria dell'utopia*, in *(a cura di Carlo Altini) Utopia. Storia e teoria di un'esperienza filosofica e politica*, il Mulino, Bologna, 9-42.

Anders, Günther. 1991. *Tesi sull'età atomica*, Centro di ricerca per la pace, Viterbo.

Armitage, John. 1999. *Paul Virilio. An Introduction*. "Theory, Culture & Society", 16, 1-23.

Bagherzadeh Samani, Bahareh, Pirnajmuddin, Hossein and Akhavan, Behnoush. 2018. *Paul Virilio's dromology and the postmodern city in Don DeLillo's Cosmopolis* "Cogent Arts & Humanities", 5, 1-12; https://www.tandfonline.com/doi/pdf/10.1080/23311983.2018.14 24600.

Balbi, Gabriele. 2022. *L'ultima ideologia*, Laterza, Roma-Bari.

Baudrillard, Jean. 1981. *Simulacres et simulation*, Galilée, Paris.

Baudrillard, Jean. 1984. *Le strategie fatali*, Feltrinelli, Milano.

Baudrillard, Jean. "Le Xerox e l'infini", 1988. Traverses: "Machines virtuelles", n. 44-45.

Bennato, Davide (a cura di). 2018. *Black Mirror: distopia e antropologia digitale*, Villaggio Maori edizioni, Valverde.

Cossi Gianugo, Maria. 2012. *La televisione fredda: la fantascienza britannica d'inizi anni '70 fra intrattenimento ed etnocentrismo*, Aracne, Roma.

Grasso, Aldo. 2011. *Prima lezione sulla televisione*, Laterza, Roma-Bari.

Guardamagna, Daniela. 1980. *Analisi dell'incubo: l'utopia negativa da Swift alla fantascienza*, Bulzoni, Roma.

Hobsbawm, Eric. 1994. *The Age of Extremes*, Michael Joseph, London.

Jameson, Fredric. 2007. *Il desiderio chiamato utopia*, Feltrinelli, Milano.

Jameson Fredric. 2007. *Postmodernismo ovvero la logica culturale del tardo capitalismo*, Fazi, Roma.

McLuhan Marshall. 1963. "Rimorso d'incoscienza", Lettera internazionale, n. 98, IV Trimestre 2008.

Palano Damiano. 2020. *Scipio Sighele e i misteri della psicologia collettiva*, in Sighele Scipio (a cura di), *L'intelligenza della folla*, Armando, Roma, pp. 7-35.

Perniola, Mario. 1985. *Transiti*, Cappelli, Bologna.

Servigne, Pablo, Stevens Raphaël, and Gauthier Chapelle. 2018. *Une autre fin du monde est possible*, Seuil, Paris.

Spanu Massimiliano. 2001. *Science plus fiction: la fantascienza tra antiche visioni e nuove tecnologie*, Lindau, Torino.

Suvin, Darko. 1985. *Metamorfosi della fantascienza*, Il Mulino, Bologna.

Virilio, Paul. 2000. *La bomba informatica*, Raffaello Cortina, Milano.

Virilio, Paul. 2002. *L'incidente del futuro*, Raffaello Cortina, Milano.

Virilio, Paul. 2004. *Città panico*, Raffaello Cortina, Milano.

Part 3:
Literary and Performing Arts

Out of Sight and beyond Speech: State of Nature and Morality in Saramago

Patricia Chiantera-Stutte

Introduction

Since the 1990s the increasing success and diffusion of dystopian literature and allo-histories has attracted the attention of political scientists. This "genre blurring" literature (Baccolini 2000, 13-34), which violates the disciplinary boundaries between art, philosophy and politics, has been defined as an essayistic genre, offering new political and ethical perspectives on human relations (Booker 1994; Eckstein 1999, Jameson 2005; Gordin et al. 2010). José Saramago's books are clear examples of a fusion between political, philosophical and literary languages and argumentations: the fascination of Saramago's literary world derives from his "essayistic touch" (Brune 2010), achieved not only through his dealing with concrete political issues and tapping into the main philosophical contemporary theories, but also through his masterly use of narrative devices, openly aiming at observing and commentinf political and social behaviour. These are the main reasons for the wide, various and even contradictory political interpretations of Saramago's novels, and in particular of his "Ensaio sobra a cegeuira" ("Blindness" in the English translation).

Here, Saramago succeeds in creating a strong feeling of estrangement in the reader, as he plays with the construction of different times, different worlds, and different voices. Evoking this feeling of estrangement is a device used in all dystopian and allo-historical texts in order to introduce a new perspective on reality and on ordinary life, by showing their tendency to breed discontent and their weaknesses and, therefore, their fragile nature (Suvin 2014). In dystopias the construction of new "settings" is the main device employed to create in the reader — via the protagonists — both a shock and a feeling of instability (Delany 1991, De Lauretis

1981). What is taken for granted and normal becomes mysterious and enigmatic, or is simply destroyed; ordinary life and reality, instead of offering a sense of familiarity and security, arouse a sense of the uncanny (Freud 2003).

Saramago skillfully constructs the setting of *Blindness* by creating a time on two levels that are simultaneously very close to and very far from the reader — and from the novel's characters. The historical period in which the story is set is extremely close to the reader — possibly almost contemporary to 1995, when the novel was written and published, and so even for readers today it qualifies as the recent past. However, the situation and the society that emerge after the catastrophe — an epidemic of blindness — is extremely distant from the experience of both readers and the characters: it is an abrupt and complete break with the civilised world, almost a return to a state of nature. But time in *Blindness* is not the future: it is an ever-present possibility; it is a possible rupture in the civilised world that can lead to a future time inversion, to a society without state, without institutions, without morality and religion. In this perspective the novel is hardly even a typical example of a dystopia: neither the time nor the place are far away from the experience and the world of the readers and the characters. And yet, *Blindness* is a perfect eternal dystopia, as it depicts the possibility that one and every society may be transformed into a state of nature. Saramago strongly emphasises the universal and exemplary nature of the tale by calling his characters not by names, but by their role (e.g. the doctor, the thief, the first blind man), their characteristics (e.g. the girl with dark glasses, the old man with a black patch over one eye) or their relationships (e.g. the doctor's wife, the wife of the first blind man).

In the time after the outbreak of the pandemic — a white blindness — a fragile humanity, deprived of institutions and dangerously akin to a state of bestiality, emerges, mirroring the primordial state of nature as described in the political literature, from Hobbes to Locke, from Rousseau to Kant. Our time, the timespan of a civilized world, appears as a parenthesis in *Blindness*, a fragile exception that can be unpredictably and abruptly swept away. The white blindness leads to the destruction of institutions and authorities, customs, morality and organization; the city is devastated, places are unrecognizable and even language has lost its power to define, to evoke or to allow communication between humans. The plague has levelled society and individuals have lost their identities (Stanley 2004; Keren 2007, Chesney 2021). In particular the moral subject finds no orientation in the new world without rules and customs.

In this novel Saramago—through the different voices and opinions of the narrator and of the characters, implicitly defines himself as a "political moralist"; he put it more explicitly in an interview with Anna Kobucka (2008), in which he affirmed that "If the moral being is shaped by his circumstances, then it is necessary to shape these circumstances humanely". The novel poses a fundamental political and philosophical question: how is morality possible in a condition almost similar to the state of nature? Saramago's answer is offered by the behaviour—and not by the language—of the doctor's wife, the only character who keeps her eyesight.

As Stanley noted, Saramago shows the difficult reconstruction of "an intersubjective relationship with other on the basis of mutual recognition and respect" in the state of nature (Stanley 2004, 294). This brief article will provide an account of the process of refoundation of individual and collective morality in Saramago's *Blindness*, observing the interdependence between the individual's and the group's regeneration of a moral world in a state of nature. This issue will be tackled from a political theoretical point of view, with a consideration of the analogies between Saramago's perspective and the political and philosophical position of such major thinkers as Jean Jacques Rousseau, Jean Paul Sartre and Fjodor Dostojewski. An awareness of the fact that Saramago was a member of the Communist party and of his militance would seem to be crucial to understanding both the model of society portrayed in *Blindness* and the critique of representative democracy and the State.

I will firstly analyse how Saramago evokes the idea of morality as an individual process, which leads to the emergence of compassion and hospitality, and then as a collective process based on the achievement of a shared idea of justice. Then I will focus on the relation between the "gaze" (or look) of the other, social rules and compassion, and refer to some contemporary and non-contemporary literature that theorizes this relation. I will then conclude with some remarks suggesting that Saramago's work might be considered utopian in nature.

Becoming a Moral Subject

Morality is an acquired quality in *Blindness*: it emerges after a collective and individual trauma, that implies different steps in the destruction of ordinary — apparent — morality, the search for individual morality though compassion and hospitality, the acknowledgement of the necessity to act — even violently — in order to affirm justice, transforming private compassion into a collective quest for justice, and finally the establishment and refoundation of collective consciousness and political action from below — the "rising" (Saramago 2017, 285). — In Saramago all moral attitudes are active, not passive: they involve responsible and risky action, a moral and mortal danger that the individual actor and actress have to face in order to achieve their moral aims. In sum, morality does not depend on the existence of institutions — in particular politics or religion: it is related to individuals and free collectives, who choose to live in accordance with their moral responsibility.

The plot begins with the rapid spread of a peculiar kind of white blindness, a surfeit of representation which develops into a pandemic. As Martel suggests, contrary to normal blindness, which is non-infective, white blindness is characterised by a surplus of light, of information. Gradually, as the story develops, white blindness will allow people to see the truth or "the blind spot" in politics and society, namely the source of political and social power and authority (Martel 2019, 36-37). This catastrophe becomes, according to Joan Tronto, a source of wisdom in an emergency situation, specifically a state of de-humanisation and de-politicisation (Tronto 2009).

The pandemic self is not seen as an unambiguous phenomenon: the narrator, who in Saramago's novel represents different points of view that are debated and juxtaposed with, connotes blindness as a pain to be inflicted on an immoral society or as a contingent catastrophe or illness. By presenting different points of view as equal arguments and using a shifting narrative that "pushes and pulls us among a variety of perspectives", Saramago disorients the readers and encourages them to set aside their certainties and cast doubt on their own moral values (Schiff 2009, 67). In one key passage, the blind people trace back the origin of the illness to fear, in a conversation in which they describe the different ways they became blind: at the end of the discussion, the last voice, that of an unidentified blind man—who, strangely, will remain unidentified throughout the novel—states "we were already blind the moment we turned blind, fear struck us blind, fear will keep us blind" (Saramago 2017, 123).

Along with the segregation of the blind from society and their confinement in an old disused asylum, the doctor's wife, who has kept her sight, begins to develop a feeling of compassion that extends from her husband, to her neighbours, to the hostile blind, who rob other blind people and abuse women. The first sign of her compassion, which does not conform to the social egotistic conduct—which, the narrator observes, is normal—is seen in her opposition to her husband's desire for her to leave him alone in order to protect her from blindness; the second step lies in her sense of compassion and guilt towards the blind, when she expresses her desire to act: "How can you of all people expect me to go on looking at these miseries, to have them permanently before my eyes, and not lift a finger to help" (idem, 127). The third step is the compassion for the evildoer: "The doctor's wife consciously wanted to think that this man had stolen ... what rightfully belonged to others... but despite these thoughts, she did not feel ... nothing other than a strange compassion for that drooping body before her" (idem, 151).

However, just after she attains universal compassion, her feelings change. Compassion is not enough for active resistance against evil—compassion would push her to comply with evil or to justify it. The options before the moral subject—the doctor's wife—are two: one is to become blind, turning "inwards more... until [her eyes] could reach and observe inside her own brain, there where the difference between seeing and not seeing is invisible to the naked eye"; the other is to act.

Compassion, as an individual and fragile feeling, a caprice that can flatter even the mind of evildoers, cannot be the source of justice because it leaves things as they are. The feeling of justice is needed and emerges only from her suffering during the collective abuse of women by the evildoers and from the building of the first informal community based on shared pain. The narrator compassionately observes the first community of women after the rape, in which the doctor's wife is included: "Deaf, blind, silent, tottering on their feet, with barely enough will-power not to let go of the hand of the woman in front... Why are you holding hands as you go, it simply came about, there are gestures for which we cannot always find an easy explanation, sometimes not even a difficult one can be found" (idem, 173). The decision to act comes naturally after the extreme violence: abuse and death. Like death and violence, the decision to act violently cannot be expressed with words and reason. So, the second turning point of the novel is the discovery of absolute evil-rape: the unnameable act which makes it impossible to go back, or in other words to refer to the old moral world and conventions. In the dialogue with her husband, the doctor's wife refuses even to use language, because evil is the unnameable: "it is foolish for anyone to ask what someone died from, in time the cause will be forgotten, only two words remain, She died, and we are no longer the same women as when we left here, the words they would have spoken we can no longer speak, and as for the others, the unnameable exists, that is its name, nothing else" (idem, 174). The unnameable leads to the breaking of the rules, to forgetting compassion and morality: she murders the leader of the blind evildoers and vows to murder again. This original violence makes the new refoundation of a collectivity possible: violence is a duty, that the moral subject does not choose—"someone had to do it and there was no one else" (idem, 184)—an act of war that makes her blind to universal compassion and, at the same time, responsible for justice.

Only after the murder, which re-enacts justice and collective dignity, does it become possible to found, step by step, a new collectivity (Vieira 2009, 14), new rituals, a new bottom-up organisation, new political and moral subjectivities (Aristodemou 2013) and a new language. This refoundation emerges not as a return to the old moral values and to the old political community; it does not lead to the re-establishment of the old political institutions. It takes place in the small communities of blind individuals, who forget about the ordinary criteria of good and evil of the pre-pandemic society, who acknowledge the reciprocal needs and desires, and who eventually reject any transcendent principle along with any superior political project of order and security. The doctor's wife, who takes on the role of a "natural chief" of the small community of blind people that she protects, states the need to break with the old concepts of evil and good after the depravation that all the blind experienced.

Sight is restored at the end of the novel, after people, believing in a possible miracle, leave a church, realizing, thanks to the words of the doctor's wife, that even the saints and holy figures depicted there have their eyes covered, have been symbolically deprived of their sight. Does the break with the transcendental authority — leaving the church — bring about the final liberation of humans from every human and supernatural power and subjugation? Maria Aristodemou believes so and suggests that the acknowledgement of the saints' blindness means the transformation of believers into "bona fide atheists" "cut off from their memories... referring to the experience of blindness" (Aristodemou 2013, 15; Frier 2001).

Morality and Gaze

Saramago's novel is not only a literary masterwork, but also a deep political and philosophical work, which tackles certain fundamental human problems by evoking concepts, metaphors and images that were widely discussed at the time.

The main character of the novel is an outsider, or rather a normal individual — a woman — who becomes the exception in a world inhabited by blind people. She can see but cannot be seen; she is the gaze that happens to be not looked at. She is the only potentially free, healthy and powerful individual but she herself perceives her power as the most terrible condemnation and feels ashamed of her privilege in being sane. However, exploiting her capacity to see, she not only realizes and points out that people were always —

morally — blind (Vieira 2009, 16) before becoming physically blind; she also takes on herself the common moral blindness when she kills and by doing so rejects her moral capacity for compassion. Compassion is transformed into a risky, openly declared claim for justice.

Her first sense of compassion is born out of the global catastrophe, the pandemic that destroys all moral values and individual positions towards good and evil, and transforms all humans into suffering beasts. It is the doctor's wife who tells the girl with the dark glasses that in the asylum "we are all guilty and innocent, much worse was the behaviour of the soldiers who are here to protect us, and even they can invoke the greatest of all excuses, fear" (Saramago 2017, 93). Fear is the animal reaction that unites the soldiers with the blind, the hoodlums with their victims. If fear is also the feeling that, according to the blind, led to blindness, then what kind of fear is Saramago referring to? The doctor's wife's evolution into a moral individual involves gaining freedom from that fear, a freedom to orient her behaviour independently from social norms and powers.

The end of the old identity and the rise of a new moral self that is achieved by the doctor's wife begins with the growth of two sentiments: compassion and hospitality. She is, as Alexei Karamazov observes in the novel *Brothers Karamazov*, the only character able to look with compassion at the crazy mass of the desperate blind, who have lost their orientation and moral sentiments. In this perspective, compassion is seen as changing and evolving along the relation of proximity-distance: the doctor's wife also discovers through experience that — as Zosimov stressed in *Brothers Karamazov* — loving your neighbour is much more difficult than loving the human species abstractly and that "the worst enemy is always the person nearest to you" (Aristodemou 2013).

Compassion oscillates, as in Rousseau's Emile, between imagination of humanity and a concrete perception of human fragility: it leads to the "attempt to see the world through the eyes of another", based on the perception of our "common miseries which turn our hearts to humanity" (Rousseau 1979, 503) and, at the same time, originates in "a disposition that is appropriate to beings as weak and as subject to as many ills as we are" (Rousseau 1964, 130). Compassion leads also to hospitality in Saramago's novel, an individual and collective practice that makes it possible for the group of blind people led by the doctor's wife, to host others.

However, compassion and hospitality cannot be the foundation of a just society — in Saramago, as in Rousseau and in Levinas. The limits of compassion in Rousseau's thinking, pointed out by Boyd (2004) and Marks (2007), are the same as in Saramago: compassion leaves things as they are, is an unpredictable and unstable individual feeling that cannot guarantee the building of a community based on justice and freedom — this is one reason why in his political work, "The Social Contract", Rousseau does not refer to the concept of pity as a foundation of democracy (Boyd 2004, 540; Marks 2007). Going beyond compassion means raising the question of responsibility; specifically, as the doctor's wife states: "The responsibility of having my eyesight when others have lost theirs" (Saramago 2017, 238) — seeing, as the only one who can see, the suffering and humiliation inflicted by some on others.

According to Levinas, also hospitality, seen as a service in the direction of the other human being, is not a sufficient moral principle in a social situation — the relation to the "third". Hospitality entails welcoming the Other and being hostage to the Other: it is substantially founded on a timeless moral imperative: "Thou shalt not murder", namely not harming the Other. From that principle derive all actions that make hospitality a concrete act of supporting the Other: nourishing, giving shelter, a home etc. (Levinas, 1961, 171). Yet, the ethical relation changes with the social relation — the relation to the third, namely the Other of the Other. Here, according to the French philosopher, the moral subject becomes responsible for the equality of the Third towards the Self and the Others — it is here that the possibilities for human fraternity emerge. As Gauthier rightly remarks "The presence of the Third entails that the Self is obligated not only to take ethical responsibility for the single, lone stranger that faces it but also the rest of humanity" (2007, 1669). In this case the moral subject has the responsibility of weighting competing moral obligations and of enlarging his/her moral concerns, in order to safeguard not only the other in the dual relation, but the

Other of the Other or, in other words, humanity. Responsibility arises here, so that the other becomes "immediately the brother of all the other men..." (Levinas 1974, 201) The interlocutor is not a Thou, he is a You (75). The relation to the Third grounds the intersubjectivity and makes the experience of sharing humanity possible; therefore it has to be addressed with responsibility and non-indifference. "The third is the evocation of politics" (Scoralick, 2021, 316). Therefore, as Levinas states, "justice and judgment are needed from the moment the third one appears" (Levinas 1998, 221).

The transformation of the doctor's wife's compassion and hospitality into a feeling of justice that not only overcomes the first two moral obligations but denies the very principle of hospitality by disrespecting the moral imperative not to murder, seems to cast new light on the moral drama in the novel. Revenge becomes the source of justice and the test of humanity, as the girl with dark glasses claims: "You killed him to avenge us, only a woman could avenge the women, said the girl with dark glasses, and revenge, being just, is something human, if the victim has no rights over the wrongdoer then there can be no justice. Nor humanity" (Saramago 2017, 242). Absolute evil breaks into reality, making the unnameable possible and, on the other hand, providing the possibility for a totally new shared experience, a new unnameable which refounds morality and, with it, a sense of community — a new "we" as Stanley remarks using Buber's terms (Stanley 2004, 301).

What characterises this Kumamoto new refoundation? What relation does it have with the old society? An answer can be given by a deeper consideration of the relation between seeing, the look and morality, in the light of Sartre's philosophy. Blindness is clearly allegorical in Saramago's novel: as the doctor's wife remarks, it is not a normal blindness, "a private matter between a person and the eyes with which he or she was born", it is rather a public or social blindness (Saramago 2017, 30). It has not to do with a malfunction of the eyes, as the doctor states; on the contrary, the eyes "are two round objects that remain inert" (idem, 232).

In the pre-pandemic society in *Blindness*, sight — as identified with moral consciousness — is malfunctioning: "The moral conscience that so many thoughtless people have offended against and many more have rejected, is something that exists and has always existed ... With the passing of time, as well as the social evolution and genetic exchange, we ended up putting our conscience in the colour of blood and in the salt of tears, and, as if that were not enough, we made our eyes into a kind of mirror turned inwards, with the result that they often show without reserve what we are verbally trying to deny." (idem, 18)

In other words, Saramago states that our capacity of seeing, of looking, and, in general, our knowledge, which is rooted in rationality and instrumentality, has reduced our moral consciousness in our civil societies (See Aristodemou 2013). As the doctor's wife asserts at the end of the novel: "I don't think we did go blind, I think we are blind, Blind but seeing, Blind people who can see, but do not see" (Saramago 2017, 309). In this regard, the pandemic is the precondition for the end of the Cartesian illusion of the autonomous self and of the panopticon gaze of others (Kumamoto Stanley 2004, 296). Seeing, in Saramago as in Sartre, has a strong relation with being seen or, in other words, with the look of the other. However, as in Sartre's philosophy, the look of the other is not per se the root of morality: it does not create moral obligation or promote a relation between the Self and the Other. On the contrary, in the capitalistic society, on the one hand it engenders conformity and the refusal to acknowledge the other while, on the other hand, the "look" becomes a powerful tool that serves to control, watch and subjugate society. As Vieira observes, the hold of power functions as "visual construct ...maintain[ing] subjects in subordination by producing and exploiting the demand for continuity, visibility and place" (Vieira 2009, 11). At the same time the look is the "fundamental connection with the Other" or, in Sartre's words, "with the Other-as-subject [who] must be able to be referred back to my permanent possibility of being seen by the Other." (Sartre 1993, 256). The look is associated on the one hand with feelings of vulnerability, disempowerment and disenslavement, but, on the other, with responsibility and reciprocity.

The gaze turning inwards, described by Saramago as a normal way of seeing in the pre-pandemic society, can be compared with Sartre's description of serial behaviour, namely a moral conformistic behaviour that makes individuals blind to others, because they are worried about their own goals and their "appearance" in societies. Serial behaviour, according to Sartre, does not imply any common praxis: in it the relation between individuals is formal, everyone acts in isolation, and everyone is a passive subject of political power and economic dominion. The action takes place elsewhere (idem 323 ff.) The bourgeois and moralistic attitude, which is the opposite of moral conduct, is embodied by some characters and by the narrator in *Blindness*, a narrative voice oscillating between the defense of bourgeois conventions and pity towards the other.

Scarcity is the fundamental condition of unfree societies whose citizens pursue material richness and power: as in Rousseau, also in Sartre, competition for material goods engenders scarcity and the power of some over others, promoting a condition of subjection of individuals to their fellows and an exterior conditioning "which determines the serial individual to do as others to make himself the same as them" (Savage Brosman 1985, 32). This is also the condition of the pre-pandemic society as it is described by Saramago, where individuals care about their material wealth, their appearance and develop a false moral relation to others.

In this regard, catastrophe in Saramago triggers a moral process that leads step by step to moral responsibility and collective action only in the event of getting rid of the old morality and serial behaviour, namely of seeing beyond the eyes. "Facing the other" — facing up to evil — becomes the only moral solution for the one who bears responsibility for action. Only the doctor's wife can take on the responsibility for murdering, as she is the only free actor who can feel compassion for the blind and decide to ignore or kill her feeling of compassion. She is, in Sartre's (1993, 553) words, "being condemned to be free" which means "carrying the weight of the whole world on h[er] shoulders; [s]he is responsible for the world and for h[er]self as a way of being". Here also the doctor's wife assumes the same role as Zosimos and Alexei Karamazov, as the one who takes on the burden of the suffering world and the responsibility for it.

Coming back to a moral world means refounding a society, a small group—and many small groups—in which reciprocity is reestablished. The reciprocity of seeing and being seen, of acknowledging the other and the other's pain, is possible, as in Sartre and Rousseau, in a collective of free individuals whose aim is "tearing away man from the status of alterity which makes of him the product of his product, to transform him... into the product of the group, ... into his own product" (Sartre 1976, 639). The small group of brothers and sisters is finally the collectivity where individuals act not egotistically but by reaching out to others. The small group is an organic unit in Saramago's description, not the coming together of different wills: "They are seated in a huddle, the three women and the boy in the middle, the three men around them, anyone seeing them there would say that they had been born like that, it is true that they give the impression of being but one body, one breath and one hunger" (Saramago 2017, 208).

The small society protected by the doctor's wife is a community, organizing itself spontaneously without—and even against—the State and the traditional powers; it is a community that has freed itself from the fear of authority and power. It is a counter-conjuration (Veiria 2009, 14) based on shared work, rituals, compassion, care and on a model of a genuine communist society. Paraphrasing Marx's ideas, both the doctor's wife and the doctor state that "We have no alternative... We shall all give up what we've got and hand over everything, And what about those who have nothing to give, asked the pharmacist's assistant, They will eat whatever the others decide to give them, as the saying rightly goes, from each according to his abilities, to each according to his needs" (Saramago 2017, 134).

If free collectives are the cornerstones of democracy, states have a deceptive and illusionary nature, being based on representative democracy. According to Saramago, "political democracy is of little use unless it is based on economic and cultural democracy", in the same way as Sartre stated that indirect democracy rendered voters powerless to effect political change. "It seems indecent—Saramago says—to talk about [democracy] in the abstract, without the stimulus given by the presence, the participation and the involvement of citizens in community life" (Saramago 1998, 219). True democracy, therefore "should begin with what is immediately to hand—the country of our birth, the society we work in, the street we live on" (Saramago 2004).

Conclusion: She Will Rise Again

If the small community of blind people restores a collective moral subjectivity and if real freedom is possible only after the demise of the ordinary world and the achievement of a subversive new politics and social life, then the end of Blindness means the end of the social experiment which has provided the opportunity to live a plain democracy and a plain morality. The frustration of the doctor's wife, as well as her tears in the final scene, when sight is recovered, may signal that the dystopia—living without seeing—was the beginning of a possible utopia—a real moral and free society—while, in contrast, the real dystopia is normal ordinary life. The pandemic is an opportunity, an earthquake which levels society and enhances individual choices and responsibilities, offering a possibility for moral regeneration or complete destruction.

Only a woman can refound society: she can overcome the rational and egotistic structures on which a patriarchal society is based. However, men and women together, choosing to live as brothers and sisters in free-chosen groups, constitute the utopian image and project that Saramago aims at portraying. It is up to the people to take the chance and to rise again: "She will rise again—cries out the doctor's wife to blind people watching her while burying an old woman—Not her, no, those who are still alive have a greater need to rise again by themselves and they don't" (Saramago 2017, 286).

Yearning for a "post-metaphysical ethics" (Stanley, 269), refusing the universal truth claims of grand narratives Kumamoto, Saramago asserts: "I do not aspire to be the savior of the world, but I live with the very simple belief that the world could be a better place, and it could very easily be made a better place.

This belief leads me to say that I do not like the world in which I live. The worldwide revolution I envision—please pardon my utopian vision—would be one of goodness. If two of us woke up and said, "Today, I will harm no one," and the next day said it again and actually lived by those words, the world would change in a short time. Of course, this is nonsense—this will never happen. All this leads me to question the use of reason in this world. This is why I wrote *Blindness*." (Saramago 1998a, 69).

References

Aristodemou, Maria. 2013. "Democracy or Your Life! Knowledge, Ignorance and the Politics of Atheism in Saramago's Blindness and Seeing". *Law, Culture and the Humanities*, 9, no.1, 169-187.

Baccolini, Raffaella. 2000. "Gender and Genre in the Feminist Critical Dystopias of Katherine Burdekin, Margaret Atwood, and Octavia Butler". In *Future Images, the Next Generation: New Voices and Velocities in Feminist Science Fiction* Ed. Marlene Barr, 13-34. LanhaM: Rowan and Littlefield.

Booker M. Keith. 1994. *The Dystopia impulse in modern Literature. Fiction as social criticism*. Westport, CT: Greenwood Press.

Boyd, Richard. 2004. "Pity's Pathologies Portrayed: Rousseau and the Limits of Democratic Compassion." *Political Theory* 32, no. 4, 519-46.

Brosman, Catharine Savage 1985. "Theories of Collectivities in Sartre and Rousseau." *South Central Review* 2, no. 1, 25-41.

Brune Krista. 2010. "The Essayistic Touch: Saramago's Version of Blindness and Lucidity". *Mester*, 39 no.1, 89-110.

De Lauretis, Teresa. 1981. "A Sense of Wonder". In *The Technological Imagination. Theories and Fiction*, edited by Teresa de Lauretis, An. Huyssen, K. Modward (eds.), 159-174. Madison Wis.: Coda.

Delany, Samuel R. 1991. "Reading Modern American Science Fiction". In *American Writing Today*, edited by Richard Kastalanetz, 517-528. Troy, N.Y.: Whitson.

Duncan McColl, Chesney. 2021. "Re-Reading Saramago on Community — Blindnes"., *Critique: Studies in contrmporary fiction*, 62, no. 2, 211-223.

Eckstein, Barbara J. 1999. *The Language of Fiction in a World of Pain: Reading Politics As Paradox*, Philadelphia: University of Pennsylvania Press.

Freud, Sigmund. 2003. *The Uncanny*, Oxford: Penguin.

Frier, David G. 2001. "Righting Wrongs, Re-Writing Meaning and Reclaiming the City in Saramago's *Blindness* and *All the Names*". *Portuguese Literary & Cultural Studies*, 6 (Spring), 97-122.

Gauthier, David J. 2007. "Levinas and the Politics of Hostpitality" *History of Political Thought* 28, no. 1, 158-80.

Gordin Michael D., Helen Tilley, and Gyan Prakash. 2010. *Utopia/Dystopia. Conditions of Historical Possibility* Princeton: Princeton Un. Press.

Jameson, Fredric. 2005. *Archaeologies of the Future, The Desire Called Utopia and Other Science Fictions* London: Verso.

Keren, Michael. 2007. "The Original Position in José Saramago's 'Blindness.'" The Review of Politics 69, no. 3, 447-63.

Klobucka, Anna. 2008. "José Saramago: A Writer's Progress", 30. September 2008, https://www.pwf.cz/archivy/texts/interviews/jose-saramago-a-writer-s-progress_1159.html

Kumamoto Stanley Sandra. 2004. "The Excremental Gaze: Saramago's Blindness and the Disintegration of the Panoptic Vision". Critique: Studies in Contemporary Fiction, 45, no. 3, 293-308.

Levinas Emmanuel. 1961. *Totality and Infinity. An Essay on Exteriority*, Pittsburg: Duquesne University Press.

Levinas, Emmanuel. 1974. *Autrement qu'être ou au-delà de l'essence*. La Haye: Martinus Nijhoff.

Levinas, Emmanuel. 1998 *Entre nous. Essai sur le penser-à-l'autre*. Paris: Grasset & Fasquelle.

Marks, Jonathan. 2007. "Rousseau's Discriminating Defense of Compassion." *The American Political Science Review* 101, no. 4, 727-39.

Martel, James. 2019. "An Anarchist Power Amidst Pessimism: The Overcoming of Optimism in José Saramago's Blindness and Seeing." *The Comparatist* 43, 125-46.

Rousseau, Jean-Jacques. 1964. *First and Second Discourse*. New York: Saint Martin's, 1964.

Rousseau, Jean-Jacques. 1979. *Emile or On Education*. New York: Basic Books.

Saramago Josè. 1998(a). Interview with Donzelina Barroso. "The Art of Fiction." *Paris Review* 40 no. 149., 55-73.

Saramago, José. 1998. *Caderno de Lanzarote V, Lanzarote Journals V*, Lisbon: Editorial Caminho, 1994-1998.

Saramago Josè. 2004. "Reinventing democracy", *Le Monde Diplomatique*, August 2004, file:///C:/Users/patri/Documents/Lavoro/distopia /Reinventing%20democracy,%20by%20Jos%C3%A9%20Saramago %20(Le%20Monde%20diplomatique%20-%20English%20edition,%2 0August%202004).html

Saramago Josè. 2017. *Blindness*. London: Vintage.

Sartre, Jean Paul. 1976. *Critique of dialectical Reason*, London, BLB.

Sartre, Jean Paul. 1993. *Being and Nothingness: A Phenomenological Essay on Ontology*. Washington: Washington Square Press.

Schiff, Jacob. 2009. "Inclusion and the Cultivation of Responsiveness." *The Good Society* 18, no. 1, 63-69.

Scolarick, Klinger. 2021. "The Other, The Third, The Justice" *Etica & Politica / Ethics & Politics*, 33, no. 1, 305-321.

Suvin, Darko. 2014. "Estrangement and Cognition". *Strange Horizons*» 24 (November 2014) http://strangehorizons.com/non-fiction/articles/estrangement-and-cognition/

Suvin, Darko. 1979. *Metamorphoses of science fiction: On the Poetics and History of a literary Genre*. New Haven, Conn.: Yale University Press.

Tronto, Joan C. August 19, 2009. "Emergency! Saramago on Blindness and Seeing".. Available at SSRN: https://ssrn.com/abstract=1458118 or http://dx.doi.org/10.2139/ssrn.1458118

Vieira, Patricia I. 2009. "The Reason of Vision: Variations on Subjectivity in José Saramago's Ensaio Sobre a Cegueira." *Luso-Brazilian Review* 46, no. 2, 1-21.

Comparing Two Italian Alternative History Novels: *Asse pigliatutto* by Lucio Ceva and *Contro-passato prossimo* by Guido Morselli

Emiliano Marra

Introduction

Alternative history is a type of storytelling based on a retrospective and counterfactual hypothesis diverting the course of the events of the historical past known by readers. This deviation in the historical outcomes, representing the basis of the alternative history tale, has been defined by critics as *point of divergence, jonbar point* or as *nexus point*. Besides being known as a subgenre of science fiction, counterfactual storytelling is characterized by a long history started from Herodotus's and Titus Livius's excursus. The term itself — and its synonyms such as *alternate history* and *uchronia* — were used in the past to define various texts.

Besides counterfactual history, also other tales based on parallel universes, and some type of time travels, were defined as alternative history. Bronisław Backzo called them uchronias because they are utopias displaced from spatial axis to time axis (Baczko 1979, 42). As far as counterfactual historiography is concerned, this is a speculative method having always been part of historians' skills and separate from the literary genre of alternative history tales. Nevertheless, the two categories often tend to be confused under a single designation, as it occurs in critical works such as the bibliography of alternative history compiled by Barton C. Hacker and Gordon B. Chamberlain in 1986 (Hacker and Chamberlain 1986); this work includes all kinds of counterfactual historical speculation of both historiographic and narrative nature. Baczko's definition of alternative history is not frequently used, although sometimes it can be applied to different types of utopian or dystopian narratives set in the future (and not only in the past). The example which Baczko refers to is *L'An 2440, rêve s'il en fut jamais* by Louis-Sébastien Mercier (1771), but it should be noted that several uchronias have not merely depicted an alternative present or a deviation in past events, but they have also succeeded in narrating future events with respect to the time these works were produced; so Baczko's understanding of the term is complied with. Examples of this kind can be found even in the Italian context and we shall mention them briefly later.

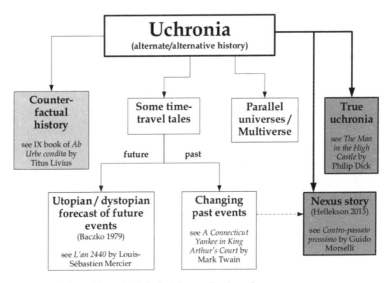

Figure 1: Various historical definitions of uchronia

In any case, the classic types of alternate history tale (as well as those with the widest fortune) are the true (or pure) uchronias and the *nexus stories*: true uchronias are tales that describe a world deeply changed following one or more divergences occurred in the historical past of diegesis, whereas nexus stories describe the ways the divergence itself occurs. Karen Hellekson, who coined the term, properly includes time travels, that change the past, in this type of uchronia (Hellekson 2013, 20-1), whereas other scholars (such as William Collins) consider nexus story as a main form of pure alternative history. However, as several critics (including Gordon

Chamberlain, Renato Giovannoli and Éric B. Henriet) claim the autonomy of the pure uchronic narrative from other kinds of alternative history, I too prefer to focus on true uchronias and on the nexus stories not based on time travel, examining the beginning of these forms in the Italian novel.

The Italian Context

The production of uchronic tales in Italian literature cannot be compared to the French and English traditions (that are the two main corpora in the Western world), yet — according to Henriet (2003, 256) — Italian literature plays an important role in the history of uchronia. In fact, the canon compiled by Hacker and Chamberlain in 1986 also includes two Italian texts, such as the first explicit counterfactual hypothesis of Italian historical writing (that is Luigi Pignotti's paragraph on Lorenzo the Magnificent) and identifies the first Italian alternative history novel in *Il tunnel sottomarino* by Luigi Motta (Hacker and Chamberlain 1986, 342-3). In this case, Chamberlain's list could not be reliable, because this novel is nothing more than an adventure story set in a parallel present, without any historical divergence. Chamberlain's error is probably due to an indirect knowledge of the novel.

Therefore, apart from *Il tunnel sottomarino*, the first Italian novel showing the formal features of pure uchronia is a text coming from the far right environment, that is *Benito I imperatore* by Marco Ramperti: this is a 1950 work approaching texts of political fantasy — such as *Storia di domani* published by Curzio Malaparte in 1949 — more than the most typical forms of this genre. Moreover, *L'ipotesi proibita* — a short story by Giovannino Guareschi, published in *Candido* magazine in 1949 — can be considered as another possible source. However, *Benito I imperatore* represents a forerunner of a remarkable current of Italian alternative history, that showing a reactionary scenario. In fact, this novel was even reprinted by Edizioni di Ar, owned by Franco Freda, former right-wing terrorist (cf. Malvestio 2018).

This narrative current is rather important in the history of Italian uchronic narratives (see Marra 2022); indeed, before the full establishment of the genre in Italy, from an ideal point of view this history can unravel between the two editions of Marco Ramperti's novel (1950-2012). Gianfranco de Turris—journalist and scholar of speculative fiction and former president of the foundation dedicated to Julius Evola's thought—would be one of the main promoters of this current he will define *fantafascismo*[1]. The idea of a uchronic scenario based on the Italian fascism overcoming the Second World War unscathed, if not actually victorious, will become one of the distinctive features of the Italian background: far-right or right-friendly publications—like the novel *Occidente* (Farneti 2001)—will be contrasted by several works of opposite political sign, such as the sagas by Giampietro Stocco and Enrico Brizzi[2], whereas in early 2000s the author Valerio Evangelisti will argue with Gianfranco de Turris about the propagandistic character of the uchronic fiction he was promoting (see Marra 2014). Indeed, some texts from this area are apologetic descriptions of fascism. Moreover, they do not merely depict it in a present or alternative past, but they also project it into the future, as in the works by Mario Farneti and Errico Passaro; thus we come back again to Baczko's definition, whereby uchronia is not merely an afterthought of the past but it can also prefigure the future.

However, the current of *fantafascismo* (capable of enhancing the debate on alternative history in Italy) will appear only in 1990s and more than twenty years will pass from the first edition of *Benito I* before the publishing of other Italian novels being classified as true uchronias, even if these novels cannot be related at all with *fantafascismo*. Early examples following Ramperti's *Benito I* include *Le armi l'amore* by Emilio Tadini (Tadini 1963) and *Aprire il fuoco* by Luciano Bianciardi (Bianciardi 1969): these works show a lot of similarities with alternative history tales, but they are experimental novels that cannot be fully framed as alternative history tales (cf Raccis 2013). So, we can wait until the '70s to read new Italian true uchronia novels. Indeed, Mondadori publishes *Asse pigliatutto* by

---

[1] The term is a portmanteau based on the Italian translation of *science fiction* (*fantascienza*), so it should be roughly translated as *fascist fiction*.
[2] Cf. Brioni and Comberiati 2019, 207-8.

Lucio Ceva in 1973 and in 1975 Adelphi will publish *Contro-passato prossimo* by Guido Morselli: these novels are more complex and characterized by a better literary structure and style, with respect to *Benito I imperatore*.

Comparing Two Italian Alternative History Novels

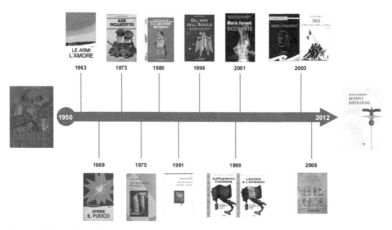

Figure 2: Timeline of Italian alternative history novel (no time-travel tales included)

Asse pigliatutto and *Contro-passato prossimo* go away from science fiction niche and they are independent from Italian or foreign models, which the two authors seem to ignore, and this is also evident in Ceva's preface:

> This book was published in 1973 by Mondadori with the title "Asse Pigliatutto". [...] In my opinion, this is the first alternative history novel concerning the Second World War published in Italy.[3]

Ceva's career as novelist is complementary to his academic production, that mainly concern military history. *Asse pigliatutto* is his second novel and it got a fair success when published, even deserving the Forte dei Marmi Prize, but then it fell into oblivion: in fact, its third edition was published by the author himself. On the contrary, Guido Morselli is posthumous author: his whole work was

---

[3] Ceva 2009, 2; my translation.

published by Adelphi some years after his suicide in 1973. Three novels of his represent a personal interpretation of some trends of mature science fiction: *Roma senza papa* is set in a future when the Second Vatican Council has attained its extreme outcomes; *Dissipatio H.G.* is an apocalyptic novel; whereas *Contro-passato prossimo* is an alternative history novel.

We must remark that both Ceva's and Morselli's novels are nexus stories: a style not frequently used at present, but quite common in the early examples of the genre, such as *Napoléon apocryphe* by Louis Geoffroy and *Uchronie* by Charles Renouvier. In my opinion, the reason why nexus stories are not very common at present is due to the success of *The Man in the High Castle* by Philip Dick appeared in 1962: this is a true uchronia representing the milestone and main model of the genre. In fact, also most contemporary Italian examples, such as *Occidente* by Mario Farneti, *Nero italiano* by Giampietro Stocco and *L'inattesa piega degli eventi* by Enrico Brizzi, are true uchronias. Unlike the first author trying to write this type of tales in Italian, all these three writers are well acquainted with the horizon of expectation of uchronia-loving readers, so the structure of their works reflects the canonical structure of true uchronia, in which the jonbar point modalities are barely sketched and the focus is the fictional universe produced by the historical divergence, rather than the divergence itself[4].

In any case, *Asse pigliatutto* and *Contro-passato prossimo* should be considered as modern nexus stories, like *The Plot Against America* by Philip Roth (Roth 2004), rather than nineteenth-century alternative history tales. Although their main focus (id est the unexpressed possibilities of war and military history) is common to a lot of the early alternative history tales, the topic is dealt under a postmodern point of view: the link between subtle satire and detailed analysis of war events — intrinsic in both novels — cannot be compared to the works of the previous century, especially when belonging to the genre of *future wars*[5].

---

[4] However, Enrico Brizzi will also try to deal with the nexus story writing the second novel of the saga, *La nostra guerra* (cf. Rossi 2021).

[5] As regards the importance of the genre of *future wars* at the beginning of modern alternate history tales, see Van Herp 1984, 57.

Asse pigliatutto and *Contro-passato prossimo* in Detail

Examining the two novels in detail, we can realize that *Asse pigliatutto* is the journal of general Triora and it describes the events experienced by him between 1937 and 1943. Triora is the assistant of general Doriani, an old-fashioned military man, but intolerant of the warlike ignorance of the fascist regime. Doriani promotes a low-cost reform of the most inadequate units of the Italian army, namely the armored regiments. Doriani's reform will be approved, but then opposed by the dictatorship (which obliges him to discharge); nevertheless, his strategic intuition — that is training the Italian armored units to a rapid movement war, thus transforming the weak spot of absence of heavy tanks into an advantage — will enable the Italian army to win the war in Africa. Then the Second World War will end in a multipolar world, even because of some secondary jonbar points (such as the Italian conquest of Kuwait), and Italy becomes a power of containment of Nazi Germany.

On the contrary, Morselli's novel is a choral tale about a different outcome of the First World War: the main protagonist is Von Allmen, an Austrian major who thinks to use an old unfinished tunnel through the Alps in order to prepare an attack against the Italian ally in case of treason. Following a series of random and grotesque circumstances, this project becomes the cornerstone of Edelweiss Operation, which will enable the Central Empires to spread across the Padan Plain, bypassing the Italian and French fronts. A secondary jonbar point — that is the chance seizure of Kaiser Wilhelm the Second by the British army and the consequent transformation of the Reich into a republic — leads to the end of the war without a bloodbath, laying the foundations for an ante-litteram European Union led by France and Germany.

Apart from the stylistic and structural differences, the research activity of the two authors on the history of the two World Wars, and their logistical and strategic aspects, is always very accurate. Besides their characteristics of nexus stories based on a divergence inherent to the military history and spiced up by an irreverent spirit towards the positivist forms of historicism, the two novels share some deeper features. For example, both authors want to defend and argue their own choices: Ceva explains that in the preface, with a bit of irony,

> [Alternative history] has already led many people to conclude that there is only one reality: not the alternative one but the other one, that is that studied by historians and explained to us by them. So what I wrote not only is completely false, but never happened for any reason. Italy and Germany could only be defeated as they were. [My] characters […] always act unreally. […] How could one believe that exponents of the Church or of our culture would have ever been sympathetic with fascism even if it had been victorious?[6]

Whereas Morselli expresses his considerations on historical determinism — and on the validity of his own invention as a means of exploring history — in a meta-narrative *Intermezzo critico* breaking the continuity of the novel:

> There are only single events, only groups of individuals, or rather, single individuals. And they analyze (their own) history in front of the mirror every morning. Otherwise, they could think that living would be nothing more than a silly repetition of mistakes. In our daily experience, the alternative to the past, though valid in itself, even overcome contingency, to appropriate a quasi-necessity.[7]

And this is a noteworthy feature, as also *The Man in the High Castle* shows meta-narrative aspects, though inside the plot itself.

The Concept of History in Ceva's And Morselli's Novels

However, the main feature shared by these two novels is the attention reserved to the choices of ordinary people and to the trends of the masses, although they are not involved actively in the decision making processes of the power. In fact, less deep alternative histories based on a single arbitrary nexus point (see Pascal's nose of Cleopatra) do not consider the underground activity of multiple variables in historical development.

---

[6] Ceva 2009, 5; my translation.
[7] Morselli 2008, 117; my transation.

But Ceva's and Morselli's novels, like *The Plot Against America* by Philip Roth, focus the chance leading unexceptional people (such as Doriani, Triora and Von Allmen) to subtly affect the epochal crossroads, without relegating the alternative history exclusively within the strategic choices of the mighty. Moreover, the literary device of partially restoring the timeline known by readers, at the end of both novels, represents an absolute novelty with respect to nineteenth-century nexus stories, whose outcomes were much more radical (Napoleon conquers the world, Europe does not convert to Christianity, etc.). On the other hand, even in Roth's novel, after Charles Lindbergh's presidency, Roosevelt's re-election brings history back to the timeline we know.

Contro-passato prossimo forecasts the birth of European Union, promoted by Rathenau, because the tragedy of the Second World War did not happen, whereas Ceva's novel ends with an illusory victory of the fascist Italy; in fact, the young people grown up during the regime will probably overturn the dictatorship with a mass movement similar to the Italian Resistance. Although these novels describe two scenarios where Central Empires win the First World War and the Axis is the winner of the Second World War, these outcomes are not necessarily worse than what occurred in the reality. For that matter, Triora himself notes how the resistance movement that would eventually counter the supposedly victorious regime would not be led by the old-guard anti-fascists, but by a generation having grown up imbued with regime propaganda (such as his son Tomaso). Indeed, the general closes his reflections with these lines:

> But Tomaso is not an old disappointed nor a mad man, that I know of. In my opinion, he cannot be compared with Mauri nor with the old Nito of Rondissone, who starts singing *Bandiera rossa* when he's drunk and is warned by carabinieri.[8]

On the other hand, Morselli ends the novel with a series of remarks (expressed by Rathenau and Von Allmen) on the lack of necessity of historical events, whereby a seemingly dystopian scenario such as the victory of the Central Empires in World War I ironically

---

[8] Ceva 2009, 309; my translation.

represents an acceleration in the rational process of European democratic cohesion which the continent will tend to after World War II. This process is ascribable not only to a single actor among many involved in the events, such as Germany, but it will be a mere possible outcome of the interlocking individual decisions of human beings (thus making the narrated story as plausible as the real history):

> Schneider. — Does the credit for having set up this Federation belong to Germany?
> Rathenau. — I wouldn't say.
> Schneider. — Whose then? Of History?
> Rathenau. — Quid, est Historia? In my opinion, there are only men who acted, or act, for their aims.[9]

Final Comments

In conclusion, these works can be considered as the first examples of an original Italian approach to alternative history storytelling, for the quasi-contemporaneity of these texts and their peculiar approach to nexus story (that is the ironic criticism of historical determinism and the reunion of the needs of history and the freedom of invention, at the end of both novels). Moreover, for distinct philosophical and ideological reasons, it must be pointed out how the gap between "expected dystopia" (such as the different outcomes of the two world wars) and the uchronic scenarios being narrated (not at all dystopic), is also common to the far-right-oriented Italian uchronic narratives, and this represents an Italian anomaly in the world uchronic landscape where the divergent outcomes of the two world wars almost exclusively display dystopian characteristics.

However, for the current of *fantafascismo*, the dystopia is that of the actual timeline; therefore, uchronias about victorious fascism become a utopian refuge. On the contrary, in Morselli and Ceva the relationship with historical reality is completely different. If Morselli wishes for Germany's victory in World War I because it would lead to a rapid European cohesion that would defeat nationalisms (in fact, the conclusion of *Contro-passato prossimo* configures an

---

[9] Morselli 2008, 239-40; my translation.

utopian outcome), in Ceva's novel the Axis victory in World War II, obtained thanks to a greater strategic ability of fascist Italy, enhances the sprouting of Italy as a regional power counterbalancing the supremacy of the Third Reich in Europe. Moreover, as noted before, the cohesion of the dictatorship already seemed to creak soon after the victory. Ceva's solution (a fascist regime capable of making shrewd strategic choices) is also present, albeit declined differently, in Farneti and Brizzi's uchronias. These examples — as the scenarios of *fantafascismo* in which fascism survives thanks to its choice of non-belligerence — represent dystopias: Brizzi deals with an actual dystopia, whereas Farneti and the other authors of *fantafascismo* describe scenarios which are dystopian only for non-right-oriented readers, but they are wholly utopic for the target readers.

On the contrary, Ceva and Morselli do not want to characterize their historical speculations in any sense, moving on a thread of subtle irony and full awareness of the complexity of historical flow and heterogony of ends. In fact, their novels do not depend on any foreign model and they stand out as unique works in the international literature of this genre, closer in spirit and outcome to particular uchronias such as *The Plot Against America* by Philip Roth than to the more stereotypical examples of this subgenre of science fiction.

References

Baczko, Bronisław. 1979. *L'utopia. Immaginazione sociale rappresentazioni utopiche nell'età dell'Illuminismo.* Translated by M. Butto and D. Gibelli. Turin: Einaudi.

Balestra, Vanni. 2013. "Origini dell'ucronia. La letteratura contro la storia." PhD diss., University of Bologna.

Bianciardi, Luciano. 1969. *Aprire il fuoco.* Milan: Rizzoli.

Brioni, Simoni and Daniele Comberiati. 2019. *Italian Science Fiction. The Other in Literature and Film.* New York: Palgrave Macmillan.

Brizzi, Enrico. 2008. *L'inattesa piega degli eventi.* Milan: Baldini Castoldi Dalai.

Brizzi, Enrico. 2008. *La nostra guerra.* Milan: Baldini Castoldi Dalai.

Ceva, Lucio. 2009. *Asse pigliatutto.* Rome: Gruppo Editoriale l'Espresso.

Chamberlain, Gordon B. 1986. "Afterword: Allohistory in Science Fiction." In *Alternative Histories: Eleven Stories of the World as It Might Have Been* edited by Charles G. Waugh and Martin H. Greenberg, 281-2. New York and London: Garland.

Collins, William Joseph. 1990. "Paths Not Taken: The Development, Structure, and Aesthetics of the Alternative History." PhD diss., University of California at Davis.

Dick, Philip Kindred. 1965. *The Man in the High Castle*. Harmondsworth: Penguin.

Farneti, Mario. 2001. *Occidente*. Milan: Editrice Nord.

Giovannoli, Renato. 1991. *La scienza della fantascienza*. Milan: Bompiani.

Guareschi, Giovannino. 1949. "L'ipotesi proibita. Se avesse vinto Hitler". *Candido*, no. 4, 5, 6, 7 (January-February).

Hacker, Barton C. and Gordon B. Chamberlain. 1986. "Pasts That Might Have Been, II: A Revised Bibliography of Alternative History." In *Alternative Histories: Eleven Stories of the World as It Might Have Been* edited by Charles G. Waugh and Martin H. Greenberg, 301-63. New York and London: Garland.

Hellekson, Karen. 2013. *The Alternate History: Refiguring Historical Time*. Kent: Kent State University Press.

Henriet, Éric B.. 2003. *L'Histoire revisitée: panorama de l'uchronie sous toutes ses formes*. Paris: Encrage.

Malaparte, Curzio. 1949. *Storia di domani*. Rome: Aria d'Italia.

Malvestio, Marco. 2018. "Cronache del fantafascismo: L'ucronia in Italia e il revisionismo storico." *The Italianist* 38, no. 1: 90-107.

Marra, Emiliano. 2014. "Il caso della letteratura ucronica italiana. Ucronia e propaganda nella narrativa italiana." *Between* 4, no. 7 (May). https://doi.org/10.13125/2039-6597/1116.

Marra, Emiliano. 2022. "Mussolini nella letteratura ucronica italiana." *Rivista di Politica* 13, no. 1: 93-103.

Morselli, Guido. 2008. *Contro-passato prossimo: un'ipotesi retrospettiva*. Milan: Adelphi.

Motta, Luigi. 1935. *Il tunnel sottomarino*. Milan: Edizioni S.A.D.E.L..

Pignotti, Luigi. 1824. *Storia della Toscana sino al principato con diversi saggi sulle scienze, lettere e arti*. Florence: Leonardo Ciardetti.

Raccis, Giacomo. 2013. "Tadini, Bianciardi, Morselli: il romanzo italiano alla prova della controstoria." *Il Verri*, no. 51: 1-33.

Ramperti, Marco. 1950. *Benito I° imperatore*. Rome: Scirè.

Ramperti, Marco. 2012. *Benito I imperatore*. Padua: Edizioni di Ar.

Rossi, Umberto. 2021. "Contro-passato prossimo: genesi di una storia alternativa in *La nostra guerra* di Enrico Brizzi." *Narrativa*, no. 43: 197-206.

Roth, Philip. 2004. *The Plot Against America*. Boston: Houghton Mifflin.

Stocco, Giampietro. 2003. *Nero italiano*. Genoa: F.lli. Frilli Editori.

Suvin, Darko. 1985. *La metamorfosi della fantascienza. Poetica e storia di un genere letterario*. Translated by L. Guerra. Bologna: Il Mulino.

Tadini, Emilio. 1963. *Le armi l'amore*. Milan: Rizzoli.

Van Herp, Jacques. 1984. *L'histoire imaginaire*. Bruxelles: Editions Recto-Verso.

Walls, Camps, State of Exception, Sweden-Enemies, and Gang-Related Individuals. A Journey into the Dystopian Sweden of Johannes Anyuru and Jens Lapidus

Luca Gendolavigna

Introduction

In present-day Sweden, the concept of national identity — imbued with the contradictions of the past — is evolving towards new political and cultural clashes, reshaping itself in a rather ambivalent way. In Tommaso Milani's words, "it is only possible to speculate about what is going to happen in the near future. What is certain, however, is that the issue of citizenship is becoming increasingly politicised in Sweden and linked ever more closely to issues of traditional values and norms" (Milani *et al.* 2022, 74). In this connection, contemporary literature captures this politicisation, narrating how people tend to physically include and exclude others from society for racial and cultural reasons.

In recent years, dystopia has become central in the Swedish literary field thanks to several novels, such as Zulmir Bečević's *Avblattefieringsprocessen* (2014, *The demigrantisation process*) Johannes Anyuru's *De kommer att drunkna i sina mödrars tårar* (2017, *They will drown in their mothers' tears*), Thomas Engström's and Margit Richter's *Nattavaara* series from 2020, and Jens Lapidus' *Paradis City* (2021, *The no-go zone*). Furthermore, Swedish literature has also produced a dystopian chef d'oeuvre in less recent times: *Kallocain* (1940) by Karin Boye.

The most recent texts provide a harsh social critique, taking current inequalities and fears, issues of tolerance, diversity, democracy, crime, segregation, and surveillance to the notably 'used and abused' extreme. In this article, the concept of dystopia will be framed, according to Frédéric Claisse and Pierre Delvenne's definition, as "the depiction of a dark future based on the systematic amplification of current trends and features. It relates to a complex narrative posture that relies on the critical observation of a threatening present that would lead to an apocalyptic future 'if nothing were done'" (Claisse and Delvenne 2014, 155-156).

Complementarily, dystopia is also understood as a complex posture able to identify "something already taking place in society and then employing the resources of imaginative literature to extrapolate to some conceivable, though not inevitable, future state of affairs" (Seeger and Davison-Vecchione 2019, 55). In other words, dystopia provides a counter-narrative to question the disturbances of the present. As stated by Dietrich Kammerer, "[b]y presenting alternative worlds, novels and films aid us in the reflection of our own situation: (How) does our society differ from what is represented? Can we discern elements of the dystopian world in our world? How are we better (or worse) off than the society portrayed?" (Kammerer 2012, 105).

Concerning what Kammerer terms as "our own situation" and "our world", we see how issues of migration, multiculturalism, and crime favour restrictions all over the Swedish political spectrum. In 2015, the then Social-democratic Prime Minister Stefan Löfven stated "Mitt Europa bygger inte murar, vi hjälps åt när nöden är stor" (My Europe doesn't build walls, we help each other in case of need),[1] while in 2020 he backtracked and claimed to "hold the borders", evidencing a conservative shift after Turkish President Erdoğan's decision to open the border between Turkey and Greece.

Sweden's strong humanitarianism makes it a moral superpower, also thanks to its moderate and relatively humane criminal justice system (Franko, Van der Woude and Barker 2019, 57). Quoting Milani, *moderate* and *humane* criminal justice refers "to the argument that generous and inclusionary welfare states are less likely to rely on coercive means to respond to social problems and are more likely to maintain mild and humane prison conditions out of

---

[1] https://www.regeringen.se/tal/2015/09/tal-av-stefan-lofven-vid-manifestat ionen-for-flyktingar-den-5-september/.

respect for persons inside" (2022, 58).These features constitute the notion of Nordic exceptionalism, namely the representation of Nordic countries as a beacon of secular values in the world (Jensen and Loftsdóttir 2022; Milani *et al.* 2022). In this connection, Sweden's core values are neutrality and a strong drive for humanitarianism, rooted in the awareness of being the 'conscience of the world' and the 'champion of human rights' by setting moral standards in international relations (Dahl 2006; Engh 2009). However, as is well known, Sweden's neutrality is lost in the light of the Scandinavian country's entry into NATO in March 2024.

The above-mentioned feature of Swedish criminal justice is central in this article, as the dystopias analysed below display a dramatic reversal of this relatively humane system. Nowadays, organised crime is injecting 'moral panic' into society, with an increased number of shootings in the whole country (388 of which 61 fatal in 2022), especially in the Stockholm region (126 of which 28 fatal in 2022).[2] In this regard, in August 2022 the leader of the far-right party *Sverigedemokraterna* (Sweden Democrats) Jimmie Åkesson stated that it is time to end a long tradition of "saft-och-bulle-politik" (juice-and-bun-politics), proposing a sharpened justice, where criminals should be punished instead of cared for, prompting a shift from *vårda* (take care) to *straffa* (punish), by proposing to rename the *Kriminalvården* (Prison and Probation Service) in *Straffverket* (Punishment Agency). Åkesson also proposed sending foreign criminals to cheap prisons abroad.[3] Against this issue, Prime Minister Ulf Kristersson (Moderate Party) is promising harsher criminal policies against murders and shootings through the proposal to introduce a system of time- and geographically-limited visitation zones (*Visitationszoner*), as already applied in Denmark through the notorious *gettoplan*.[4] The aim is to intensify the work against gangs and prevent shootings and explosions. As a matter of fact, Swedish

---

[2] https://polisen.se/om-polisen/polisens-arbete/sprangningar-och-skjutningar/.
[3] https://www.expressen.se/nyheter/akesson-bort-fran-saft-och-bullar/.
[4] Danish government's proposal for a Denmark without Parallel societies and no ghettos within 2030. See https://www.berlingske.dk/politik/nedrivning-dobbeltstraf-og-udvisning-af-foraeldre-her-er-regeringens-22-markante.

Parliament has approved this legislative proposal, which have come into force in April 2024.[5]

Following the riots aroused after the April 2022 Quran-burning demonstrations by Rasmus Paludan (leader of the Danish far-right party *Stram Kurs*), Liberal Party's leader Johan Pehrson raged against alleged, separatist Muslim forces that are growing up beyond integration: "Det är krafter som vill kontrollera delar av befolkningen som bor i Sverige och separera människor från vår livsstil och samhället i övrigt" ("There are forces that want to control parts of the population living in Sweden and separate people from our way of life and society in general").[6]

Looking at how discourse is changing, we see how homeland security and the sovereign right to exclude bodies are justified and necessary in Sweden, currently ranked as the OECD country with the "fastest growth of social inequality" (Ålund, Schierup and Nergaard 2017, 12), and the most segregated country in Europe (Tunström and Wang 2019).

Scholars show how non-white people in Sweden experience exclusion, discrimination, and the constant need to prove themselves as Nordic people (Hübinette and Lundström 2011; Osanami Törngren 2022). This increased difficulty is linked to a collapsological discourse of Swedish welfare embodied in the *folkhem* (The people's home), defined as a metaphor for an ethno-culturally homogeneous Sweden as a once efficient welfare State (Önnerfors 2022).[7] In recent times, we see the re-appropriation of the *folkhem* concept by the Swedish right-wing to blame the growing number of migrants for a shrinking welfare, effectively leading to conceptualizations of the *folkhem* as a cultural and material heritage under "siege" (Andersson 2009, 240). As the Utopia where things and bodies had their own place, "[t]he Swedish People's Home [...] was without doubt meant for ethnic Swedes, although this was never

---

[5] https://www.regeringen.se/pressmeddelanden/2022/12/system-med-visitationszoner-utreds/.
[6] https://www.svd.se/a/BjawaG/johan-pehrson-fortsatter-varna-for-separatister.
[7] For reasons of transparency, the original term will be used instead of its translation (people's home).

acknowledged or thought to be necessary to acknowledge" (Hettne, Sörlin and Østergård 2016, 400).

This leads to a sort of resurrection of *folkhem* as a retrotopian, and nostalgic dimension of Swedish society as a *paradise lost* to globalisation, and multiculturalism, something organically linked to *our* way of life and society, as stated by Pehrson above). By *retrotopia* is meant a spatial-temporal dimension based on the nostalgic restoration of the past, presented as an alluring retreat from an implicitly less desirable present. In Zygmunt Bauman's words, retrotopia thrives on "visions located in the lost/stolen/abandoned but undead past" (2017, XV), where the main concerns are no longer political issues of equality, but "personal security, something that can be linked indirectly to [...] law and order, and any punitive regime of securitization" (Önnerfors 2022, 70).

Theoretic Background and Aim of the Study: The Collapsological Turn in Swedish Dystopias

This article will analyse how bodies are disciplined according to a technological regime of security, where walls and internment camps are dominant architectures, and how the novels enclose detailed legal frameworks and statutes of citizenship to frame a white, retrotopian, Islamophobic Swedishness. The main argument is that Anyuru's and Lapidus' works embody a *collapsological turn* in Swedish fiction, definable as the depiction of an age of extremes, in which social stability and security shrink while the boundaries between people grow.

Against the backdrop of Cathrine Thorleifsson's concept of Swedish Dystopia, coined as a sociological tool to construct an image of Sweden as an example of the dangers posed by pursuing naïve migration policies (2019), this article frames the dystopian representation in fiction of Sweden as a risk society exposed to (1) Islamisation, threatened by a 'great ethno-religious-cultural displacement' (Juhász and Szicherle 2017); (2) the resulting criminalisation of Swedish citizens with foreign, most frequently extra-European, background (Jensen and Loftsdóttir 2022);[8] (3) Collapse of human rights and neutrality, jeopardised by growing support for populist, banally racist policies, and NATO membership respectively.

In the novels, we see a shift to brutally realistic pragmatism, where social problems related to crime and culture are drastically tackled in order to save a lost *folkhem*, which may describe what Achille Mbembe called "the nomos of the political space in which we [already] live" (2003, 14).

From a theoretical-methodological point of view, as Anyuru's and Lapidus' novels seem to be in a dimension of *extremised* continuity with current discourses and political orientations, they are both to frame as examples of what Claisse and Delvenne defined as 'enlightened catastrophism', namely "a realistic depiction of the future as if it had already happened and nothing could be done to stop it" (Claisse and Delvenne 2014, 166). Linked to this concept is the ethical approach to catastrophe, theorised by the French scholar Jean-Pierre Dupuy (2012): to become aware of the catastrophe, we must believe in the certainty that it will take place, and adjust our behaviour accordingly. Therefore, an enlightened approach to catastrophe interprets this event, whatever it may be, as perpetually imminent. In fact, Dupuy explains, catastrophe always seems improbable to us, relegated to the realm of uncertainty and, when it comes, we always find ourselves unprepared (ivi, 587). Nevertheless, in order to prevent it, the catastrophe needs to be necessary, because thinking of it as inevitable allows us to acquire a critical awareness of it.

Within this dimension, this article also draws on Michel Foucault's theories of surveillance, punishment, and biopolitics (1995, 2003) to show how both novels fit into a growing cultural critique of Sweden as a "white nation in crisis" (Lundström and Hübinette 2020), afflicted by nostalgic melancholia for an irretrievable *folkhem* (Barrling and Garme 2022).

---

[8] This acronym refers to people from Middle-East (ME), and North-Africa (NA).

Two Paradigmatic Cases: De Kommer Att Drunkna I Sina Mödrars Tårar and Paradis City

Both Anyuru and Lapidus read the future "as a distorted projection of the present" (Claisse and Delvenne 2014, 158), which is a particularly topical perspective in terms of what might be the possible consequences of a progressive suspension of recognised institutional authorities. The age of extreme informing the collapsological turn is found, in both authors, in the attempt to reflect on what it might look like if an organised far-right were to take power in Sweden, inspired by an extremisation of current trends of intolerance, crime, and segregation.

Johannes Anyuru was born in 1979 in Borås, Sweden. He is a poet, novelist, and essayist who debuted in 2003 with the poetry collection *Det är bara gudarna som är nya* (2003, Only the gods are new). His latest novel *Ixelles* came out in September 2022. *De kommer att drunkna i sina mödrars tårar* is not only his most widely read and famous work, but it was also awarded the Augustpriset in 2018.

Anyuru's s novel is influenced by several traumatic events that occurred in the 21st century: The Twin Towers attack, the Abu Ghraib scandal, Jyllands-Posten and Charlie Hebdo's anti-Islamic caricatures, the Stockholm bombings in 2010, and the terror attack on Drottninggatan in Stockholm in 2017. As a result, Anyuru critically observes the growing concern for anti-terrorist security and suspicion of citizens from Islamic countries, stating that, while we live in the "saga om människans okränkbarhet" (fairy tale of human inviolability) (2018, 194), on the other hand, it is impossible to hide that "vi lever och skriver återigen i den öppna tortyrens tidsålder" ("we live and write again in the age of open torture") (ibid.), where the aim of torture acts on the body through control, security, and surveillance (ivi, 195).

Jens Lapidus is a Swedish lawyer born in 1974 in Stockholm who now works as a professional writer. Traditionally regarded as an exponent of Nordic noir, he debuted as a novelist with *Snabba*

Cash (2006, Easy Money), and his latest work is *Mr. Ett* (2022). *Paradis City* is his first dystopia.

In the wake of what inspired Anyuru in 2017, Lapidus defines his dystopia as "en ironisering och en kommentar till det vi brukar kalla folkhemmet. Och jag kanske har sett trender i dag med segregering och polarisering och så drar jag ut de trenderna riktigt åt helvete i den här boken" (an ironisation and a comment on what we usually call the *folkhem*. And I perhaps have seen trends today of segregation and polarization and so I pull those trends out really badly in this book).[9]

Analysis and Discussion

4.1 de Kommer Att Drunkna I Sina Mödrars Tårar

Anyuru's novel weaves in concern about a future where Sweden turns into a fascist and xenophobic country. The story is composed of two timelines, one in the present and one in the future. It opens in the present in Gothenburg, where three terrorists plan to execute a Swedish satirist, who they believe has desecrated Islam, but one of them, Nour, prevents this before it is too late. After the trial, she is placed in a psychiatric clinic and diagnosed with schizophrenia as she claims to have come from the future to stop this attack.

The future she describes forms the second timeline of the novel, narrated in the first person by Nour, who actually bears a different name in the dimension she claims to have come from: Annika. In this future, the terror attack ends with the satirist's murder, and consequently, Sweden becomes a fascist regime. As a matter of fact, the satirist's murder works as a catalyst for power to further inflame anxieties about Islam, which is increasingly portrayed as a threat to Sweden. In this future, the original Arabic Quran is banned and only allowed in a Swedish version.[10] New laws, known

---

[9] https://www.svtplay.se/video/30478544/babel/babel-jens-lapidus-stina-wirsen-ellen-sundberg-fernanda-melchor.

[10] Anyuru's fantasy is interestingly relatable to the recent episodes of Paludan burning the Quran in Sweden, which until January 2023 have been publicly allowed by Swedish authorities based on the principle of freedom of expression.

as *Februarilagarna* (February Acts), force people to sign a *Medborgarkontrakt* (Citizen contract), committing to vaguely defined Swedish values. Not doing it marks them as *Sverigefiende* (Sweden-Enemies), who end up in Kaningården (Rabbit Yard), an internment camp where Sweden-Enemies are exposed to torture and trained in 'Swedish values' such as democracy and freedom of expression.

Kaningården is divided into different zones, as explained by Nour-Annika: "Jag och pappa bodde i en linjerad zon [...] i ett av höghusen [...]. Om vår säkerhetsklass höjdes—det hände till exempel om du bar religiösa kläder [...] inte samarbetade på lektionerna i Hus K eller hade vissa sorters skägg—[...] skulle vi vara tvungna att flytta till en rutad zon, vilket antagligen skulle betyda att vi inte längre fick ha en egen lägenhet, utan måste bo i ett parkeringsgarage [...]. Om vår säkerhetsklass höjdes ännu mer skulle vi hamna i en svart zon, och bara få vistas på de öppna fält som drönarna kunde filma (Anyuru 2017, 154) ("Dad and I were living in a striped zone in one of the buildings [...]. If our threat level was raised—which could happen if you wore religious clothing, [...] didn't cooperate in class at Building K, or had a certain style of beard, [...]—we'd have to move to a checkered zone, which apparently meant we wouldn't have our own apartment, but we'd have to live in a garage instead [...]. If our threat level was raised even more, we'd end up in a black zone and only be allowed out on the open fields where the drones could film us").[11]

Reading these lines, we notice a certain discipline of space through the creation of special architectures, such as Building K, but we also note an aesthetic discipline related to appearance, in which precise religious dress codes are sanctioned. As explained by Nour-Annika: "Varje dag hade vi lektioner i Hus K [...], typ en gång var det en svensk kille i min egen ålder som pratade om att män måste byta blöjor och dammsuga, och nästa gång satte en av väktarna på en tecknad film om hur barn blir till [...]. Lärarna kallade sig för demokratientreprenörer och yttrandefrihets coacher och samtalsaktivister och skrev upp sina namn på whiteboarden"

---

[11] All translations from Anyuru's novel are by Saskia Vogel's 2019 edition *They will drown in their mothers' tears*.

(ivi, 152) ("We had daily classes in Building K [...]: one time there was a Swedish guy my age who talked about men having to change diapers and vacuum; the next time one of the guards put on a cartoon about how children are made [...]. The teachers called themselves 'democracy entrepreneurs' and 'free speech coaches' and 'dialogue activists', and wrote their names on the whiteboard").

Building K mirrors an oppressive architecture emphasizing the insignificance of the individual in the camp. Thus, life therein is "focused on the body as machine" (Foucault 2007, 242), which makes Building K a place where bodies are trained, optimized, and disciplined by what Michel Foucault defines as "the procedures of power that characterized the disciplines: an anatomo-politics of the human body" (ibid.). As such, in Building K bodies are disciplined and segmented by a biopoliticised surveillance within a well-delimited space, in which bodies are humiliated to learn basic, civil activities based on the assumption that prisoners are unable to execute them. Borrowing Giorgio Agamben's terminology, Kaningården is a place where 'bare life' (2003) rules. Sweden-Enemies, mostly Muslims, are deported into a surveillance regime and required to attend courses to facilitate social integration. Here, a subtle form of nationalism takes shape, including civic and secular values into the national narrative, which in turn reproduces the *exceptional* superiority of Swedish (The West) culture vis-à-vis the culture of Sweden-Enemies (the Rest) (Milani *et al.* 2022), which (ironically enough) should be educated in the simplest daily activities such as changing diapers and cleaning.[12]

A widespread intolerance surrounds Sweden-Enemies, confined into a heterotopia of deviation (Foucault 1986), and believed to have no notion of hygiene, civility, democracy and fundamental freedoms. Framed as 'the political paradigm of modernity' (Agamben 2003), Kaningården represents the tragic landmark of the Northern European civilizationist turn in defence of secularist values against threats from Islam (Brubaker 2017).

---

[12] These aspects are also present in Bečević's novel *Avblattefieringsprocessen*, where a young boy is tutored by a Swedish educator called *Avblattefierare* (Demigrantiser) in small daily actions considered 'typically Swedish'.

Sweden-Enemies relate not just to a political, but to a cultural, and racialised category, identified with Islam and non-whiteness. As the text reads, a Sweden-Enemy is disciplined to the passive acceptance of his own non-Swedishness: "Du var svensk om svenskarna tyckte att du var svensk, det var det vi lärde oss på värdegrundslektionerna. Jag var inte svensk eftersom jag var muslim och så. Men vem var egentligen den första svensken, som hade bestämt att de andra var svenskar? Han fanns inte, och där han borde stå fanns ett hålrum, ett hål inne i ordet svensk [...]. En tomhet" (Anyuru 2017, 75) ("You were Swedish if the Swedes thought you were Swedish—that's what we learned in our Core Values class. I wasn't Swedish because I was Muslim or whatever. But I mean, who was the first Swede anyway—the one who'd decided who got to be Swedish? He didn't exist, and there was a hole where he was supposed to be, a hole inside the word "Swedish" [...]. An emptiness").

Through this distinction, the ruling regime proves to be based on the existential division between citizens reputed to be human, and citizens not reputed to be human. As expressed in this dialogue between Nour-Annika and her mother: "'De delar in människor i vänner och fiender'. 'Det är värre än så [...] De delar in oss i människor och djur' (Anyuru 2017, 84-85) ("'You're either an enemy or a friend'. 'No, I'm afraid it's worse than that', [...] You're either human or an animal'"). In accordance with dystopia as a critique of hopeless degeneration from existing problems, Anyuru emphasizes the issue of diversity and the monstrosity of the Other: "Jag bar på skärvor av en annan värld, en annan grammatik för att ordna tid och rum. Jag var muslim, och de där åren började jag tro att det gjorde mig till ett monster i Sverige" (Anyuru 2017, 157) ("I was carrying shards of another world, different grammar in which I ordered space and time. I was Muslim, and it was during those years that I started to think this made me a monster in Sweden").

Anyuru problematises the *folkhem* notion focussing on the exclusion of groups who are reduced to bare life, which has not just an animalising dimension but rather, drawing on his essay collection *Strömavbrottets barn* (Blackout Children), it stems from an attempt to eliminate the foreign trace that bodies carry on their very surface (2018, 226).

The rule of law is guaranteed by a vigilantist ethos: "I min tid kunde en ladda ner en app som kontrollerade ditt passnummer mot ett register över sverigefiender, och enligt februarilagarna fick alla medborgare göra kontroller på varandra" (Anyuru 2017, 45) ("In my time, you could download an app that checked a passport number against a registry of enemies of Sweden, and according to the February Laws citizens were allowed to screen each other").

This quote shows the totalitarian ubiquitousness, represented by passports, biometric apps, and Swedes who check other citizens to report Sweden-Enemies. In Foucauldian terms, we notice how power works as a circulating grid spread in the masses. Thus, there is no need for extensive surveillance when the civilians themselves are already part of it.

4.2 Paradis City

The second novel, *Paradis City* by Lapidus, represents a "brave 'New' Sweden, which has gone through a profound, paradigmatic economic transformation since the early 1990s, [with] no classes, no collectives, not even institutions, just individuals, according to the dominating paradigm" (Hellgren 2019, 157).

In detail, the novel is a critical distortion of *folkhem*, where a 'Special Areas Act' is in force, and a wall separates Stockholm from the Northern suburbs of Järva.[13] Most of the national companies are privatised, residential areas are owned by China, and the four richest people in the country own much more than the rest of the population. Society is deeply polarised with strong neo-nazist organisations, violent protest movements of religious, criminal, and ecologist networks. The story moves around the kidnapping of the Minister of Interior Eva Basarto Henriksson in Järva, and it displays a complex triangulated plot, as it follows the actions of three different but deeply linked protagonists, who alternate on parallel tracks: Emir Lund, a gang-related criminal of Kurdish origin raised in

---

[13] A geographical area north of Stockholm, including, among others, the municipality of Solna.

Järva; the sisters Fredrika and Nova Falck, a policewoman and an influencer respectively, whose fate is bound together by the task of rescuing the Minister. Lapidus describes a scenario where sophisticated surveillance devices regulate the circulation of bodies, highlighting socio-spatial divisions that undermine human equality and dignity. The presence of investigative elements and the distortion of Swedish social reality as we know it (Ciaravolo 2019, 625), make the novel a 'dystopian noir'. The novel opens with the text of the 'Special Areas Act', a law imagined to come into force in 2025, which defines: 1) a Special area, where identity checks are run; 2) a Particularly Gang-related Individual, to whom health insurance can be revoked; 3) a Comfort divider, which surrounds special areas for segregative population management. As a political grammar of the crisis, this Act mirrors a shift towards the pathologisation of securitarianism capitalizing on collective conflicts and fears.

Lapidus openly stated that he was inspired by the above-mentioned Danish *Gettoplan*, borrowing the term *Særlige områder* to forge his own *Särområde* (Special Area), framing the idea of aggravating penalty in such areas. The 'Special Area' comes to be what Foucault defined as a *heterotopia*,[14] that is, a place outside of and different from any other place, located within a specific territory, on the margins of society, and serving as its negative: a "counter-space" (Foucault 1986, 24). In *Paradis City*, the suburbs take a heterotopic form as they hardly communicate with the rest of society, and access to the centre is limited for those who live inside. As a parallel society with issues related to crime and shootings, this initially *provisional* heterotopia becomes a place of *permanent* exclusion: "Varenda polis visste hur de här särområdena hade vuxit fram: gängvåldet, skjutningarna och sprängningarna. Parallellsamhället, klansväldet, tystnadskulturen: staten som till slut hade reagerat. [...] Så hade särområdeslagen kommit till, först som en interimistisk krislösning, senare blev den permanent" (Lapidus 2021, 83-84) ("Police knew how these special areas developed: gang violence, shootings and explosions. The parallel society, clan rule,

---

[14] The concept derives from Greek ἕτερος (different/other) and τόπος (place).

culture of silence: the state that had finally reacted. [...] In this way the Special Areas came to life, first as a crisis solution *ad interim*, and then as a permanent one").[15]

The Act defines also a SGI, the short form of *Särskilt Gäng-relaterad Individ* (Particularly Gang-Related Individual, PGI), a Special Area resident with at least three prior crimes and proven gang affiliation. This legal category is not entitled to free healthcare and cannot leave the Area. As Emir is SGI-marked, he experiences the dehumanising treatment of the Social Insurance Agency: "Dessutom pissade Sverige på honom. När de klassat honom som SGI hade de kastat ut honom ur systemet. *Din allmänna sjukförsäkring har upphört att gälla* [...]. Från den dagen fick han betala all vård ur egen ficka" (Lapidus 2021, 35) ("In addition, Sweden pissed on him. By the time they had classified him as a PGI, they had thrown him out of the system. *Your general health insurance has expired* [...]. From that day on, he had to pay for all his care"). As Emir suffers from kidney failure and is no longer entitled to free treatment, we see here the shift from care (*vårda*) to punish (*straffa*) advocated by Åkesson in August 2022, which takes the distorted shape of vindictive exclusion of bodies within a 'necropolitical' system (Mbembe 2003). In a very similar way, the Citizen Contract developed by Anyuru works as a structured political tool of marginalisation and deletion of fundamental rights from bodies.

Finally, the Act defines a *Trevnadsdelare*, literally a Comfort Divider, the wall that implements separation as the most concrete solution to protect the *folkhem*: "trevnadsdelarna som byggdes var bara en fysisk manifestation av något som redan existerade. Problemen kanske inte löstes, men de kapslades i vart fall in, i väntan på bättre alternativ. [...] Trevnadsdelaren var inte bara en mur: den var en uppfinning för att sprida rädsla" (Lapidus 2021, 154) ("the Comfort Dividers that were built were just a physical manifestation of something that already existed. The problems may not have been solved, but they were at least encapsulated, while

---

[15] Although there is a published English translation, in this article all translations from Lapidus' novel are provided by the author.

waiting for better alternatives. [...] The Comfort Divider wasn't just a wall: it was an invention to spread fear").

What we find in the text shapes a conceptual link with Massimo Recalcati's psychoanalysis of the wall as a fortress that defines the incivility of our time and the urge to delimit one's territory as a primary securitarian character against the permanent threat of "internal outsiders", namely those living in our midst who are not seen as belonging to the nation (Recalcati 2020, 17). Thus, yielding to what Recalcati calls the 'temptation of the wall', governmental power in *Paradis City* does not even try to solve problems anymore, but to enclose them within a delimited space, ensuring that the crime-contaminated world does not destroy the image of *folkhem* entrenched in the centre.

As the novel reads: "Men det var omöjligt att motstå konflikter för alltid. Det var logiskt egentligen: Sverige var inte annorlunda än resten av världen—så man hade varit tvungen att bygga en mur runt problemen, runt dem som förstörde stabiliteten" ("But it was impossible to resist conflicts forever. It was actually logical: Sweden was not different from the rest of the world—so a wall had to be built around the problems, around those who were destroying stability") (Lapidus 2021, 354)

As it comes out from both novels, the root of evil is in the suburbs (such as Kaningården and Järva) and, as in a surgical operation, it must be excised. As the last alternative left, the circumscription of space provided by the wall prevents evil from overflowing, protecting the *folkhem* from the intrusive and embarrassing presence of "barbarian at the gates that should be excluded from the Swedish future" (Milani 2020, 20).

Conclusions

This article has aimed to show how fiction may provide critical tools for the analysis of current populist-illiberal turns in Swedish democracy, acting from the nowhere of literary fantasy through anticipatory illumination to prompt critical reflections in the extra-textual reality.

Anyuru and Lapidus problematise the notion of *folkhem* as "mainly a reference back to [...] prosperity, high levels of social security, and low exposure to globalisation. [...] adopted by populist and right wing [...] as a means to advance [...] ideas of Sweden as a closed society" (Götz 2019). In this sense, both authors address the progressive shift towards nostalgia for traditional Nordic exceptionalism and welfare that are now catalysts of a retrotopian sentiment. Thus, research needs to shed light on the recent dystopian-collapsological turn in Swedish contemporary literature, as authors such as Anyuru and Lapidus can "enable political communities (public opinion, experts, industrials, policy-makers, stakeholders) to react and take steps to prevent dark futures from happening" (Claisse and Delvenne 2014, 166).

Introducing figures such as Sweden-Enemies and SGI, and architectures such as the internments camp and the wall-delimited Special Area, the novels show the progress of necropolitical mechanisms within a securitarian distinction between deserving/human and undeserving/non-human citizens. These human and spatial dimensions are to comprehend beyond the layer of right, but rather as a new structured normality shaped by new governmental tools in times of crisis. Thus, while citizenship becomes something to deserve by virtue of class, race, culture, and religion, some groups are forced into criminalised subalternity, where internment and segregation could not be remote possibilities anymore, but rather a plausible political solution, and where whiteness continues to be inevitably seen as "the central core and the master signifier of Swedishness and thus of being Swedish" (Hübinette and Lundström 2011).

References

Agamben, Giorgio. 2003. *Stato d'eccezione*. Torino: Bollati-Boringhieri.

Ålund, Aleksandra, Schierup, Carl-Ulrik, and Nergaard, Anders. "Reimagineering the Nation: Crisis and Social Transformation in 21st Century Sweden: An Introduction". In *Reimagineering the Nation: Essays on Twenty-First-Century Sweden*, edited by Aleksandra Ålund, Carl-Ulrik Schierup, and Anders Nergaard, 9–40. Frankfurt am Main: Peter Lang, 2017.

Andersson, Jenny. 2009. "Nordic Nostalgia and Nordic Light: The Swedish Model as Utopia 1930-2007". *Scandinavian Journal of History* 34, no. 3: 229-245.

Anyuru, Johannes. 2017. *De kommer att drunkna i sina mödrars tårar*, Norstedts.

Anyuru, Johannes. 2018. *Strömavbrottets barn – Texter om konst, våld och fred 2010-2018*. Stockholm: Norstedts.

Barrling Katarina and Garme Cecilia. 2022. *Saknad – På spaning efter landet inom oss*. Stockholm: Mondial.

Brubaker, Roger. 2017. "Between nationalism and civilizationism: The European populist moment in comparative perspective". *Ethnic and Racial Studies*, 40, no. 8: 1191-1226.

Bauman, Zygmunt. 2017. *Retrotopia*. Bari: Laterza.

Ciaravolo, Massimo (ed.). 2019. *Storia delle letterature scandinave. Dalle origini a oggi*. Milano: Iperborea.

Claisse, Frédéric and Delvenne, Pierre. 2014. "Building on anticipation: Dystopia as empowerment". *Current Sociology*, 63, no. 2: 155-169.

Dahl, Anne-Sophie. 2006. "Sweden: Once a moral superpower, always a moral superpower?". *International Journal: Canada's Journal of Global Policy Analysis* 61: 895-908.

Dupuy, Jean-Pierre. 2012. "The precautionary principle and enlightened doomsaying", *Revue de Métaphysique et de Morale* 4, no. 76: 577-592.

Engh, Sunniva. 2009. "The Conscience of the World? Swedish and Norwegian Provision of Development Aid", *Itenerario* 33, no. 2: 65-82.

Foucault, Michel. 1986. "Of Other Spaces", *Diacritics*, 16, no. 1: 22-27.

Foucault, Michel. 1995. *Discipline and Punishment. The birth of prison*. London: Vintage.

Foucault, Michel. 2003. *Society Must Be Defended: Lectures at the College de France*, 1975-6. London: Allen Lane.

Foucault, Michel. 2007. *Security, Territory, Population. Lectures at the Collège de France 1977-78*. Palgrave MacMillan.

Franko, Katja, Van der Woude Maartje, Barker, Vanessa. 2019. "Beacons of tolerance dimmed? Migration, criminalization and inhospitality in welfare states" in Bensixsen, Synnove and Wyller, Trygve (eds.), *Contested Hospitalities in a Time of Migration – Religious and Secular Counterspaces in the Nordic Region*, London-New York: Routledge.

Hellgren, Per. 2019. *Swedish Marxist Noir: The Dark Wave of Crime Writers and the Influence of Raymond Chandler*, Jefferson: McFarland.

Hettne Björn and Sörlin Sverker, Østergård, Uffe. 2006. *Den globala nationalismen: Nationalstatens historia och framtid*. Stockholm: SNS Förlag.

Hübinette, Tobias and Lundström Catrin. 2011. "Sweden after the Recent Election: The Double-Binding Power of Swedish Whiteness Through the Mourning of the Loss of 'Old Sweden' and the Passing of 'Good Sweden'", *NORA – Nordic Journal of Feminist and Gender Research* 19, no. 1: 42-52.

Jensen, Lars and Loftsdóttir, Kristín. 2022. "Welfare state colonialism in the Nordic countries and Britain", in *Exceptionalism*, edited by Lars Jensen and Kristín Loftsdóttir, 76-108. London-New York: Routledge.

Juhász, Attila and Szicherle, Patrik. 2017. *The Political Effects of Migration-Related Fake News, Disinformation and Conspiracy Theories in Europe*. Budapest: Friedrich Ebert Stiftung, Political Capital.

Kammerer, Dietmar. 2012. "Surveillance in literature, film, and television". In *Routledge Handbook of Surveillance Studies*, edited by David Lyon, Kevin D. Haggerty and Kirstie Ball, 99-106. London-New York: Routledge.

Lapidus, Jens. 2021. *Paradis City*. Stockholm: Bonniers.

Lundström, Catrin and Hübinette, Tobias. 2020. *Vit Melankoli – En analys av en nation i kris*. Göteborg: Makadam.

Milani, Tommaso M. 2020. "No-go Zone in Sweden – The infectious communicability of evil", *Language, Culture and Society* 2, no. 1, pp. 7-37.

Milani, Tommaso M. et al. 2022, "Civic orientation for adult migrants in Sweden – A multimodal critical discourse analysis of Swedish values and norms in the textbook About Sweden". In *Didaktiska perspektiv på språk och litteratur i en globaliserad värld*, edited by Pia N. Larsson, Cecilia O. Jers and Magnus Persson, 57-77. Lund: Nationella nätverket för svenska med didaktisk inriktning och författarna.

Önnerfors, Andreas. 2022. "*Folkhemmet*: 'The Peoples Home' as an Expression of Retrotopian Longing for Sweden before the Arrival of Mass Migration". In *Migration and Multiculturalism in Scandinavia*, edited by Eric Einhorn, Sherrill Harbison, and Markus Huss, 60-79. Madison: University of Winsconsin Press.

Osanami Törngren, Sayaka. 2022. "If I Can't Say I Am Swedish, What Am I? Freedom within Limits of Choosing Identity, *Journal of Critical Mixed Race Studies* 1, no. 2, pp. 129-144.

Recalcati, Massimo. 2020. *La tentazione del muro – Lezioni brevi per un lessico civile*. Milano: Feltrinelli.

Seeger, Sean and Davison-Vecchione, Daniel. 2019. "Dystopian literature and the sociological imagination", *Thesis Eleven*, 1, no. 155, pp. 45-63.

Thorleifsson, Cathrine. 2019. *Nationalist Responses to the Crises in Europe: Old and New Hatreds*. London: Routledge.

Tunström, Mora and Wang, Shinan. 2019. "The segregated city — A Nordic overview, Copenhagen: Nordic Council of Ministers". Accessed February 1, 2023. https://nordicwelfare.org/wp-content/uploads/2019/03/The-segregated-city-A-nordic-overview-1.pdf.

From Natural to Cyber.
A Transmedia Approach to
Body Representation in Techno-Dystopias

Silvia Leonzi, Fabio Ciammella, Grazia Quercia

Technodystopia, Cyberpunk and the Body Representation

The dystopian literature, so the various media evolutions of the dystopian genre, by definition describes the failure, disillusionment, and tragedy of society in all the possible forms through which they manifest themselves: environmental, political, social, post-apocalyptic, etc. (Claeys 2017). In this essay, we would like to examine a particular strand that has come to be defined as the evolution of science fiction, namely the one which refers to the field of science and technology. Science fiction, from the earliest literary works, has described the mutations of society by exaggerating their consequences in a future perspective, for example, in the period of the Industrial Revolution, the machine in central, intended as the artefact representing technological progress, as the dominating power that dehumanises the individual (Di Minico 2018). In the evolution of the genre, the relationship between man and machine becomes almost a game of mirrors in which the human being wants to overcome his own weaknesses by using technologies as an extension of his body, while the machine tends to resemble and imitate man. An example could be HEL, the female android in *Metropolis* (Lang 1920) which is perhaps the first and peculiar example of this duality.

This essay is not intended to reconstruct the historical relationship between man and machine, but to present a proposal for analysis derived from a specific reading of the dystopian genre with a science-fiction connotation. Since the Second World War, many of the authors that can be traced back to such an offshoot of two literary genres, namely science fiction and dystopia, have proposed stories that aimed to describe and criticise the society in which they lived, describing how certain choices made in the present can lead to radical consequences in imaginary future societies, exemplary are George Orwell, Aldous Huxley, but also and above all the works of Philip K. Dick.

A literary movement that has represented the synthesis of sci-fi critique to society since the early 1980s has been cyberpunk. Among its defining narrative topics there is the exasperation of the trajectories and trends that characterise contemporary society (postmodern, late modern, risk, etc.) in a fast and swirling change, for example: embedded technology, information technology, synthetic drugs, mega corporations imposing themselves as new nation states. Also: electronic music, cyberspace, network cowboys, body alterations through surgery both for aesthetic purposes and for the improvement of the individual, but also for the social control of the person. For example, Case, the protagonist of the genre's manifesto book Neuromancer, is excluded from the common environment, the cyberspace, through an alteration of the nervous system, as he is a network cowboy.

Thus, it is indisputable that the sub-genre defined as Techno-dystopia, from the 1980s onwards, is largely linked to the work of William Gibson, Bruce Sterling and the other *Mirroshades* authors, a term derived from the first anthology of the Cyberpunk genre, and, by extension, also from the works of Philip Dick, which became mainstream through the many film and television adaptations such as *Blade Runner* (Scott 1982), *Total Recall* (Verhoeven 1990), *Screamers* (Duguay 1995), *Minority Report* (Spielberg 2002), *The Man in the High Castle* (Amazon Studios 2015-2019). This is not to praise the predictive abilities of the above-mentioned authors as new Cassandras describing the future/present by anticipating technologies, but their sociological sensitivity, expressed in their narrative creativity applied to the imagination of controversial near futures, allows us to identify social and cultural representations of our present. Seeger and Devison-Vecchione's (2019) reading of the genre appears interesting: according to them, the dystopian works and so the techno-dystopian works can act as a bridge to interpret, sociologically, the context in which they are created since, in this type of narrative, connections are generated between private and public problems. Furthermore, this vision helps to imagine a link between the biographical dimension and History and, finally, emphasises the great ability of dystopian narratives to describe the influence between objective and subjective dimensions, i.e. "how elements of social structure and individual experience influence each other, thereby capturing how it feels to inhabit a particular social world with a vividness that even a qualitative ethnography that strives for the 'thickest' description can arguably never quite achieve" (Seeger and Davison-Vecchione 2019, 61).

Thus, technodystopia can be considered, in its narrative topoi, a radicalisation of social representations in the context in which the works, ascribable to the genre, take shape. As Claeys states

> Works of dystopian fiction sometimes appear as counterfactual "future histories," which project narratives from the present into the future. They are often combined with technological and scientific projections of various kinds and are sometimes described as a subset of science fiction (Claeys 2022, 54).

A central narrative element in the social, political and cultural critiques of science fiction, and one that has become absolutely central from cyberpunk onwards, is the representation of the body. Indeed, this becomes the sensitive element capable of making explicit the connections between subject and object, society and individual, public and private. The body is the terrain of conflict for the assertion of rights and the means of manifesting one's identity, as in issues regarding gender, medicine, science, the self-assertion of the individual in the civil and political spheres. It also is the narrative element trough which explore themes in relation to overcoming human frailty, the advance of ageing, illness, death. In science fiction representations this translates into bodies modelled according to science, supported by machines that enhance their potential. Dyers, using science fiction works as a model, describes the cognitive evolution of the body from a post-biological perspective: according to this perspective it is possible to consider the body "as a mosaic of biological, viral, technological, cultural and political dynamics"

(Dyens 2000). The author notes how the representation of the body in science fiction works calls into question classical archetypal figures such as life, death, sexual desire, etc. In cyberpunk works, the cybernetic invasion of body and mind becomes a distinctive feature as mechanised prosthetic limbs, cerebral sensors, aesthetic surgery appear:

> In the cyberpunk universe, the body (the whole body) is a schizophrenic construct; its identity is a centerless amalgam of informational systems (such as DNA, viruses, genes, memes, etc.). In the cyberpunk model of the body the homogenous whole is replaced by a supple and permeable mosaic, one whose selfhood is diffuse; the whole is only a series of heterogeneous elements grafted to one another (Dyens 2000, 75).

Hence, it does not only refer to the body as technological integration, but, considering how science fiction operates by projecting society's anxieties, criticisms and problems into a future world, the body is a manifest and radicalised cultural representation of contemporary society.

As proof of this, a recurring theme in technodystopias is eugenics, a conflicting topic regarding both technological and cultural aspects related to the human being. As Di Minico points out, in this case, the body becomes a significant medium of control, through which power relations, social structures, and politics are enacted (Di Minico 2018).

Studying the representation of the body in works belonging to the Technodystopian genre allows us to wonder about how human evolution is thought of in its physicality, in relation to cultural and ideological extents expressed in the relationship with technology. In this case, technology, as in every work of science fiction, has the function of representing the construct of the human, opening to a form of reflexive narration.

The proposed analysis put its starting point on the selection of works that fell within a genre, not yet clearly codified, such as Technodystopia. Therefore, first of all, all of the distinguishing characteristics of the genre were framed, taking as model the specific works that certainly refer to a dystopian narrative. Moreover, the technological aspect in these narrations should not embody just a narrative setup to trigger the story but must represent the content of the fictional universe. Taking cyberpunk as a reference model, (cyber) technology must invade and interact with all the elements that make up the narrative universe (setting, social aspects, values, existents, events). Finally, the selection of works fell on products distributed mainly after the year 2000, in order to identify a key to understand the representation of the body in contemporary works, considering how "dystopia increasingly defines the spirit of our times" (Claeys 2017, 498).

Our corpus was composed of 31 selected audiovisual texts (films, TV series, anime)[1], to which we applied a transmedia approach (Ciammella *et al.* 2019), meaning we considered the entire corpus as a single storyworld capable of generating a secondary worldness (Leonzi *et al.* 2019), an idea of a shared narrative universe. In this way, representations of the corpus were analysed starting from the features that make up the storyworld such as mythos, ethos and topos (Klastrup and Tosca 2020) and the elements of itself (Wolf 2014; Ryan and Thon 2014).

A hermeneutic analysis of the corpus was carried out (Montesperelli 2014) starting from an outline composed of three aspects: the themes of the narrative, i.e. the set of symbols and meanings it carries in general; the identity of the characters, i.e. the role they play in the narrative; the aesthetics and ethics of the body, i.e. the representations it takes on.

Through analysis, we categorised the dimensions of the representation of the body in relation to technology by placing them on a continuum composed of three main still points: Natural body, Hybrid body, Artificial body/disembodied body.

---

[1] Below are the texts that constitute the corpus. Franchise: *Ghost in the hell* (3 animated movies, 1 live action, 4 anime series), *Matrix* (4 movies, 1 animated series). Movies: *Aeon Flux* (2005), *Alita: Battle Ange* (2019), *Blade Runner 2049* (2017), *Elysium* (2013), *Equilibrium* (2002), *In time* (2012), *Looper* (2012), *Ready Player One* (2018), *The Island* (2005), *Total Recall* (2012). TV/Animated series: *Altered Carbon* (2018-2020), *Black Mirror* (2011-in production), *Dark Angel* (2000-2003), *Ergo Proxy* (2006), *Oats Studios* (2021), *Sweet Tooth* (2021-in production), *Wayward Pines* (2015-2016), *Westworld* (2016-2022).

The Body Representation: Natural, Hybrid, Artificial/Disembodied

Considering the spectrum within which the body is represented in Technodystopias, it is possible to consider the three main nodes: the natural body, which rejects technology and preserves the naturalness of the life cycle (and mortality) of human biology; the hybrid body, which uses or grafts technology to improve performance and, often, life expectancy; the totally technological body, made up almost exclusively of non-biological parts and which makes use of tools that deprive it of the aspects that characterise being human, such as mortality and caginess, all the way to a dematerialised body, completely inhuman, but nonetheless conscious.

The natural body, as the first category of this study, is often opposed or correlated to the machine-integrated body, a partly or completely artificial body.

Westworld (HBO 2016–2022) in its first season encapsulates the theme of conflict and power play between humans and androids within an immersive amusement park. The series is set in 2050 and Westworld is one of the theme parks of the Delos Inc. company. This is themed on the American Old West and truly reproduces the spaces and styles of the time, with an ad hoc setting and the presence of *residents*, androids serving guests. The latter simulate human skin and attitude, but remain immortal machines that can be repaired, reprogrammed and restarted for each new narrative cycle of the park. Some residents, however, manage to retain memories of their experiences and become sentient: this is the moment when the machine is set against the natural body, placing the clash between sentient artificial intelligence in a mechanical body and human beings, characterised by free will and creativity in a mortal body, at the centre.

The body becomes the element that distinguishes, even more than the mind, the factions of visitors and residents, the two different mainly in the physical. Thus, it oscillates between presenting itself as an element to be preserved and protected, when the residents are not sentient, to a fallacious and imperfect enemy to be destroyed and replaced with a perfectible technology that simulates humanity.

The natural body confronting an artificial body is the common thread that also characterises the episode *Be Right Back* (2013) of the show *Black Mirror* (Brooker 2011 — in production). Martha, in a techno-dystopian present, after the funeral of her husband Ash, first chooses to use an online service that, thanks to personal data, allows her to stay in touch with a digital, disembodied version of the deceased. After numerous e-mails and telephone contacts, thanks to the voice simulation of an AI, Martha, who is pregnant and addicted to the husband's presence, convinces herself to acquire a synthetic flesh body in the image and likeness of her husband, on which is implanted the bot with which she has been conversing up to that point. The human simulation is, however, always lacking in elements such as unpredictability, spontaneity, survival instinct and free will, or simply human needs such as breathing, eating and sleeping. Although the artificial body succeeds in overcoming brain and physical death, it seems nothing more than an object to be used and easily disposed of, opposed to a natural body, whose presence and absence is sought after, perceived, valued.

The natural body, confronted with a technological reality, is properly honoured and defended in *Altered Carbon* (Netflix 2018-2020), a series based on the novel *Bay City* by Richard Morgan. The show's first season presents a technodystopian world in which human consciousness, uploaded into an implanted device, can pass from body to body, called a shell, which can be preserved while waiting for a new user. Once again, the augmented body overcomes death, but loses its identity and authenticity, its roots and image. This is the reason why there is a religious movement that, in particular, stands up in defence of the pure, authentic and mortal human, therefore, valued in the time and place in which it lives, as opposed to the careless life of a disposable body. The religious element and the preservation of the body is a recurring narrative topos in cyberpunk-derived narratives, such as in the anthological series of short films called *OATS Studios* (Blomkamp 2021). Particularly, it is central in the episodes that structure the *Adam* narrative, where a war between humans and robots is generated and which seems almost reminiscent of the crusades for the blind faith and the liturgical rituals of the warring factions.

The set of biological elements of skin, blood, organs is also the benchmark of technological innovation, which attempts to resemble and replicate the human being in mind and body. The line becomes particularly blurred in *Blade Runner 2049* (Villeneuve 2017) where the replicants, rebellious humanoid androids, perfect themselves to the point of being able to emulate even reproduction: in the film, it is revealed that the artificial Rachel had two children, but this was only possible thanks to her partner, the first *Blade Runner* (Scott 1982) Rick Deckard, a human with a natural body. This union evokes the game of supremacy between androids and humans, putting the fate of all life forms in the hands of the 'natural'.

The struggle between humans and conscious androids is also played out in the anime series *Ergo Proxy* (Manglobe 2006), which places some of the humans inside a dome to protect them from the inhospitable environment outside. In the dome live the AutoReiv androids, first servants then rebels, while outside other less wealthy humans fight for survival: the natural body seems defended, preserved and at some point threatened, once again, by conscious technology emulating the human desire for supremacy, but this is dependent on social and economic position, valuing the bodies inside the dome and leaving humanity outside to its own inauspicious fate.

The social discourse of different classes and unequal chances of survival recurs in techno-dystopian narratives, such as in *Elysium* (Blomkamp 2013), in which the natural body is exalted and defended even from its own weaknesses only in an Eden destined for the wealthiest, leaving the rest of humanity exposed to increasingly deadly risks, such as the gamma radiation to which the protagonist Max Da Costa is exposed in an accident that will mark his death sentence. The protagonist's goal will be to combat inequality by curing himself thanks to the devices, special capsules, found on Elysium, a futuristic space station where the highest levels of society thrive. The natural bodies, but also animal and plant life forms, are cured, respecting their natural needs, but trying to minimise their weaknesses. In this case, the body remains natural in its features but begins to hybridise with machines that enable its improvement.

This is the reason why it is not possible to speak of categories, but it is more appropriate to refer to a spectrum of representation of a body that is increasingly artificial and technological.

Hybridisation can therefore be internal, external and more or less visible. For example, in the *Black Mirror* episode entitled *The entire history of you* (2011), the mnemonic activity of the brain is enhanced, indeed replaced with a device called the *Grain*: it is implanted in the brain to allow it collect all images and sounds perceived by the senses, simulating an always available hard drive. This is also used to provide security, verify identities, and assess skills, although the story exposes the risks of such a device when used for personal purposes. The triangle between the protagonist Liam, his wife Ffion and lover Jonas will lead a family to disintegration precisely because of the re-examination of each other's memories; the peculiarity, however, lies in the substitution of real experiences for memories, in the dependence on the device that takes away the pleasure of ever new experiences, flattening life solely to the memory of the best moments, without building new ones. Once again, a distinction is drawn between the unpredictable human and the programmable machine, in a struggle, in this case, within the body: the protagonist will decide, in the finale, to free himself from the Grain, to escape from his past.

The dystopian series often place at the centre of their narrative the mingling of man and machine, imagining different threats to natural human life: this is the case of *White Christmas* (2014), also part of the *Black Mirror* series, in which, in flashbacks, Matt and Joe tell of the Z-eye, a device implanted in the eye and connected to the network with numerous functions, including that of blocking another person and seeing, in its place, a white silhouette, so as to protect certain victims, resolve disagreements and create, for those who are blocked, a sort of social prison without bars. Also in the *Arkangel* (2017) episode, the device is implanted in the eye, but in this case of children and young people so that they are watched by their parents and guardians, with results that are sometimes life-saving, but ultimately disastrous; in the *Men against fire* (2017) episode, devices are implanted in soldiers to manage their ability to detect and recognise the enemy, whom the soldiers see as zombies threatening humanity, but who are actually civilian targets of the invasion campaign by the state.

Technology, in these cases, controls, excludes, discriminates, under the guise of improving human capabilities.

The devices also represent a dualism between threat and defence, as in *Rakka* (2021), an episode of the *Oats Studios* series, in which the technological superiority of alien reptiles succeeds in subduing humanity on a devastated Earth, except for a few resistance groups wearing brain shields, the only hope for the preservation of a necessarily hybridised body. Even in *Ghost in the Shell*, a franchise that imagines a post-apocalyptic world, technology, especially physical technology such as bionic limbs, is integrated in order to survive in a world put to the sword by political and social unrest; it appears to be the same dynamic whereby in Altered Carbon a natural body is replaced like a suit, on which the same personality is installed.

The body then loses its value: it can be changed, repaired, integrated, so it begins to be dispersed in the tumult of the technological wars of dystopian narratives.

If, on the one hand, the body is easily mistreated, in other narratives it is defended and preserved, usually by attempting to circumvent mortality: as in *Elysium*, also in *In Time* (Niccol 2012) longevity is destined only for the very rich. A device determines everyone's life time, set canonically at 25 years and extendable indefinitely through the purchase of additional time: the body is not mistreated, indeed after hybridisation with the device it becomes the most valuable asset.

The body is hybridised not only with technology, but is also denatured through genetic engineering operations, as in *The Island* (Bay 2005), in which the body is cloned, artificially creating a duplicate of the living being, so that it can be used as a reservoir of organs and for procreation. In *Sweet Tooth* (Netflix 2021- in production), where only some are born half-human half-animal due to a virus, the theme of the body hybridised by the results of genetic engineering clashing with natural bodies is recurrent. This is also portrayed in *Æon Flux* (Kusama 2005), in which the head of the new state of Bregna, who impersonates the highest power, practises cloning without the knowledge of an almost completely sterile citizenship, which became unable to procreate because of the vaccine the state developed, which saved 1% of the population from a deadly virus but not without consequences. Ultimately, in the *Dark Angel* series (Cameron, Eglee 2000-2003), child soldiers are genetically modified and a group of these, fugitives, become the resistance against classist social systems.

Access to technology is very often underpinned by economic possibilities or stemming precisely from a lack of wealth. Examples of this are *Ready Player One* (Spielberg 2018), in which the protagonist escapes from a problematic situation of limited access to resources, climate crisis and his own neighbourhood made up of container homes stacked in the poorest part of the city. The escape takes place in a virtual world, dematerialising the body thanks to physical devices such as a visor and haptic gloves: the body goes from hybridised to disembodied thanks to the desire to escape from an inhospitable reality. This time, the *Black Mirrors* episode *USS Callister* (2017) also represents the escape from a context, in this case social, depicting a world in which it is possible to reproduce real subjects in the virtual reality of certain video games, through the insertion of personal DNA into the machine.

The body is no longer flesh and bones when interfacing with this type of technology, but becomes immaterial and formed by pure consciousness and perception, which can, however, be falsified when reality itself becomes, unconsciously, virtual, as in the *Matrix* franchise (Wachowski 1999-2021)[2]. In the famous narration, the reality of the protagonist is a simulation, an illusion of life to hide a reality composed of cultivated humans, fed with the corpses of the dead, of which only Neo, the Chosen One, becomes aware.

The simulation of experience is also an element of confusion in the aforementioned episode *White Christmas*, whose plot twist is

---

[2] With reference to four movies (*The Matrix*, 1999; *The Matrix Reloaded*, 2003; *The Matrix Revolutions*, 2003; *The Matrix Resurrections*, 2021) and one animated series (*The Animatrix*, 2003).

based on the discovery that the interactions between the protagonists have taken place in a virtual place, that their existences have been replicated through web cookies, and that even the prison to which Matt will be relegated will be virtual, with the condemnation of perceiving the time unit of a minute as a thousand years, driving him to madness.

The self hence takes on completely digital, dematerialised traits, including hybridised bodies. For instance, in the *Ghost in the Shell* franchise (1989-2022)[3] a recurring theme is the relationship between the perception of the self as Soul, the Ghost, and the cybernetic shell that hosts it. In the film, Motoko, the protagonist, merges with an artificial intelligence to save herself and transcend her existence. Or, again in the franchise, people's cybernetic brains are often attacked by hackers or computer viruses that can also create false memories.

Conclusions

To conclude this brief reading of the representations of the body within the Technodystopian works, we would like to present some considerations on common characteristics or tendencies that emerged in the narrations examined.

From a point of view closely linked to the relationship between man and machine, there is a loss of biological identity when the first hybridises with machines/technology. In particular, technology aims at hyper-humanisation, used to reach immortality and wellbeing. But paradoxically, both machines and humans tend towards a simulation of human behaviour and needs, as if these were ritual behaviours useful to define identity-building practices, in which connections to the human self through objects take shape.

---

[3] In this case, reference was made to three animated movies: *Ghost in the Shell* (Oshii 1991) and *Ghost in the Shell 2 – Innocence* (Oshii 2004), *Ghost in the Shell: S.A.C. Solid State Society* (Kamiyama 2006); one live action: *Ghost in the Shell* (Sunders 2017); four animated series: *Ghost in the Shell: Stand Alone Complex* (Production I. G. 2002-2003), *Ghost in the Shell: Stand Alone Complex 2nd GIG* (Production I.G. 2004-2005), *Ghost in the Shell: Arise* (Production I.G. 2013-2014), *Ghost in the Shell: SAC_2045* (Production I.G. 2020-2022).

From a broader point of view, the body is the explicit manifestation of the social conflict and becomes a mean to exercise power. Some manifestations are found on the critique of the radicalisation of capitalism (the body to be bought and maintained): the access to technologies and well-being becomes an extremization of the class division, building groups taken apart by wealth but also confined in different physical (or virtual) locations. The high classes seem to embody an Apollonian vision, being the only ones who can act under an idea of progress for the humanity, while the lower classes represent, on the other hand, the Dionysian values, stuck into an eternal present with no hope for a brighter future.

In conclusion, the representations of the body in Technodystopian worlds are still a narrative element not limited to fiction, but tools that allows us to wonder on the social discourses that are generated in our present, recognised as a time characterised by an outstanding advancement of technology.

References

Ciammella, Fabio, Giovanni Ciofalo, and Silvia Leonzi. 2019. «"It's a trap". Transmedia Screen-Storytelling: dall'esperienza immersiva all'interattività partecipativa = "It's a trap". Transmedia Screen Storytelling: from the immersive experience to participatory interactivity». University of Salento. https://doi.org/10.1285/I22840753N15P89.

Claeys, Gregory. 2017. *Dystopia: a natural history: a study of modern despotism, its antecedents, and its literary diffractions*. First edition. Oxford, United Kingdom: Oxford University Press.

Clayes, Gregory. 2022. «Dystopia». In *The Palgrave Handbook of Utopian and Dystopian Literatures*, di Peter Marks, Jennifer A. Wagner-Lawlor, e Maria de Fátima de Sousa Basto Vieira, 54–64. Palgrave Handbooks. Cham: Palgrave Macmillan.

Di Minico, Elisabetta. 2018. *Il futuro in bilico: il mondo contemporaneo tra controllo, utopia e distopia*. Linee 39. Milano: Meltemi.

Dyens, Ollivier. 2000. «Cyberpunk, Technoculture, and the Post-Biological Self». *CLCWeb: Comparative Literature and Culture* 2 (1). https://doi.org/10.7771/1481-4374.1061.

Klastrup, Lisbeth, and Susana Tosca. 2020. «An Experience Approach to Transmedia Fictions». In *The Routledge Companion to Transmedia Studies*, a cura di Matthew Freeman e Renira Rampazzo Gambarato, First issued in paperback, 392–400. Routledge Companions. London New York: Routledge, Taylor & Francis Group.

Leonzi, Silvia, Fabio Ciammella, and Elisabetta Trinca. 2019. «Transmedia is coming. Il caso FantaGot e la storyworld interactivation». *Indistinti confini. Transmedialità nei processi culturali e comunicativi* 13: 56–71.

Montesperelli, Paolo. 2014. *Comunicare e interpretare: introduzione all'ermeneutica per la ricerca sociale*. Prima edizione. Alfaomega. Milano: EGEA.

Ryan, Marie-Laure, and Jan-Noël Thon, a c. di. 2014. *Storyworlds across media: toward a media-conscious narratology*. Frontiers of narrative. Lincoln: University of Nebraska Press.

Seeger, Sean, and Daniel Davison-Vecchione. 2019. «Dystopian Literature and the Sociological Imagination». *Thesis Eleven* 155 (1): 45–63. https://doi.org/10.1177/0725513619888664.

Wolf, Mark J. P. 2014. *Building Imaginary Worlds: The Theory and History of Subcreation*. New York: Routledge.

Beyond Fiction and Reality. Contemporary Performance Discovers Fairy Tales in the Works of Lina Majdalanie and Rabih Mroué

Jovana Malinarić

Can Dystopian Help Us Better Understand Our World?

Before utopias and dystopias became imagined futures, they were imagined pasts or imagined places. *Mundus Novus* is a Latin phrase meaning "New World" and it was mentioned initially in Amerigo Vespucci's letters, printed in Florence in 1503, in which an Italian merchant and explorer described his voyages across the Atlantic: "I have found a continent more densely peopled and abounding in animals than our Europe or Asia or Africa, and, in addition, a climate milder and more delightful than in any other region known to us." (Northup, George T., 1916) Soon after, in 1516, Sir Thomas More used the term *utopia* for the very first time as the title of his best-known work, which created a blueprint for an ideal society with minimal crime, violence and poverty. More's book imagines a complex, self-contained community set on an island, in which people share a common culture and way of life. He coined the word 'utopia' from the Greek *ou-topos* meaning 'no place' or 'nowhere'. And so, his secular and intellectual construct was still an expression of desire for something lacking the here and now. This place, according to the perception of the author, represents both a good place and a bad one. A utopia is a planned society and as various writings from all over the world will repeatedly confirm, the planned societies are often disastrous. "Every eutopia contains a dystopia, and every dystopia contains a eutopia". (More, Thomas, 2012) More pointed out the fact that elements of one can be found in the other and vice versa. Nevertheless, there are certain elements that we can often find in a dystopian narrative and which make it a clearly distinguishable genre. Some of them are: uncontrolled fear, tyrannical governments, environmental disaster, complete control over the people in a society through the use of propaganda which brings the denial of free thought and the complete loss of individuality. They make dystopia mostly immortal and of continuing interest in cultural debate. A large number of every-day issues have been explored through the dystopian lens which bring us to reflect about it in the reverse way: how can the dystopian help us better understand and navigate our world?

Different scholars have noted that the concept of dystopia existed many centuries ago in Dante's *Inferno*, even if placed in a religious framework rather than in the future of the mundane world, as modern dystopias tend to be. Dante's famous inscription *Abandon all hope, ye who enter here* would have been equally appropriate if placed at the entrance to Orwell's "Ministry of Love" and its notorious "Room 101". This makes us realize that there has always been a pouring of the dystopian elements into narratives, which brought discourses into imaginative realms seemingly far removed from what we understand as reality.

These examples are noteworthy because in a very similar way, I will approach the concept of dystopia in this study. I will treat it as an umbrella term that gathers together thematically close concepts, that often intertwine in the artistic works which make use of dystopian to investigate the mechanisms of reality. These concepts are reality and truth, representation strategies and their perception. More precisely, I will analyze in which way they are employed in the performative writings of two artists from Lebanon, Lina Majdalanie and Rabih Mroué. I will focus especially on their performance Sunny Sunday that I had the chance to see during the Spring Festival 2022 in Utrecht, and thanks to the correspondence with the dramaturg of the performance, Grzegorz Reske, I was able to confront the materials engaged in the making of the play. This made it possible to get closer to how the artists' thinking and writing processes make use of the dystopian elements as useful tools for investigating contemporary political narratives.

Rabih Mroué and Lina Majdalanie: Investigating Reality through Performance Practice

In the introduction of his own work Mroué says: "When I was young, the civil war started, which lasted for 15 years. When we started working, we started to do works about the war. But we started to escape from telling what happened during the war and we started to do art works that are reflecting on the war, and trying to analyze, to understand what happened." Lina Majdalanie and Rabih Mroué were both born in Beirut and currently live and work in Berlin. The event that radically informed their work was the Lebanese Civil War: "So we were not interested in telling about the horrors of the wars. We were much interested in *ideas* and *questions.*" Theater in Beirut revived in the years after the war, but Mroué and Majdalanie, who frequently collaborate, were among the first to push into *avant-garde* territory (and away from European influences), using venues such as the Russian Cultural Center, makeshift halls and private homes. Their work since the late 1990s blurs and confounds the boundaries between theater and the visual arts, often using screens and projected images. Mroué declared: "For me the theater is always like where I have to provoke myself. I find something that challenging me, something that makes me afraid of, and when I feel such kind of things, then I would say, okay, now I'm on the right track." Their performances are designed to appear more like improvised works in progress, reflecting their continuing theme of inquiry focused more on provoking thought than presenting spectacle. They explore the medium of documentary, performance, and video art, blending facts and fiction, historical tragedy and biographical issues.

Almost all of their performances deal with issues regarding the current political situation in Lebanon, investigating censorship, social and political taboos about sexuality in *Biokhraphia* (2002), or about why the Middle East banished any kind of bodyart in the '60s and '70s in the performance called *Who's Afraid Of Representation?*(2005). In *The Pixelated Revolution* (2012), for example, Mroué reflects about how death is represented in the images of war during the first years of the Syrian revolution.

Sunny Sunday, on the other hand, represents a different chapter in their work. It is the first time that these two artists worked on a subject regarding the political scene of another country: Poland. The work on this subject arose from the exchange between two dramaturgs, Grzegorz Reske and Marta Keil. It presents the same density of elements and topics that interweave with Mroué and Majdalanie's previous work. Concurrently with their early meetings and exchanges on the work, the right-wing populist party had firmly risen to power once again in Poland. In the affirmation before the performance premiere during the Spring festival, Reske declared:

"Sunny Sunday is a very special work for me. Not only because I was directly involved in its creation and it partly shows reasons I decided to leave Poland and move to Utrecht. But first of all, this is performance about techniques of manipulation of culture and history in order to impose certain narration over people. A warning against those manipulations should be sound today as much in Poland or Lebanon, as in Netherlands."

What it is the object of vision, how it is presented, and how the audience is involved in the vision are the things that Mroué and Majdalanie investigate in Sunny Sunday. The concept of truth is anatomically dissected while its component particles demonstrate its own porosity and fragility. I will argue how the dystopian, in this operation, appears as a quality, aspect or characteristic of what is seen, involving the process of spectatorship. More specifically, in this work, the dystopian element is used as a relational tool emerging from the intersection between the spectator and what they see, which constantly challenges the viewer's cognitive process. This leads us to reflect on the consequential relationship between storytelling strategies and arising vision and perception.

Sunny Sunday: To Trust or Not to Trust?

Through the strategies of Arabic fairy tales, the different uses of propaganda's narration, and the conscious interrogation of spectatorship, Mroué and Majdalanie reflect on the meaning of a certain event that took place on the 8th of May, 2016 in Poland. One sunny

BEYOND FICTION AND REALITY 273

Sunday in 2016, in a small village in Poland, a very strange wedding took place. The two people involved in the wedding ceremony were both dead, one of whom had died in 1948 and the other in 2002. Both of them were well known to the Polish people, since one of them was the famous national hero, Witold Pilecki and the other, his fiancée, Maria Ostrawska. Pilecki's fame is due to his heroic behavior during the resistance movement in the period of Nazi occupation in Poland. As an intelligence agent, he infiltrated himself directly in Auschwitz and secretly drew up reports about the reality of the camp. Once inside, he organized a resistance movement, including hundreds of inmates, which brought him into a situation of severely high risk. He managed to escape from Auschwitz, but soon after he was interned in a German prisoner-of-war camp. After the communist takeover of Poland he remained loyal to the London-based Polish government-in-exile. In 1945 he returned to Poland to report to the government-in-exile on the situation in Poland. Before returning, Pilecki wrote Witold's Report about his Auschwitz experiences, anticipating that he might be killed by Poland's new communist authorities. In 1947 he was arrested by the secret police on charges of working for "foreign imperialism" and, after being subjected to torture was executed in 1948. His remains have never been found. His life and death has been the subject of several monographs, books and films, and a number of streets, institutions and monuments have been named after him. In a sense, the figure of Pilecki has become inscribed in the collective imagination by associating with what is called the national identity.

During the commemoration of his life in 2016 through the celebration of his wedding day, there were present both historical figures and people from current society. Mroué and Majdalanie have found both interesting and curious that the event involved both the actual Polish Minister of Culture, the bishop of the church and Pilecki's son. This moment of commemoration staged the wedding day of the national hero by mixing the past with the present, confounding the boundaries between what is perceived as fiction with what is seen as reality. What the two makers tried to do with their performative action is to raise from this narrative two basic questions: what is fiction and whose is reality? How this narrative construction spreads its meaning and in what ways it directs the perception of recipients, are also points of interest in Mroué's and Majdalanie's work.

"Every dystopia is a history of the future" wrote Margaret Atwood. She added "It's a sad commentary on our age that we find dystopias a lot easier to believe in than utopias. Utopias we can only imagine; dystopias we've already had." Jill Lepore in her article for the New York Times wrote that "dystopia used to be a fiction of resistance, but now it becomes the fiction of submission, the fiction of an untrusting, lonely twenty-first century, the fiction of fake news and info-wars, the fiction of helplessness and hopelessness, the fiction poisoned by polarized politics." What she is trying to bring in front of us is similar to what we can see in Pilecki's commemoration. For example this kind of dystopian narrative is not meant to imagine "a better future" but to consolidate old presumptions and beliefs. Mroué and Majdalanie recognized dystopian as something that has to be revealed from the fictional hideout, to be used as a tool for investigation and knowledge. Something in which we don't have to believe, but to comprehend.

During the performance, two artists notice that the strange commemoration wedding had all the proprieties of a theatrical event: it places on stage the actors; it has a precise narrative construction; everyone who was present wore costumes. Theatricality intrinsic in this event makes that distinction between spectators and what they see, between reality and fiction, suddenly ceases to be self-evident. The commemoration of the national hero among the participants was not perceived as a theatrical event. It was a symbolic representation that has different meanings for the people that were present there. The actual presence of the Minister of Culture of Poland, real bishop of the church and Pilecki's son, together with actors and audience materialized the distant past into the current present. It had nearly all the properties of a theatrical event but it was recognized as a political event and almost a dystopian one. In a diametrically opposite way, the performance Sunny Sunday does not seek to delude the spectators by recreating the space for the representation. There is no set up, just a stage with a huge screen in front of the audience. Because of the apparent absence of any kind of action on scene, the major importance was placed on how it could be transmitted to the public. There were no particular lights, just one big screen with the title of performance, and a table with a chair, waiting for performers. When Mroué and Majdalanie entered they brought with them one very large, at first sight—ancient book. That element acquired an almost mystical meaning due to the importance that the makers gave to it. They read it for the whole duration of the performance, it was there to remind the audience that every sentence is a construct of narration, as seen in the first sentence, "Based on true events this performance is purely fictional." With this statement the authors lead the audience to consider fiction as a tool through which they can investigate the trueness of the reality. Lewis acknowledged in Postscript B that some people value fiction "mostly as a means for the discovery of truth, or for the communication of truth" (Lewis 1983: 278). Learning from fiction is not easy, since it requires an ability to tell whether an apparently factual claim in a work of fiction has been included in the fiction because of its truth or for other reasons. In this specific case, the authors utilize different narration strategies, reflecting also on the fairytale tradition of storytelling, showing how the same story can be distinctively told by different people. *Yeki bud, jeki nabud* is the common opening of Persian fairytales, whose equivalent in Arabic reads: *fi yawm min al'ayaam*. And while both phrases are usually translated into English as "Once upon a time..." the real meaning is much more fluid: "There was, and there was not or this happened, and it did not happen." This strategy comes from the tradition of Arabic fairytales, but was lost in European translation and adaption. Mroué and Majdalanie recognized that it is an investigative and imaginative force, and reintroduce it as a sub-construct of the whole narration. The audience constantly moves between fact and invention, whereby in some moments the difference between the two is blurred and confounding. To make it even more confusing, the authors constructed as many possible points of view on the same event, mixing together historical events, biographical facts and cultural phenomena and pushing them to the dystopian. As with the opposite of classical dystopian narration, where the reader is confronted with an unambiguous vision, in this case the dystopian needs to dislocate it and in that way deconstruct any possibility of imposing one particular narrative over the audience. In the following example from the script, it is possible to observe how the multiplication of viewpoints carries a strong investigative tone.

409-	His post-mortem wedding in 2016, (or wedding re-enactment or wedding commemoration, whatever it was)
410-	was not done on April 7 as it should have been, but on May 8, which is exactly the day of his capture...
411-	Symbolically the day of his death.
412-	Were they really trying to commemorate him?
413-	Or to kill him again, symbolically?

This use of storytelling techniques embraces what is commonly called literary cognitivism, which claims that literary fiction can contribute to the reader's knowledge in a way that adds to the literary or aesthetic value of a work (Davies 2007; Gaut 2005). It provides a phenomenal amount of knowledge: knowledge of what it is like to be a certain kind of person or to be in a certain kind of situation, and this knowledge can help us understand other people or the moral complexity of situations (Kieran 1996; Currie 1998; Putnam 1978; Carroll 2002; Swirski 2007). On the other hand it provides us a critical distance that, according to Brecht, is essential for navigating our contemporary world: "The attitude is a critical one. Faced with a river, it consists in regulating the rivers, faced with a fruit tree, in spraying the fruit tree; faced with movement, in constructing vehicles and airplanes; faced with society, in turning society upside down." (Brecht, 1964) The authors unveil the characters while presenting them, revealing their fiction to show the things in themselves, the things that cease to represent the other than the essence of themselves.

74-	Actually, I am from another world.
75-	I am fictional, I have been written by the great novelist Henryk Sienkiewicz,
76-	and I have a strong presence among the Living:
77-	I'm taught in schools,
78-	my character has been played in theater,
79-	and in films that are broadcast every year, on Christmas, Easter and all National holidays.

This method is that of alienation, firstly used by Russian futurists and then practiced and made notorious inside the brechtian Epic theatre. What gains particular importance is the mode of address and modes of engaging the audience, therefore the alienation effect could be explained as the performative invitation to engage with the narrative environment. It is a mixture of both intellectual and empathic engagement aimed to induce responses and interaction of the audience. In Sunny Sunday we can immerse ourselves in the texture of the narrative elements that gives substance to the fiction of the story and at the same time provides the necessary tools for the audience to move away from just identification and immersion. The authors create such an interweaving by telling the same story from different points of view, creating a *living* storytelling body which clearly demonstrates how single points of view, frequently used by polarized politics, synthesizes and simplifies the reality. They show how propaganda creates its own narration through an unambiguous view on events and history, and how the sentences like "His remains have never been found" can easily become an endless source of inspiration and conspiracy.

Stories May Not Actually Breathe, but They Can Animate

Sleeping through the warning signs is another problem that dystopia presents. "I was asleep before," the heroine of "The Handmaid's Tale" says in the Margaret Atwood's novel. "That's how we let it happen." Sunny Sunday may be easily called Snowy Monday, as each country has its own similar narration. The warning signs are not so difficult to recognize if everyone is awake. Being awake to Mroué and Majdalanie means to pay attention to stories, wondering who narrates them and how they are narrated. The use of different narrative elements such as fairytale and dystopian, does not arise to match one of present-day dilemma. Instead of painting reality by depicting it, in Sunny Sunday we can observe the interruption and suspension of the progress of the story: everything is focused on a single event. The narrative elements cease to be the support of the narrative by becoming the tools for the audience, necessary to activate their attentiveness and comprehension of what happened. Majdalanie and Mroué, through the narrative use of a different fictional genres and points of view show us how populist powers manipulate historical facts and pop culture to influence our thinking. Focusing on a story that happened in Poland in 2016, their elaboration ultimately takes the audience by surprise by revealing the true events that occurred that sunny Sunday in 2016. It points out that the elements from dystopian genre, fairytale tradition, historical events and storytelling can relate to each other and construct the tools that challenge the unambiguous political narratives in which we are all immersed. Not surprisingly, their writing is performative, meaning that it becomes body and voice, it becomes living matter, and as such relates to the living body of the audience. As Arthur Frank remarked "Stories work with people, for people, and always stories work *on* people, affecting what people are able to see as real, as possible, and as worth doing or best avoided."

References

Atwood, Margaret. 1985. *The Handmaid's Tale*, Toronto: McClelland & Stewart.

Brecht, Bertolt. 1964. *Brecht on theatre: the development of an aesthetic*, New York: Hill and Wang.

Carroll, Noël. 2002). "The Wheel of Virtue: Art, Literature, and Moral Knowledge", *Journal of Aesthetics and Art Criticism*, 60(1): 3–23.

Currie, Gregory. 1998. "Pretence, Pretending and Metarepresenting", *Mind and Language*, 13(1): 35–55. doi:10.1111/1468-0017.00064

Davies, David. 2007. *Aesthetics and Literature*, London, New York: Continuum.

Frank, W. Arthur. 2010. *Letting Stories Breathe: A Socio-Narratology*, Chicago: University of Chicago Press.

Gaut, Berys. 2005. "Art and Knowledge", in Levinson 2005: 436–450.

Kieran, Matthew. 1996. "Art, Imagination, and the Cultivation of Morals", *Journal of Aesthetics and Art Criticism*, 54(4): 337–351. doi:10.2307/431916

Lepore, Jill. 2017. "A Golden Age for Dystopian Fiction- What to make of our new literature of radical pessimism", The New Yorker, «Books» June 5 & 12. Available online: A Golden Age for Dystopian Fiction | The New Yorker (accessed 19 March 2023).

Lewis, David. 1983. "Truth in Fiction", American Philosophical Quarterly, 15(1): 37–46.

Northup, George Tyler. 1916. trans. *Mundus Novus: Letter to Lorenzo Pietro di Medici*, New Jersey: Princeton University Press. Available online: *Internet Archive*, Mundus novus. Letter to Lorenzo Pietro di Medici; : Vespucci, Amerigo, 1451-1512 : Free Download, Borrow, and Streaming : Internet Archive (accessed 21 March 2023).

More, Thomas. 2012. *Utopia*, London: Penguin Books.

Orwell, George. 1977. *1984*, London: Penguin Books.

Putnam, Hilary. 1978. "Literature, Science and Reflection", in *Putnam Meaning and the Moral Sciences*, London: Routledge & Kegan Paul, pp. 83–94.

Swirski, Peter. 2007. *Of Literature and Knowledge: Explorations in Narrative Thought Experiments, Evolution and Game Theory*, London: Routledge.

Clothes and Costumes: Dystopian Storytelling through Fashion

Maria Teresa Zanola

Introduction

Among the omnipresence of security monitoring, totalitarian states, and climatic cataclysms, fashion also reflects the anxieties of the present.

In July 2018, the runways of fashion weeks were filled with new shapes of women: the exhibited outfits were costumes that delineated roles, following a utilitarian function of clothing. Jeans, dungarees, jumpsuits, sweatpants... *Haute couture* features terminologies, forms and fabrics that respond to ecological anxieties, thus becoming a laboratory for both new textile inventions and semiotic messages about the future. In fashion, dystopia depicts a future where nothing is possible anymore: the dystopian register transpires a fear that the future could be worse than the present.

It is important to highlight the role of fashion, which has always been able to anticipate the dystopian anxieties of society, and which has been able to announce the trends of fears and anxieties throughout history. Examples from across the centuries will illustrate this anticipatory function of fashion in dystopian visions.

Dystopian Fashion in the 21st Century

Dystopian motifs in fashion have always expressed fears and anxieties about the fragility of bodies exposed to the threat of war, catastrophe, and destruction. They were quite popular in the 2020 autumn fashion show in Europe, when the presented outfits ranged from black cloaks to full-on face coverings: it was as if fashion were preparing for the 2021-2022 pandemic period and the war that followed.

Fashion can also be used as a means of expression or telling a story about a current situation or event: dystopian fashion is designed as a form of a post-apocalyptic, cyber first world wear. Dystopian fashion mostly involves boiler suits, camping-ready parkas, fire prints, oversized cargo pockets, futuristic leather trench coats, roomy jackets and pants that are mostly proposed in black or ashen colours. This trend was originally made popular by soldiers wearing durable, functional and resilient clothing. To survive in this harsh world in fact, these garments are shields suited to protect and help in facing any difficulties that may arise (Evans, 2003; Kwon and Ha, 2013). Let examine some dystopian runways over the past sixty years.

In the 1960s, Paco Rabanne anticipated the "end of the world" (later predicted in the book *Le feu du ciel*, 1999) by dressing his models in metallic dresses designed like armour. During the Comme des Garçons' autumn/winter 1982 Rey Kawakubo's show featured a substantially all-black collection called *Destroy*.

For the autumn/winter 2009-2010 Lee Alexander Mc Queen imagined a post-apocalyptic future: the runway, titled "The Horn of Plenty", displayed a large pile of trash, composed of pieces from the stages of Mc Queen's past shows as the centrepiece. The models also wore sculptural trash on their heads and garments made from trash ranging from plastic bags to umbrellas and lampshades. Inspired by Charles Darwin's *On the Origin of Species* (1859), the spring/summer 2010 collection called *Plato's Atlantis* presented a narrative centred not on the evolution of humankind but rather on its devolution. Mc Queen predicted a future in which "the ice cap would melt... the water would rise and... life on earth would have to evolve in order to live beneath the sea once more or perish". This experience of nature was paralleled with and supplanted by that of technology and the digital age.

> It was the idea of sort of the reversal of evolution (...). So what he would do is he would have an engineered print, and with that print he would place it on the form, and he would pin and construct these pieces that looked like they'd morphed out of the body themselves.
> And only by taking the fabric and seeing how the fabric moved, you could come up with something new — by creating it on a body because clothes are

to be worn; they're not two-dimensional things. They are something that has to sit and mold onto a human being[1].

Karl Lagerfeld's Chanel autumn/winter 2011 collection proposed a darker vision; the same dystopian scenario was chosen by Marc Jacobs for his spring/summer 2014 collection; for the autumn/winter 2017 session, Gareth Pugh staged an all-black dystopic show.

In April 2017, some characters with enigmatic names like Zenoba, Shipley, Ejaw Bolsorg and Xeod appeared on Gucci's social networks. They are between 2 and 7000 years old, and come from distant planets; a few months later, they appeared in apocalyptic settings with menacing monsters, or aboard the legendary spaceship borrowed from the science fiction series "Star Trek". The images from the "#GucciandBeyond" autumn-winter 2017 campaign are accompanied by an eschatological speech detailing the brand's motifs. This collection is thus transported to a parallel universe where a mixed cast of humanoids, aliens, robots, and terrestrials with metallic makeup in view of Gucci's invasion of a distant galaxy.

In February 2018, Raf Simons' runway show for Calvin Klein was inspired by Todd Haynes' film *Safe*, where Julianne Moore plays a woman who is dying from pollution. The runway presents contemporary fashion stirred by apocalyptic narratives woven around an anti-disaster wardrobe of balaclavas, firefighter suits and anti-radiation gloves and waders. This collection focusses on protective clothing to avoid contact with a poisoned and hostile earth.

Fashion communicates an encroaching sense of doom: Raf Simons brought pieces that looked like something from a horror film come to life for the Calvin Klein autumn/winter 2018 collection. Miuccia Prada also explored hazmat suits with oversized rubber coverings for Prada; John Galliano was inspired by the idea of personal protective equipment for Maison Margiela, armouring his models with giant, oversized windbreakers.

In winter 2018, Demna Gvasalia prepared his Balenciaga clientele for extreme weather conditions by layering jumpers, parkas, and faux fur coats. The following season, he set up his show for the

Parisian fashion house in a tunnel lined with screens that simulated the effects of molten lava and seemed to announce the scorching temperatures that could soon suffocate the Earth while speeding up the melting of the ice caps. The Balenciaga spring/summer 22 runway was called *Clones*, so an alienating virtual event was created through the interplay of cloning and disruption, based on the presentation of alternative realities and the inability to distinguish the 'real' reality from the crafted one. The protagonist of the show was Eliza Douglas, the American performer and painter known for her interdisciplinary take on art. In the video directed by Quentin Deronzier[2], Eliza Douglas appears wearing womenswear and menswear on an all-white runway as if there a series of digital clones in front of an imaginary audience. The video opens with this text:

> We see our world through a filtered-perfected, polished, conformed, photoshopped. We no longer decipher between unedited and altered, genuine and counterfeit, tangible and conceptual, fact and fiction, fake and deepfake. Technology created alternative realities and identities, a world of digital clones.

The show itself is non-existent and uses different narrative tools, starting with cloning and deepfakes, as all the models have Eliza's face, and continuing with a soundtrack that takes parts of *La vie en rose* ("Quand il me prend dans ses bras/Qu'il me parle tout bas/Je vois la vie en rose/Il me dit des mots d'amour/Des mots de tous les jours/Et ça m'fait quelque chose"....) and replays them with a metallic, anonymous, and empty voice, thus completely wiping out any emotion from this famous song.

On the whole, it is post-apocalyptic fashion bordering on punk, steampunk, grunge, gothic and military. Even if this style has not been entirely adopted, there are details for everyday clothes that influence our own clothes: chunky zips, hoods, dark neutral colours, multiple textures, buckles, tabs, and large exterior pockets. Fashion is moving towards darker palettes and themes to describe and define a grimmer mood.

Dystopian Fashion in Movies

Costume design in a science fiction film tells us a lot about the spirit of the times: in *Brazil* (1985), the future is depicted as a totalitarian state that constantly monitors, tortures, and uses disquieting bureaucratic euphemisms to define government murders (people who are killed are "classified"). The characters dress in plain 1940s outfits, such as suspender suits and straight dresses so costumes lose their colours.

The costume design in *Clockwork Orange* (1971) conveys the disorders of the 1960s. Pants sporting the Renaissance-style crotch pocket that men wore were the focal point of the costumes of the "droogs", a small band of thugs. The rest of their outfits (a bowler hat, braces, and a cane) exhibited the quintessence of British sophistication. *Clockwork Orange* is set in the future but reveals the anarchist atmosphere of the 1960s.

The Matrix's iconic costumes embodied a futuristic sleek look that has continued to live on in mainstream consciousness. The film's aesthetic consists of long leather trench coats, combat boots, slicked back hair and tiny sunglasses. *The Matrix*'s impact as a film was reflected on the runway: for Dior's autumn 1999 show, creative director John Galliano dressed the models in leather-heavy ensembles that were clearly inspired by the film. The list of films and shows influenced by this trend, from *Dune* to *The Matrix Resurrections*, is very long. In fact, all characters involved in futuristic settings, gothic revival, the development of the world and stories connected with injustice, represent fashion styles embodying their bold and emerging personalities.

This analysis could be expanded with other details, but we believe that we have made it clear that the atmosphere of fashion influences trends imbued with dystopian elements, and conveying dystopian imagery. This situation is not completely new: in the following section, we will point out cases demonstrating the role of fashion as a precursor of dystopian events and a forerunner of disruptive transformations in society. We are going to analyse the case of the female garment *par excellence* of the 18th century, the *robe à la française*, and of some clothes dating back to the French Revolution with the aim of revealing an incredible dystopian history.

Fashion Influence and Dystopian Prediction: The "robe à la française" (18th Century) and the Phrygian Cap

Elisa Urbain Ruarte (2017, 92) reminds that taste for the clothing known as *négligés* (loose garments worn by women in their private space) emerged in France during the 1680s and rapidly spread throughout Europe. By the 1780s, almost 20% of the fashion plates from the journal *Gallerie des Modes* included the word *négligé*:

> The first fashion plates showing négligé clothes appear at the end of the 1670s and during the 1680s.
> Some engravers are well known, such as Jean Dieu de Saint Jean or the Bonnard family, and most of the plates are published alone or in the *Mercure Galant*. Some of these négligés look like dressing gowns, and others are black dresses that are used to go outside and visit friends.

At the end of the 17th century, Madame de Montespan appeared at the Royal court wearing a flapper dress to conceal the fact that she was pregnant: it was a dress without a belt, a sort of dressing gown, which Boursault refers to in his comedy *Mots à la mode*, calling it 'innocent' (Quicherat 1877, 520). On November 6th, 1703 Marie Carton Dancourt appeared at a theatre performance of Terence's *Andrienne* dressed according to this new fashion: she wore a wide pleated brim flowing from shoulder to toe and widening into a wide train, something like a *négligé* as a matter of fact. It must be noticed that this dress was originally an indoor dressing gown, so it was unimaginable that an indoor dress would be worn outside in the street. The actress' choice to wear this outfit in public stirred surprise and the desire to emulate her.

The elegant women of Paris adopted the *robe volante* (or *robe battante*) — which was the name given to this *négligé* — and took the opportunity to dress like this while they were out on their walks. The floral and arabesque brocade fabrics of the court gowns of the time could not be adapted to the needs of the new *parure*. In contrast, taffetas or light satin allowed the *robe volante* — which became known as the *robe à la française* (see https://madparis.fr/10-frise-chronologique) — to undulate gracefully at the slightest movement.

This dress was also called the *robe Watteau*: Watteau's talent in depicting the flat folds of the back of the *robes à la française* led to this garment being given his name. In *L'Enseigne de Gersaint* (1720)[3], these folds intersect with those of the skirt lifted by the young woman walking up the step marking the boundary between the street and the art dealer Gersaint's shop. This garment features something less formal and rigid, consisting of a bodice fitted to the bust, a coat over this top, and a skirt made of the same fabric as the coat. The back has two series of large flat pleats, known as "Watteau pleats", falling to the floor and sometimes continuing into a train.

This dress was transformed into the emblematic dress of the reign of Louis XV, which was highly prized in the 1730s and worn until the 1780s[4]. Leloir (1938, IX, 46) quotes the following comments:

> En mars 1729 on lit ceci dans le *Mercure* [*de France*] : "Les robes volantes sont universellement en règne. On ne voit presque plus d'autres habits". [...] De 1730 : "[...] Pour les habits habillés qu'on ne voit guère qu'aux jeunes personnes et aux nouvelles mariées, il en a paru cette année en étoffe de couleurs unies avec beaucoup de prétentailles de la même étoffe découpées avec deux rangs de falbalas à la jupe"[5].

At the 1720 wedding in Modena of Princess Charlotte Aglae of Orleans and the Duke of Modena Francis Mary, the princess was criticised for wearing an 'andrienne', the Italian name for the *robe volante /robe à la française* (sack gown). The elegance of this dress helped to launch the fashion in Italy (Levi Pisetsky 1967, IV, 53): on a visit to Venice in 1721, the princess appeared in an open *robe à la française*, which provoked strong reactions from the Venetian ladies, who immediately adopted this new model (Orlando 1993, 21).

The history of the *robe à la française* highlights a case of dystopian fashion thanks to the theatre: a bourgeois dress typical of family intimacy becomes the dress of Parisian bourgeois ladies and makes its way from the streets of Paris to court (Zanola 2018). It is an announcement of the French Revolution: clothes of everyday life passed through the centuries without leaving a trace, and fashion is not only the result of the pomp and circumstance of the courts and ambition of rich social categories. This fashion rebellion emerged at the beginning of the 18th century and moved from Paris to Versailles, where it sparked an initial sign of the 1789 revolution of.

Another symbol of dystopian fashion is represented by the Phrygian cap, or liberty cap. Worn by the Phrygians, it was the felt cap of the emancipated slaves of ancient Rome and an attribute of the goddess Libertas. In 1675, the anti-tax and anti-nobility Revolt of the papier timbré erupted in Brittany and North-western France, where it became known as the *bonnets rouges* uprising because of the blue or red caps worn by the insurgents. The name and colour remained as a symbol of revolt against the nobility and establishment. In 1793, red berets entered the Tuileries Palace in Paris, and anyone wearing the red beret could enter the guillotine guild.

This sinister cap owes its fame to a story: the amnesty law of March 28th, 1792 granted freedom to the Swiss of the Châteauvieux regiment, which had been condemned to prison following the Nancy brawl. While being taken to Paris, these soldiers wore the headgear of convicts, a red beret. The people looked upon this red beret as the symbol of tyranny, so a headgear initially symbolizing infamy became the symbol of freedom.

The Phrygian, or liberty, cap was worn by the executioner at the guillotine and became a symbol of revolutionary France. Even the national allegory of France, Marianne, is shown wearing a red Phrygian cap. Moreover, the 2024 Olympic Phrygia and the Paralympic Phrygia are depicted as two red Phrygian caps with eyes in the shape of a tricolour cockade.

Conclusions

In the 21st century, designers are no longer telling fairy tales, but rather dystopias. From *haute couture* to *prêt-à-porter* collections, fashion trends prove that the dystopian invasion is underway.

Fashion has the power to change our vision of the world, if not to anticipate it, by showing projections of a distant or near future.

Marine Serre's autumn-winter 2019-2020 *Radiation* collection was presented in the former chalk pits of Issy-les-Moulineaux in the South-west of Paris. Here, toxic green lasers lacerate the confined, smoke-filled space featuring a tribe of survivors dressed in pollution masks, fluorescent parkas with reflective stripes and ultra-covering suits to protect themselves from the unbreathable air. For the same season, Rick Owens introduced another type of survivor: mutants perched on platform shoes with disfigured faces and augmented bodies, and equipped with external airways and horn-like implants. These are fantastic visions of what the human physique might evolve into to survive the apocalypse.

Our analysis is limited to a few examples, but it allows us to understand the relevance of the study of fashion as a semiotic space of anticipation of social facts and strategic interpretation. From this perspective, fashion leads to a semiotisation of people and a status of signs. Ecological disaster, caused by pollution, resource depletion, pandemic emergency and war, has oriented fashion towards designs with printed messages on environmental issues or protecting from the abuse of technology or expressing concerns on environmental devastation (Kwon and Ha, 2013: 13), war disasters and sinking economies.

The idea of dystopia shaped by these socio-cultural changes, continues to inspire fashion. By expressing the fears of the times and giving the public the opportunity to face issues without shying away from their way of life, fashion encourages everybody to reflect on our current situation and shows how to read these phenomena and react. A significant trend in this dystopian fashion is grounded in Simmel's observation (1957, 541) that fashion is changing: "The élite initiates a fashion and, when the mass imitates it in an effort to eliminate the external distinctions of class, abandons it for a new mode". Dystopian fashion is both *haute couture* and *prêt-à-porter*, a complex thought that has to express itself as positive or negative, as a definite hope or hopeless fear, and a question to come back to in the near future.

References

Burton, Sarah. 2011. *Plato's Atlantis, spring/summer 2010*. https://blog.metmuseum.org/alexandermcqueen/tag/plato-atlantis/.

Deronzier, Quentin. 2022. *Balenciaga Spring/Summer 22 Clones*. https://www.youtube.com/watch?v=O2XVFT7ep6M.

Evans, Caroline. 2003. *Fashion at the edge: Spectacle, modernity and deathliness*. New Haven and London: Yale University Press.

Galant, Justyna. 2017. "Fashion Triumphant and the Mechanism of Tautology in Two Nineteenth-Century Dystopias". *Utopian Studies* 28, no. 3, special issue: 428-450. https://www.jstor.org/stable/10.5325/utopianstudies.28.3.0428.

Gershon, Livia. 2021. "How to Dress for Dystopia". *JSTOR Daily*, 30 April, 2021. https://daily.jstor.org/how-to-dress-for-dystopia/.

Kwon, Sanghee, and Ha, Jisoo. 2013. "A Study of Fashion Influenced by Dystopian Ideas". *Journal of the Korean Society of Clothing and Textiles* 37, no. 7: 837-851. http://koreascience.or.kr/article/JAKO201336161059614.pdf.

Leloir, Maurice. 1938. *Histoire du costume de l'Antiquité à 1914, t. XI Epoque Louis XV. 1725 à 1774*. Paris : Henri Ernst.

Levi Pisetzky, Rosita. 1967. *Storia del costume in Italia, t. IV, Il Settecento*. Milan: Istituto Editoriale Italiano.

Orlando, Flavio. 1993. *Storia del vestire nel Granducato di Toscana ai tempi dei Lorena*. Milan: Idea.

Quicherat, Jules. 1877. *Histoire du costume en France depuis les temps les plus reculés jusqu'à la fin du XVIIIe siècle*. Paris: Hachette.

Simmel, Georg. 1957. "Fashion". *American Journal of Sociology*, 62, no. 6: 541-548.

Stephan, Charlotte. 2014. *La robe en France, 1715-1815: nouveautés et transgressions*. Paris: Ecole du Louvre. https://dumas.ccsd.cnrs.fr/dumas-01547219.

Rabanne, Paco. 1999. *Le feu du ciel*. Paris: Michel Lafon.

Urbain Ruarde, Elisa. 2017. "The Négligé in the Eighteenth-Century French Portraiture". *The Journal of Dress History*, I, no. 1: 92-99.

Zanola, Maria Teresa. 2018. "Les relations synonymiques du lexique spécialisé dans la tradition lexicographique entre XVIIIe et XIXe siècles : le cas de l'habillement féminin". *Etudes de Linguistique Appliquée*, 189: 35-48.

Part 4:
Transmedia Narratives

Sliding Towards an Uncertain Future. *Years and Years* and the Ever-Closer Dystopia

Luca Barra

Introduction

On Tuesday 14 May 2019, in the 9 pm prime-time slot, Britain's main public TV channel, BBC One, aired episode one of the six-part miniseries *Years and Years*, which would conclude just over a month later on 18 June. In less than a minute, the series promo put together numerous fragments: pieces of a family puzzle and allusive shards of a social and political perspective. The audience had little to go on besides an indication of the timeline, a sense of years flying by, the launch tagline—"the future is loading"—, the audio backdrop of "Somebody to Love" by Jefferson Airplane and the reputation of series creator Russell T. Davies. These hints would coalesce into an inventive, unpredictable series that presents an original look at today's world and its future. Its dystopian vision is close at hand, already coming true before our heedless eyes, and it will ultimately have a powerful impact on both the society we live in and our tiny individual lives. This article offers an in-depth analysis of the text and its context (the author, the genre, the distribution, the critical reception), highlighting some specific aspects of this British miniseries' "ever-closer dystopia" and its take on our society's slow, inevitable slide into negative extremes and on the (im)possible escape routes that might be found when people come together.

Contexts. Production and Distribution

Years and Years is part of a strong, long-established tradition of British-made drama series that balance a public-service broadcaster's all-round requirements with the need to tell engaging, exciting, spectacular stories (Bignell and Lacey 2014; Cooke 2015) while updating its imaginary to meet the challenges in the contemporary social and media scene (Chapman 2020; Korte and Falkenheyner 2021). For limited series and multi-season titles alike, British series are often structured over a small number of episodes; this serves both industrial and creative needs, supporting quality writing and production values while enabling a more varied offering (McElroy and Noonan 2019). The six-part *Years and Years* is a case in point, where sequels or follow-up seasons have been excluded at the outset. Series are a centrepiece product with high-value content distilled into just a few weeks, a welcome departure from a largely entertainment- and news-based programming flow. And the one-shot miniseries with top writers and actors further reinforces this rarity value, the idea of a pleasurable exception. *Years and Years* has a full-hour format, clearly indicated as drama and scheduled on the flagship public-service channel, BBC One, at 9 pm, the slot with the largest, broadest mainstream TV audience.

As well as fitting seamlessly in with the formats and trends in British television drama, *Years and Years* is also the latest in a long line of transatlantic coproductions (Weissman 2012; Hills, Hilmes and Pearson 2019). Although the British system with its "European" public-service-inspired approach is profoundly different from a purely commercial set-up, it is the closest to the US model in an industrial sense, with frequent sharing of templates, talent and expertise; many dramas are hybrid UK–US coproductions. A huge high-value production, the dystopian miniseries was made by the BBC with the crucial financial support of premium American cable operator HBO, which has been making quality original series for years. Lately, it has topped up its schedules and library with high-concept, lower-cost European content—like *The Young Pope*, *The New Pope* (Barra 2020), *Chernobyl* and *My Brilliant Friend*. *Years and Years* aired in the States from 24 June to 19 July 2019, just weeks after its UK run, on Monday at prime time, an evening that HBO often reserves for co-production premieres. (US originals are generally screened on Sundays.) Here, the promo was longer, less allusive and more descriptive, playing out the initial scene and foreshadowing many of the themes in a kind of overall view.

Another point that enables us to contextualise the project and understand it better is that it forms part of another contemporary media trend: the renaissance in European drama driven by the pay operators and on-demand audiovisual platforms (Barra and Scaglioni 2021), especially at the premium end of the spectrum, but with significant impact on free public and commercial television too. Drama, therefore, now enjoys a wider circulation on many national markets and can build a shared imaginary (Bondebjerg and Redvall 2019). Although the phenomenon is deeper-rooted for UK series, *Years and Years* also benefitted from a greater receptiveness in the linear schedules and on-demand libraries. The BBC distributed it on its Belgian and Dutch channels, while HBO took the title to Spain and Poland (along with Mexico and Latina America). It aired in Germany on the leading public channel, ZDF, and in France on the pay network Canal+ (a central asset for the StudioCanal group, which also owns the series producer, Red Production Company). Italy was a partial exception, where the title was broadcast belatedly (from 5 March 2020) on a minor on-demand platform with a small audience, StarzPlay, garnering minimal critical comment and a limited pirate circulation. Interestingly, this production by the British PSB almost always appeared elsewhere as a pay series, both in the US partnership and on the European rounds. It became part of a prestigious global, cosmopolitan television offering, thus emphasising the quality of the story but confining its impact to a niche audience of largely cultured, affluent viewers, without the UK original's (at least in theory) across-the-board appeal.

Contexts. The Author, the Genres

The promotional push to build the hype for the miniseries in Britain and around the world centred on its author, creator, screenwriter and showrunner, Russell T. Davies. The authorial dimension is key to a quality/prestige series: in the UK, his name was the first thing mentioned in the BBC promo. Davies is one of the most important figures in contemporary British TV, with a long and impressive CV, multiple awards, a high profile and good name recognition (Aldridge and Murray 2008). He can be termed an author-brand, adept at drawing attention to his projects before they are made, a sure-fire ticket for fans and the general public alike. In his 40-year career since debuting in children's TV, the creator and showrunner has bestridden an array of series genres for a multitude of commissioners: the commercial (ITV), the experimental (Channel 4) and the institutional (the BBC). In the 1990s, he devised numerous titles exploring sexuality or offering a lay perspective on religion, through soap operas, comedies and miniseries, earning a big international hit with *Queer as Folk* (Channel 4, 1999-2000), about the lives of some young gay men from Manchester, subsequently remade for America (Showtime, 2000-05). In the mid-2000s, he was the executive producer behind the relaunch — after a 15+ year hiatus — of one of the longest-running and most important series on British television, *Doctor Who* (BBC, 1963-89 and 2005-); he did not stop at a straight revival but expanded the franchise with several spin-offs, including notable *Torchwood* (BBC, 2006-11). Latterly, after an interlude in the US, he gave voice to different generations of the gay community with *Cucumber* (Channel 4, 2015) and *Banana* (E4, 2015) before telling queer stories from the past with his adaptation of *A Very English Scandal* (BBC One, 2018), a novel set in the '60s, and the story of the AIDS crisis in the 1980s and '90s with *It's a Sin* (Channel 4, 2021). Simplifying a little, *Years and Years* fits perfectly into this authorial journey with its three recurrent themes: a sci-fi look to the future through contemporary eyes; the everyday detail of queer (in a broad sense) lives and families; and an original perspective on fragments of forgotten or marginal shared stories. The 2019 miniseries successfully mixed all these elements, also thanks to its layered treatment of genre.

For on one hand, *Years and Years* is clearly a drama series, in both the format and its construction of the system of expectations in the UK and elsewhere; on the other, it is also a more complex, sophisticated and in some ways contradictory story, and that is also where its relevance lies. Davies' miniseries is a dynamic melting pot of easily recognisable classic genres with their distinctive traits, all meeting and clashing and combining in original blends and unusual ways. A core ingredient is science fiction — a perspective on a different (albeit often not very different) future sliding towards dystopia with all its potential scenarios, high-tech add-ons, different geopolitical contexts and unexpected ramifications. But *Years and Years* is also a crime drama and, in the later episodes, a prison drama. It portrays a struggle between order and chaos, between good and evil (in imperfect, changing forms), the discovery of a great global conspiracy, and some characters' attempts to escape and even overturn the seemingly impregnable new order.

A hallmark of the series, the story's heartbeat below the surface, is the family drama. The great changes in the background world and the developments in the crime plot are always reflected in detail in the action, the dialogue, the way the characters behave. And even in the mere presence of a family, the Lyons, comprising four siblings with complicated lives and relationships: Stephen (Rory Kinnear), a financial analyst living in London with his wife, Celeste (T'nia Miller), and two daughters; Daniel (Russell Tovey), a housing officer in a long-term relationship with his partner (Dino Fetscher); Edith (Jessica Hynes), a globetrotting activist; and Rosie (Ruth Madeley), a canteen worker and single mother of two, with a spinal condition that requires her to use a wheelchair. They gather, at least on special occasions, under same roof in the welcoming if sometimes challenging atmosphere of granny Muriel (Anne Reid)'s house. The narrative structure closely resembles a soap, most of the action (involving the characters and what goes on in the world) playing out around the family lunches and dinners, the calls between siblings, and the holidays punctuating the various gatherings in the grandmother's home. Redemptive yet oppressive, compassionate yet judgemental, the family network is the web that holds them all together and attempts to protect them from a dystopian future society and its threats.

Besides this already multi-faceted rich mix, *Years and Years* also has a strong comic streak, its nuanced political satire and black humour eliciting a bitter, strained, anxious kind of laughter. The many scenes where the characters comment on events viewed on television or a smartphone are laced with irony, sarcasm, a typically contemporary apathy—beguiling yet profoundly problematic, as David Foster Wallace (1993) highlights—and the characters' (and viewers') mirth gradually becomes muted, hollow and guilt-wracked. The phone calls between brothers and sisters work in the same way, as a time for gossiping, sharing thoughts, teasing the others, helping to release the everyday stresses with a chuckle. Blending with the drama storylines, the humour's strange, guilty relief provides a constant counterpoint; this mixing of tones is the wellspring for the highly original tale of dystopia in progress that *Years and Years* presents.

A Way of Interpreting it All

Russell T. Davies' story begins in the present day (2019 when aired) and immediately moves forward into the future in gradual steps indicated on screen by the year in question, culminating fifteen years later. It weaves together two levels: the micro level of the many ordinary or exceptional events occurring in a complicated yet fundamentally close family group; and the macro level of a changing world slipping incessantly and inevitably into a future blighted by wars, pandemics, populism and conspiracy theories, represented by various public figures and above all by their many ramifications and impacts on the characters' and their families' lives, the violent and brutal consequences of macro changes on micro existences. This two-level structure also offers a way to read the whole series, and it is there right from the start of the pilot episode.

The very first words we hear are: "I just don't understand the world any more." They are pronounced by Vivienne Rook (Emma Thompson), the public protagonist from the outside world that is butting heads with the Lyons' private family life. Rook is a political commentator on talk shows, a pundit who revels in the conviction that she is the voice of everyman common sense standing up to the experts and the usual vested interests. She becomes famous, just seconds after those first words, for uttering an insult on live television; this notoriety will be her springboard to a successful political career, from starting a new party to entering government itself. Rook is the antagonist, the villain that the Lyons see only through the papers, TV shows, rallies and public events. Sometimes they find her captivating; on other occasions, they firmly disagree. Either way, she will end up having a huge influence on their lives and everyone else's. The inability to understand a changing world compared to a more straightforward, idealised past is a widespread sentiment that Rook represents on television and then exploits in the political arena. It is an eternal part of how everyone feels, a common denominator of the human experience. And it is also a useful way to begin interpreting the series, as a long meditation on this bewilderment and these incomprehensible things: everyone in its narrative world, and probably everyone in the audience, experiences this sense of disorientation and disconnect at some point.

Among the things that people are unable and maybe unwilling to grasp, three great crises are highlighted, factors that make our world more uncertain and problematic in this brutal version of our everyday experience. There is an economic crisis, with a gradual rise in unemployment due to technology, recession and pressures on the banks. There is a humanitarian crisis, due to migration driven by war, poverty, a lack of security, and border control—in an especially powerful and unexpected scene, one of the characters drowns while attempting to cross the English Channel on a makeshift dinghy. And there is also a political crisis, both national and global, with the emergence and explosion of populism and nationalism, leading to wars, instability, and suffering. The three crises, in the miniseries as in the real world, are linked. And in this dark, supercharged version of the present, the results are a monkey flu pandemic and secret concentration camps.

Beyond this diegetic world on the brink of catastrophe (or maybe it has already happened), the most interesting aspect of *Years and Years* is its success in staging a dystopia in the near future—not a far-off, alien world that is hard to picture as true, but a dystopia that is actually unfolding bit by bit before our eyes, almost without our realising. Starting from the present day (2019, when first broadcast in the UK and US), the series portrays a slow, gradual slide where each step seems natural until its problematic side becomes clear, as change plays out in broad daylight for all to see. *Years and Years* explains how the dystopia develops through incremental changes that are downplayed or ignored or that pass unnoticed, and how this infiltrates the minutiae of daily life, those little things in everyone's everyday existence, their personal freedoms and lives, the close relationships within a family or community.

Which makes this approaching near-future dystopia all the more disturbing, traumatic and effective.

The series moves swiftly forward in time through front-page headlines, breaking-news stories on 24-hour all news channels, and little clues sprinkled in the background that keep track of what is changing, thus presenting a world where the immediate future is getting worse. The dystopia is at hand, and if we carry on as we are, then we run the risk of sleepwalking into it. As Daniel Lyons emphasises in a scene from the pilot episode, it is about more than being unable to understand what is happening any more but also feeling powerless in the face of recent, unstoppable change:

> I don't know if I could have a kid in a world like this. [...] Things were OK a few years ago, before 2008. Do you remember back then? We used to think politics was boring. Those were the days. But now, I worry about everything. I don't know what to worry about first. Never mind the government, it's the sodding banks. They terrify me and it's not even them, it's the companies, the brands, the corporations. They treat us like algorithms, while they go around poisoning the air and the temperature and the rain, and don't even start me on Isis. Well, now we've got America. Never thought I'd be scared of America in a million years, but we've got fake news and false facts and I don't even know what's true anymore. What sort of world are we in? If it's this bad now, what's it going to be like for you, huh? 30 years' time, 10 years, 5 years? What's it going to be like?

The character's words, looking ahead to those years and those changes, betray an idealisation of the past, a sense of the profound revolutions that are under way, the preoccupations of adulthood and fears for the future that are constructed and manipulated by the news media and triggered by uncertainty and change in the economy, in technology and in the political and social spheres.

Dystopia, One Step at a Time

The process that eases the narrative world of *Years and Years* (and, in essence, our world) into dystopia, step after step, works on several major themes. Without claiming to offer an exhaustive analysis, these mainly are the following three. First, as is clear from the opening scene with Rook, there is politics and its perverse permeation of the news and media. The trigger is real: a world where Leave has beaten Remain in the Brexit referendum and where celebrity entrepreneur Donald Trump has been elected President of the USA. Politics is widely debated in the media although reduced to a theatrical clash of opposite extremes, with a disregard for what happens abroad. Rook becomes famous because she "simply does not give a fuck" about Yemen, Qatar, tensions between Israel and Palestine, or Russia's threat to Kyiv (a foreshadowing of the war that reflects an understanding of the dynamics already under way in the contemporary world). When challenged "You can't say that!", she simply replies: "But I mean it". Her rise exploits the porous borders between the media and politics, as she founds the Four Star Movement (a clear reference to the Italian party founded by comedian Beppe Grillo), presenting herself as an independent candidate from outside the political arena. She loses the first election but wins the second, coming to power with the clandestine support of an unscrupulous establishment. The miniseries charts this ascent of political populism, linked to the great geo-economic changes of the day (Sorolla-Romero 2021), and the growing politicisation and polarisation of a public life (Faure and Taïeb 2022) increasingly at the mercy of reactionary elements and incapable of fostering social cohesion.

A second and similar development unfolds in relation to technology. Here too, the springboard is the reality of the Western world today, where everyday life is propped up by smartphones, global personal connections on social media, the debate agenda imposed by Twitter (now X), and interaction with the digital personal assistants that infiltrate people's homes. Things evolve from here in small yet important steps, as Davies makes an interesting imaginative foray into modern tech (Pandelakis 2021). There are the visor called Vision for watching films, the dependency on telephones both in doom scrolling about the real world and in the interactions with other people, pervasive fake news and conspiracy theories (flat-earthism, for one), and a proliferation of artificial intelligence and humanoid robots. Some of the miniseries' fictional enhancements to existing technologies (Zermeño-Flores and Cornelio-Marí 2023) have already materialised for real in the years since it aired, but there are also some more radical ideas. One such is the "filter" that replaces your face with emojis, to conceal your emotions in a kind of caricature; another is the diffusion of a transhumanist movement, which invites people to become data, to replace parts of their body with digital surrogates and finally to enter the cloud.

The same trajectory is also applied to foreign affairs, the inevitable backlash from a wilfully one-eyed, dumbed-down political discourse that fixates on national matters in an attempt to pander to voters. The miniseries does not hang back on issues like war and migration. Ukraine is invaded by Russia while the world barely notices; an authoritarian regime is installed in Kyiv, prompting an exodus towards the (initially) more democratic and tolerant United Kingdom. Emergency camps appear, with foreigners unable to live normal lives, kept apart from the "normal" citizens—not everyone welcomes the new arrivals; some are fearful of them; the camps turn into prisons. Migration is the other face of globalisation, and both come under heavy fire from politicians and their henchmen in the media (Mora-Ramírez 2022). In this climate, as familiar certainties gradually crumble, people feel at sea, unable to tell what is real from what is not. The same applies on another war front, as China builds an artificial island, Sha Dao (a clear allusion to the Taiwan situation) and clashes with the United States. The Americans drop nuclear warheads on the island, precipitating a global crisis, but it is unclear whether the bomb has actually exploded, whether the situation is actually dangerous, whether it is a trick aimed at justifying authoritarian moves in democratic societies. The near future in the miniseries portrays a perverse society of risk (Barnes 2021) in "an excess of trivialised cruelty" (Fernández-Rodríguez and Romero-Rodríguez 2021). And, faced with risks and cruelty, the series has no clear, definitive answer.

Some Conclusions

The rich mix that is *Years and Years* can be viewed on multiple levels: as part of the evolution of the British television industry and its author Russell T. Davies' career; in the context of the scenario in which it is set; in the ways the story has been developed, with its characters and their narrative world that is dystopian yet very close to reality. And also in terms of its critical and audience reception. The initial ratings of 4 million UK viewers settled back to a highly respectable 2.6 million, while in the USA, the premium commercial channel HBO achieved a live audience of around 200,000. But interestingly, the response can be analysed into two distinct stages. In the first, just after the 2019 release, critics and journalists used terms like "dystopia", "future" and "shock". Right from the opening titles, *Years and Years* is a series where "things fall apart, fast" and "can be too overwhelming" (Poniewozik 2019) and which "is meant to serve as an alarm, an alert to what's going on in front of our eyes and where it might lead" (Nussbaum 2019), "personalizing a global sense of doom" (Stuever 2019) and finding "entertaining family-drama in the dystopian near-future" (Lloyd 2019). The series' originality is discussed, its sense of realism and unusual mix of genres. In early 2020, though, the global Covid-19 pandemic put the series in the spotlight for a second time, both in markets where it was distributed later (like Italy, with its mid-lockdown release) and in those where it was revisited and reappraised partly because of several resonances, primarily the viral pandemic that it presaged. Thus it became both "the perfect series for these days" (Palmieri 2020) and "the worst show to watch right now [... a] mistake" (Delaney 2020), "a dystopian fantasy [that] has become all too real" (Miller 2020). Its "oracular" power has also been discussed since, for example for its foretelling of Queen Elizabeth II's death in 2022.

Several conclusions can therefore be drawn from this fertile case study. First, it is very useful to draw a distinction between what might be termed "classic" dystopias based on far-off scenarios and a much nearer dystopia that is not just imminent and growing closer but probably already happening, which unfolds differently but also more easily than one might expect, making it all the more worrying. Second, the anxiety for the future is built here primarily on everyday trivialities, minimal changes in daily life and family relationships, on seemingly innocuous yet revealing comments. The dystopia, in other words, is not something "other": it is normal; it is near. It can happen. Third, the passage of time and the story's multiple perspectives allow for various interpretations, adding further value and significance to a text that is already lavishly rich and layered to start with. Finally a sense of impotence, incomprehensibility and inevitability is constructed, staged and put to the test (in its relationship with the viewer) as a cautionary tale and survival guide for how to grapple with a possible future. When sliding into dystopia, a sense of desperation is normal, as embodied in the pilot episode by a worried, frantic Rosie, who asks herself "What happens now? What happens now?". But *Years and Years* does try to offer a hint of relief: elsewhere in that episode, a conversation underlines how "stories help [...] to make sense of the world". And that goes not just for the characters, but for us viewers too.

References

Aldridge, Mark, and Murray, Andy. 2008. *T is for Television: The Small Screen Adventures of Russell T Davies*. Richmond: Reynolds & Hearn.

Barnes, Naomi. 2021. "The *Years and Years* of Late Modernity: Ulrich Beck and Risk Society". In: Barnes, Naomi, and Bedford, Alison (eds.). *Unlocking Social Theory with Popular Culture. Critical Studies of Education, vol 15*. Springer, Cham. DOI: 10.1007/978-3-030-77011-2_6.

Barra, Luca. 2020. "*The Young Pope* Goes to Washington. Percorsi distributivi di una serie 'italiana' nella televisione statunitense". *Cinergie. Il cinema e le altre arti*, 18, pp. 25-35. DOI: 10.6092/issn.2280-9481/10922.

Barra, Luca and Scaglioni, Massimo (eds.). 2021. *A European Television Fiction Renaissance. Premium Production Models and Transnational Circulation*. London: Routledge.

Bignell, Jonathan and Lacey, Stephen (eds.). 2014. *British Television Drama. Past, Present and Future*. London: Palgrave Macmillan, II ed.

Bondebjerg, Ib, Redvall, Eva Novrup, et al. (eds.). 2017. *Transnational European Television Drama. Production, Genres and Audiences*. London: Palgrave Macmillan.

Chapman, James. 2020. *Contemporary British Television Drama*. Bloomsbury, London.

Cooke, Les (2015), *British Television Drama. A History*. London: BFI. II ed.

Delaney, Brigid. 2020. "*Years and Years* Is Riveting Dystopian TV – and the Worst Show to Watch Right Now". *The Guardian*, 7 April.

Faure, Antoine, and Taïeb, Emmanuel. 2022. "*Years and Years*. Temps et politisation". *ReS Futurae. Revue d'études sur la science-fiction*, 19, online. DOI: 10.4000/resf.10955.

Fernández-Rodríguez, Carlos, and Romero-Rodríguez, Luis M. 2021. "The Cinema of Cruelty in Streaming: Elements of Perversity in *Chernobyl* and *Years and Years*", *Journal for Cultural Research*, 25:2, pp. 202–219, DOI: 10.1080/14797585.2021.1937250.

Hills, Matt, Hilmes, Michelle, and Pearson, Roberta (eds.). 2019. *Transatlantic Television Drama. Industries, Programs, & Fans*. Oxford: Oxford University Press.

Korte, Barbara, and Falkenheyner, Nicole. 2021. *Heroes in Contemporary British Culture. Television Drama and Reflections of a Nation in Change*. London: Routledge.

Lloyd, Robert (2019), "Review: HBO's *Years and Years* Finds Entertaining Family Drama in the Dystopian Near-Future". *Los Angeles Times*, 24 June.

McElroy, Ruth, and Noonan, Caitriona. 2019. *Producing British Television Drama. Local Production in a Global Era*. London: Palgrave MacMillan.

Miller, Adam. 2020. "*Years and Years* Is Really Freaking People out: Russell T. Davies' Dystopian Fantasy Has Become All Too Real". *Metro*, 3 April.

Mora-Ramírez, Pedro. (2022. "(De)Constructing Identities: the Depiction of Post-Brexit Migration in *Years and Years* (2019)". *Journal of Artistic Creation & Literary Research*, 10(2), pp. 1–22.

Nussbaum, Emily. 2019. "*Years and Years* Forces Us Into the Future", *The New Yorker*, 22 June.

Palmieri, Attilio (2020). "Perché devi assolutamente vedere *Years and Years*, la serie perfetta per questi giorni". *Esquire Italia*, 27 March.

Pandelakis, Saul. 2021. "Disappearing Bodies, Disappearing Objects: What *Years and Years* Can Teach Us About Design". *Temes de Disseny*, 37, pp. 132–156.

Poniewozik, James. 2019. "Review: In *Years and Years*, Things Fall Apart, Fast". *The New York Times*. 23 June.

Sorolla-Romero, Teresa. 2021. "Iconographies of the Present. Political Populism, Economic Instability and Migratory Crisis in *Years and Years* (BBC and HBO, 2019)". *Communication & Society*, 34(2), pp. 281–296. DOI: 10.15581/003.34.2.281-296.

Stuever, Hank. 2019. "How HBO's *Years and Years* Triumphed at Personalizing a Global Sense of Doom". *The Washington Post*, 30 July.

Wallace, David Foster. 1993. "E Unibus Pluram: Television and U.S. Fiction". *Review of Contemporary Fiction*. 13:2, pp. 151–194.

Weissman, Elke. 2012. *Transnational Television Drama. Special Relations and Mutual Influence between the US and the UK*. London: Palgrave Macmillan.

Zermeño-Flores, Ana-Isobel, and Cornelio-Marí, Elia-Margarita. 2023. "A Multilevel Analysis of the Representations of Technology in *Years and Years*". *Communication & Society*, 36(1), pp. 113–126. DOI: 10.15581/003.36.1.113-126.

Sisters in Arms against the Pandemic. Female Figures in the TV Series *The Rain* and *Anna*

Stefania Antonioni

Contagion, Dystopias and Young Female Heroines

The narrative of the viral spread of the contagion, which has always characterized fictional production, has over time become linked to the dystopian genre (Conti 2020), giving rise to a multiplicity of novels, films and, in recent years, TV series. More specifically, the latter have catalysed the attention of global audiences who have often praised their success, leading to the production of titles extending over several seasons, with their spin-offs and the creation of actual transmedia narrative universes[1].

We can definitely note that these types of products are dramatically timely and thought-provoking when framed in the recent contemporary global scenario that dealt with the spread and subsequent containment of the Covid-19 epidemic. And, in fact, many of these television series, conceived and produced in a period before that of the pandemic, were somewhat foretelling of the contagion, of the containment measures, and more generally of the suspension of the state of 'normality'.

Another interesting point to consider is that dystopias constitute one of the ways in which a society represents its fears and anxieties, somehow similar, in a way, to what happens within the horror genre, but also within science fiction, incorporating a warning function, which makes them particularly interesting objects of study because they have the power to provide a social and cultural reading of present days fear and anxieties. Referring specifically to

---

[1] Consider, just to mention the most popular examples, the eleven seasons of *The Walking Dead* (2010-2022) and its various spin-offs, the four seasons of *The Strain* (2014-2017), the five seasons of *The Last Ship* (2014-2018), up to the most recent *The Last of Us* (2023), renewed for a second season.

the horror genre, but as mentioned, this discourse can also be applied to science fiction and dystopian narratives, Noel Carroll states:

> "What presumably happens in certain historical circumstances is that the horror genre is capable of incorporating or assimilating general social anxieties into its iconography of fear and distress" (1990, p. 207).

And it is precisely the similarity of these narrative elements, which originate from fears and concerns that are crystallised in certain periods of social crisis, that often leads these genres to hybridise and merge with each other, giving rise to 'new' genres.

Some authors, noting the proliferation of these dystopian narratives on television, have referred to a "dystopian turn" (Woytina 2018), precisely to emphasize the emergence of this narrative trend that has led to a multiplication of titles that can be ascribed to this genre, probably also implying its appeal to an audience that is increasingly confronted with challenges and anxieties concerning the environment, health issues and the relationship with science, each of which may be a pivotal element of a dystopian narrative. All these issues are increasingly interlinked from a social point of view and, in the meanwhile, are also represented in audiovisual products that draw on this type of shared imagery. As Woytina points out:

> "The proliferation of dystopian fictions in contemporary narrative TV series proves both the increasingly high ambitions of TV storytelling and a large, unorthodox capacity of dystopias to permeate any fabric of contemporary cultural discourse" (2018, p. 170).

Thus, according to the author, the large presence of dystopian narratives in contemporary TV series can be explained on the one hand by the ability of dystopian narratives to capture a set of social tensions already present in the contemporary social and cultural imaginary, and on the other hand, by the fact that it is a type of narrative particularly suited to the complexification and ambitions of contemporary seriality from an artistic, narrative, visual and thematic point of view, which makes it the natural outlet for this type of discourse.

Another remark we can make while considering the themes and narrative trends on which contemporary audiovisual narration focuses, concerns the increasingly conspicuous presence of what have been called from time to time "tough girls"(Inness 1999), "women warriors" (Early and Kennedy 2003), "modern Amazons" (Mainon and Ursini 2006), "supergirls" (Madrid 2009), all concepts dating back to the 1960s and 1970s when a generation of physically and psychologically strong heroines began to feature in film, television and comic narratives, as Inness recalls in his book on tough girls (1999). Although the ultimate popularisation of the heroine figure occurred in the 1970s and 1980s, with the second wave of feminism and, referring to television seriality, with characters such as Wonder Woman, The Bionic Woman, Charlies' Angels (Knight 2010).

Many of the female action heroes who emerged from the late 1990s reflected the spirit of third-wave feminism, "with its advocacy of looking good and being powerful" (Knight 2010, XXI) and, later on, some super heroines will represent, in a certain way, the popularization of feminism. A further development was brought about, indeed, by the third-wave feminism, according to which identities are intersectional, they "co-mingle and overlap" and it is an error to think that women "can be described by certain discrete categories" (Fixmer and Wood 2005, p. 238).

Therefore, women can be and are represented in all their contradictions, in a constellation of power, strength, vulnerability, anxiety, determination, courage, care, as well as problems with attachment. Some new characteristics that have come to define female action heroes are youthfulness, girlishness and combativeness, which have emerged since the late 1990s and are exemplified by the character of Buffy, the protagonist of *Buffy the Vampire Slayer* (1997-2003), who ushered in a new trend prominent in nowadays' TV series.

An intersection between contemporary dystopian narratives and the presence of characters of young female heroines, represented in a more complex way, while also making a series of apparent contradictions fit together, typical of the third wave of feminism, is what is pointed out by Adrienne Boutang, who claims that one can observe a "recent trend of young adult dystopian fictons featuring teenage heroines who resort to violence to defend their freedom and protect the ones they love" (2020, p. 134). And here the author refers to examples, which she then analyses, of the franchise *Hunger Games, Divergent, Fifth wave*. Therefore if

> "Dystopias thus interrogate the now and offer warnings and sometimes prophecies about the future... But sometimes they offer glimmers of hope... often stemmed from a lone (sometimes heroic) figure" (Sargisson 2013, p. 40).

this heroic figure is often represented in contemporary seriality by complex characters of young girls, which will be discussed more specifically in the following section.

New Heroines for a New World: The Cases of The Rain and Anna

To explore this 'new' type of character, I will take as examples two contemporary TV shows that are in some ways different but in others very similar, namely *The Rain*[2] (2018-2020) and *Anna*[3] (2021), which can be analysed using the same angle of observation applied by Adrienne Boutang to the aforementioned films. These two European series, one Danish and the other Italian — although the former is explicitly designed for an international circulation given its production and distribution by Netflix — indicate how much the presence of two young or very young heroines who are somehow referring to an idea of third wave feminism has found its expression, indeed also in the European context.

---

[2] The TV series was created by J. Tai Mosholt, E. Toft Jacobsen and C. Potalivo and it's the first Danish series produced by Netflix. The critics has often compared *The rain* with the film *28 Days Later* and the Tv show *The Walking dead*.

[3] *Anna* was created and directed by Niccolò Ammaniti, who scripted it with Francesca Maniera adapting it from his 2015 novel with the same title. The TV series was distributed by Sky and produced by Wildside, in co-production with ARTE France, The New Life Company and Kwaï. It's noteworthy saying that the COVID-19 epidemic spread out six months after the beginning of the shooting that were completed at the end of the lockdown.

The events recounted by the two series have various points of contact and similarities: basically, they narrate the stories of the two protagonists (Simone in *The Rain* and Anna in the homonymous TV series) who take on the burden of their survival and that of their respective siblings, who were entrusted to them upon the death of their parents due to a pandemic that decimated the population. In the case of *The Rain*, the vehicle of transmission of a mysterious virus is the rain, which significantly turns from a source of life into a source of death, while in *Anna*, the epidemic, called the Red because its manifest symptoms are red spots on the body, has decimated the adult population, leaving alive only children and adolescents who have not entered yet the puberty phase, the threshold representing sexual maturation and access to adult life, not even so metaphorically.

The deaths of Simone's parents, whose father is a scientist from the Apollon company who turns out to be somehow involved with the spread of the virus, and Anna's mother, with whom the young girl lives with her step-brother, place them in the uncomfortable and sometimes rejected position of surrogate or vicarious mothers, called upon to take unexpected, unprepared and sometimes recalcitrant care of younger and immature brothers or step-brothers who, in various ways, manage to get into trouble. This issue of surrogate motherhood that is not always happy, we can recognise is another of the traits of a representation of the contemporary feminine, in which even bad mothers can become new heroines (Vallorani 2005) and motherhood is not always portrayed as idyllic, peaceful, happy, in other words one-dimensional.

Simone's and Anna's Journeys

The Rain, spanned over 3 seasons for a total of 20 episodes, can count on a longer narrative arc than that of *Anna*, which is instead a 6-episode miniseries, and thus also on an evolution of the character and co-protagonists, which allow to focus on other issues and characters embodying ideal types, as well as various types of relationships with Simone. One of these is Martin, a former soldier leading a small group of young survivors, who will weave a romantic relationship with Simone, whom he decides to follow and recognises as the new leader of the group. The pole star, the only one able to save everyone, as Lia defines her in the first season. Lia is the religious and naive young woman, the innocent soul, to mention another typified character. Other relevant female characters with whom Simone relates and teams up are Kira, the true warrior woman, armed with a machine gun, disillusioned and pragmatic, and Fie, a medical biologist who represents the good side of science, ready to question itself, dedicated to research and the collection of data and proofs, as opposed to the figure of the Promethean scientist, who compares himself to god, represented in some way by both Simone's father and the Apollon company CEO, Stie, not by chance two male figures.

Anna, like Simone, also meets her first love, Pietro, who helps her when he can but refuses to follow her when the girl wants to go and look for her brother, kidnapped by the blues, a gang of lost, hungry and unruly kids, in the mansion that became their headquarters, judging this to be a suicide mission. Anna, unlike Simone, cannot count on the help and support of a group, but is more a solitary girl, in heroic action against many, who according to Wim Tigges (2017) represents the highest stage in the scale of audiovisual representation of female empowerment. The other female figures with whom Anna is confronted (and clashes) are Angelica, the spoilt, fatuous and cruel girl who grew up watching reality and talent shows and became the 'queen' of the blue, the equally cruel and violent little girls who hold Anna captive, like Cinderella's evil stepsisters, and Picciridduna, who in pre-pandemic life was the tailor Katia, and now is the only surviving adult because she is hermaphrodite. She is the only one with whom Anna seeks an alliance and whom she would be willing to take with her.

Simone and Anna move through the de-humanised, desertified space typical of dystopian scenarios. It is an inhospitable environment, in which uninhabited cities are now in ruins, motorways are populated by abandoned vehicles, roads now are completely useless. On one side are the ruined buildings of Copenhagen and on the other those of Palermo, so reminiscent of the deserted London landscapes of the film *28 Days Later* (2002). The decaying buildings are reused and resemantitised by their new inhabitants, reduced to a pre-social state, now unaccustomed to any kind of comfort. Exemplary from this point of view are the Bagheria's mansion that has become the refuge of the blues in *Anna* and the Ballardian building where a gang of children dressed as urban Indians lives, who appear in *The Rain*'s third season, and who resemble and recall the blues in their behaviour as a hungry tribe on the rampage and in their clothing. This similarity is particularly striking because it depicts an environment barbarised by the absence of rules, in which the only imperative one obeys is one's own survival by getting organised into atomistic gangs, which have nothing to do with a sense of community.

In addition to the abandoned urban and peri-urban landscapes cluttered with ruins, waste and abandoned cars, another leading character in the geography through which the two girls move is wild nature, which regains its spaces. The connection with nature and wilderness, which re-establishes a topical intimate bond between nature and woman, is demonstrated by the way in which both Simone and Anna move through the woods, in the midst of nature that has now regained its space, taking revenge against excessive anthropisation. Simone, after seeking salvation first in the bunkers, then beyond the containment wall against the contagion, and later in Sweden, realises that the only salvation lies in nature, the mysterious purple flower that secretes a liquid that is the only one that can defeat the virus.

Anna, on the other hand, at ease even in the ascent to Mount Etna, a strenuous journey in which she accompanies Pietro to fulfil his last wish, understands that her and Astor's salvation can only derive from her ability to 'dominate' the sea by crossing it with a pedal boat. The two girls' journey is one that, after crossing desolate urban spaces, takes them back to nature, signaling the need to return to a more archaic state of nature, which obviously applies not only to the two girls but is also suggested as an escape route and a real alternative to the audience. A journey that is also, clearly, a journey of growth for the two girls, who find themselves on the threshold of a new world from the point of view of their identity under construction, and who also experience the world through the first love relationships that they weave but which never undermine their independence. Meaningfully Simone at one point says to Martin: "You play superhero? I don't need you" (season 2, ep. 4). And in the same vein Anna says to Pietro: "You saved me because you feared to be alone, but I'm not your girlfriend. I won't play your little wife. Go away" (ep. 3).

As with the others young heroines mentioned by Boutang, violence is considered as an extension for a more general and altogether positive protective impulse. When requested, both Anna and Simone shift to survival mode, enabling them to shoot and kill only when extremely needed, to defend themselves or their beloved ones (their respective brothers Rasmus and Astor or their lovers). The sensitivity of the protagonists is not a trait that downgrades them as heroines, on the contrary. According to Sonya Sawyer-Fritz (2006) the merging of a traditional feminine trait (hypersensitivity) with a progressive one (the ability to convert emotions into action) gives way to blur the distinction between the heroines of classical melodramas and the ones of contemporary action movies.

One aspect on which both these series do not dwell except implicitly (*Anna*) or fleetingly (*The Rain*) is the generational clash or conflict. In *Anna*, in fact, the adults have disappeared, they have, in spite of themselves, left the world to children and adolescents, a world in which they are in danger of being unable to navigate because, in addition to their inexeperience, they are neither socialised nor culturally educated by anyone. And Anna's ability to survive and to know how to juggle in the midst of enormous difficulties, including raising a little three-year-old brother, probably depends on that guide to life that her mother, aware of her own imminent death, manages to leave her, "The Book of Important Things", together with the admonition to teach her brother to read. In other words, culture must be preserved and passed on as a legacy because it is the only one that will save us.

In *The Rain*, on the other hand, the only moments of conflictual relationship with adults are Simone and Rasmus' relationship with their own father and with the father of Luna, a little girl who appears in the third season, representing a generation selfishly closed in the defense of their own family and their own benefit, a compulsion that is anti-social and therefore questioned by Simone. The other adult with whom both Simone and her brother Rasmus are confronted is the scientist who believes himself to be all-powerful, Stien, whose bad intentions Simone immediately understands and by whom, on the other hand, Rasmus is initially beguiled.

Girls, in these two TV series as well as in the films analysed by Boutang, are emotional, caring, sensitive but also very strong-minded and confident in their own ideas, which will manage to make them survive and, particularly in Simone's case, lead them into a new world that has defeated the pandemic.

In conclusion we can say that the characters of Simone and Anna, illustrate the ambiguities of postfeminist girl culture, begrudgingly endorsing the role of collective hero because of the special circumstances of a pandemic in a dystopian scenario, but secretly longing for a more traditional, private, and maybe even conservative destiny. Witnessed in the case of *Anna* by the arrival in a possibly 'new family' and, in the case of *The Rain*, by the birth of Fie's son, the child of science, rationality and post-dystopia, and by the reconstruction of a large family made up of young people and children with different characteristics, a group that has shown itself capable of staying together thanks to the guidance of a young woman, the only one capable of saving humanity.

References

Boutang, Adrienne. 2020. "Girls against Women. Contrasting Female Violence in Contemporary Young Adult Dystopias". In *Women Who Kill. Gender and Sexuality in Film and Series of the Post-Feminist Era*, edited by Cristelle Maury and David Roche, 135-153. London: Bloomsbury.

Carrol, Noel. 1990. *The philosophy of horror. Or paradoxes of the heart*. New York-London: Routledge.

Conti, Valentina. 2020. "Il contagio distopico". *Comparatismi*, 5: 163-172.

Curtis, Neal, and Cardo, Valentina. 2017. "Superheroes and third-wave feminism". *Feminist Media Studies*, 18:3, 381-396.

Early, Frances and Kennedy, Kathleen (eds). 2003. *Athena's Daughters: Television's New Warriors*. New Yook: Syracuse UP.

Fixmer, Natalie, and Wood, Julia T. 2005. "The Personal is Still Political: Embodied Politics in Thirs Wave Feminism". *Women's Studies in Communication*, 28(2): 235-257.

Innes, Sherrie A. 1999. *Tough Girls: Women Warriors and Wonder Women in Popular Culture*. Philadelphia: University of Pennsylvania Press.

Knight, Gladys L. 2010. *Female Action Heroes. A Guide to Women in Comics, Video Games, Film, and Television*. Santa Barbara: Greenwood.

Madrid, Mike. 2009. *The Supergirls: Fashion, Feminism, Fantasy and the History of Comic Books*. Exterminating Angel Press.

Mainon, Dominique, and Ursini, James. 2006. *The Modern Amazons: Warrior Women On-Screen*. Limelight Editions.

Sawyer-Fritz, Sonya. 2016. "Girl Power and girl activists in the fiction of Suzanne Collins, Scott Westerfeld and Moira Young", in S.K. Day, M.A. Green-Barteet, and A.L. Montz (eds), *Female Rebellion in Young Adult Dystopian Fiction*, London and New York: Routledge.

Sargisson, Lucy. 2013. *Dystopias Do Matter*, in Fatima Vieira (eds), *Dystopia(n) Matters: On the Page, on Screen, on Stage*, 40-42. Newcastle Upon Tyne: Cambridge Scholars Publishing.

Tigges, Wim. 2017. "A Woman Like You? Emma Peel, *Xena: Warrior Princess*, and the Empowerment of Female Heroes of the Silver Screen". *The Journal of Popular Culture*, vol. 50, n. 1.

Vallorani, Nicoletta. "2017. "Of women and children. Bad mothers as rough heroes". *EIC*. XI, n. 20.

Wojtyna, Milosz. 2018. "Solidarity, dystopia, and fictional worlds in contemporary narrative TV series". *Beyond Philology*, n. 15/3 (2018): 163-180.

Dystopian Nostalgia.
Oxymorons in Pandemic Television.

Daniela Cardini

Introduction

March 2020 seems a century away. Nowadays, we prefer not to think about lockdown and Covid-19 anymore. Nevertheless, all of us went through it and, willing or not, it did change all of us, our private lives as well as the global mediascape. After the pandemic, the very meaning of "dystopian world" has become an inescapable challenge for researchers: in spite of ourselves, we have lived firsthand in a de-humanized society, in ghostly, deserted and silent cities incredibly similar to the terrifying scenarios of well-known dystopian literary and audiovisual narratives.

In the long days and nights of the lockdown, television played a double fundamental role: it was the main source of information on the progress of the pandemic (medical bulletins, politicians' statements, news appointments, ...), and the main provider of individual and family entertainment. Through an unpredictable reversal, the much neglected small screen returned to the center of segregated daily life, becoming relevant and indispensable even to audiences who were traditionally distant from it. Furthermore, when reality turned dystopian, nostalgic feelings were a natural and common refuge to the uncertainties of a frightening present (and future), a valid response to fear, boredom and loneliness (Ellis 2021).

In such an unusual and emotionally complex situation, nostalgia pushed many people to turn back to the reassuring classic and much loved serials of the past: not only lighthearted sitcoms and TV series of the Eighties and Nineties took the stage, but also other traditional serial genres changed their looks and their targeted audiences: it is the case of teen drama, that refreshed its popularity for the youngest audiences, but became unexpectedly attractive for adult audiences too, usually not interested in the stories of coming-of-age characters; but a nostalgic and reassuring plunge into their teens was a quite common choice for adult audiences to the uncertainties of a dystopian pandemic present and an unpredictable future.

Dystopia, the Pandemic and Television

Along with boosting the relevance of nostalgia, the pandemic has radically questioned the very idea of dystopia. Its commonly accepted definition refers to the reality of a near future, imagined but credible and predictable on the basis of the negative tendencies of the present. In contrast to utopia, dystopian society is characterized by oppressive socio-political conditions, where technology plays a relevant part in taking to extremes some dangerous environmental conditions. The references are countless: dystopian novels, from Aldous Huxley's *Brave new world* (1932) to George Orwell's *1984* (1949), from Anthony Burgess' *Clockwork Orange* (1962) to Margaret Atwood's *The Handmaid's Tale* (1985); dystopian movies, from Fritz Lang's *Metropolis* (1927) to Stanley Kubrick's *2001: A Space Odissey* (1969), from Ridley Scott's *Blade Runner*(1982) to Wachowski Brothers' *Matrix* (1999); dystopian tv series, from *The Twilight zone* (CBS 1959-1964) to *Star Trek* (NBC 1966-1969), from *The Walking Dead* (AMC 2010-in production) to *Black Mirror* (Channel 4-Netflix, 2011- in production), from *The Handmaid's Tale* (Hulu 2017-in production) to *Squid Game* (Netflix 2021-in production).

According to Baccolini and Moylan (2003, 1), dystopian narratives assume a central role in contemporary cultural production and are typically defined by those stories concerning *"places worse than the ones we live in"*. Sargent (1994, 9) referred to the fictional dystopian world as *"a non-existent society, described in considerable detail and normally located in time and space, that the author intended a contemporaneous reader to view as considerably worse than the society in which that reader lived"*.

However, March 2020 totally reversed these definitions: our present was by far worse than any possible dystopian storytelling. In an essay on the relationship between utopia and dystopia,

Garcia-Siino and Guynes (2021, 3) say: "*2020 makes many dystopian tales seem tame by comparison*". The harshness of the dystopian pandemic present deeply affected the usual role and perception of television in everyday life: a medium that was usually ignored and considered as outdated by a large part of the young and the adults, became a sort of "shelter-good" for all, a precious opportunity to help people afford the gloomy days and nights of the lockdown. As Amy Holdsworth says: "*In the context of public service broadcasting, television has worked as a social glue – imagining, building and reasserting community relations in response to 'stay at home 'orders, shielding and social distancing* (Holdsworth 2021, 240).

As a consequence, the lockdown produced a conspicuous increase in the total audience and in the per capita daily consumption of television, and a substantial variation in the socio-demographic profiles of the audience itself. Television became the most influential medium both for information and for entertainment. The increase in the total audience and the extension to the younger age groups enhanced the practices of shared viewing, both within families and through comments on social networks (Scaglioni 2022).

The news became the pillar of the television schedules, recovering a long-lost centrality for a large part of the population in favor of online information and social media. Forcibly locked at home, a large number of people looked out for long hours at that single "window on the world" which, especially for the youngest audiences, was no longer considered an option, surpassed by social networks, YouTube, streaming platforms (Cardini, 2020).

As for the entertainment genre, pandemic television played a fundamental role for families and individuals. Formulaic and reassuring forms of serial television renewed their popularity: sitcoms and procedurals were (re)discovered by new and old audiences both on linear tv and on streaming platforms:

> "*I've been rewatching 'Gilmore Girls' while knitting, the epitome of lockdown.*"
> "'*The O.C.' brings me 'light relief' – a feeling I also experience when looking at old photos on Facebook or Instagram.*"

"I've been scrolling through the archives because it's nice to remember how times used to be. I think these TV shows help you do that too."[1]

Tv series played a central role, showing up to be a valuable content during the lockdown. A survey conducted in Italy in May 2020 on a representative sample of the population between 18 and 74 years of age through online interviews, highlighted a 47% increase in TV consumption in the considered period; 34% of respondents used streaming platforms more frequently than usual. The increase in Netflix data is evidenced by the unexpected increase of 15.8 million new subscribers worldwide, recorded in the first three months of the year, which therefore only includes the first weeks of the lockdown. In Italy, in the first weekend of total closure (13-16 March 2020) there was a 46% increase in the viewing of tv series/films on demand since the beginning of the quarantine.[2]

However, the pivotal role of television during the Covid-19 pandemic[3] also showed its ambiguity: through the genres of entertainment, television provided reassurance and distraction; but through information, it conveyed scary and distressing news, which makes an interesting parallel with the perception of the changing experience in the meaning of "home": on the one side, home was perceived as a safe haven from the dangers of the virus that was circulating outside, but on the other side, it turned out to be a claustrophobic cage, a prison from where it was impossibile to escape (Holdsworth 2021).

---

1 Isabelle Aron. 2021. "The pandemic and nostalgia: how lockdown left us longing for the past". *Independent*, 18 March. https://www.independent.co.uk/life-style/nostalgia-pandemiclockdown-b1818605.html.
2 Manolo De Agostini. 2020. "Netflix, il lockdown fa bene: boom di abbonati". *Quotidiano.net*. https://www.hwupgrade.it/news/web/netflix-il-lockdown-fa-bene-boom-di-abbonati_88789.html
3 Gianluca Roselli, 2020. "Coronavirus, tutti davanti alla tv: volano tg, film e fiction, ma cala il "trash". *Il Fatto Quotidiano*, 28 march. https://www.ilfattoquotidiano.it/in-edicola/articoli/2020/03/28/tutti-davanti-alla-tv-volano-tg-film-e-fiction-ma-cala-il-trash/5751967/

The Pandemic, Seriality and Nostalgia

TV series represented a sort of "comfort food" during the lockdown. The reasons are clearly expressed by the main characteristics of seriality, which perfectly matched the viewers' needs in such a particular period: the reassuring feeling of being involved for a long time in a well-known fictional universe (Mittell 2015) became a common remedy to fear and isolation.

During the lockdown, not only the role of television underwent significant transformations, but also did some common viewing habits which were usually associated with TV series. For example, the practice of binge watching lost some of its reasons related to social discourse, replaced by the need for not to finish a good series too soon. The forced lack of the "watercooler effect" (the possibility to discuss and share opinions with friends and colleagues during breaks at work after a serial marathon) was partially replaced by slower practices of viewing: less episodes per day in favor of a slow immersion into a comfortable narrative universe, that often replaced the lack of real relationships in the outside world.

The obsession with novelty that characterized the practices of serial viewers of platform series in pre-pandemic times was replaced, in many cases, by the (re)watching of classic series, both in their linear scheduling and/or thanks to their presence in streaming platforms' menus. To face a distressing present and an unpredictable future, the rewatch practice became a precious escape to a carefree and happy past, represented by much beloved series. The practice of rewatching was mostly driven by nostalgia, both for a past that was perceived as joyful and perfect, and for a future that was impossible to imagine: nostalgia for "normal life", for being able to plan the future, even if future was nothing but organizing a trivial weekend at the seaside.[4]

In the United States, the most (re)watched series was *Friends* (NBC, 1994-2004), no longer on air since sixteen years: a reassuring and comforting experience of "the way we were". In general,

---

[4] Marilena Pirrelli. 2020. "I consumi culturali durante il lockdown? Tv, libri e musica". *Il Sole 24 Ore*. 4 July. https://www.ilsole24ore.com/art/i-consumi-culturali-il-lockdown-tv-libri-e-musica-AD1kKAc

comedy has been the most (re)watched genre, from *How I met your mother* (CBS, 2005-2014) to Seinfeld (NBC, 1989-1998), from *Gilmore Girls* (The WB-The CW-Netflix, 2000 -2016) to *The Fresh Prince of Bel Air* (NBC, 1990-1996). Even the traditional battleship titles of the networks still in production, such as the family drama *This is Us* (NBC, 2016-2022) or the medical *Grey's Anatomy* (ABC, 2005-in production) recorded a marked increase in audience rates compared to the pre-Covid period. The preference for classics is quite meaningful, from *Law & Order* (NBC, 1999-in production) to *Shameless* (Showtime, 2011-2021), but also the rewatch of *Breaking Bad* (AMC, 2008-2013) or even the first historical series of *Star Trek* (NBC, 1966-1969).

Needless to say, dystopian tv series such as *Black Mirror* (Channel 4, 2011-in production), *Westworld* (HBO, 2016-in production) or *The Handmaid's Tale* (Hulu, 2017-in production) have not been rewatched, in favor of more reassuring and comfortable classics, such as *Mad Men* (AMC, 2007-2015) or *Lost* (ABC, 2004-2010).[5]

Teen Drama as a Nostalgic TV Genre in Dystopian Times

Among all the genres that nostalgic television proposed during the pandemic in response to the dystopian present, teen drama seems particularly interesting for several reasons, the most important of which is its capacity to evoke nostalgia in different and distant generations, notably boomers, millennials and GenZ.

During the pandemic, many teen dramas were watched not only by teenagers, but also by adult audiences, thus provoking an interesting switch in the viewers' habits and a deep change in the identity of the genre. Some tv series have been re-watched by adult audiences and watched for the first time by GenZ viewers, such as *The O.C.* (Fox, 2003-2007), while more recent titles were followed by both adults and young people together. Needless to say, for older

---

[5] Eleanor Stanford. 2020. "Comforting Streaming TV Shows for Stressful Times". *The New York Times*. 16 March. https://www.nytimes.com/article/comforting-streaming-tv-shows.html

viewers the theme of youth is strictly linked to nostalgia; but in the pandemic, also for young adult viewers the stories in different teen dramas worked as strong activators of nostalgia, because of their representation of a "normal" daily life that was impossible to live during the lockdown.

So, during the pandemic the teen drama has become a sort of a cross-generational nostalgia activator, that can be analyzed through Svetlana Boym's brilliant definition (2001).

Boym identifies two different types of nostalgia: *restorative nostalgia* and *reflective nostalgia*, each of them characterized by specific political and ideological implications.

Starting from the etymology of the word "nostalgia", Boym points out that, on the one hand, restorative nostalgia emphasizes the idea of *nostos* (returning home) which refers to the wish to rebuild the lost home and patch up all the memory gaps; reflective nostalgia, on the other hand, emphasizes the idea of *algia*, that is pain, longing and loss, in the imperfect and individual process of remembrance:

> "The past for the restorative nostalgic is a value for the present: it is not a duration but a perfect snapshot (...) a politically reactionary mode that romanticizes the past by refusing to critique or even acknowledge this earlier period's negative aspects, and presenting it as an alluring retreat from an implicitly less desirable present (...).
> Reflective nostalgia lingers on ruins, the patina of time and history, in the dreams of another place and another time. (...) It is more concerned with historical and individual time, with the irrevocability of the past and human finitude. The focus here is not on recovery of what is perceived to be an absolute truth but on the meditation on history and passage of time.
> (...) They can use the same triggers of memory and symbols, the same Proustian Madeleine pastry, but tell different stories about it." *(Boym 2001, 42-49).*

In order to underline the appeal of teen drama to different audiences during the lockdown, due to its capacity to activate different experiences of nostalgia, Boym's definition can be applied to some teen dramas aired during that dystopian period of our lives.

The appeal of teen drama for different audiences in the lockdown thanks to its capacity to activate different experiences of nostalgia is clearly shown by applying Boym's definitions of nostalgia to some teen dramas that were much appreciated during the pandemics.

Stranger Things is one of the big titles for Netflix. Its first season was released in 2016, the second season in 2018, the third one in 2019 and the fourth one in 2022. The two creators Matt and Ross Duffer conceived the series with the aim of paying tribute to the classics of cinema and fantastic literature of the Eighties, trying to convey to modern viewers the same sensations generated by works such as the classics by Steven Spielberg and John Carpenter or the novels by Stephen King.The series is a celebration of a sort of "warm and welcoming nostalgia" to honor the works from which it is inspired by telling a story that is both scary and sweet.

Even though neither season was released during the lockdown, it was one of the most re-watched tv series during that period by young adults and adults.

Following Boym's definition, *Stranger Things* is a perfect example of restorative nostalgia *("a politically reactionary mode that romanticizes the past by refusing to critique or even acknowledge this earlier period's negative aspects"*, 42) because it depicts the neoconservative politics of the 1980s with no critical engagement. Some scholars harshly criticize its partial and optimistic portrayal of the period: instead of dealing with the racist, sexist and homophobic issues so widespread — and accepted — in such a controversial decade, the series relates to the Eighties in a nostalgic mood that is more celebratory than critical:

> *"'Stranger Things' is fun for almost all the family, depending on your juvenile cohorts' response to occasional gory scenes. The pace is (just about) fast enough to keep younger viewers hooked, and anyone old enough to remember 1983 for real is in for a richly enjoyable retro-feast whose cockle-warming abilities make up for (what is for us) a slightly predictable narrative and inadequate explanation of the underlying mythology by the end."* [6]

Other scholars appreciate *Stranger Things* 'evocative period aesthetics for its being positively reassuring:

---

[6] Lucy Mangan. 2016. "Stranger Things Review: A Spooky Shot of 80s nostalgia straight to your heart". The Guardian, 15 July. https://www.theguardian.co m/tv-and-radio/2016/jul/15/stranger-things-review-a-shot-of-80s-nostalgia-right-to-your-heart-winona-ryder

"If Stranger Things and other nostalgic television programs can work to generate positive feelings within the present, provide a temporary safe haven from current troubles, and serve as a source of ispiration for the future, then (...) that is good nostalgic television." (Sirianni 2019, 196–7).

A good example of what Boym defines reflective nostalgia, focused on *"the patina of time and history, in the dreams of another place and another time... The focus is ... on the meditation on history and passage of time"* (Boym 2021, 49), is another Netflix teen drama, located in Italy, *Summertime* (Netflix 2020-in production), whose first season was released on April 29th, 2020, in the midst of the first lockdown.

The story is based in Cesenatico, an Italian seaside town on the Adriatic coast that was a renowned summer holidays spot in the Sixties, and is focused on the love story between two teenagers, Summer and Alessandro. The shy and introverted Summer works as a waitress during her school vacations; her parents are artists and she likes listening to old 60s' Italian songs. Alessandro is a rich Roman boy, a professional motorcycle rider, in eternal conflict with his father; his mother is the owner of the hotel where Summer works. Their tormented—but predictable—relationship unfolds through a pleasant balance between a lighthearted "teenage" tone of voice and a hint of sadness and melancholy.

Scenes are dominated by golden and sepia colors, the characters have a clean look and decent behavior, the location is the perfect symbol of what summer teenage vacations should be, the storylines deal with predictable love troubles and friendships, the score is composed by the most famous Italian love songs of the Sixties loved by the main character Summer, who shows a peculiar nostalgic and retromaniac attitude—but very appreciated and nostalgia-boosters for adult audiences (Cardini and Sibilla 2021).

Everything in this series sounds perfect, delicate and wrapped in memories of that "normal" habits so different from the restrictions due to the pandemic captivity. *Summertime* is the portrait of a never-ending summer, a never-ending youth that appeals more to the adult audiences than to the teens; an idealized portrait of teenage years and of summer vacations that is perfect for eliciting nostalgia in pandemic dystopian times.

In the early 90s, the genre was born thanks to *Beverly Hills 90201* (Fox, 1990-2000) and created *ex nihilo* the teen audience as a commercial target in American television; from then on, the teen drama has undergone such a deep transformation as maybe none of other serial genres did, even though some scholars in recent works still consider it "not a foundational genre to television such as the soap opera, western, or episodic action series. (...) Teen television is mostly concerned with its targeted demographic" (Marghitu 2022).

It could be said, however, that the Covid-19 emergence reversed this statement: due to the central role played by nostalgia in dystopian pandemic times, this peculiar genre has become relevant and interesting also for adult audiences. Much better than other tv serial genres, during the lockdown it fulfilled the needs of different generations of viewers, who were equally involved in the difficult task of coping with an unexpectedly dystopian daily life.

References

Aron, Isabelle. 2021. "The pandemic and nostalgia: how lockdown left us longing for the past". *Independent*, 18 March. https://www.indep endent.co.uk/life-style/nostalgia-pandemiclockdown-b1818605.ht ml.

Baccolini, Raffaella, and Tom Moylan, eds. 2003. *Dark Horizons: Science Fiction and the Dystopian Imagination*. New York-London: Routledge.

Boym, Svetlana. 2001. *The Future of Nostalgia*. New York: Basic Books.

Cardini, Daniela. 2020. "Locked Down. Strategie (seriali) di resistenza durante la pandemia". *Sociologia della Comunicazione*, 60: 57-66.

Cardini, Daniela, and Gianni Sibilla. 2021. *La Canzone nelle Serie TV. Forme Narrative e Modelli Produttivi*. Bologna: Pàtron.

Ellis, John. 2021. "Provocations, I: What do we need in a crisis? Broadcast TV!'. *Critical Studies in Television* 15(4): 393-98.

Garcia-Siino Leimar, and Sean Guynes. 2020. "Introduction: Screening Utopia in Dystopian Times". *Science Fiction Film and Television* 13(3): 317-21.

Holdsworth, Amy. 2021. "The Homesick and the Sick Home". *Journal of Popular Television* 9(3): 239-99.

Holdsworth, Amy. 2021. *On Living with Television*. Durham, MA: Duke University Press.

Marghitu, Stefania. 2022. *Teen TV*. New York-London: Routledge.

Mittell, Jason. 2015. *Complex TV. The Poetics of Television Storytelling*. New York-London: New York University Press.

Negra D. 2020. "Pandemic Television". *Film Criticism*, 44(4). DOI: https://doi.org/10.3998/fc.13761232.0044.407

Sargent, Lyman Tower. 1994. "The Three Faces of Utopianism Revisited". *Utopian Studies* 5(1): 1-37.

Scaglioni, Massimo, ed. 2022. *La Televisione nella Pandemia. Intrattenimento, Fiction, Informazione e Sport nell'Anno del Covid-19. Annuario 2021*. Roma: Carocci.

Sirianni, Joseph. 2019. "Nostalgic Things: *Stranger Things* and the Pervasiveness of Nostalgic Television". In *Netflix Nostalgia. Screening the Past on Demand*, edited by Kathryn Pallister, 167-90. Lanham, Boulder, London, New York: Lexington Books.

The Potential and the Use of the Radio in the Construction of a Dystopian Imaginary

Miriam Petrini

Radio Potential

Why talking about radio and dystopia? Because of radio's potential in creating worlds, images and being as close to the public as to appear realistic. In this way it shifts from fiction to reality as dystopian narrations do.

At the same time, the radio can create intimacy with the listeners because it surrounds them and, like the music, takes the audience into different realities where there are no limits of space and time. So the public could be easily transported to fantasy, sci-fi, dystopian dimensions. The language of the radio has not a material body and everything becomes a suggestion. Without a body, only evocations remain and the radio can go beyond reality. Magic, fantasy, horror, everything that is unbelievable could happen: the imagination is free and emancipated.

According to German scholar Rudolf Arnheim:

> "[The radio] Although wireless, when it wished to, could beat the theatre at sound realism, yet those sounds and voices were not bound to that physical world whose presence we first experienced through our eye, and which, once perceived, compels us to observe its laws, thus laying fetters on the spirit that would soar beyond time and space and unite actual happenings with thoughts and forms independent of anything corporeal". (Arnheim, 1936).

That is why dystopian matters can be very powerful in radio-theatre and the most famous radio-drama *The War of the Worlds* by Orson Welles is an example of how the potentiality of the radio could operate.

In 1938, while radio-drama in Italy was still at the beginning and slowly developing, the American CBS radio-channel transmitted *The War of the Worlds* based on the story published on Pearson's

Magazine in 1897 by Herbert George Wells. For a long period it was believed that this radio-play created a traumatic impact which spread all over the USA. Indeed, even if this is fake news, it is important to focus on the fact that it was believed true for many years, also by the academic critics. *The War of the Worlds* radio adaptation was, in fact, quite realistic, thanks to its success in playing with the two dimensions of time and space and an implicit agreement of trust between the radio speaker and the audience.

"Ladies and gentlemen, we interrupt our program of dance music to bring you a special bulletin from the Intercontinental Radio News. At twenty minutes before eight, central time, Professor Farrell of the Mount Jennings Observatory, Chicago, Illinois, reports observing several explosions of incandescent gas, occurring at regular intervals on the planet Mars". (Welles, 1938)

In this way the speaker described, with a game of sounds, noises, echoes and screams far away from the audience, that in another place, but at the same time, an alien invasion was happening. This created a short-circuit between real time and the time of narration.

However the traumatic impact of the radio-play was fake news created by journalists, as recent researchers Brad Schwartz, Jefferson Pooley and Michael Socolow proved.

"Far fewer people heard the broadcast (and fewer still panicked) than most people believe today. How do we know? The night the program aired, the C.E. Hooper ratings service telephoned 5,000 households for its national ratings survey. -To what program are you listening?- the service asked respondents. Only 2 percent answered a radio "play" or "the Orson Welles program". (Pooley, Socolow, 2013).

But we should not minimize the great echo of the phenomena. In fact, in 1938, the journalists had already noticed the great potential of the radio in manipulating the mass. At that time there was the Great Depression and newspapers tried to reduce this potential, but they just succeeded in increasing the popularity of radio and radio-theatre.

"Radio had siphoned off advertising revenue from print during the Depression, badly damaging the newspaper industry. So the papers seized the opportunity presented by Welles' program to discredit radio as a source of news. The newspaper industry sensationalized the panic to prove to advertisers, and regulators, that radio management was irresponsible and not to be trusted". (Pooley, Socolow, 2013).

Italian Examples

Between the 30s and the early 40s, without even pretending a dystopia, the fascist EIAR (Ente Italiana Audizioni Radiofoniche) tried to recreate a fake reality both by telling a rarefied reality of Italian socio-economic and political situation and trying to influence people lives with a botched version of Orwell's Big Brother. We do not have many recordings of war time ordinary transmissions (except, of course, for Mussolini's speeches), but we can read Radiocorrere's planning of the time, or watch a propaganda radio-television documentary made in 1940 entitled *Ecco la Radio!*, to notice how hard the fascist radio tried to come inside households and give directions to ordinary people. There are gymnastic programs, working-class programs, praying times, suggestions to housewives, and many special programs with the same purposes.

This connection between a cruel reality and a dystopian world, the power of the radio and radio theatre was also noticed by an Italian author who had experienced real cruelty: Primo Levi. No one more than him could perceive what a dystopian world could be like, and maybe, that is why he chose to realize some sci-fi, "soft dystopian" stories (as I call them), and he chose to give them to radio narration even before having them published.

Levi had written for the radio since the 50s, but his interest in it increased when he received a recording from Canada, the radio version of his masterpiece *Se questo è un uomo* (1964). He was impressed by the way the authors of this radio version succeeded in creating the harshness of the concentration camp and the confusion of the people who were there, confusion recreated with a multilingual game. Levi said that it was a real revelation: "Authors had understood everything of the book and even something more [...] They had succeeded in realizing for the radio a spoken meditation, with a high technical and dramatic level, and at the same time strictly faithful to the reality as it was". (Levi 2016, LXXIV) [NB: personal translation].

He then decided to curate the Italian radio-version of *Se questo è un uomo*. About his radio adaptation of his work he said:

> "For me it was a peculiar way to live again, on my skin, the environment of the time, because the purpose of this radio-version was to give life again to the multilingual world of the concentration-camp. Therefore there were many actors—non actors—amateur actors, French, Hungarian, Yiddish, Polish and Russian. Living this renewed Babylon was for me a jump again with deep effects on that time". (Levi 2016, LXXIV) [NB: personal translation].

Thanks to this first radio-version he became more involved in radio-plays, not only for his experiences in the concentration camp but also for other kinds of stories. In the meantime, while he was still writing his concentration camp chronicles, even before writing *La Tregua* (1963), in the early 50s, he started his sci-fi stories. Many years later, he published them in a volume entitled *Storie naturali* (1966) with the false name Damiano Malabaila, but some of those stories were already adapted for the Radio Rai.

Two of these sci-fi stories, in particular, show what I mean by "soft dystopian" dimension. The first one is *La Bella Addormentata nel frigo*. It is a story that appears in Levi's notes for the first time in 1952 but it was adapted for the radio in June 1961. The second one is *Il versificatore*. We have a 1960's recording of it, and it is preserved at Centro Internazionale di studi Primo Levi, in Turin, but it was broadcast only in 1967; the director was Andrea Camilleri.

The first script, *La bella addormentata nel frigo*, is set in a futuristic middle-class evening party, in Berlin in 2135: the owners of the house, the Thols' family, have inherited a peculiar valuable thing, that is the "Beauty in the fridge", Brunilde. Brunilde is a smart woman who, in 1995 took part to an experimental project whose intention was to take someone up to the future. The way Brunilde can travel to the future is living in a fridge from where she goes out twice or three times a year, for ceremonial events. Anyway when Brunilde goes out of the fridge, her presence causes many problems to the family. The wife, Lotte is annoyed by Brunilde's snobbery, and a little bit jealous of her eternal youth and eternal life. Besides, Lotte also noticed something wrong in the relationship between Brunilde and her husband, Peter. On the other hand one of the dinner guests, Baldur, fell immediately in love with Brunilde and in the same night he decides to free her forever. He took this decision with her. Brunilde, in fact, had confessed him to be bored with all these continuous freezing and warming and she was also tired of her renouncing life. At the end of the story, anyway, we will discover that Brunilde, though really annoyed of her situation, did not want to flee with Baldur. She only wanted to leave the Thols, because, as she confessed, she had been abused by Peter many times in those moment in which she was warming but she was not enough warm to react.

> "Baldur I feel that I owe you a confession. I am really annoyed, you know, freezing and warming, freezing and warming...for a so long time that is becoming tiring. And there is more...his visits, when I was 33 degrees, when I was just warm but not enough to defend myself ". (Levi 2017, 18) [NB: personal translation].

The end of this story is quite harsh and it focuses on problems such as violence, worries about the future and other matters that are even got worse at present times (as Levi predicted): the obsession of the eternal beauty, youth and appearance. Another important consideration is also on the quality of life because in her "life/no life", Brunilde feels lonely, and this makes her appear snobbish. She is not really loved: she is famous, she is admired, but in this futuristic society she is not even considered a real woman, she is just treated as a luxury item.

> "We don't often receive friends, twice or three times a year and we seldom accept invitations...Well, that's obvious, nobody can offer the guests what we can offer them. There are people who can show ancient pictures, such as Renoir, Picasso, Gottuso [...] There are also people with a bar full of the most modern drugs, but we have Brunilde" (Levi 2017, 3) [NB: personal translation].

The second Levi's sci-fi story is less dark, but extremely contemporary. In fact, through the radio-version of *Il versificatore*, Levi could experiment and have fun with sounds and noises. He also changed the original story. At the beginning, in his notes, the story was a monologue, but for the radio adaptation it became a dialogue between the two main characters, the poet and his secretary.

Il versificatore may have taken inspiration from George Orwell's *1984* where there was a writing machine called "The Versificator" which created lyrics and music for the proles. Levi's versificatore, in fact is a machine which creates poetry from some internal dictionaries.

The main point of the story is the different idea that the poet and his secretary have about the machine. The poet was very happy because thanks to it he was able to delegate the most boring poetry commissions and focus on what he really liked to write. Instead, the secretary was strongly shocked by the machine and afraid of it. Not only she did not trust the machine capacity of creating poetry, but she was also terrified by the danger of losing her job.

> "If I were you, I would never do anything like that. I don't say for me, but a poet, an artist like you...How can you resign yourself to putting a machine at home? How can it have your taste, your sensibility?" (in Pantheon, min. 15.12) [NB: personal translation].

The two main characters try the machine in many ways and with many experiments: the noises and the mechanical voice of the machine are well performed by the radio (which makes the radiodrama funny). At the end on the story the listeners find out that the poet has already been using the versificator for two years and they have been told that the machine works perfectly: in fact the story was written by the versificator itself!

> "I have owned the Versificator for two years. I can't say I have already amortized it, but it has become essential for me. It has proved to be very versatile: not only it does a great part of my job as a poet, it also keeps my accounts and wages, it notifies the expiring dates. I taught it to compose in prose and it is really good. The text you have listen to, for example, has been created by it" (Levi 2016, 513) [NB: personal translation].

This second Levi's sci-fi story is much funnier and lighter than *La bella addormentata nel frigo*, but also *Il versificatore* deals with present times. The most famous example of modern versificator is, of course, *ChatGPT,* the artificial intelligence chatbot developed by

OpenAI and released in November 2022. But before, firms have already created and put into operation their own "versificators" such as the project "DeepQA" by Lexus, a luxury car brand which, in 2018, wrote a spot based on an algorithm using the main successful elements of car advertising.

Another versificator instead created a rudimental novel inspired by Jack Kerouac's novel *On the road* (1957). The book is entitled *1 the Road*: it is a project by Ross Goodwin (a technologist and a ghost writer for the President Barack Obama's administration). In 2017 he put a AI machine on the back seats of his car and drove from NY to New Orleans while the machine recorded all sounds and words it could capture and it also registered the time and space of the journey. At the end, with all these data, the machine created the story of *1 the Road*.

These examples of modern versificators generated a debate on the human imagination, a debate similar to the one between the secretary and the poet in Levi's story.

Il versificatore and *La bella addormentata nel frigo* radio-versions are good examples of Levi's ability of using different media. He was not only a great writer but also a storyteller: he used to tell his concentration camp experiences in schools and to friends. That is why he saw in the radio a new possibility of giving evidence of the Holocaust and his doubts on society: he had very clear in his mind the danger which the distortion of reality can cause and the danger caused by an exaggerated intervention on nature and human beings. So, although in the Italian language the word "dystopia" was not yet used, he already perceived the concept.

In reply to the accusation of conflict between his main novels and his sci-fi stories, Levi said:

> "As for me I don't feel any contradictions between the two themes and I don't believe I have betrayed anything or anyone. Instead I believe that it is not difficult to find signs of the concentration camp in some stories: such as the accepted evil, the geometric madness". (Levi 2016, 1509) [NB: personal translation].

In another interview Levi said: "According to me there is an intimate link between the previous play and my latest book. In both there is a man reduced to slavery, on one side "the nazi thing" and on the other side – the object thing –. Always the sleep of reason generates monsters" (Levi 2016, 1509) [NB: personal translation].

Levi was an avant-garde man who could understand which medium could be better for the stories he intended to tell and he liked to try as many different media as the many stories he told us. About the radio:

> "It is extremely subtle, more subtle than television: it suggests to the listener emotions and feelings through imperceptible channels" (Levi 2016, LXIII) [NB: personal translation].

Radiotheatre in Pandemia

What about the use and connection between radio and dystopia in recent times? An interesting example is the initiative called *Scienza e fantascienza dal Valle*.

This early 2021 project was carried out by Teatro Valle in Rome during the pandemic period: it included nine sci-fi radio-dramas recorded in the theatre and broadcast as podcasts. There were nine different directors and for some of them the project was the first experience with radio theatres. Francesco Villano and Giacomo Bisordi, two of the nine directors, in an interview, said that the aim of the initiative was, on one hand, to exorcize the dystopian atmosphere emerged with the covid pandemic and, on the other hand, to keep theatres alive when they were actually closed in Italy.

Francesco Villano's contribution consisted in a re-adaptation of the Russian playwright Mikhail Durnenkov *The War Has Not Yet Started*. The most interesting element of this 2015 play is its foresight because it starts with Russian troops entering Ukraine. "Russian troops enter Ukraine. But the war hasn't started yet. Not officially. Meanwhile, protestors take to the streets, parents lose their children, strangers find lovers, journalists lie on television, cancer patients crack jokes about the absurdity of existence, the downtrodden dream of rising up against their oppressors and everyone everywhere is addicted to something"(in Playpiepint).

Another radioplay to be considered is *The Republic of Happiness*, by the British playwright Martin Crimp. The play deals with capitalisms crisis seen by the hypocritical point of view of a middle class family. Giacomo Bisordi, the director of the radio re-adaptation, had already brought it into theatres (traditional theatre, of course). In my interview we talked about the differences in the direction of a drama in theatre and in radio. For example, according to Bisordi, the first act of *The Republic of Happiness* which is set during a Christmas Eve's dinner, is quite realistic, and it worked better for the theatre than for the radio. Instead the second and third acts which are more surrealistic were of greater success on radio adaptation that in the theatre version. The results of the adaptation surprised the director who was greatly appreciated.

Conclusions

A hundred years later its invention, radio is still a powerful way of spreading narrations and the medium is suitable to different opportunities, from the idea of contributing to create dystopian realities, to the ability of creating intense experience of dystopian narrations, up to the positive ability, during covid pandemic, to make theatrical shows possible, even when theatres were closed[1].

References

AI Wordcar. 2018. *1 The Road: by an Artificial Neural Network*, Jean Boîte Editions.

Arnheim, R. 1936. *Radio*. Faber and faber LTD.

Levi, P. 2016. *Opere complete vol. 1*. Torino: Einaudi.

Levi, P. 2017. *La bella addormentata nel frigo*, Torino: Einaudi.

Pooley Jefferson, Socolow Michael J. 2013. *The Myth of the War of the Worlds Panic* in SLATE.com https://slate.com/culture/2013/10/orson-welles-war-of-the-worlds-panic-myth-the-infamous-radio-broadcast-did-not-cause-a-nationwide-hysteria.html

Welles Orson. *The War of the Worlds* in *https://www.wellesnet.com/the-war-of-the-worlds-radio-script/*

---

[1] I would like to give my special thanks to Francesco Villano and Giacomo Bisordi who have let me listen to their podcasts and gave me the possibility to interview them.

Sitography:

Lexus (newsroom.lexus.eu), November 18th 2019, *Driven by Intuition: Car by Lexus, Story by Artificial Intelligence, Camera by Oscar-Winning Director*, https://newsroom.lexus.eu/driven-by-intuition-car-by-lexus-story-by-artificial-intelligence-camera-by-oscar-winning-director/ *accessed on* 03-17-23.

Playpiepint (playpiepint.com), May 2015, *The War Hasn't Started Yet*, https://playpiepint.com/plays/the-war-hasnt-started-yet/, *accessed on* 03-17-23.

Podcast:

Primo Levi alla radio, in Patnheon, by Pavolini Pantheon, Marras Diego, Barozzi Federica, aired on 03-18-2017, broadcast by Rai Radio3 (then loaded on RaiplaySound). *accessed on 03-17-23.*

Youtube:

Archivio Luce Cinecittà *Ecco la radio*, on Youtube, 04-19-2019 https://www.google.com/search?q=ecco+la+radio+youtube&rlz=1C1YTU H_itIT1003IT1003&oq=ecco+la+radio&aqs=chrome.0.69i59j46i512j0i22i30j0i10i22i30j0i22i30.2816j0j7&sourceid=chrome&ie=UTF-8#fpstate=ive&vld=cid:5963f0d5,vid:IjG_9XWWoVk *accessed* on 03-18-23.

Lexus ES – Driven by Intuition, loaded by Lexus Belux, on Youtube, 02-13-2019. https://www.youtube.com/watch?v=4WY9_1b4gDE *accessed on* 03-17-23.

Primo Levi. *La bella addormentata nel frigo [da Primo Levi, Racconti fantastici]*, loaded by So Chison, on Youtube, 1st December 2015. https://www.youtube.com/watch?v=4nYfsYp15nw *accessed on* 03-17-23.

Primo Levi. *Racconti fantastici di Primo Levi "Il Versificatore"*, loaded by Fictionfilm2, on Youtube, 03-07-2015. https://www.youtube.com/watch?v=vHjpYYmvjs8 *accessed on* 03-17-23.

Walls, Animals and Drones: Concept Albums and Transmedia Dystopic Narratives in Popular Music

Gianni Sibilla

Introduction

This paper aims at analyzing the narrative models used in popular music to represented dystopian societies. Why are dystopic tales so relevant and frequent among pop-rock artists and audiences? Why do this tales assume the particular form of the "concept albums"? What is the role of performances and media in this peculiar form of storytelling?

Popular music is a complex *transmedia* narrative form: artists tell their stories not only through songs, but with different and interconnected media: performances, images, videos, movies and digital platforms. One of the most interesting expressions of this storytelling is indeed the *dystopic concept album*: a group of songs with recurring characters and connected events, used to represent dehumanized societies.

The origins of the concept album can be traced to the Sixties: this narrative form was explored by those musicians who wanted to move beyond forward the boundaries of a single song, creating more complex stories, also including concerts, theatrical staging, movies, videos in their storytelling (Shuker 2022, 5).

"Concept albums" may be me perceived as outdated form of music, linked mainly to the 60's and the 70's: as I will analyze in more detail later, in this period the "album" form became more and more relevant in the music industry; on the contrary, today artists and record company focus on releasing single songs on streaming platforms. But even in this digital landscape of music distribution and consumption, artists still produce concept albums; the two best selling and most streamed titles in Italy in 2022 were two concept albums: "Taxi driver" by Rkomi, and "Persona" by Marracash[1]. Also dystopian references and tales in today's popular music are very frequent, even today. Just to name an example: in 2022 Muse introduced their latest album "Will Of The People" with a press release that used the definition "dystopian glam-rocker".

This paper traces the origin of dystopic concept albums analyzing classic examples such as Pink Floyd's "Animals" (1977, based on George Orwell's *Animal Farm*") and "The wall" (1981) but also more recent ones, such as Coldplay's "Mylo Xyloto" (2011) and Muse's "Drones" (2015).

The narrative complexity of these dystopian concept album will also used to show the relevance and peculiarity of popular music in the media landscape.

The analysis will focus on answering a double question. On one side, why are dystopic tales so present in popular music and why do these narratives take the shape a transmedia concept album? On the other side, and on a more general level—what can dystopic concept albums tell us about the *transmedia* narrative models of popular music? A narratological approach, with tools derived from both media studies and popular music studies, can be useful to make sense of the various interconnected media that popular music artists use to tell their story, from recorded music, to theatrical performances, to TV, cinema, and social media.

A Narratological Approach to Popular Music

Given this complexity how is it possibile to make sense of the communicative forms of popular music? How does it works on a narrative level? Popular music is much more than "simple" songs. It's a powerful and complex *transmedia* narrative form, in which songs

---

1 Cfr. "Top of the music 2021: trionfa la musica italiana—crescono i consumi", FIMI.it, 7/1/2022, https://www.fimi.it/news/top-of-the-music-2021-trionfa-l a-musica-italiana-crescono-i-consumi.kl and "Top of the music 2020: 'Persona' di Marracash è l'album piú venduto", 7/1/2021, https://www.fimi.it/ news/top-of-the-music-2020-persona-di-marracash-e-l-album-piu-venduto.kl

are the basic narrative unit, but they're just the top of the iceberg (Sibilla 2003).

Songs themselves tell stories, through lyrics set to music, of course. But these stories are transformed into theatrical stage performances, into music videos or into movies and/or tv series scenes. And into social media content: the use of songs in micro videos on Instagram and TikTok has become the primary tool to launch a song and or to rediscover an artist. In other words, popular music is a narrative media system made of interconnected different forms of communication.

From a methodological point of view, the scientific study of Popular music is relatively recent, compared to the analysis of other forms of popular culture such as cinema and television. The term "Popular music" denotes a field of study made of different disciplines and methods. They are often ideological, in the sense that they focus on a single aspect of popular music, as if it represented the whole phenomenon.

An *Immanent* method/approach, derived from musicology and semiotics of classical music, is focused mainly on musical structures in songs and how meaning is constructed within the popular musical text. This is a consolidated method derived from the study of classical and contemporary music which are, of course, radically different from popular music in the way they are produced, communicated and consumed.

The second approach is a *trascendent* one, grounded in sociology and focused on the consumption of popular music, whose meaning is to be found outside the text, in the way songs are used by a particular group of people. The sociological approach to popular music reflect the methodology used to study different cultural process and focuses on context, on the way songs and artists reflects and constructs social discourses and social interactions.

Speaking of social discourses, there is also a non-scientific, journalistic approach that focuses on lyrics, that are often connected to gossip, to the singer's personal lives. In this perspective, songs are often considerate an autobiographical texts, not narratives.

If popular music is considered as a complex *transmedia* storytelling, a narratological approach to music helps us to make sense both of text and context: it analyzes the way a narrative is produced and distributed through artist, by music industry and media.

Transmedia is "the increansigly popular industrial practice of using multiple media technologies to present information concerning a single fictional world through a range of textual forms" (Evans 2011: 1). As Paola Brembilla recalls, "The music industry too has embraced not only cross-media distribution principles, but also world building and transmedia storytelling models, mixing and remediating itself with other media languages in order to produce narratives and experiences that are centered on music" (Brembilla 2019, 82-83)

Concept albums and their complex with they intertextual and intermediate narrative form, show us that moreover the music was a *transmedia* storytelling before this definition, introduced by Henry Jenkins (2006), was even used. To comprehend how they build a fictional—and often dystopical—world, it is necessary to consider textual narrative structures through different languages and media platforms, but also the context of production models, distribution and reception.

Most of all, all these aspects interact to build a complex storytelling must be considerer: this is the case of dystopian concept albums.

From Albums to Concept Albums

Popular music too is part of what Nieborg and Poell (2018) call the "platformization cultural production": the predominance of streaming services imposes that recorded music industry and artists focus on producing texts and narratives that satisfy precise requisites, such as singles songs released more frequently, to be consumed by human-curated and algorithmic playlists (Bonini and Gandini 2019). But in this digital music landscape, albums nonetheless are still relevant in how artists tell their stories and build their credibility.

The idea of the "album" itself has profoundly evolved. The name itself recalls a photograph album that collects pre-existing pictures: its origins can be traced to collection different and already published songs, with no connections with one another. (Shuker 1998, 5).

But, as once Tom Waits said, "If you can put some songs all together on the same disc you can perceive them as a collection: they ultimately will develop a logic, even if you hadn't endowed them with that. It's like a group of people that just got off the bus, and they seem to be united on some type of a tour: you assume they have relationships" (Montandon 2005, 123-124). In other words, it is assumed that songs grouped and sequenced in a album have a narrative connection: the sequence becomes a small narrative plot even if there is not a real *fabula*.

In the second half of the '60s, a shift happened in the music industry and in consumption models: the importance of 7 inches singles—vinyls with one song per side or (or "45rpm", referring to the speed of 45 rounds per minute they needed to be played on turntables) began to diminish. Artists and bands began to focus on collection of songs written and recorded together: LPs ("Long playing") or 33rpm (they needed to be played at slower speed in order for the vinyl support of 12"to contain more music). Albums gave musicians the chance of a broader artistic expression and the industry more revenues: by the end of the decade they sold more than singles. 7" began to be used not only as stand-alone publications, but a songs distributed to promote the album which they came from (Shuker 1998, 271-273).

In a period when popular music needed cultural recognition, musicians turned to concept albums as means of expressions similar to consolidated narrative forms. They wanted to tell more complex stories and push forward the boundaries of a single song, and their narratives expanded from recorded music to theatrical performances on the stage, in movies, in videos and TV, and so on. They aimed at demonstrating that popular music was a cultural form comparable to literature, cinema, theatre, classical music: their first name was indeed "Rock operas", a clear reference to classical music.

The birth of the concept album is commonly associated with *Sgt. Pepper's Lonely Hearts Club Band* (1967). The Beatles's LP was not a concept album *per se*, but it had different interconnected elements that served as a narrative framing: the cover artwork depicting the characters; an introduction with a prelude in which one can hear sounds from a theater (voices, an orchestra tuning) and then a title-track that introduces the same characters. That song is reprised at the end before the last track, "A day in the life", which ends with the sound of tape rewinding to the start and then an outro with some voices looped backwards. John Lennon denied publicly in different interviews that band was not aiming at making a concept album, but the songs created narrative world that was more than the sum of the single parts.

From here on, artist began to produce albums as "operas", with a unifying concept. Album that have a concept, a unifying theme, telling a single story through connected songs like chapters of a novel, with recurring characters. Follero (2009, 103) has identified 5 models of concept albums:

1. *Thematic concept album*
   A group of songs develops around a single theme, from different angles, even without a narrative sequence.
2. *Literary concept album*
   Interconnected songs that aim a greater narrative dimension, inspired by a pre-existing literary or musical work, directly referenced and quoted.
3. *Semi-concept*
   A story or theme that often assumes the form of the suite, on only one side of the record.
4. *Instrumental concept album*
   No songs, but a conceptual plot that evolves only through music and melody with no lyrics
5. *Rock Opera with a dramatic structure*
   Songs that are interconnected with a precise dramatic structure: scenes, recurring characters and events.

Popular Music and Dystopian Tales: Pink Floyd

Far more than the space of this essay would be needed for a list, even an incomplete one, of concept albums produced in the late '60s and '70s. But names such as The Who, David Bowie, Genesis, Frank Zappa, King Crimson should at least be mentioned: these artists set their stories stories in dehumanized societies and dystopia was from one of popular music's preferred subject from the birth of concept albums. It has been a recurring way uses to express personal unease in an unfair and greedy society — a recurring and fundamental theme of popular music.

In this category there's a name that stands above the others: Pink Floyd. between 1973 and 1983 the band recorded and released five concept albums: "The Dark Side of the Moon" (1973), "Wish You Were Here" (1975), "Animals" (1977), "The Wall" (1979), and "The Final Cut" (1983).

Phil Rose (2015) notes that all this albums have dystopic elements: they are explorations of what he calls "anti-life pressures" in contemporary existence, such as corporate machinations, institutionalized and entertainment warfare, dehumanization of personal relationships, celebrity culture.

Rose, who uses a musicological approach, notes that what makes the concept albums of Pink Floyd both complex and popular is not necessarily the lyrics themes, but the music, the way the concept is represented in an aural dimension. But if the concept album is analyzed as a form complex *transmedia* storytelling, there is need to expand the point of view beyond songs and their inner lyrical and musical structures: what makes these albums interesting is the way their story has been powerfully told not only through recorded music, but constructing what Lori Burns (2016) calls a "transmedial storyworld" that integrates different forms of expression, including performance and audiovisual narrative. From this point of view, Pink Floyd were pioneers of music *transmedia* storytelling: popular music dystopian concept albums are not just fixed musical "texts", they are often rewritten with different means and media and updated over time with new technologies.

This is well exemplified by two albums by Pink Floyd, "Animals" (1977) and "The Wall" (1979). George Orwell's dystopic novels have been a constant source of direct and indirect inspiration for concept albums, from Bowie's "Diamond Dogs" (1974; the artist was denied the rights to adapt "1984" into music, but its still remained a huge influence to his work of the time) to Pink Floyd's "Animals" (1977). This album is loosely based on "Animal Farm": pigs, dogs and sheep are the characters used to represent a dehumanized society of extremized capitalism. Central to the storytelling was not only its famous cover, with a giant pig flying over London's Battersea Power Station, but also its *live* representation: the album was transformed into a performance with inflatable pigs flying over the audience. This albums also shows as concept albums are narrative rewritten and expanded with new technologies and linked to contemporary events: in 2017 and 2018 Roger Waters recreated the Battersea Power Station for the *Us + Them Tour*, with a giant structure that in arenas was hung up on the audience, while outdoor became a 80 meters backdrop for the stage; the songs and the concept were connected to contemporary events, such as Trump's presidency in the United States. This is another example of how a musical dystopian tale was updated both with new technology and content. "The Wall" (1979), on the other side, tells, the story of Pink, a rockstar that closes himself behind a wall to hide from an oppressive dystopian society. It not's just an album, though: it first became, in 1980, a stage performance in which a 12m wall built and then tore down before the audience. This representation of the wall grew bigger and bigger: It became a movie by Alan Parker in 1982 and has been brought on stage by Roger Waters alone several times: with 219 dates tour in 2010-2013 but more famously with a 1990 performance in Berlin, staged to celebrate the collapse of the real wall. These different adaptations have been documented in concert films shown in cinemas in the classical music adaptation "Another Brick in the Wall: The Opera" (2017-2018). Dystopian concept albums such as those by Pink Floyd are are never-ending stories, told through different media and technologies.

Contemporary Popular Music and Dystopian Tales: Coldplay and Muse

During the following decades, the concept album popularity expanded beyond rock music: many pop artist explored this model, often dwelling with dystopian themes and using new media spaces. For example, in 1981 MTV opened its programming with "Video killed the radio star" by Buggles, which was part of a dystopian concept album called "The plastic age" (1980). Concept album transcended music genres, from rock to hip-hop to pop to r'n'b: it was explored by divers artists such as Radiohead, Green Day, Kendrick Lamar, Jay-Z, Eminem, Björk, Beyoncé, Daft Punk, Nine Inch Nails, Janelle Monáe, just to name a few.

Two more recent big examples of transmedia storytelling of dystopian tales are Coldplay's "Mylo Xyloto" (2011) and Muse's "Drones" (2015). "Mylo Xyloto" is set in the dystopian world of Silencia, were a war against sound and color is happening, while Muse's "Drones" is set in a society were flying robots rule the world. As Lori Burns, notes, "The storyworld emerges in and through the totality of the materials, as individual parts focus on specific elements of the narrative. We do not receive the full narrative by means of the songs on the album, nor do we receive the complete story by means of the videos that were released or the comic book series. These parts of the whole work together, and rely upon multimodal, intermedial and transmedial storytelling strategies to build the complete storyworld" (Burns, 2016, 98-99) On one side, Coldplay's dystopic narrative, for example comprehends more than 50 different texts: 14 songs, 6 comics book, music videos, specific performances, singles and artworks. On the other side Muse's tale is augmented through videos, social media specific content and a world tour that featured flying drones over the audience — a reference to Pink Floyd's "Animals". In these and other cases, artwork, videos, performances are not just paratexts (Genette 1987) or "paraphonography", as musicologist Serge Lacasse (200) calls them, but central part of the storytelling as songs themselves: "Paraphonographic practices are a critical aspect of the reception and promotion of any popular music album, however in the case of a concept album, the paraphonographic materials can be considered as integral to the mediation of the conceptual theme, narrative, or persona of the work. Paraphonographic materials can take many forms and can function in relation to each other in a variety of ways. We can consider the artwork, graphics and texts that are available in print and digital media: album covers and liner notes, promotional materials and booklets that document the concert tour associated with the album, comic books and graphic novels, posters and clothing that feature images and graphics related to the album and tour. We can also include the film media that are developed for the concept album: music videos, concert footage, and documentary footage from the production of the album, video, or tour. In an expanded consideration of paraphonographic materials, I would also include the stage materials and design of the concert tour as an important vehicle to mediate the concept album" (Burns 2016, 96) This dystopic concept albums are *transmedia* stories, an evolution of the complex storytelling envisioned by rock operas in the 70's, augmented by today's tools and media.

Dystopian Concept Albums as a Complex Transmedia Narratives

So why are dystopic concept albums still relevant in popular music? The first reason is that popular music, especially the rock genre, is rooted in counter-culture and has historically given voice a to discomfort distress and to outcasts who don't see themselves represented in society and its dynamics (Shuker 2022). Concept albums are powerful way to address this social discomfort traditionally expressed by literature, cinema and series.

But there's more: through dystopic concept albums, music aims at putting itself on the same level as more consolidated and recognized cultural and narrative forms. Dystopian concept albums showcase the complexity of musical transmedia narratives and are historically used a proof the relevance of popular music in the media landscape. Concept albums show how music and media are inseparable: media studies should deal more with popular music and music studies should deal more with media. They are produced, distributed and consumed together. Music helps us understand media, and media help us understand music: and that is particularly true for dystopian concept albums.

References

Bonini Tiziano, and Gandini Alessandro. 2019. "First Week Is Editorial, Second Week Is Algorithmic": Platform Gatekeepers and the Platformization of Music Curation". *Social Media + Society*, 5(4): 1-11.

Burns Lori. 2016. "The Concept Album as Visual-Sonic- Textual Spectacle: The Transmedial Storyworld of Coldplay's Mylo Xyloto". *IASPM@Journal* vol.6 no.2: 91155

Brembilla Paola. 2019." Transmedia Music: The Values of Music as a Transmedia Asset". *The Routledge Companion to Transmedia Studies*, edited by Freeman, and Renira Rampazzo Gambarato. 82-89, New York/London: Routledge

Evans Elizabet. 2011. *Transmedia Television. Audiences, New Media, and Daily Life*. New York/London: Routledge,

Follero Daniele. 2009. *Concept Album*. Bologna: Odoya.

Genette Gerard. 1987. *Seuils*. Paris: Seuil.

Lacasse Serge. 2000. "Intertextuality and Hypertextuality in Recorded Popular Music. *The Musical Work: Reality or Invention?*, edited by Michael Talbot. 35-58. Liverpool: Liverpool University Press.

Montandon Mac. 2004. *Innocent when You Dream. The Tom Waits Reader*. New York: Thunder's Mouth Press.

Poell Thomas, and Nieborg David. B. 2018." The Platformization of Cultural Production: Theorizing the Contingent Cultural Commodity". *New Media & Society*, 20(11): 4275-4292.

Rose Phil. 2015. *Roger Waters and Pink Floyd: The Concept Albums*. Madison/Teaneck: Rowman & Littlefield.

Shuker Roy. 2022. *Popular Music Culture. The Key Concepts*. New York/London: Routledge.

Sibilla Gianni. 2003. *I linguaggi della Musica Pop*. Milano: Bompiani.

Build Your Own Dystopian Nightmare: The Case of Civilization VI

Andrea Piano

Introduction

Games can be viewed from a variety of angles. As a multidisciplinary field, game studies combine the perspectives of many other disciplines: semiotics, sociology, architecture, and even eco-nomics. Each approach brings a specific definition of "what a game is" and thus "what a game can (or cannot) do." Thus, games have been considered social activities (Huizinga 1949), texts (Aarseth 1997), processes (Bogost 2008b) and more. Despite these differences, games have been found to have an impact on players, as they can be used for learning, changing perspectives, and gathering information (Rollinger 2020; Squire 2006).

The ability of games to communicate or even persuade the player through procedural arguments has already been highlighted by scholars (Bogost 2008a; 2010; Frasca 2001; Schrape 2019). From this perspective, procedural rhetoric is the way games can argue about something by letting the player fill in the gaps between processes, instead of textual arguments. Often, the activities that the game allows players to engage in create the conditions for players to understand what is behind them.

One of the best-known examples of this practice is the game *Monopoly*. In this game, two to six players must compete for financial dominance. To achieve this, the game's mechanics force them to build real estate and—by doing so—extort money from opponents, in a capitalist scheme that eventually results in one player owning the most real estate while the others struggle financially.

Monopoly was conceived as a critique of capitalism (Dodson 2011). The rules of the game and the dynamics that emerge when players interact with each other are all means of conveying how dystopian a capitalist society can eventually become. In the same way, modern video games often have an underlying meaning, a connection between the processes they construct that can be seen as an argument for — or against — something.

Dystopia and Video Games

Video games and dystopias have a long relationship: *Space Invaders* (Taito 1978) is a game in which the player must defend planet Earth from a hostile alien invasion. Perhaps the ability of games to create safe spaces in which to experiment with speculative scenarios makes them a perfect medium for dystopian authors and designers.

Over the last twenty years, dystopian video games have proliferated. The *Fallout* series grew in popularity from game to game. *Bioshock* (Irrational Games 2007) set a precedent for combining audiovisual representations of dystopia with a procedural form of it (Hocking 2009). *The Last of Us* received very positive feedback, leading to a TV adaptation ("The Last of Us (TV Series) " 2023). Games such as *This War of Mine* (11 Bit Studios 2014), *Papers, Please* (3909 LLC 2013), and *Cyberpunk 2077* (CD Projekt RED 2020) have approached dystopias from different angles and perspectives.

However, video games sometimes even let players actively build their dystopias. The entire genre of "god games" sets the stage for this possibility: *Black & White* (Lionhead Studios 2001), Spore (Maxis 2008), and *Sim City* (Maxis 1989) are just a few examples of how video games allow players to plan and manage entire populations. These games have much in common: they all simulate societies and present the player with challenges — required for the game's playful component — that often require drastic solutions and lead to fairly dystopian outcomes.

In some cases, this is unintentional: designers simply implement the features that can sell more copies of their games. Sometimes this approach can hide something, or it can be seen as an argument against certain practices or processes. *Sid Meier's Civilization VI* (Firaxis Games 2016) may be an example of this: through its game mechanics, it highlights and procedurally argues against some dystopian aberrations of human progress and society.

Build Dystopias in Civilization VI

Sid Meier's Civilization (from now on *Civilization*) is one of the most influential and famous franchises in the history of video games. It was launched in 1991 as a turn-based strategy game and now counts more than a dozen iterations, including a board game, mobile games and several spin-offs. *Civilization VI* is the latest installment in the series and continues to be supported by the development team with new content and updates.

In *Civilization VI* the player takes control of a civilization from prehistory to the future. Over the course of the game, she must build a balanced system that will allow her to achieve a series of goals called victory conditions. Originally there were five victory conditions (Science, Culture, Domination, Religion, Points/Time), but with the *Gathering Storm* expansion (Firaxis Games 2019) a new one was introduced (Diplomacy).

Unlike *Monopoly*, there is no victory condition related to financial dominance. However, money is a common denominator shared by all possible objectives in *Civilization VI*. In the game, wealth is power: it allows the player to buy all sorts of resources, including land, military units, rare units, buildings and even more. Despite an initial disadvantage in terms of other resources, earning gold — and storing it wisely — can be the only way to keep up with other players. For example, if the player is unable to accumulate enough points to obtain a Great Prophet (a rare unit needed to establish a religion) for her civilization, this character can be bought with gold.

Another universal problem solver in this game is military strength. No matter what the player's goal, a strong army is always a good idea. Primarily because of the automatic attacks that both barbarians and AI-controlled opponents will conduct, but also because military strength is often the only leverage left when things get out of hand. If another player builds too many wonders, i.e., gives himself an advantage, a possible solution in the game is to conquer her territories and eventually annex them.

These premises show how the game inevitably leads to the creation of global dystopias, literally: a social condition in which great injustice prevails, often a totalitarian realm. The latter, in a sense, lies in the soul of *Civilization VI* and all the god games: in this genre, players play God and enforce their decisions on the non-playing characters portrayed. This paper, however, focuses on the first part: a social condition in which a great injustice prevails. created by the player in pursuit of the game's proposed goals

Only one player — or a coalition of players — can achieve a victory condition per game. This means that in each game there will always be defeated civilizations or different nations that will be subjugated to the dominant states in one way or another. The fact that the game does not allow peaceful coexistence between all civilizations triggers a competitive dynamic that leads to often hysterical or overly aggressive decisions by the players or the AI-controlled factions.

The result of this interaction between players is a world where famine, war, surveillance, corruption, and mass degradation are just some of the undesirable elements of daily life. Despite an apparent variety of final objectives, each victory condition requires competition and questionable decisions, and therefore forces the player to build a dystopian society. In the following sections of this contribution, all victory conditions and their dystopian effects will be examined in detail.

Science Victory

"The Science Victory is achieved by the first player to establish a colony on an extrasolar planet," reads the Civilopedia, an encyclopedia included with the game, where the player can often learn more about certain elements of the game. However, there are a few obligatory intermediate steps: launch a satellite, land a human on the Moon, and establish a Martian colony; only after achieving each of these objectives can the player launch an exoplanet expedition.

All these goals are called technologies in the language of the game: symbolic milestones of progress that each civilization can achieve as it expands and grows. They are represented as steps in a so-called technology tree, a branching roadmap of evolution built according to a deterministic approach. Technologies are used to unlock certain bonuses, units or buildings in the game. Each of them requires a certain amount of science to be "discovered".

Science, just like culture or gold, is a resource in the game. Thus, to achieve scientific victory, players must aim to collect as much science as possible per turn and eventually discover all necessary technologies before their opponents. Collecting science requires exploiting certain natural resources, building special infrastructures (campuses, universities, etc.), recruiting great scientists or building wonders that guarantee unique bonuses.

At some point during the simulation of human history in the game, it is almost necessary for the players to establish a working surveillance network over their opponents. Otherwise, opponents can exploit them and steal resources, including technologies. This mechanic allows the players to do the same by creating spies and sending them out to sabotage other civilizations: stealing technologies from opponents becomes a basic mechanism for scientific victory. Information is crucial in *Civilization VI*, and so are spies: the result is a world in which the leaders of each country try to exploit every weakness of their opponents to pursue their own goals and eventually prevail.

Scientific progress is also closely linked to military power. A scientific advance often translates into a stronger, more efficient army. After all, fighting tanks with arrows and sticks makes a big difference. Subjugating other players or free cities gives an advantage in the form of land that can be exploited, allowing for more science points per turn and creating a situation where a player begins to accumulate an advantage that grows exponentially over time.

Scientific victory could have been presented in many forms: the cure of all diseases, the elimination of world hunger, and many other goals that humanity imagines in utopian dreams to this day. *Civilization VI* instead encourages players to be the first to colonize a new space, dominate new lands and thus strengthen political and economic power. This also implies that Earth cannot be saved and that we will eventually be forced to find a new home.

This victory condition stems directly from the Western notion (Ilardi 2010) of colonization, frontier, and the conquest of space. It represents the space race at its best. Moreover, Science Victory almost explicitly aims to show a world in pain that must be abandoned for humanity to survive. A world that the player has helped to create through the game's mechanics.

Domination Victory

The victory condition "Domination" is probably the most dystopian of all. To fulfill it, the player must conquer the capital of every other civilization in the game. As simple as this may seem, it depends on certain key factors and resources: mostly land, science and gold. The more land the player conquers, the more resources she can collect. Scientific progress and financial power are, as we have noted, crucial elements of military growth.

Nevertheless, the victory condition "Domination" is easier to achieve than many others. If the player builds a strong army, she can take advantage of the game's snowball effect. Conquering a capital gives several resources — including ecological values — that are converted into new military strength. The more capitals conquered in succession, the larger the empire the player has built. Again, the advantage is ultimately exponential.

Interestingly, the player is not allowed to commit war crimes in the game — at least not explicitly — with one exception. In fact, the only atrocity allowed is nuclear war, which has also spawned some rather odd contradictions, such as Nuclear Gandhi (Alejski e Kowalska 2021). Atomic bombs are a great military advantage, but as expected, have devastating consequences. But even if the player does not use these weapons again, just the possibility of doing so is a great deterrent and leads to another simulation of the Cold War.

Culture Victory

Culture victory is probably the most difficult to achieve. This condition requires players to attract tourists to their civilization by generating high amounts of culture and tourism. Culture points work the same way as science points, leading to "civic progresses" that are very similar to technologies. They are also distributed on a branching roadmap that is almost identical to the one used for scientific progress.

This victory condition is very controversial. It stands — almost literally — for the cultural domination of one civilization over all others, as measured by tourist flows, which also implies a kind of economic hegemony. However, to attract tourists, players must fulfill some conditions (build wonders or train units) and collect certain resources, called Great Works. These objects are often masterpieces of art, music and writing, but also religious relics or archeological artifacts.

These important elements of the game are kept in palaces and museums and can be traded or even stolen. Conquering a city where Great Works are kept also allows players to take possession of them. Apart from the implications of this dynamic, which represents very clearly colonialism, the pursuit of cultural victory encourages the player to take over all the identity elements of other civilizations.

Religious Victory

Like the "Domination" victory, the religious condition requires the player to subjugate her opponents. In this scenario, however, the battles are not fought with weapons, they require faith. Religious victory is achieved when a player has a religion that eventually finds the most followers in the world. The first step towards this goal is obtaining a Great Prophet, a rare unit in the game whose only purpose is to establish a religion. Then the player must earn faith points by building temples, exploiting resources, and training religious units such as missionaries or apostles.

These units act as religious mediators: they can be sent out to convert a certain number of citizens to their religion. However, the game also lets such units fight against each other: religious battles are represented with thunder and lightning and have two outcomes: the losing unit dies, and the surrounding area receives a boost from the winning religion, while the losing one is weakened. The player can also ban other religions from his territories by creating inquisitors: stronger units with the ability to eradicate unwanted faiths.

Time and Score Victory

If a game goes on too long and no player achieves another victory condition, Civilization VI will rank the remaining active players and determine a winner based on their score. Points are calculated based on factors such as the number of wonders the player has built, the number of technologies they have discovered, the number of citizens, and much more. The game does not put any emphasis on the status of the population, the number of wars the player has fought, or the number of tribal villages defeated.

Diplomatic Victory

Diplomatic victory was introduced to the game in the *Gathering Storm* expansion (Firaxis Games 2019), and can be achieved by scoring 20 diplomatic points. These points can be earned through a variety of actions: some are credited to the player for supporting an opponent in times of need, for punishing an aggressive leader after a war, or for winning diplomatic resolutions, for example.

There are also ways to trade points and use cunning and deception to determine how they are awarded. By allying with the right nations, the player can prevent dangerous opponents from winning and reduce their diplomatic influence. Voting against carbon dioxide emissions to gain diplomatic points, for example, is a viable way to win the game and achieve diplomatic victory.

Conclusions

Sometimes video games give the player insight into our world. They offer perspectives and new information, and they can also change our perspective. Just as Monopoly tried to teach how dangerous capitalism can be, Civilization VI lets players learn how society can be distorted when nations try to take advantage of each other. Sid Meier's game simulates the random distribution of resources on the map that has influenced the history of the world as we know it. When resources are in short supply, the player must act, either diplomatically or by force.

The competition demanded by the rules of the game creates the conditions for a cruel race for supremacy, which in any case has dire consequences. Whether it is an attempt to reach for the stars or to impose the only true creed, players are encouraged to build dystopian worlds. The whole concept of the game, which emphasizes culture-based differences by featuring famous historical figures as leaders, is a way of saying that we are all different, in our cultures, goals, and philosophies of life.

However, by forcing players to fight each other in a variety of ways and suggesting that peaceful coexistence is not possible, Civilization VI takes a stand. It takes a stand on our society and the dystopian trajectory it may take if leaders continue to follow their individualistic interests. It is up to the players to recognize this, understand the procedural argument and finally interpret it.

References

11 Bit Studios. 2014. «This War of Mine». PC.

3909 LLC. 2013. «Papers, Please». PC.

Aarseth, Espen. 1997. Cybertext: *Perspectives on Ergodic Literature*. JHU Press.

Alejski, Jakub, e Elżbieta Kowalska. 2021. «How Gandhi Went Nuclear: Potentiality of Archiverse in Sid Meier's Civilization VI». *Studia Humanistyczne AGH*, fasc. 2: 7–21. https://doi.org/10.7494/human.2021.20.2.7.

Bogost, Ian. 2008a. «The Rhetoric of Video Games». In *The Ecology of Games: Connecting Youth, Games, and Learning*, a cura di Katie Salen, 117–40. The John D. and Catherine T. MacArthur Foundation Series on Digital Media and Learning. Cambridge, MA, USA: MIT Press.

Bogost, Ian. 2008b. *Unit Operations: An Approach to Videogame Criticism*. MIT Press.

Bogost, Ian. 2010. *Persuasive Games: The Expressive Power of Videogames*. MIT Press.

CD Projekt RED. 2020. «Cyberpunk 2077». PC.

Dodson, Edward J. 2011. «How Henry George's Principles Were Corrupted Into the Game Called Monopoly».

Firaxis Games. 2016. «Sid Meier's Civilization VI». PC. It. Civilization.

Firaxis Games. 2019. «Sid Meier's Civilization VI: Gathering Storm». PC. It. Civilization.

Frasca, Gonzalo. 2001. «Videogames of the oppressed: Videogames as a means for critical thinking and debate.» https://ludology.typepad.com/weblog/articles/thesis/FrascaThesisVideogames.pdf.

Hocking, Clint. 2009. «Ludonarrative Dissonance in Bioshock: The Problem of What the Game Is About». In *Well Played 1.0: Video Games, Value and Meaning*, 255–62. Pittsburgh, Pa.: ETC Press.

Huizinga, Johan. 1949. *Homo ludens*. G. Einaudi.

Ilardi, Emiliano. 2010. *La frontiera contro la metropoli. Spazi, media e politica nell'immaginario urbano americano*. Liguori.

Irrational Games. 2007. «Bioshock». PC.

Lionhead Studios. 2001. «Black & White». PC.

Maxis. 1989. «Sim City». PC.

Maxis. 2008. «Spore». PC.

Rollinger, Christian, a c. di. 2020. *Classical Antiquity in Video Games: Playing With the Ancient World*. London ; New York: Bloomsbury USA Academic.

Schrape, Niklas. 2019. «The Rhetoric of Game Space». In *Ludotopia: Spaces, Places and Territories in Computer Games*, a cura di Espen Aarseth e Stephan Günzel, 245–69. transcript Verlag.

Squire, Kurt. 2006. «From Content to Context: Videogames as Designed Experience». *Educational Researcher* 35 (8): 19–29. https://doi.org/10.3102/0013189X035008019.

Taito. 1978. «Space Invaders».

«The Last of Us (TV Series)». 2023. United States: HBO.

Part 5:
Catastrophic and Apocalyptic Imaginaries

Loving the Futures We Hate: The Ubiquity of Dystopias in Popular Culture[*]

Joe Trotta

Introduction

Dystopian themes are notably pervasive in today's popular culture. We typically encounter them via various modes of storytelling (e.g., literature/film/TV), as a central, often genre-defining setting for a narrative, but they also feature explicitly or implicitly in many other forms of cultural expressions, such as advertisements, board games, video games, fine art, graffiti, song lyrics, podcasts, and fashion, among others. Moreover, the power and appeal of the 'dystopia' construct are not confined by language, culture, time period, or creative medium. *Dystopia* as a theme has a malleable and transformative quality, evolving and allowing alignment with diverse social/political/cultural paradigms and artistic expressions, which can be articulated across a spectrum of platforms and formats in a truly transmedial fashion. These qualities are not limited to imaginative texts as there has been a noticeable rise the use of *dystopia/n* as a descriptor in non-fictional contexts, for example in news reportage, political discourse, science journalism, business/financial news, likely for its powerful rhetorical effect (among which is the so-called 'fear appeal', cf. McAlear, 2010; Panay, 2017).

The ever-evolving ways in which the concept of dystopia is used, along with the increasing popularity of dystopias in general, has attracted considerable attention from a broad spectrum of academic disciplines, including but not limited to media studies,

---

[*] This article is based on a keynote speech delivered at the international conference *Dystopian Worlds beyond Storytelling,* held in Milan, 15-16 September 2022. It follows the main points delivered in that speech, but it has since been revised and adjusted for its inclusion in this anthology. I extend my gratitude to the conference participants for their invaluable comments and suggestions.

politics, literature, linguistics, sociology, and cultural studies. This attention speaks to the importance of understanding what the meaning of a dystopia is and the role and impact of such themes in shaping our perception of reality and potentially our future.

Against this background, the primary objective of the present work is to scrutinize the term *dystopia/n*, assessing its substantive usage and questioning whether over-flexibility in its application to an expanding variety of imagined and real-life scenarios has caused a kind of semantic inflation, resulting in a depreciation, or 'bleaching' of its essential meaning. In doing so, the present study has two main parts:

First, I aim to provide a concise background and overview of the issue at hand, namely the coinage, meaning, development and application of the term *dystopian*. My aim is to be productively disruptive by challenging its ever-broadening use in academic work and in popular culture, in this manner prompting us to critically examine what we truly mean when we describe (or analyze) a work as *dystopian*. By questioning the normative boundaries we often unthinkingly draw around the term *dystopia*, the present work also invites a more rigorous and nuanced understanding. Has the term's current usage been broadened or inflated to the point at which it lacks substantive meaning? And if so, what are the implications of this dilution on our collective understanding and the discourse surrounding the topic?

Thereafter, the discussion shifts to our seemingly paradoxical attraction to dystopias. What lies beneath this drive us to repeatedly craft, disseminate, and engage with bleak visions of futures we ostensibly hate? No one-size-fits-all explanation can suffice, but in this section, I summarize and evaluate selected insights from both scholarship and popular discourse into our captivation with dystopian worlds, probing into the psychological and sociocultural dynamics that might help clarify our apparent fascination for such narratives.

Setting the Stage—from Ad Hoc Term to Literary Genre. Who Cares about Genres Anyway?

As the following sections will show, the word *dystopia* has evolved from an ad hoc, one-off expression to become a significant label in the broader landscape of genre categorization rooted in the fabric of 20th century literature. However, in an era where the usefulness of *genre* as a meaningful conceptual category can trigger heated scholarly debate, it is crucial to first discuss the problematic nature of genre categories, acknowledging the pitfalls but also offering a common-sense defense of genre classifications and their integral role in understanding how they frame dystopian works.

Skeptics questioning the validity of genre labels argue that genres are not insular, well-defined categories. Artistic works often transgress genre boundaries, blending elements of various genres in a single work, which casts genre classifications as subjective, misleading, inadequate, and therefore flawed and untenable.

Critiques of genre also center on the dismantling of fixed meanings and rigid boundaries typically associated with traditional genre classifications. Genre-theory critics question the power dynamics embedded within these classifications and underscore the interplay of reading, language, and intertextuality in shaping meaning. These viewpoints challenge the traditional notion of genres as possessing inherent meanings, positing instead that meaning is not embedded within the text, but is constructed through the act of reading. This notion unsettles conventional genre classifications predicated on the belief that texts within the same genre bear intrinsic similarities.

Other criticisms of genre classifications relate to how such classifications can perpetuate prevailing power hierarchies. They critique, for example, the favoritism shown to certain genres or the influence a text's genre classification exerts on its interpretation and valuation. Post-structuralist scholars like Roland Barthes (1974) highlight the critical role of language and intertextuality—the interplay among texts—in crafting meaning. This perspective further problematizes genre, as a text's meaning is not solely a function of its compliance with genre norms but is also shaped by its connection to other texts.

Postmodern and post-structuralist critiques, while illuminating the fluid nature of genres and the power dynamics inherent in their creation, do not inherently deem genre labels futile or discussions about their significance unfruitful (cf. Fish, 2021; Hutcheon, 2003; Jameson, 2007). Instead, they highlight the necessity for continuous critical examination of genre definitions and applications. Consequently, even within a post-structuralist framework, the genre concept can preserve its practicality, provided we admit its inherent adaptability and responsiveness to cultural shifts.

Considering the present study, genre is a valuable tool as it offers crucial insights into the historical and cultural milieu surrounding a work's creation. The surge in popularity of certain genres often mirrors societal anxieties or obsessions; the expansion of dystopian literature in the 20th and 21st centuries is of particular importance as it echoes widespread apprehensions about authoritarianism, technology, environmental degradation, and more.

Additionally, genre classifications allow academics to situate a piece of work within an expansive literary and historical tradition. Identifying a work as a 'dystopian' novel, a 'western' movie or a 'detective' series, for instance, allows us to contextualize it within a lineage of similar works, deepening our understanding of thematic, stylistic, and ideological evolution within that genre. In this way, genres also act as a convenient shorthand for discussing and comparing various works. Labeling a novel/film as a 'dystopian techno-thriller' instantly sets expectations about the work's setting, themes, and potential plot structure, enhancing efficient communication among readers, writers, and scholars.

In a similar fashion, genre classifications foster comparative and interdisciplinary studies, enabling scholars to examine various works through the genre lens, shedding light on diverse expressions and explorations of similar themes, settings, or character types across various texts and media.

Lastly, as new genres surface and existing ones morph, they create platforms for ongoing discussions and debates about these genres' meanings. Understanding genre conventions is crucial to appreciating contemporary works that subvert, blend, or evolve these conventions. Thus, genre studies is not a static field but a dynamic discipline that adjusts to cultural changes and artistic novelties. Acknowledging this allows for a more nuanced comprehension of genre hybridization and the socio-cultural factors propelling genre evolution.

Mapping the Territory: The Impossible Becomes Good and Good Leads to Bad

The terms *utopia* and *dystopia* are intrinsically linked in origin and evolution. When used to describe fictional narratives, some scholars even consider them as facets of one and the same genre (see, for example, Donawerth, 2013), distinguished primarily by perspective. Both often hinge on social criticism, and both often explore the balance between individual freedoms and the benefits of a structured and secure society. A comprehensive examination of their historical trajectories is beyond the ambit of this article (see Claeys, 2016 for an in-depth analysis), I instead outline the pivotal points in their evolution with a focus on *dystopia* as a genre descriptor, leaving any examination of utopia as a form of dystopia to further research. The overview that follows below is thus best understood as a sketch that aims to set the stage for more nuanced discussions in subsequent sections.

The term *dystopia* is commonly attributed to British philosopher John Stuart Mill during his 1868 parliamentary speeches in which he used the word in passing as an ad hoc way to describe Britain's future overpopulation issues. However, attested uses of the word can be traced further back in literary history, cf. Budakov (2010), who cites instances from as early as the 1740s. Regardless of the exact authorship and the precise date of its first use, *dystopia* is largely formed in contrast to its semantic analog *utopia*, a term first attested in English by Sir Thomas More in his 1516 fictional work, *Utopia*.

Though forever linked by their superficial similarities and analogous word formation, the semantic relationship between *utopia* and *dystopia* is not straightforward; More's *utopia* is a derived from the Greek prefix *ou-*, meaning 'not', and *topos*, meaning 'place' and thus literally signifies an 'unreal' or 'non-existent' place. More's fictional narrative served as a critique of his own society, using the utopian moniker as label for an unreachable, unrealistically idealized alternative[1] that served to underscore the flaws of his contemporary European society. *Dystopia*, on the other hand, is derived from the Greek prefix *dys-*, meaning 'bad', and *topos*, meaning 'place' and thus literally means 'bad place'. At the risk of pedantry and overstating the obvious, technically speaking, *dystopia* and *utopia* in their original, literal meanings are not antonyms, which raises the question of how 'bad place' came to be the antithesis of 'no place.'

In current English usage, the *utopia/dystopia* contrast makes some sense; in present-day dictionaries and usage guides, *utopia* is primarily defined as meaning 'an ideal place' (see, for example, Cambridge University Press, n.d.-a.; Literary Devices, n.d.-a.; Merriam-Webster, n.d.-a) which is a significant departure from More's original intention of signaling unattainability and non-existence[2]. But given the shift in meaning, then so far, so good—if the contemporary understanding of *utopia* is that it means 'good place', then a word which means 'bad place' is a logical antonym.

However, *dystopia* has also undergone a shift in meaning, a so-called 'semantic narrowing', and in present-day English the word is typically used and defined more specifically as a label to characterize societies marked by oppression, degradation, and the collapse of societal norms and values (for consistency, see again, Cambridge University Press, n.d.-b; Literary Devices, n.d-b.; Merriam-Webster, n.d.-b)—undoubtedly an antithesis to the now idealized concept of *utopia* but with a more specific meaning than simply 'bad place'. Thus, the evolution of *utopia* and *dystopia* in the cultural and

---

[1] In fact, before its publication, Thomas More referred to his book as *Nusquama*, which is Latin for 'nowhere.' It was only later that the title was changed to *Utopia*, possibly from a suggestion by Erasmus, who helped in the publication process (see Vieira (2010).

[2] Naturally, many dictionaries also include information about the original etymology of the word, but I take it as a matter of course that in current usage, its default meaning is a perfect or ideal place.

literary lexicon demonstrates their lexical dissonance and entrenched antithetical relationship, which is one of the essential factors that contribute to confusion about how the terms can be applied with academic rigor and precision.

Dystopia as a Literary Genre

It is difficult to accurately pinpoint the first attested usage of the word *dystopia* to describe literary works, but it is clear that in the 20th century, the semantically narrowed sense of *dystopia* had gained currency and the term had begun to signify something more specific than just a 'bad place'. Very clearly, in conjunction with the publication of influential works like Yevgeny Zamyatin's *We* (1924), Aldous Huxley's *Brave New World* (1932), and George Orwell's *1984* (1949)[3], *dystopia* as an identifiable, coherent genre label began to solidify (cf. Moylan, 2018). Because of the importance of these three works in establishing *dystopia* as a recognizable and specific genre label, these early works are henceforward referred to in this study as *proto-dystopias*.

I take it as a matter of course that dystopian themes existed before these works, I am merely emphasizing that the term *dystopian* crystalized as a genre label in connection with the above-mentioned proto-dystopias (which then, in turn, established a template for all future works which could be considered as belonging to this genre). The concept of a dystopian theme could, of course, be applied retroactively to stories written well before the novels of Zamyatin, Huxley and Orwell. For lack of a better term, this ex post facto application of the term could be referred to as 'retroactive categorization', i.e., a new genre or category is established and codified, then works that were produced before the creation of the genre label are recognized as fitting within that genre. This is quite common in literature, film, music, and other artistic fields, as our understanding of genres evolves and becomes more nuanced over time (cf. Altman, 1999; Fowler, 1982; James, 1995).

---

[3] Please note that for all the primary works, e.g. books, movies, TV series, etc., I do not provide bibliographical information at the end of this text. Please contact the author if more detailed information is desired.

So, while the term for a particular descriptive label for a genre may be relatively new, the ideas, themes, and styles that are characteristic of that genre can predate the term itself, leading to a retroactive categorization of a work, which in turn lends a new perspective and understanding of said work. In the case of utopian/dystopian narratives, one of the most cited examples of a precursor or forerunner of the dystopian genre is Plato's *Republic* (see Morrison, 2007). Other works could also be seen retroactively through the lens of dystopian storytelling such as the ancient Greek epic poem *Works and Days* by Hesiod, Lucian's *True History*, and perhaps the biblical *Book of Revelation* could conceivably be interpreted and analyzed as dystopian narratives. Additionally, and somewhat confusingly, even works published after the terms *utopia* or *dystopia* had entered the English lexicon, like Jonathan Swift's *Gulliver's Travels* (1726) and Jack London's *The Iron Heel* (1908), which were typically referred to as political satire previously, would eventually be seen as utopian/dystopian after the genre labels had gained currency (cf. Fromm, 1961; Houston, 2007).

What Characterizes a Dystopia?

Stated simply, our understanding of *dystopia* today is quite broad and can cover a variety of works, which I argue could lead to an unthinking depreciation and devaluation of the term. However, despite any cavalier post-structuralist attitude toward genre labels, there is reasonably high justification to treat three paradigmatic works as having indelibly shaped our collective understanding of the dystopian narrative: namely the proto-dystopias *We*, *Brave New World*, and *1984*. By first analyzing the narrative fabric of these foundational stories, one can distill the quintessential characteristics that typify these exemplars of dystopian fiction, generalize them, and then discuss any inflation in meaning that has accrued over time[4].

---

[4] For a concise and insightful overview of this topic, see Baccolini and Moylan, 2003.

One unmistakable feature is the oppression/suppression exerted by an authoritarian government or entity. In *We*, we witness a future society dominated by the One State, which regulates every facet of its citizens' existence. This suffocating control is visually represented by a city encapsulated in a mammoth glass dome. Similarly, *Brave New World* paints a vision of the World State that meticulously governs every stage of a citizen's life, from birth—or rather, 'decanting'—to death. *1984* introduces us to the Party, helmed by the enigmatic Big Brother, wielding unrelenting authority over Oceania, where even the slightest hint of dissent is brutally quelled.

Another commonality is the prevalent theme of dehumanization and the consequent loss of individuality. In *We*, this is evident in the practice of addressing citizens by numbers instead of names—a system that protagonist D-503 often lauds for its precision. *Brave New World* offers a bleak vision where the Bokanovsky process churns out identical individuals, and a caste system is strictly adhered to. This, coupled with the ubiquitous use of the drug 'soma,' ensures a population devoid of emotions and individual desires. Meanwhile, *1984* presents a society where personal bonds and emotional connections are systematically eradicated. All forms of love and loyalty, save for those directed at Big Brother, are considered treachery.

The control of information is also a key feature in these works; this control can take various forms, but is primarily exercised through surveillance and/or propaganda. *We* projects a society where the One State's vigilance is inescapable; homes crafted from transparent glass leave no room for privacy. The Benefactor and his clandestine police force are ever-vigilant against state dissenters. While *Brave New World* may not employ traditional surveillance tactics, the state ensures compliance through conditioning and 'Hypnopaedia' from an early age. Contrastingly, '1984' is a nightmare of constant scrutiny. Telescreens are ubiquitous, and the Thought Police's watchful gaze ensures unwavering allegiance to Party mandates. The narrative also introduces us to the Ministry of Truth, which alters every media form to perpetuate the Party's propaganda, thereby manipulating public perception.

I am suggesting here that dystopian narratives are anchored by these core features which may be present to varying degrees, but numerous secondary elements offer depth and nuance to the genre, providing readers a spectrum to gauge the degree to which a work can be deemed dystopian. The features/themes that follow here are not organized in any particular order, nor is this intended to be an exhaustive list.

The setting of a dystopian narrative is often a future society or an alternate universe. In these ostensibly 'alienized', but relatably parallel settings, current societal trends can be extrapolated to their grimmest extremes. It is not uncommon for these societies to masquerade initially as paradises—false utopias—only for their deep flaws or oppressive natures to be unveiled as the narrative unfolds.

The time frame for these tales frequently leans towards the future. This projection serves a dual purpose—it is distant enough to envisage substantial societal or technological shifts, yet proximate enough to echo eerily familiar parallels with the present world. This balance ensures that readers remain uncomfortably anchored in the reality of the tale.

The protagonist is typically an average individual who is grappling with the unsettling truths of their society, nurturing seeds of dissent or rebellion against the oppressive status quo. Conversely, the antagonist often embodies an oppressive force, be it in the form of a singular dictator, entities such as governments, corporations, religious groups, etc., or simply suffocating societal norms.

With the above-noted loss of individuality, there is typically an emphasis on uniformity, pitting societal expectations of conformity against individual desires for autonomy. This friction frequently births pockets of resistance, in which characters dare to defy the dominant structures, even if it is a perilous endeavor.

Advanced and/or unfettered technology commonly plays a role in dystopian narratives, but this may be expressed in a number of ways. For example, it can emerge as the catalyst for unforeseen repercussions that spiral societies into dystopia, as seen in narratives like *Snowpiercer*. Alternatively, it can play a role as a potent tool in the hands of the oppressors, utilized for surveillance, control, or punishment. Such technology-driven dominance often gives rise to stark social disparities, creating a landscape where power and wealth are concentrated among a privileged few, reminiscent of worlds portrayed in *Altered Carbon* and *Elysium*.

As regards aesthetics, the dystopian universe often oscillates between two extremes: the sterile, monochromatic rigor of uniformity, or the chaotic decay of a post-apocalyptic world. This visual representation often dovetails with the narrative's tone, predominantly somber and desolate, though punctuated by fleeting glimmers of hope.

Prototypicality and the Relevance of Hammers in Fiction

The preliminary set of the defining features of dystopias, as outlined above, offers an intentionally idealized and neat list of criteria. Yet, as acknowledged above, the boundaries of genres are known to be porous, which requires some flexibility in how we understand the term and its application. While some works may encompass recognizable dystopian features to varying degrees, they might also combine with elements from other genres. As such, a work of fiction might include dystopian elements or themes without squarely fitting the mold of a 'dystopian novel' in the strictest sense, like in the case of works such as *2001: A Space Odyssey*, in which one might see the setting as a 'bad place' along with the AI character HAL as potentially a commentary on the dangers of technology and surveillance,. However, there is no oppressive society, no systematic dehumanization and ultimately, the story is more about humanity's potential and destiny than about a degraded future society.

Taking a brief detour into cognitive linguistics, the concept of a 'prototype' stands out as particularly relevant in this context. A prototype represents the most typical example within a category. For instance, when contemplating the term *bird*, one might envision a sparrow before a penguin, despite both rightfully being birds. This inclination stems from the fact that sparrows align more aptly with our generalized view of birds, as they exhibit the most common characteristics we associate with the category, as was most famously noted in Rosch (1973) and is echoed in other major works like Lakoff (2008) and Taylor (2003).

Drawing parallels back to literary genres, a similar argument can be posited. Just as there are quintessential representations of birds and their less typical counterparts, fiction too houses both prototypical dystopian works and those that diverge. Classic fictions like George Orwell's *1984* or more contemporary narratives like Margaret Atwood's *The Handmaid's Tale*, Susan Collin's *The Hunger Games* or Veronica Roth's *Divergent*, sit firmly as hallmark dystopian tales. They resonate with the well-known attributes of the genre: suppressive societies, curtailed individual freedoms, and rampant dehumanization[5].

Conversely, works that only weave in some dystopian elements could be perceived as less characteristic of the genre. For example, Cormac McCarthy's novel *The Road* is considered by many to be a dystopian narrative — while it has some of the features of a dystopian tale (most of which are those that frequently overlap with post-apocalyptic stories, see Trotta, 2019), its status as a dystopian work is not clear-cut. The setting of *The Road* is a dismal 'bad place' for sure and there is dehumanization in abundance, but it lacks oppression by a regime or entity (the oppression in *The Road* is the result of cataclysmic events). In content, it is more focused on the intimate relationship between the father and son, their love, and their survival rather than the overarching societal critiques typically present dystopian fiction.

Classifying a work as dystopian mirrors the challenge of using labels that are scalar in nature, as is the case if we designate someone as 'tall.' While scalar descriptors like these have clear extremes — most would concur when someone is decidedly tall or decidedly not tall — the intermediary points on the spectrum blur. Just as there is ambiguity about what height range qualifies as 'medium tall' or 'somewhat tall,' determining the exact degree to which a narrative embodies dystopian qualities can be subjective and open

---

[5] Some scholars, like Moylan (2018) might reserve the term 'critical dystopias' for those works that are closer to the prototype.

to interpretation. This inherent fuzziness underscores the complexity of such categorizations[6].

Pushing these comparisons further, consider how big a subset of dystopian features would be sufficient to label a work as dystopian. For example, if we collected every story that includes a hammer, we would not have a genre of 'hammer fiction', but if we collect every book about an oppressive society, we may have a core of stories that will include 'dystopia' but this will be to varying degrees. Just as the mere presence of a hammer in a story does not make it hammer fiction, the presence of dystopian elements does not automatically make a story a dystopian work. It is the centrality and significance of these elements to the narrative, as well as their interaction with other thematic and stylistic elements, that determine whether the label of 'dystopian ' is appropriate and to what extent it can be used meaningfully.

Approaching dystopia as a scalar concept or as a construct that conforms more or less with a prototype illuminates the diversity and depth of narratives that employ dystopian themes. While some works may use dystopian motifs more superficially and symbolically, merely as a backdrop for action or drama, others may plunge readers into the heart of societal decay, emphasizing the need for precise definitions and academic discrimination as to how closely a story adheres to the prototypical characteristics of dystopian fiction. This spectrum emphasizes that genre classifications, like 'dystopian', are not rigid boxes; they are fluid categories subject to interpretation and context. Authors may weave in dystopian elements to critique real-world issues or subvert genre norms. As such, understanding and classifying a work's dystopian attributes becomes a nuanced task, blending subjective judgment and context. Scholars must discern how closely a story aligns with prototypical

---

[6] The concepts discussed here bear resemblance to the notions of **crisp sets** and **fuzzy sets** in set theory. While a crisp set has a clear boundary, defining whether an element does or does not belong to the set, a fuzzy set allows degrees of membership, meaning that an element can belong to the set to a certain extent, rather than absolutely. This idea of graded membership challenges traditional binary categorizations and can be applied to numerous fields beyond mathematics, such as linguistics, artificial intelligence, and social sciences. See Zadeh (1965) for the seminal, foundational paper on this topic.

dystopian characteristics and, ideally, clarify their criteria, deepening the discourse on the genre's significance and its myriad manifestations.

It is precisely the complexity and variability outlined here that make the concept of dystopia so rich and interesting. Discussion about what constitutes a dystopia, and which works should be classified accurately as dystopian are necessary and will typically mirror the dynamism and diversity of artistic works themselves. Indeed, even though I make the case that our understanding of the dystopian genre was lastingly influenced by the proto-dystopias of Zamyatin, Huxley and Orwell, the concept is not inherently rooted in a historically static set of texts or practices. Rather, its nature and boundaries shift over time and are, to some extent, shaped by the very act of theoretical examination. The need for academic discussion on these topics is further accentuated by the fact that various theoretical perspectives often zoom in on specific facets of the dystopian concept, thus adding layers of complexity to its definition and understanding.

Why Do We Love These Futures We Hate?

It is not surprising that dystopian narratives capture our attention; at their best they are entertaining, thought-provoking and resonate with relevant social issues. It is a genre that challenges readers, making it an engaging, immersive, and stimulating form of storytelling that blends the familiar with the foreboding. At their core, dystopias grapple with quintessential existential queries found in all great literature, but against a more dramatic, attention-grabbing background. They ponder the essence of identity, the dynamics of societal belonging, the intricacies of free will, and the delicate equilibrium between individual liberty and collective security. Such themes tap into our intrinsic human need for self-understanding and societal placement. As with any examination of what is popular at any given time, there is no one-size-fits-all explanation for exactly why audiences are drawn to it, but rather it discussed below as a confluence of numerous factors, some apparent and others more subtle.

Starting with a relatively superficial observation, excitement and escapism are clearly a part of the appeal of many dystopian stories. Despite their bleakness, dystopian narratives often feature thrilling plots with high stakes, action, and suspense, which can be entertaining and gripping for readers. At the same time, the drastically different imagined worlds or societies provide a form of escapism, despite their typically grim nature. In this way, some dystopian stories have strong similarities with action stories and thrillers (e.g., *The Maze Runner* or *Altered Carbon*), while others, though less cinematic in their action are equally tense in plot (e.g., *The Handmaid's Tale* or *The Giver*).

In both popular and academic spheres, the appeal of dystopian fiction is often attributed to its ability to reflect and amplify societal fears and anxieties relevant to its time. Whether it is rooted in concerns over technology as depicted in Lang's *Metropolis* or Gibson's *Neuromancer*, pandemics in Saramago's *Blindness* or Flynn's *The Companions*, the threat of climate change as in Butler's *The Parable of the Sower* or Lob's graphic novel *Snowpiercer*, or fears of extremist ideologies seen in Zamyatin's *We* or Atwood's *The Handmaid's Tale*, these narratives tap into the zeitgeist, reflecting societal evolution, existential anxieties, technological advancements, or prevailing ideological trends.

As a natural consequence of dystopia's reflection of societal anxieties, they are particularly well-suited vehicles for socio-political commentary (cf. Moylan, 2018)[7]. Positioned as both protest and forewarning, dystopias can critique societal architectures, compelling audiences to reevaluate the world around them and inspire audiences to recognize and take action to rectify real-world challenges. Setting these narratives in speculative futures or alternate (but relatable) realities facilitates critiques that remain abstracted from direct censure of contemporary political entities, thus avoiding immediate controversy.

---

[7] Naturally, a narrative that reflects social anxieties about technological overreach can simultaneously critique the political and corporate entities enabling this scenario. However, the distinction lies in the primary focus and intent of the narrative. While one might primarily aim to mirror societal feelings, the other seeks to interrogate the structures creating those feelings.

Some analysts relate the popularity of dystopias with the general popularity of Young Adult (YA) fiction as this genre is undeniably well represented in YA literature (consider the enormous success of *The Hunger Games* as well as other YA dystopias like Marie Lu's *Legend* trilogy or Scott Westerfeld's *Uglies* series, among many others). YA dystopias appeal to young adult audiences as they metaphorically reflect the transitional phase of adolescence, where one begins to critically question societal norms and parental authority. This stage in life can sometimes feel oppressive, as young people navigate the rules and structures placed upon them by parents, teachers, and society. Hence, the authoritarian regimes seen in dystopian societies may resonate strongly with this demographic, as they too are seeking to understand their place in the world. These stories mirror their struggles, validate their experiences, and encourage them to question the status quo and inspire them to believe in their potential to effect change. Themes like inequality, corruption, environmental degradation, and loss of privacy are presented in exaggerated settings, allowing young readers to engage with these complex issues without the discomfort of addressing them directly in their current reality.

Despite their grim settings, many dystopian stories feature elements of hope and resistance. Protagonists often fight against their oppressive circumstances, providing the audience with someone to root for. The struggle against a dystopian society can highlight the power of human spirit, courage, and determination, which can be inspiring to readers. Young adults in particular, often full of idealism and a strong sense of justice, can resonate with the themes of resistance and rebellion against oppressive systems found in dystopian literature. They are often at a stage in their lives where they are developing their own political and moral beliefs. Seeing characters fight against injustices can inspire young readers and foster a sense of activism.

In line with themes of hope and resistance in dystopian fiction is the recurring trope of the 'ordinary hero' (such as, for example, Guy Montag in *Fahrenheit d451* or Theo Faron in *Children of Men*). The portrayal of commonplace protagonists struggling against formidable odds resonates among audiences in general, but especially among younger ones. Eschewing the extraordinary abilities characteristic of superheroes, these figures exemplify that true courage emanates from choices, determination, and moral integrity, rather than innate powers. This paradigm can inspire readers, suggesting that heroism is within everyone's grasp.

A more speculative (and to my knowledge overlooked) explanation for the popularity of dystopian themes is the so-called 'negativity bias' of human psychology (see Baumeister et al., 2001 for a robust discussion of this concept). This is the idea that we are wired to pay more attention to negative experiences than positive ones as a survival mechanism. We, as humans, are future-oriented and we are naturally inclined to be curious and concerned about what lies ahead, and dystopias tap into this forward-looking disposition. Together with this forward-looking inclination, the negativity bias suggests that our ancestors needed to be hyper-aware of potential threats in their environment in order to survive and pass on their genes. Applying this concept to storytelling, we might be inherently more drawn to narratives that depict danger, conflict, and adversity, like those found in dystopian stories. These narratives stimulate our sense of threat and risk, engaging our attention more effectively than utopian narratives might. Dystopian stories allow us to engage with worst-case scenarios in a safe environment, exercising our problem-solving skills and allowing us to mentally prepare for potential real-life crises.

The popularity of the dystopian construct it is not solely a result of its intrinsic features, cultural trends or its appeal to human psychology, but is also a product of market dynamics and industry practices. The entertainment industry, like other sectors, operates within a market system where supply responds to demand. When a particular work, such as *The Hunger Games* or *The Handmaid's Tale*, becomes a commercial success, it signals a strong market demand for that genre or style of storytelling. Industry producers are thus incentivized to create more works that align with this demonstrated preference.

In connection with any successful franchise, imitation and derivation will naturally come into play. Following a major success, studios, publishers, and other content creators often seek to replicate that success by producing works that mimic the successful formula. This leads to a proliferation of similar works, which can give the impression that a certain genre or theme has suddenly risen in popularity. The release of the *Divergent* series following the success of *The Hunger Games* is an apt illustration of this phenomenon. This process of imitation and derivation also serves to reinforce the popularity of the genre. As more similar works are produced and consumed, audiences become more familiar and comfortable with the genre conventions, creating a self-reinforcing cycle of demand. This process continues until the genre becomes oversaturated, at which point audience interest might begin to wane, and a new trend could take its place. While this process of mimicking a popular formula often leads to the production of derivative works, it can also spur innovation within the genre. Creators seeking to capitalize on a trend might experiment with genre conventions, blend genres, or introduce fresh narrative approaches in an attempt to stand out within a crowded market. This can lead to the evolution of the genre and the emergence of sub-genres, keeping the genre dynamic and preventing it from stagnating.

The commercial trajectories of the dystopian construct, its potential for screen adaptations, and even associated merchandise can bolster a genre's visibility. The staggering success of *The Hunger Games trilogy* and its subsequent film versions underscore how these market forces can elevate and broaden the reach of dystopian tales, which leads us to the role of transmediality in accounting for the popularity of dystopias. If a dystopian book becomes a bestseller, there is a market incentive for creators in other media to build upon that narrative. If consumers are fascinated by dystopian themes and eager to explore them in different media, this demand drives the creation of more diverse and widespread dystopian content. For example, a novelist might write a dystopian book; a filmmaker might adapt that book into a movie; this may inspire a TV series, a play or or a podcast; a graphic novel may reinterpret the story; a game developer might then create a video game grounded in the book and the wider universe of the narrative, and so on and so on.

At first blush, expansive, multi-platform variants of dystopian narratives can appear to be the result of a premeditated design. However, much like the so-called 'invisible hand' in economics, it's an organic outcome shaped by a confluence of individual creators, consumers, cultural trends, and market forces. This decentralized, emergent dystopian construct, guided by the collective self-interest of myriad stakeholders, attests to the adaptive and expansive nature of dystopian themes in our contemporary culture. Particularly important to the present discussion is the ways in which dystopian themes have undergone a kind of commodification. Dystopia, in essence, has become a commercial, saleable construct and a useful tool in the art of persuasion. The apprehensions and anxieties it builds on are powerful emotional levers that can be exploited in non-fictional contexts by actors such as marketers, politicians, journalists, religious leaders and social commentators in general, among others.

In direct ways, consumers buy into the allure of dystopian-themed entertainment, be it through books, video games, TV series, or even themed live events. This is direct since the commodification is based on a marketings strategy in which there is an assumption that promoting a work as dystopian will generate sales. Indirectly, familiarity with dystopian tropes and/or any semiotic/aesthetic features associated with this genre can be used to persuade or garner attention in other kinds of discourse and even in the marketing of unrelated products. A noteworthy instance is Apple's 1984 Super Bowl commercial, in which Apple used the imagery of a dystopian society to position its product as a tool of liberation and individual empowerment against a monolithic, oppressive regime represented by its competitors, presenting itself, of course, as a beacon of hope and resistance (cf. Van Den Berg, 2012; and, in connection to other tech products, Jung et al., 2021). Another example can be seen in the field of environmental and sustainable products, where the fear of a dystopian future due to climate change and environmental degradation is used to promote products that are 'eco-friendly', 'sustainable', or 'green' (cf. Gunster, 2004).

The commodification of dystopia in popular culture, particularly in film and literature, has made the term and its connotations widely recognizable. This broad familiarity with dystopian themes makes it a powerful rhetorical tool, especially in political discourse. A full examination of this phenomenon is beyond the scope of this study, but rather a few common patterns will suffice here. For eampple, a politician might present a rival's policy proposal as leading to a dystopian future to galvanize opposition against it. Dystopian constructs can be employed to suggest that a particular action or policy, even if seemingly benign or minor, could set society on a path to a dystopian future. This is the classic 'slippery slope' argument, where one event supposedly inevitably leads to a cascade of negative outcomes. Politicians can use dystopian rhetoric to idealize the past and present the current or future situation as bleak or dystopian. This can be especially effective in nationalist or populist campaigns that hinge on the idea of returning to a golden age. Additionally, dystopian narratives in popular culture often simplify complex societal issues into clear-cut battles between good and evil. Politicians can use this black-and-white thinking to reduce nuanced policy debates to simple dichotomies where they represent the 'good' or 'right' choice and their opponents represent the path to dystopia. Lastly, when a politician's warnings echo themes familiar from popular movies, books, or TV shows, it can make their messages more resonant and compelling; consider, for example, how words/phrases like *Orwellian, big brother, newspeak, thought police* as well as visual or implied references to *The Handmaid's Tale* can be used astutely by politicians and activists.

Ultimately, while the commodification of dystopia can be an effective tool for selling products, promoting ideas, and supporting political agendas, it is important to question how it affects our perception and understanding of dystopias and the potency of the concept. Does it trivialize the meaning of the term and thus minimize serious social and environmental concerns? Or does it raise awareness and drive action?

Summary and Final Remarks

As we continue to engage with, produce, and study dystopias, it is imperative to approach them with a discerning lens. The ever-growing and increasingly multidisciplinary academic interest further underscores the genre's enduring importance, but also raises questions about the currency of terminology and the parameters of genre classification. In presenting this 'disruptive' discussion about the essential meaning of *dystopia*, it has not been my goal to discourage new understandings of the term, but rather to stress the importance of recognizing the layers of meaning involved, the legacy of the word, and the implications of its broadened application. The discussion about what constitutes a dystopia and why we are fascinated by this topic is far from over, but continuous examination of the term along with scholarly precision and careful consideration about how we apply it, are vital to ensure that the concept of 'dystopia' maintains its relevance and efficacy.

References

Altman, Rick. 1999. Film/genre. *British Film Institute*.

Baccolini, Raffaella, and Tom Moylan. 2003. Introduction. Dystopia and histories. In *Dark horizons: Science fiction and the dystopian imagination* (pp. 1-12). London-New York: Routledge.

Barthes, Roland. 1974. s/z (R. Miller, Trans.). New York: Hill and Wang.

Baumeister, Roy. F., Ellen Bratslavsky, Catrin Finkenauer, and Kathleen D. Vohs. 2001. "Bad is stronger than good". *Review of general psychology*, 5(4), 323-370.

Budakov, Vesselin M. 2010. Dystopia: an earlier eighteenth-century use. *NOTES AND QUERIES-NEWARK NJ-OXFORD UNIVERSITY PRESS-*, 57(1), 86-88.

Cambridge University Press. (n.d-a). Utopia. In *Cambridge Dictionary*. Retrieved September 6, 2023, from https://dictionary.cambridge.org/us/dictionary/english/utopia

Cambridge University Press. (n.d.-b). Dystopia. In *Cambridge Dictionary*. Retrieved September 6, 2023, from https://dictionary.cambridge.org/us/dictionary/english/dystopia

Claeys, Gregory. 2016. *Dystopia: a natural history*. Oxford: Oxford University Press.

Donawerth, Jane. 2013. Genre blending and the critical dystopia. In *Dark horizo Dark horizons: Science fiction and the dystopian imagination* (pp. 29-46). London-New York: Routledge.

Fish, Stanley. 2021. Is there a text in this class?. In *Campus wars* (pp. 49-56). London-New York: Routledge.

Fowler, Alastair D. S. 1982. Kinds of literature: An introduction to the theory of genres and modes. *(No Title).*

Fromm, Erich. 1961. Afterword in 1984. ORWELL, George. *Nineteen Eighty Four.* Florida: The New American Library.

Gunster, Shane. 2004. "'You belong outside': Advertising, nature, and the SUV". *Ethics and the Environment, 9*(2), 4-32.

Houston, Chloe. 2007. "Utopia, dystopia or anti-utopia? Gulliver's Travels and the Utopian mode of discourse". *Utopian Studies, 18*(3), 425-442.

Hutcheon, Linda. 2003. *A poetics of postmodernism: History, theory, fiction.* London-New York: Routledge.

James, Edward. 1995. *Science fiction in the 20th century.* Oxford: Oxford University Press.

Jameson, Fredric. 2007. *Archaeologies of the future: The desire called utopia and other science fictions.* London: Verso.

Jung, Jaesuk, Jihye Yu, Yuri Seo and Eunju Ko. 2021. "Consumer experiences of virtual reality: Insights from VR luxury brand fashion shows". *Journal of Business Research, 130,* 517-524.

Lakoff, George. 2008. *Women, fire, and dangerous things: What categories reveal about the mind.* Chicago: University of Chicago press.

Literary Devices. (n.d.-a). Utopia — Examples and Definition of Dystopia as a Literary Device. Retrieved September 6, 2023, from https://literarydevices.net/utopia/

Literary Devices. (n.d.-b). Dystopia — Examples and Definition of Dystopia as a Literary Device. Retrieved September 6, 2023, from https://literarydevices.net/dystopia/

McAlear, Rob. 2010. "The value of fear: Toward a rhetorical model of dystopia". *Interdisciplinary Humanities* 27 (2): 24-42.

Merriam-Webster. (n.d.-a). Utopia. In Merriam-Webster.com dictionary. Retrieved September 6, 2023, from https://www.merriam-webster.com/dictionary/utopia

Merriam-Webster. (n.d.-b). Dystopia. In Merriam-Webster.com dictionary. Retrieved September 6, 2023, from https://www.merriam-webster.com/dictionary/dystopia

Morrison, Donald. 2007. The Utopian Character of Plato's Ideal City. In Giovanni R. F. Ferrari (Ed.), *The Cambridge Companion to Plato's Republic* (Cambridge Companions to Philosophy, pp. 232-255). Cambridge: Cambridge University Press. doi:10.1017/CCOL0521839637.009

Moylan, Thomas. 2018. *Scraps of the untainted sky: Science fiction, utopia, dystopia*. London-New York: Routledge.

Panay, Andrew. 2017. "Fear appeal construction in the Daily Mail online: A critical discourse analysis of Prime Minister Corbyn and the 1000 days that destroyed Britain". *Critical Approaches to discourse Analysis across Disciplines*, 9(1), 45–62.

Rosch, Eleanor H. 1973. "Natural categories". *Cognitive psychology*, 4(3), 328-350.

Taylor, John R. 2003. *Linguistic categorization*. Oxford: Oxford University Press.

Trotta, Joe. 2019. "A corpus-informed study of apocalyptic/dystopian texts". In *Broken Mirrors* (pp. 179-201). London-New York: Routledge.

Van Den Berg, Thijs. 2012. Nineteen Eighty-Four and "1984": Apple's Use of Dystopian Poetics in iCommodification. *Journal of literature and Science*, 5(1), 98-124.

Vieira, Fàtima. 2010. "The concept of utopia". *The Cambridge companion to utopian literature*, 3-27.

Zadeh, Lofti A. 1965. "Fuzzy sets". *Information and control*, 8(3), 338-353.

Dystopia in Your Eyes! Retro-Mediation as Retroactive Remediation of Pandemic Visual Imaginaries

Mario Tirino and Lorenzo Denicolai[1]

Introduction

Various novels, films and TV series have imagined a future in which viruses have mowed down mankind, altering the structures of contemporary Western societies. In some ways, therefore, the COVID-19 pandemic could be experienced as the reversal of a dystopian future turned into concrete everyday reality. The COVID-19 pandemic is classifiable as a 'total social fact' (Mauss 1924), since it reconfigures all the rites of passage of human beings and all spheres of social action. The pandemic produces visual imaginaries (Pintor Iranzo 2020), organised around objects such as masks, disinfectant gels, syringes containing vaccines, and practices such as disciplining access (the queue), immunisation, sanitisation.

Starting with the concept of premediation (Grusin 2004, 2010), our paper intends to reflect on a new media logic, which we call *retro-mediation*. Retro-mediation is shaped by the forces of premediation. The latter are produced both by the narratives that prefigured the pandemic, and by the daily rituals of institutional and mainstream communication. Premediation contains and fuels anxiety about the management of the pandemic: in this way, it fosters emotional alertness and constant familiarity with the visual cultures of the virus.

Retro-mediation can be defined as a media logic of reimagining the past. On the basis of the reversal of dystopia in the present, it operates as retroactive remediation, through which users project

---

[1] The text was conceived jointly by the two authors. Lorenzo Denicolai wrote paragraphs 1 and 4, Mario Tirino wrote paragraphs 2 and 3. The paragraph 'Introduction' was written jointly by the two authors.

symbols, icons and dystopian symbols, icons and elements. Thus, retro-mediation can be conceived as the embodiment of a mass dystopian gaze on pre-pandemic cultural products, experienced in the light of the emotional experience of viral catastrophe and its aesthetics.

1. The COVID-19 Media Era

In these last years, humankind has known a particular condition: it has had to face a pandemic with direct and indirect consequences on everyday life. Studies from different scientific areas have illustrated how COVID-19 has changed our experience in many areas, from education to work, from health (physical and psychological) to social relations, not forgetting political and economic aspects, both locally and globally[2].

Moreover, periods of lockdown and social distancing have inevitably also contributed to changes in our relationship with the media experience: technology has become a viable alternative to human contact and a helpful tool for overcoming prohibitions dictated by the emergency, as well as having assumed an essential role in educational and professional dynamics. This general condition has thus affected media consumption, the relative increase in problems associated with such an abundance of use (Boursier *et al.* 2020), but also a gradual increase in the media use to create content and to reorganize the fabric of cultural business (Flore *et al.* 2021; Khlystova *et al.* 2022). In this context, we hypothesized that COVID-19 also influenced the development of a media and social imaginary capable of influencing everyday life and fostering a reinterpretation of audiovisual fiction that users enjoyed in the months following the pandemic condition. In this way, it is possible to attribute particular objects and 'signs' a different meaning than the original one, declining them in the direction of the pandemic. This contribution, therefore, seeks to attempt to introduce this dynamic, to which we have given the name of *retro-mediation*, drawing on media theories,

---

[2] See Chakraborty 2020; Ratten 2020; Osofsky *et al.* 2020; Singh and Singh 2020; Cuce *et al.* 2021; Shaw *et al.* 2021; Devoe *et al.* 2022; Rossette-Crake and Buckwalter 2023; Ryan 2023; Saqib *et al.* 2023.

film studies and sociological theories for the introductory exploration of these phenomena.

2. Social Imaginaries and Affective Mediation

Our paper starts from two closely related research questions.
First. How has COVID-19 changed the way we perceive social imaginaries?
Second. Can we identify a new mode, called retro-mediation, by which we perceive post-COVID-19 visual imaginaries? What is the role of media imaginaries in these processes?

What is and was COVID-19? As mentioned earlier, we believe that this global event can be defined as a 'total social fact,' in the meaning given to this concept by Marcel Mauss (1924). Indeed, it affects every sphere of human activity (political, economic, judicial, artistic, etc.) and every meaningful stage of individual life (birth, marriage, funeral, etc.). It pushes sociologists and media theorists to rethink the conceptual tools with which to interpret transformations of the social imaginaries.

According to Charles Taylor (2004, 23), by social imaginary, we mean "the ways people imagine their social existence, how they fit together with others, how things go on between them and their fellows, the expectations that are normally met, and the deeper normative notions and images that underlie these expectations".

These modern social imaginaries has three main characteristics: 1) "The way ordinary people 'imagine' their social surroundings (...) is carried in images, stories, and legends (...) 2) the social imaginary is shared by large groups of people, if not the whole society (...) 3) the social imaginary is that common understanding that makes possible common practices and a widely shared sense of legitimacy".

Social imaginaries and media imaginaries are thus not the same thing, although the latter can help in the spread (but also the destruction) of the former.

Both social and media imaginaries are part of a larger collective imaginary, made up of conflicting tendencies. It is therefore necessary to ask the question about the relationship between these two foundational social and symbolic structures.

According to Alberto Abruzzese (1973, 2007), we can conceive media imaginaries as a processual and myth-making machine fed by media narratives (literature, cinema, television seriality, comics). They contribute to shared definitions of reality, just as social imaginaries do. In fact, increasingly the social construction of reality is being replaced by a media construction of reality, as Nick Couldry and Andreas Hepp (2016) explain. In this perspective, we have to reconsider the concepts of premediation and retro-mediation, in relation to the transformation of imaginaries (social and media) triggered by COVID-19 pandemic.

The concept of premediation was developed by Richard Grusin (2004, 2010). It refers to the work of the news media (especially television) when during catastrophic events (natural disasters, war events) they pre-mediate the future by predicting various possible scenarios. Premediation has the function of containing and, at the same time, feeding anxiety about the unknown developments of a catastrophic event. However, in the digital mediascape there is no longer one dominant media type and media logic. We are faced with a media manifold (Couldry and Hepp 2016), consisting of multiple different media that contaminate and hybridize each other. This logic of remediation, identified by Bolter and Grusin (1999), enables the evolution of the mediascape. In the digital age, the main feature of the mediascape is the multiplication of communication and information spaces. However, this also produces an intensification of premediation processes, which run through the whole of contemporary media.

On the one hand, we have digital media. They are affective environments (Farci 2019) in which we mediate collective affectivity. On the other hand, mainstream media such as television still play a significant role in premediation processes. During the pandemic, this set of media continuously pre-mediated future scenarios on the growth of infection curves, the number of deaths, the effectiveness of vaccines, and so on. As for Italy, we can cite the ritual of the Civil Defense's daily bulletin or Premier Giuseppe Conte's regular press conferences.

In the current mediascape, there is an evident conflict between different forms of premediation. Indeed, the scenarios foreshadowed are of different kinds. Some reinforce the legitimacy of institutional health policies. Other scenarios challenge the legitimacy and the prevailing definitions of reality, fueling phenomena such as conspiracy and denialism. These different forms of premediation fuel different ways of imagining social relations.

In addition to intensive premediation, there is 'slow' premediation. This is provided by media narratives different from those of the news media. Novels (*The Bladerunner*, 1974, *The Stand*, 1978), films (*12 Monkeys*, 1995; *Contagion*, 2011), and TV series (*See*, 2019 – 2022); *The Walking Dead*, 2010-2022; *The Last of Us*, 2023 – present) have created dystopian fictional worlds in which a pandemic forever changes the social, political and economic arrangements of Western societies.

Even studies in the field of Future Studies, virology and popular science and para-science had prefigured scenarios in which the entire planet would face a pandemic. We refer to these narratives as a kind of slow premediation of pandemic visual imaginaries. In some ways, therefore, the Covid-19 pandemic could be conceived and experienced as the reversal of a dystopian future turned into concrete everyday reality. The effect of this dual movement of premediation, slow and intensive, is that many individuals experience the feeling of a total reconfiguration of their social life. Indeed, COVID-19 has completely reconfigured the essence of sociality and lifestyles. The new normal involves a reprogramming of physical and cultural spaces, including the most intimate and personal.

With respect to our work, we are interested in emphasizing that media narratives about COVID-19 have imposed a clear visual imaginary of the pandemic. The essential elements of this imaginary are the masks, physical distancing, disciplining all access to public activities, coffins, mass graves, personal protective equipment, helmets for artificial ventilation, intubated individuals, syringes with vaccines, places where subjects could vaccinate, empty streets and squares, and so on. Such media imaginary has profoundly affected social imaginaries. In particular, it has altered the way we imagine the system of social interaction and relationship with others. In turn, this violent reconfiguration of social imaginaries transforms the way we relate to media narratives, particularly movies and TV series. In this sense, we can conceive of retromediation as the outcome of a short-circuit between media imaginaries and social imaginaries. Media imaginaries produce a premediation of catastrophe, causing the restructuring of social imaginaries. Such reconfiguration of social imaginaries, in turn, generates a transformation in the way we perceive media narratives.

What we call retro-mediation is exactly this movement of retroactive and affective re-mediation, aimed primarily at cultural products of the past. More specifically, retro-mediation consists of the projection of feelings and emotions about our new ways of understanding post-pandemic social existence onto movies, TV series and other cultural objects.

3. TV Series and Retro-Mediation

We will now proceed with a quick analysis of four empirical cases of retro-mediation. But first we want to briefly discuss two Facebook posts. These are obviously items without any statistical value. Nevertheless, they help to understand what psychological, media and cultural processes are involved in retro-mediation.

The first post is related to watching the film *Capri-Revolution* (2018):

> Tonight while watching a beautiful movie (*Capri-Revolution*) I felt like I was reliving the same feelings I was experiencing during the lockdown. When I saw a movie it felt strange for people to kiss, strange for them to hug, strange for them to eat all together. As if the normal world is ours. As if that relational normalcy that we can now only see in movies was a dystopia. Instead, the dystopia is the real world we are in. The movie was beautiful. The feeling was not.

The second post is related to watching the TV series *Emily in Paris* (2020 — present) and *We Are Who We Are* (2020):

> Lately, especially when I was watching series such as *Emily in Paris* or *We Are Who We Are* in which we often switch between outdoor and indoor environments, I felt displaced by the fact that the characters would go into offices, bars, supermarkets, and stores without their masks on. It's normal, you'll say, especially since it probably doesn't happen to just me but to so many other people. However, it is also proof that this pandemic has changed something in the way we view movies and TV series and that certain things don't speak to us as much as they used to, partly because they show a pre-pandemic or pandemic-free world that simply doesn't concern us.

Stasera, mentre vedevo un film bellissimo (Capri re-volution), mi è sembrato di rivivere le stesse sensazioni che vivevo durante il lockdown. Quando vedevo un film mi sembrava strano che le persone si baciassero, strano che si abbracciassero, strano che mangiassero tutti insieme appiccicati. Come se il mondo normale fosse solo il nostro e basta. Come se quella normalità relazionale che ora possiamo vedere solo nei film fosse una distopia. Invece la distopia è il mondo reale in cui siamo. Il film era bellissimo. La sensazione no.

Ultimamente, specie mentre guardavo serie come Emily in Paris e We Are Who We Are in cui si passa spesso da ambienti esterni a interni, mi sono sentito spiazzato dal fatto che i personaggi entrassero negli uffici, nei bar, nei supermercati e nei negozi senza la mascherina. È normale, direte voi, soprattutto perché probabilmente non capita solo a me ma a tantissime altre persone. Tuttavia è anche la dimostrazione che questa pandemia ha cambiato qualcosa nel nostro modo di vedere i film e le serie TV e che certe cose non ci parlano più come prima anche perché mostrano un mondo pre-pandemia o senza pandemia che semplicemente non ci riguarda (e questo ci dice anche

Both posts (Fig. 1 and Fig. 2) testify to the ability of audiovisual narratives to short-circuit everyday experience. Locked in their homes, unable to relate to others in person, and forced to use masks in every interaction outside, the two authors of the posts certify the shock they felt while observing audiovisual fictional worlds in which all possibilities of experiencing social relationships were virtually untouched. The authors of the two posts, then, express a more general sense of despondency, fueled by the comparison between the post-pandemic dystopian world and the fictional world told in movies and TV series made before Covid-19.

Let us now analyze four cases of retro-mediation related to television seriality.

The selected image (Fig. 3) depicts a mass grave in New York City. The site houses the bodies of those who died from COVID-19 unclaimed by their families. The image of a mass grave is connected to a network of historically encoded meanings through which a connection is established between COVID-19 and and past pestilences.

The second frame (Fig. 4) is from *Acting Up*, the first episode of the second season of the TV series *POSE*, aired in 2019. *POSE* is an American drama television series about New York City's Ballroom culture scene, an LGBTQ subculture in the African-American and Latino communities, throughout the 1980s and 1990s.

At the beginning of this episode two main characters, Pray Tell and Blanca, travel to Hart's Island. Upon arriving at the supervisor's office, they explain that they want to visit the grave of Pray's former partner, Keenan. The two went to the grave site, observing men in protective suits carrying numerically marked wooden boxes in a collective pile. Buried in this mass grave are the bodies of all AIDS deaths unclaimed by their families. The viewer who saw the episode after the pandemic experiences a direct connection between the AIDS outbreak in LGBTQIA+ communities and the COVID-19 pandemic outbreak. In both cases, the dramatic dimension of the phenomenon can be visually translated into the communal burial of human beings, deprived of the *pietas* they would have deserved.

The second example is from the famous sitcom *The Big Bang Theory*. Protagonists of the series are young nerdy scientists. The episode cited is *The Engagement Reaction*, the twenty-third episode of the fourth season, aired in 2011. Sheldon goes with his friends to the hospital where Howard's mother is hospitalized. Sheldon is on his way back from the toilet when he sees a coughing man being wheeled through the hallway. In order to escape the coughing, Sheldon ducks into a room (bearing a biohazard warning sign), before turning and seeing an astonished medical staff who declare he cannot leave as he has been exposed. Sheldon covers his face with his shirt and insists he is fine.

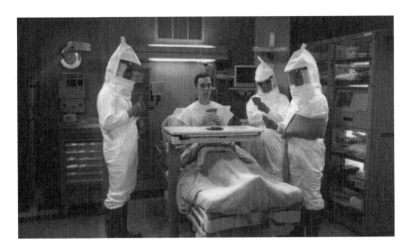

In the final scene (Fig. 6), Leonard, Howard and Raj put on a hazmat suit and play a card game, in the same room where Sheldon is quarantined because he has been exposed to a deadly virus. This scene calls to viewers' minds the various images of patients with COVID-19 admitted to the intensive care (Fig. 5).

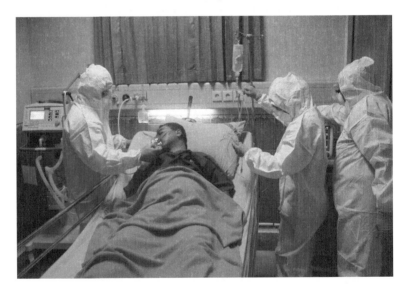

In a pre-pandemic era, the storyline would have elicited only hilarity because of Sheldon's paranoia. But in a postpandemic world, the dystopian gaze with which we view protective suits, distancing, and viruses immediately calls to mind the risk of infection. In such a world, even Sheldon's obsessive germophobia appears as an acceptable weapon of defense.

The third example is from an already dystopian series, *The Handmaid's Tale*. The plot features a dystopia following a Second American Civil War wherein a theonomic, totalitarian society subjects fertile women, called 'Handmaids', to child-bearing slavery.

In the episode *Unfit*, eighth episode of the third season, aired in 2018, inside the only supermarket where the Handmaids can go, one of the Handmaids, OfMatthew, loses control, steals a gun from one of the guardians and threatens to kill Aunt Lydia, a kind of overseer of the Handmaids (Fig. 8).

In this case, retro-mediation operates by projecting the tension and anguish of disciplining for COVID-19 onto this sequence, which has specific significance within the framework of the series' narrative storylines. The analogy that retro-mediation establishes between the present of the pandemic and the fiction of Gilead's world is based on the common disciplining in access to stores. The difference is that the retro-mediation makes us perceive as general that imprisonment which in the series is reserved only for women and the Handmaids in particular. The tension that suddenly erupts thus recalls the many fights that occurred during lockdowns inside supermarkets (Fig. 7).

The fourth example is one of the most interesting of all. *Pushing Daisies* is an American comedy-drama television series created by Bryan Fuller that aired on ABC from 2007 to 2009. The series tells the story of Ned, a pie-maker who has the gift of resurrecting dead living beings with a single touch. This gift, however, comes at a very high price: a second touch from Ned, in fact, brings irreversible death to people. When Ned resurrects his unconfessed love, Chuck, he must face the painful condition of not being able to have any direct physical contact with her. Ned and Chuck invent a variety of devices, such as hugging machines and improvised protective suits (Fig. 9, 10, 11, 12).

Such devices are known to have been used during the COVID-19 pandemic to enable fragile and isolated individuals to have minimal contact with loved ones, avoiding the risk of infection. Retro-mediation operates here in two ways. On the one hand, the tools Ned and Chuck invent to have physical contact in the series had a romantic overtone. Instead, our dystopian gaze makes us perceive them as everyday tools for avoiding contagion, depriving them of any loving, dreamy undertones. On the other hand, Ned's absolutely singular condition is brought back to the new normal. In this way, the post-pandemic viewer can experience a deeper empathic relationship with the character, as he experiences his own daily anxieties through the impossibility of being able to touch and be touched.

Retro-mediation can be defined as a media logic of reimagining the past. It operates as retroactive and affective remediation, through which users dystopian symbols, icons, and visual elements, drawn from pandemic visual culture, onto audiovisual images of the pre-pandemic years.

These examples highlight the sociocultural processes involved in retro-mediation. It shapes the forms of production, reproduction, and reconversion of social imaginaries (Marzo and Meo 2019) by transferring into the past the distressing feelings caused by pandemics. It can be conceived as a dystopian response to the total presentness and impossibility of imagining a different future. In contrast to Zygmunt Bauman's retrotopia (Bauman 2017), retromediation does not stimulate individuals to find comfort in an idealized past, but extends the projection of a dystopian present onto cultural objects of the past.

4. The *retro-mediation*: Several Basic Questions

The change that COVID-19 has brought to everyday life also concerns the media and audiovisual world to some extent. The discourse is not absolute, but it is clear that the wave of communication and information that has arisen around the pandemic has constituted an agent of reshaping certain communicative practices and has seen the emergence of others, not always oriented towards a correct scientific disclosure, as shown by the emergence of the so-called *infodemic* (Zarocostas 2020).

In the more strictly communicative sphere, the need to make the coronavirus explicit and to give it 'a face' that is also recognizable visually has caused the proliferation of various modes of representation. Moreover, the need to make explicit and concretize in images a phenomenon that would otherwise be difficult to perceive (such as viruses, microorganisms, and abstract concepts in general) also responds to the average human's need to rely on the media in order to understand the phenomenon under analysis better, as shown, for example, by specific studies relating to the teaching of scientific concepts and concerning the understanding of reality in general (Mayer 2003, 2009; Manches and O'Malley 2011; Manches and Ainsworth 2022). In the first instance, COVID-19 created new media and visual artifacts (videos; posts; reels on SNSs, etc.) that fed new social and media imaginaries. At the same time, media have remediated information about the virus—by relocating it in multiple contexts—through a series of images created specifically to make it perceptually and cognitively visible and accessible: these are veritable media or *postmedia* devices (Eugeni 2021) with which users enter into a relationship and from which they can also feel influences on the affective side.

Indeed, during the pandemic, viewing images of the virus changed our perceptive experience of the concept of illness and danger, acting mainly on an emotional level. Synthesizing this first passage, we can say that COVID-19 acted as a prompt (Floridi 2014) to construct new visual artifacts; such objects are also delineated as techno-media devices (in the sense of Eugeni 2021) that act on and with the user (i.e., the one who visualizes and enjoys such images), forming a bio-technological assemblage.

The hypothesis is that the effect exerted by these devices is mainly affective and that it acts retroactively, modifying the very narrative of COVID-19 and, above all, other audience experiences that the user may have, experiences which are, however, linked to visual and media objects prior to the pandemic outbreak. Therefore, it is a circular trend capable of influencing all the elements that make up this media-ecological system.

COVID-19 — visual & media artifacts — viewers

Let us briefly examine some theoretical underpinnings of our hypothesis called 'retro-mediation'. As we explained previously, according to Grusin's (2010) premediation, a medium can 'pre-act' on its users: in this way, a user can feel and emotionally experience the impact of a mediatized phenomenon on him/herself, which, as we know, may or may not occur. COVID-19 and its representations — according to the circularity just described — have generated a series of collective feelings and reactions (of anxiety, fear, etc.) also conveyed and fuelled by media artifacts and practices, i.e., by media and *postmedia* devices. These, in turn, played a role in modifying that collective feeling. In Film Studies, Carl Plantinga (2009) introduced the concepts of 'emotional contagion', 'memory traces', and 'learned associations' that are functional to our hypothesis. Emotional contagion is "the phenomenon of 'catching' the emotions of those around us or of those who we observe" (Platinga 2009, 125): the scholar thus explains the emotional sharing of an event, such as the viewing of a film, and the collective reaction that one can have to a particular scene; the reaction is thus also stimulated by the collectivity that participates in the event.

Similarly, it is clear that in social media circles, for example, the general reaction to news about COVID-19 played a significant role in the constitution of a familiar feeling, thus forming the basis of collective affectivity conveyed mainly by images. On the other hand, 'memory traces' and 'learned associations' are phenomena that act on our experience, modifying it. The emotions that come from watching a film are "partly the product of learning" (Platinga 2009, 75): this means that the elements that characterize a film (music, narrative lines, etc.) — and, by extension, any audiovisual fictional work — are associated with previous real-life experiences. Watching a film or media product can initiate these associations linked to memory traces. Often, moreover, such memories — which Plantinga refers to Sanskrit poetic tradition — act not only as representations but also and above all, emotionally. In practice, the memory is often only affective, which makes it not necessarily linked to a specific representation but rather to an emotional intensification uncoupled from the object from which it initially originated (Plantinga 2009; D'Aloia and Eugeni 2015). According to our proposal, retro-mediation acts the opposite of the one described here, as it materializes an emotional state from experiential memory traces (those generated by emotional contagion and personal reaction to the virus) that influence audiovisual texts that predate the appearance of COVID-19. In some ways, postmedia devices born with the virus activate these involvement processes and emotional feedback on film and media experience.

Regarding activation, a brief reference to Alfred Gell's anthropological theory of the *agency* concept (1998) in ritualistic visual artifacts seems interesting. For the English anthropologist, every object — like every event — can exert an intentionality that has effects at the cognitive level: these are retroactions that arise in a continuous dialectical exchange between human and non-human agents, thus placed in reciprocal modification. To simplify: according to Gell, a human agent acts on the non-human agent (e.g., a totem or an image, etc.), which retroactively acts on the human (thus, the totem or idol acts on the human, making him feel 'changed'). In the same way, retromediation acts on both an emotional and a cognitive level and, simultaneously, is a result of these two levels. It derives from emotion because COVID-19 and its images 'act' by emotional contagion, including from memory traces and learned associations.

Furthermore, it derives from cognition because artifacts and human agents influence each other. As mentioned above, retro-mediation materializes emotional states by reviving them in the enjoyment of visual objects prior to the event itself. Retro-mediation, thus, is an experience of media affection, which has an emotional and cognitive nature and a retroactive value, mainly when applied to media and visual attendance. It is an even illusory mechanism (perhaps a kind of *pareidolia*?) that concerns a retroactive reading that arises from the object we see: a film, a series, an image, etc. This retroactivity is motivated by mediation that generated an imaginary and contributed to making it recognizable. It has modified, for example, a standard surgical mask into a COVID-19 symbol. This artifact (the mask, its representation in a visual object, images, and videos about the pandemic condition, etc.) becomes an agent capable of activating an associative memory, perhaps produced by the emotional contagion, which can influence the same emotional contagion too. Of course, other users can participate in the emotional contagion (as Plantinga says). However, the medium could also generate it when it has contributed, with premediation, to explode this event/phenomenon emotionally.

Finally, we point to two possible developments in our research. First, the following could be investigated more deeply the interferences between premediation processes and retro-mediation processes: how do the two modes of perception of audiovisual narratives influence each other? Second, the phenomenon of retro-mediation could be explored over a broader time frame to test the symbolic-affective reach of the pandemic on media processes.

References

Abruzzese, Alberto. 1973. *Forme estetiche e società di massa*. Venezia: Marsilio.

Abruzzese, Alberto. 2007. *La grande scimmia. Mostri vampiri automi mutanti*. Roma: Sossella.

Bauman, Zygmunt. 2017. *Retrotopia*. Cambridge: Polity.

Bolter, Jay David, and Richard Grusin. 1999. *Remediation: Understanding New Media*. Cambridge: MIT Press.

Boursier, Valentina *et al.* 2020. "Facing Loneliness and Anxiety During the COVID-19 Isolation: The Role of Excessive Social Media Use in a Sample of Italian Adults". *Front. Psychiatry* 11: 586222. doi: 10.3389/fpsyt.2020.586222.

Bryan, Michael, ed. 2023. *Pandemic Pedagogies: Teaching and Learning during the COVID-19 Pandemic*. New York: Routledge.

Chakraborty, Nandini. 2020. "The COVID-19 pandemic and its impact on mental health". *Prog. Neurol. Psychiatry* 24: 21-24. https://doi.org/10.1002/pnp.666.

Couldry, Nick, and Andreas Hepp. 2016. *The Mediated Construction of Reality*. Cambridge: Polity.

Devoe, Daniel J. *et al.* 2022. "The impact of the COVID-19 pandemic on eating disorders: A systematic review". *International Journal of Eating disorders* 56, 1: 5-25. https://doi.org/10.1002/eat.23704.

Eugeni, Ruggero. 2021. *Capitale algoritmico. Cinque dispositivi postmediali (più uno)*. Brescia: Morcelliana.

Farci, Manolo. 2019. "La cultura digitale affettiva: folle, pubblici e comunità". *Sociologia* 3/2019: 7-14.

Flore, Jacinthe, *et al.* 2023. "Creative arts workers during the Covid-19 pandemic: Social imaginaries in lockdown". *Journal of Sociology* 59, 1: 197–214. https://doi.org/10.1177/14407833211036757.

Floridi, Luciano. 2014. *The Fourth Revolution: How the Infosphere reshaping Human Reality*. Oxford: Oxford University Press.

Gell, Alfred. 1998. *Art and Agency: An Anthropological Theory*. Oxford: Oxford University Press.

Grusin, Richard. 2004. "Premediation". *Criticism* 46(1): 17-39.

Grusin, Richard. 2010. *Premediation: Affect and mediality After 9/11*. New York: Palgrave Macmillan.

Khlystova, Olena *et al.* 2022. "The impact of the COVID-19 pandemic on the creative industries: A literature review and future research agenda". *Journal of Business Research* 139: 1192-1210. https://doi.org/10.1016/j.jbusres.2021.09.062.

Manches Andrew, and Shaaron Ainsworth. 2022. "Learning About Viruses: Representing Covid-19". *Frontiers in Education* 6: 1-18. doi: 10.3389/feduc.2021.736744.

Manches, Andrew, and Claire O'Malley. 2011. "Tangibles for Learning: A Representational Analysis of Physical Manipulation". *Pers Ubiquit Comput* 16 (4): 405–419. doi:10.1007/s00779-011-0406-0.

Marzo, Pier Luca and Milena Meo. 2019. "Cartografie dell'immaginario". *Im@go* 2(1): 4-17.

Mauss, Marcel. 1924. "Essai sur le don. Forme et raison de l'échange dans les sociétés archaïques". *Année Sociologique* 1: 30-186.

Osofsky, Joy D. *et al.* 2020. "Psychological and social impact of COVID-19". *Psychological Trauma: Theory, Research, Practice, and Policy* 12(5): 468–469. https://doi.org/10.1037/tra0000656.

Pintor Iranzo, Ivan. 2020. "Iconographies of the Pandemic". *CCCBLAB*. https://lab.cccb.org/en/iconographies-of-the-pandemic/.

Ratten, Vanessa. 2021. "Coronavirus (Covid-19) and entrepreneurship: cultural, lifestyle and societal changes". *Journal of Entrepreneurship in Emerging Economies* 13(4): 747-761. https://doi.org/10.1108/JEEE-06-2020-0163.

Rosette-Crake, Fiona, and Elvis Buckwalter, eds. 2023. *COVID-19, Communication and Culture Beyond the Global Workplace*. New York: Routledge.

Saqib, Kiran *et al.* 2023. "COVID-19, Mental Health, and Chronic Illnesses: A Syndemic Perspective". *International Journal of Environmental Research and Public Health* 20(4): 3262. https://doi.org/10.3390/ijerph20043262.

Shanuga Priya, Selvanathan *et al.* 2021. "A perspective of COVID-19 impact on global economy, energy and environment". *International Journal of Sustainable Engineering* 14(6): 1290-1305. https://doi.org/10.1080/19397038.2021.1964634.

Shaw, Philip *et al.* 2023. "A Daily Diary Study into the Effects on Mental Health of COVID-19 Pandemic-Related Behaviors". *Psychological Medicine* 53(2): 524–32. doi:10.1017/S0033291721001896.

Singh, Jaspreet, and Jagandeep Singh. 2020. "COVID-19 and Its Impact on Society". *Electronic Research Journal of Social Sciences and Humanities* 2(I): 168-172.

Taylor, Charles. 2004. *Modern Social Imaginaries*. Durham-London: Duke University Press.

Zaracostas, John. 2020. "How to fight an infodemic". *The Lancet* 395. https://doi.org/10.1016/S0140-6736(20)30461-X.

Our Dystopian World.
Catastrophic Storytelling in Virtual Reality

Anja Boato

The proliferation of dystopian narratives is a sign of the uncertainty of the times. As an apocalyptic prediction of possible futures, the dystopian genre exaggerates some contemporary fears by depicting terrifying worlds worse than the contemporary one. The sub-genre of technological dystopias is somehow the consequence of widespread doubts about the future of robotics and computers (Clayes 2017, 490-491), even if nowadays these devices are helping to convey new dystopian forms of storytelling.

Virtual reality (VR) began its history in the science fiction imagination of authors and creators. In this paper, I will reverse the perspective to see how the devices of virtual reality are used to represent dystopian worlds. VR will therefore be considered here as a medium, and not just as a multifunctional technology (Bolter, Engberg and MacIntyre 2021). However, the wide range of immersive technologies includes endless possibilities and problematic issues. Within this paper, I will attempt to draw a comprehensive overview of the applications of VR to the narrative arts and describe the medium's peculiarities in creating dystopian worlds. Several case studies help highlight VR's abilities to draw immersive worlds, which generate embodiment, empathy and a sense of presence that has a deep impact on the viewer's ability to take in the story and its messages. Focusing on the medium is the first step in understanding how a story and its set of meanings is received by the user-spectator. Consequently, it helps to understand also how an effective narrative system can trace dystopian worlds with great emotional impact.

A Simple Taxonomy for Many Complex Immersive Realities

Despite the obvious interest of both industry and scholars in immersive technologies, there are still many difficulties in developing a shared terminological framework. This paper may not be the right context for proposing a definitive interpretation of the definitions and boundaries of immersive realities, but the topic is nonetheless an excellent starting point for a focus on VR storytelling.

One of the most influential attempts to suggest a taxonomy of immersive realities dates back to 1994, when Milgram and Kishino worked on their *virtuality continuum*. According to them, we could place immersive technologies along a continuum ranging from the greatest adherence to the real environment and the greatest adherence to the virtual environment. *Real* and *virtual* are opposite values and points of reference. The authors complicate the taxonomy by including a number of criteria that define new poles of the continuum and can help establish the differences between immersive technologies — *Extent of World Knowledge, Reproduction Fidelity*, and *Extent of Presence Metaphor*. Focusing on the simplest level of the continuum between *real* and *virtual*, they identify in Augmented Reality (AR) the closest form of immersive reality to the real environment. On the opposite, the virtual environment is mainly reached by the so-called Augmented Virtuality (AV), which has commonalities with the concept of VR but they are not the same. We could rethink the *virtuality continuum* by adapting it to more recent taxonomies, which tend instead to recognize the duality between AR and VR (Muhanna 2014, Rauschnabel et al. 2022).

Augmented Reality could be defined as "a real time direct or indirect view of a physical real-world environment that has been enhanced/augmented by adding virtual computer-generated information to it" (Carmignani and Furht 2011, 3), so it involves the use of devices to add some computer-generated elements to the real-world view. Therefore, it requires a certain closeness to the real environment. On the opposite, Virtual Reality is related to "computer-generated simulations of three-dimensional objects or environments with seemingly real, direct, or physical user interaction"

(Dioniso et al. 2013) and tends to exclude any reference to the real world so as to simulate total immersion in another computer-generated environment. We can therefore think of AR and VR as the two opposites of the continuum of immersive technologies or as two independent and separate technologies. However, it is still necessary to remember that many other kinds of immersive environments could be mentioned. Although there is not yet a universally accepted definition, in these pages we may use the concept of Mixed Reality (MR) to identify the hybrid forms of AR and VR. Some scholars use the term to refer to the entire set of immersive technologies (Milgram and Kishino 1994; Suh and Prophet 2018), with several terminological complications that need not be addressed here. According to this perspective, VR and AR are just subclasses of MR, and not different forms of immersive technologies. However, the Extended Reality (XR) or xReality concept is more often used as an "umbrella term" for covering both AR and VR, along with MR.

Each of these different forms of immersive realities can be used as media to convey messages and tell stories, even if fiction is certainly not the field where they have been most successful so far. In the preface to the second edition of her book, *Narrative As Virtual Reality* (Ryan 2015), Ryan complains that the early enthusiasm for VR's narrative potential died out in the first decade of the 2000s, leaving room for other areas, such as military and scientific simulations. Today, however, this enthusiasm has been partially rekindled thanks to two complementary trends. First of all, the interest of some major filmmakers or digital artists in immersive technologies. The premiere at the Cannes Film Festival for *Carne y Arena*, a VR work directed and produced by Alejandro González Iñárritu in 2017, was a key turning point (D'Aloia 2018, 119-134). Secondly, the recent enthusiasm for VR has also been driven by the emergence of immersive art sections within prestigious film festivals, as well as new festivals devoted entirely to virtual technologiesIn 2016, the Venice International Film Festival introduced an Immersive section, which developed into a core Virtual Reality (VR) competition the following year. Festivals represent sites of cultural legitimacy and can set standards for future productions (De Valk, Kredell and Loist 2016).

The consumer market seems to be projected toward AR and the Metaverse, which are seen as the forms of immersive reality most likely to enter into consumers' daily lives. Museums, VR theaters, and other permanent or semi-permanent local exhibition spaces mostly require a particular form of VR that we might call "360-degree video", which is technically simpler. In contrast, festivals encourage and reward Virtual Reality in its most sophisticated forms. Of course, VR also has different nuances that make further taxonomies necessary. Internal differentiations are built on several levels. Suh and Prophet (2018) start with a basic distinction between Non-immersive VR and Immersive VR. The first one indicates "technology that displays virtual content via a computer screen without additional equipment to amplify the immersive experience" and the second one "allow users to interact the technology via more complex tracking systems, such as head-mounted displays that track motion and provide deeper immersion because displays change in accordance with minute movements" (Suh and Prophet 2018, 77-90). This elementary distinction connects to a number of taxonomies based on the type of hardware used to generate and enjoy virtual environments. For simplicity, we consider only Immersive VR as real Virtual Reality and associate it with the fundamental use of Head-Mounted Displays (HMD) for the visual immersion. The hundreds of VR headsets on the market can be divided into three main categories. First of all, Mobile HMDs are wireless devices that can be used without computers and are just able to screen 360-degrees videos and panoramas (Anthes, García-Hernández, Wiedemann and Kranzlmüller 2016, 1-19). On the opposite, wired HMDs could be partially immersive if they only support the screening of 3DOF (three degrees of freedom) experiences, that are not able to track the movement of the user in the space, or totally immersive if they allow 6DOF (six degrees of freedom) experience, that indicate room-based works in which the headset is able to map the user-spectator's movements in physical space and reproduce them in the digital world. This is an important distinction because it inevitably involves different experiences, with different narrative strategies and unique settings. This principle is applicable to any form of VR story, so even dystopian ones.

Four Keywords for Understanding VR Storytelling

VR works presented at festivals are hybrid forms with other arts, including theater, video games, dance or cinema. The term most often used to talk about the interconnections between cinema and immersive realities is Cine-VR, short for *cinematic virtual reality*. Although many scholars and professionals consider only 360-degree videos to be Cine-VR, we can expand this definition to all those works related to cinematic visual and narrative imagery. The history of Cine-VR begins so recently that it is somehow still experiencing the so-called *early virtual (post)cinema of attractions* (Dalpozzo 2018, 87-107), since many of the works in VR aspire to seek the awe and fascination inherent in the medium.

Because of this search for wonder, some genres are preferred over others. Among these, documentaries are particularly successful – the physical proximity to characters and environments helps generate empathy, so VR is considered an excellent medium for conveying socially and humanly engaged messages. Equally fortunate are stories set in fantastic, dreamlike and spectacular environments, because they inspire awe through eye-catching graphics whilst building believable but extraordinary worlds. These two categories also tend to meet often, telling true stories in imaginative environments. Dystopian stories in VR are a symbolic consequence of this encounter.

At the risk of simplifying boundless literature, we can summarize the dominant features of any VR storytelling into four key concepts, immersion, presence, embodiment and empathy (Arcagni and D'Aloia 2021, 1-7). These principles constitute the main characteristics of the medium and thus the first reference points in the construction of the experience and its aesthetic. All of them have been deeply analyzed from both psychological and technological perspectives.

The aesthetics of the medium are related to the ways in which immersive technologies affect our senses, so in this case to the specifics of hardware and software. As for VR, we could focus on the "aesthetics of immersion and visual illusion" which are " [...] pursued through constant improvements in the technology and through design techniques that encourage the user to lose herself in the flow of the game or experience. " (Bolter, Engberg, MacIntyre 2021, 46). In fact, *Immersion* is the first key concept. As a technological quality of the medium itself, the illusion of psychic and sensory immersion is the goal of any VR experience. Following Calleja's theories, this immersion can occur by *absorption* if guided by a psychologically engaging story or by *transportation* if determined by a physical projection into another world. Virtual Reality is a sophisticated technology that can simulate the sense of immersion, even if this concept has some cognitive connotations that deserve further and deeper investigations (Modena and Parisi 2021). *Presence* is the first consequence of immersion and the second key concept. As a perceptual medium, VR is based on the user-spectator's belief that he or she is physically present in another world (Micalizzi and Gaggioli 2018). The creators of these experiences have to balance external and internal stimuli in order to make their virtual environments as credible as possible. This goal could be achieved only if the experience includes a physical process of *embodiment*, the third key concept. The user-spectator has both a physical body and a virtual one, but it is necessary for him or her to delude themselves that they are only in one place with one body. Therefore, stories told through VR are based on the dual concept of ambient storytelling and embodied narrative (Ruszev 2021), due to the centrality of this process.

Through the combination of the technical feature of immersion, the psychological feature of presence, and the physical feature of embodiment, virtual reality experiences can generate *empathy*, the fourth key concept. The idea of VR as an empathy machine has been both appreciated and criticized (Modena 2022). Empathy is a multifaceted term whose reproducibility through media is often questioned. Despite this, there are many scholars who insist on the ability of VR to create a sense of physical proximity that stimulates the sharing of emotions and feelings. The effective VR storytelling starts from the emotional power of the medium.

Obviously, the specifics of the medium and the four key principles described above have important effects on the development of storytelling. We can take two examples to demonstrate how different forms of VR can create different experiences even starting from the same genre, namely the successful case of dystopian worlds—*The Key* by Celine Tricart, and *The Sick Rose* by Zhi-Zhong Tang and Yun-Hsien Huang).

Our World, but Worse. The Cases of *The Key* and *The sick rose*

Cinematic Virtual Reality works often combine elements of the documentary or docu-fiction genre with fantastic and dreamlike environments. As already anticipated, both genres are particularly suited to be told through the medium of Virtual Reality. VR is always a process of world-building, although the modes may change according to its forms—those worlds could be both computer-generated or filmed through traditional cinema techniques using 360-degree cameras. The user-spectators are immersed in these worlds thanks to specific devices. Their ability to interact with the environment leads to the development of a hybrid figure between the traditional spectator and the gamer. The elements of active participation, which obviously subsist even in more traditional forms of spectatorship, are further encouraged by the VR medium.

Cine-VR abandons many of the cardinal principles of cinema. First, the very important idea of the frame is replaced by the concept of field (Arcagni and D'Aloia 2021). As a result, if there is no frame decided upstream by one or more authors or professionals, responsible for the product-film, then the viewer has to choose his or her own frame, building up a personal experience. The same product may be enjoyed completely differently by several people or even by the same person at different times. Likewise, the concepts of film editing, camera movements, zooms, shots and so on disappear or change radically. So how can VR features affect the development of immersive experiences? More importantly, how can these features add new elements to the history of dystopian stories?

To answer these questions, I will consider two case studies. Both works use Virtual Reality to portray frightening worlds, starting from very different narrative techniques. The first case is one of the most discussed and analyzed works in the contemporary immersive arts scene (Grossi 2021). *The Key* is an immersive experience directed by French artist Celine Tricart. The experience takes the user-spectator into a dreamlike and cruel world inhabited by ghostly creatures and terrible monsters. The user experiences the trauma of losing their home and being driven to flee in search of a better future. Only at the end of the experience, the monstrous world turns out to be a metaphorical representation of the real experience of refugees, with a final scene that includes their direct testimonies. *The Key* premiered at the Venice Film Festival in 2019, with a strong theatrical dimension, including the performance of an actress and some exhibition spaces thought to make the experience as realistic as possible. The version available today on the Oculus Quest' store is adapted for home video consumption, where there is no control of the space and obviously no involvement of real and physical actors. However, both versions are 6DOF experiences, which thus provide for the ability to explore the environment with realistic tracking of the user's movements.

The Key draws a dystopian world to tell contemporary problems. The user-spectator is more than a viewer, because active participation is required, and it is something else than the common user, because its spatial freedom is strongly driven by the experience, which is inspired by cinematic storytelling. The dystopian world of *The Key* is unique and interesting precisely because of this ability to make the most of the medium. In particular, we can consider four very significant aspects: the use of the first-person shot, the attention to the environment, the anti-cinematic editing and the interaction.

The concept of first-person shot refers to "the transformation of the classical figure of point of view shot — or subjective shot —, within the contemporary intermedia network" (Eugeni 2012, 20). This term comes from the world of video games, where it is used to describe the subjective point of view when the player impersonates a character and performs in-game actions by simulating the character's own vision. According to Eugeni, the first-person shot is both an intermedia figure and an experiential figure — both concepts provide a perfect understanding of how first-person shot is used for virtual reality storytelling. In *The Key*, the first-person shot makes the user-spectator a physical character. The virtual world exists just because the *user* exists; it is built around his or her perspective and bodily presence. So the experience exploits the aforementioned processes of presence and embodiment to elicit empathy, building the environment around the user-spectator and deluding them that they are in full control of the world.

In the same way, *The Key* pays great attention to the environment, making it graphically appealing and believable in the eyes of the user-spectator. The setting is not overly detailed, but there was no need to overload the environment with information. Firstly, 360-degree animations involve higher costs than the same product designed for a flat screen. This makes a clean and simple graphic style quite advantageous. Secondly, the user-spectator immersed in the environment from a first-person shot point of view will pay less attention to detail than a traditional viewer. The setting is not intended to be realistic, but verisimilar, in order to foster the development of a sense of presence and embodiment. Although the world is not real, it must seem real in the eyes of those who experience it.

Presence and embodiment are also possible thanks to a smooth editing. The story proceeds at a slow pace in order to allow the user-spectator to adapt to changes in the environment. The editing is obviously not about the frame but about the field, so the changes from one setting to another involve the whole environment. The user-spectator of a first person shot VR experience would not be comfortable with very sudden jumps in space or time. *The Key* balances them with slow, smooth transitions. For this reason, we could define VR editing as anti-cinematographic. The VR experience is based on immersive world-building that exists, according to the perception of the user-spectator, beyond his or her physical presence in the space. Editing could break this illusion.

Finally, *The Key* is an interactive experience, so its development is possible only if the user-spectator performs a series of actions that are partly already predicted by the experience itself. At the same time, the freedom of the user-spectator interaction with environment and prompts does not interfere with the storytelling. The opportunity to actively relate to the environment is another key aspect of fostering immersion, presence, embodiment and thus empathy. At the same time, a cinematic narrative rhythm implies that its development is not tied to this interaction. In this sense, Cine-VR lies along a fine line that separates cinema from other forms of expression, such as video games. At the moment, we could just say that there is a narrative rather than a ludic goal in VR works' interactions.

The sick rose (2021) is a quite different example that reaches the same conclusions. The experience is a 360-degree stop-motion video; it does not involve any interaction with the environment or tracking of the user-spectator's body movements. The experience follows the story of Rose, a young lady who had a fight with her mother in a pandemic and apocalyptic world inhabited by monsters. Again, the directors Zhi-Zhong Tang and Yun-Hsien Huang portray a dark and disturbing dystopian world in which the user-spectator is immersed through the devices of VR. Yet, there are important differences to the case of *The Key*. First, the headset does not track the viewer's movements in physical space. The experience enacts other mechanisms to achieve the same results regarding immersion and sense of presence. First of all, it gives up the first-person shot. The position of the user-spectator is closer to that of a traditional viewer because no practical identification with a character is required. The viewer still has freedom in deciding which elements of the scene have priority importance in the 360 degrees field and can exclude one part of the environment in favor of another. However, this time the viewer does not perceive himself as an agent, the world exists regardless of his presence, and there is no illusion of control over the environment.

In a 360-degree space, attention to the graphic appeal of the setting is still a central element. In this case the user-spectator, less physically involved, will pay more attention to details. Indeed, the dystopian world of *The sick rose* is rich in detail, unlike the simplest setting of *The Key*. The interactive element obviously changes as well, because *The sick rose* does not require the direct participation of the viewer except in terms of sectional viewing—in other words, the spectator can break up the environment with his or her viewing choices, but cannot actively interact with its elements. The spectator is not required to participate in the storytelling, nor does the experience incentivize embodiment by the viewer's identification with a character's physical body. The four key principles of immersion, presence, embodiment and empathy consequently rely on only two factors: the environment, that should be detailed and impressive, and the editing. In fact, as in the case of *The Key*, *The sick rose* has to work on an editing as smooth and as invisible as possible in order to be believable in the eyes of the viewer-spectator. Together, environment and editing help to delude the user-spectator into thinking he or she is immersed in a dystopian world.

Conclusions

There are some common traits between the dystopian worlds portrayed by both the case studies described in this paper. First of all, they aim to denounce problems of our contemporary world—*The Key* is a social dystopia about the journeys of refugees, while *The sick rose* is an environmental dystopia that describes a city affected by a pandemic like COVID-19. The depiction of social or environmental problems in imaginary worlds is a common feature of the dystopia genre, but it is even more common in stories told through the medium of virtual reality. VR indeed has two advantages. On the one hand, the physical proximity between viewer, environment, and characters stimulates a process of empathy. This makes virtual reality a suitable medium for documentary storytelling, but also a perfect device to convey messages of social protest. On the other hand, VR involves the construction of computer-processed digital environments, which are unlikely to achieve convincing levels of realism, at least for now. Thus, VR is particularly suited to building fantastic worlds. Combining these two elements makes it easy for many experiences set in alternative, monstrous and cruel worlds to tell stories that are close to us and arouse empathy.

The concept of empathy in relation to VR has supporters and detractors, but at the moment it is particularly useful in describing the medium's ability to bring the user-spectator emotionally closer to the social and environmental context depicted by the experience itself. This emotional closeness is the result of the medium's technical, psychological and physical abilities to generate immersion, presence and embodiment. *The Key* and *The sick rose* approach this process in very different but equally effective ways. Thanks to this process, they create new worlds that are terrible yet fascinating, expanding the perspectives of the dystopia genre to immersive technologies.

References

Arcagni, Simone, and Adriano D'Aloia,. 2021. "VR Storytelling: Potentials and Limitations of Virtual Reality Narratives." *Cinergie – Il cinema e le altre arti* 11, no 9: 1-7.https://doi.org/10.6092/issn.2280-9481/13412

Anthes, Christoph, Rubén Jesùs García-Hernández, Markus Wiedemann, and Dieter Kranzlmüller. 2016. "State of the Art of Virtual Reality Technology." *IEEE Aerospace Conference*: 1-19. doi: 10.1109/AERO.20 16.7500674

Bolter, Jay Davis, Maria Engberg, and Blair MacIntyre. 2021. *Reality Media. Augmented and Virtual Reality*. Cambridge: Massachusetts Institute of Technology Press.

Carmignani, Julie, and Borko Furht. 2011. "Augmented Reality: An Overview". In *Handbook of Augmented Reality*, edited by Borko Furht, 3-46. Boca Raton, Florida: Springer.

Clayes, Gregory. 2017. *Dystopia: A Natural History. A Study of Modern Despotism, Its Antecedents, and Its Literary Diffractions*, Oxford: Oxford University Press.

Dalpozzo, Cristiano. 2018. "Cinema e realtà virtuale, ovvero "The early virtual (post)cinema of attractions". In *La realtà virtuale. Dispositivi, Estetiche, Immagini*, edited by Cristiano Dalpozzo, Federica Negri, and Arianna Novaga, 87-105. Sesto San Giovanni: Mimesis.

De Valk, Marijke, Brendan Kredell, and Skadi Loist. 2016. *Film Festivals. History, Theory, Methods, Practice*. New York: Routledge.

Dioniso, John David, William Burns III, and Richard Gilbert. 2013. "3D virtual worlds and the metaverse: current status and future possibilities", *ACM Computing Surveys* 45, no. 3, 1-38. http://dx.doi.org/10.1145/2480741.2480751

Eugeni, Ruggero. 2012. "First person shot. New Forms of Subjectivity between Cinema and Intermedia Networks." *Anàlisi Monogràfic*: 19-31. Https://doi.org/10.7238/a.v0iM.1499

Grossi Giancarlo. 2021. "Dreamlike Environments: "Story-living" in Virtual Reality Installations." *Cinergie – Il cinema e le altre arti* 10, no. 9: 147-155. https://doi.org/10.6092/issn.2280-9481/12321

Micalizzi, Alessandra, and Andrea Gaggioli. 2018. "Il senso di realtà del virtuale e i "principi di presenza". In *La realtà virtuale. Dispositivi, estetiche, immagini*, edited by Cristiano Dalpozzo, Federica Negri, and Arianna Novaga, 55-67. Sesto San Giovanni: Mimesis.

Milgram, Paul, and Fumio Kishino. 1994. "A taxonomy of mixed reality visual displays." *IEICE transactions on Information and Systems* 77 (12): 1321-1329.

Modena, Elisabetta. 2022. *Nelle storie. Arte, cinema e media immersivi*, Roma: Carrocci Editore.

Modena, Elisabetta, and Francesco Parisi. 2021. "Exploring Stories, Reading Environments: Flow, Immersion, and Presence as Processes of Becoming". *Cinergie – Il cinema e le altre arti* 10, no. 19: 69-82. https://doi.org/10.6092/issn.2280-9481/12399

Muhanna, A. Muhanna. 2014. "Virtual reality and the CAVE: Taxonomy, interaction challenges and research directions." *Journal of King Saud University – Computer and Information Sciences* 27: 344-361. https://doi.org/10.1016/j.jksuci.2014.03.023

Rauschnabel, P. A., Felix, R., Hinsch, C., Shahab, H., and Alt, F. (2022). "What is XR? Towards a framework for augmented and virtual reality". *Computers in human behavior*, 133. https://doi.org/10.1016/j.chb.2022.107289.

Ryan, Marie-Laure. 2015. *Narrative As Virtual Reality 2. Revisiting Immersion and Interactivity in Literature and Electronic Media*. Baltimora: Johns Hopkins University Press.

Ruszev, Szilvia. 2021. "Tracing Embodied Narrative in VR experience." *Cinergie – Il cinema e le altere arti* 10, no. 19: 9.20.

Suh Ayoung, and Jane Prophet. 2018. "The state of immersive technology research: A literature analysis." *Computers in Human Behavior* 86: 77-90. https://doi.org/10.1016/j.chb.2018.04.019

"The end times may really be night". Science Fiction and Nuclear Dystopia between the 1950s and 1960s

Giovanni Bernardini

In his recent and controversial work on the history of dystopia, Gregory Claeys identifies a discontinuity in science fiction literature after 1945. Such discontinuity does not concern so much as its canons, which continue to revolve around the fear of the degeneration of civil coexistence due to the dissolution of social order or to excessive control, and to the upper hand of technology over humanity. The novelty, rather, was due to the widespread and obsessive feeling in the literature that "the end times may really be nigh" (Claeys 2017, 447). Claeys himself identifies in the specter of the rapid and brutal self-destruction brought by a nuclear conflict both the symbol of the fears of the time, and the almost obligatory direction for the collective and literary imagination. The coming of the atomic age after 1945 had presented humanity with the concrete prospect on a technical level that for the first time in its history "a phenomenon of exclusively anthropic origin [was] able to wipe it out completely" (Malvestio 2021, 29). Science fiction literature was among the first to grasp this urgency and, thanks to its well-established acquaintance with the technical-scientific imagery, contributed more than other genres of speculation to shaping the atomic dystopia through characters, images and dynamics destined to remain in the collective imagination well beyond the boundaries of the literary genre.

Yet, for the prospect of a nuclear apocalypse to become plausible or even likely in the short term, it had to find nourishment in an irreducible political conflict, apparently destined to explode in a battle with no holds barred. Thus, the progressive affirmation of the ideological and geopolitical confrontation between the United States and the Soviet Union, soon defined "Cold War", fueled these reflections much more than the atomic bombings of Hiroshima and Nagasaki. Indeed, large part of the US media initially did not seem to fully understand the epochal rift that August 1945 had opened. Nuclear fission was hailed as proof of US technological superiority and as a promise of undiscovered benefits. This was reflected in popular culture, which at every level experienced "an almost compulsive post-Hiroshima effort to trivialize the event and avoid its deeper implications" (Boyer 1998, 10). The use of atomic energy in the military field was reduced to an accident in history and to the urgency of ending the "good fight" against tyranny and menace as soon as possible. Science fiction literature did not deviate from this dual trend: on one hand, enthusiasm for the technological progress embodied by the mastering of the secrets of the atom; on the other, poor understanding of the epochal consequences for its foreseeable implications in war (Boyer 1984, 253). Not even the first escalation of the confrontation with the Soviet Union, which occurred with the Korean War (1950-1953), seemed to change immediately the tendency to underestimate the seriousness of the nuclear threat. The plausible explosion of a direct conflict with Moscow became part of the collective imaginary without the use of atomic bombs appreciably subverting the canons experienced during the first half of the century. This is proved by the special issue that "Collier's", a magazine with a large circulation, dedicated in October 1951 to the "Preview of the War We Do Not Want" (Collier's October 27, 1951). The contributions of illustrious intellectuals from various backgrounds (including the science fiction writer Philip Wylie, to whom we will return shortly) traced the dynamics of the Korean conflict by imagining that the United States would lead a contingent of the United Nations against the Kremlin, which was responsible of promoting a regime change to stop the neutral tendency in Yugoslavia. The chapters linger over the following four years of war, sporadically mentioning the use of atomic bombs by both sides without attributing to it the ability to change the fate of the conflict: the latter, in fact, was finally resolved by an insurrection in the USSR and by the victory of the "free world". On the other hand, at the time, much literature did not fill the distance from the new enemy by futuristic long-range weapons but rather by the prospect of an internal subversion produced by communist propaganda and by the presumed moral weakness of the nation in rejecting it. The most obvious example, which soon became a reference for the decades to come, was "The Body Snatchers", a novel by Jack Finney in which a small Californian town was invaded by mysterious seeds, capable of replicating and replacing each citizen, Expect for empathy and individual initiative. The metaphor of communism seen through American eyes could not be more evident (Finney 1955).

The (Cold) War at Home

However, during the same years the "home front" of the Cold War was becoming an object of concern for other reasons directly linked to nuclear weapons. The novelist Kurt Vonnegut, earlier and more effectively than other authors, already anticipated in the early 1950s the consequences that a growingly sophisticated war technology would have on society. In his first novel "Player Piano", the United States had conquered world primacy thanks to the technological advances of its nuclear arsenal and of the computational equipment necessary to manage it (Vonnegut 1952). However, the automation process would also extend to other fields, excluding most citizens from productive life and handing over the leadership of society to a caste of technicians who are obsessively isolated from the rest of the population and increasingly self-referential in their decisions. In the following years, the theme would become commonplace also thanks to the surprising denunciation of the President of the United States Dwight D. Eisenhower: in his farewell speech from the White House (1961), he recalled the need for a massive defensive apparatus but also warned against the risk that "the acquisition of unwarranted influence [...] by the military-industrial complex" could "endanger our liberties or democratic processes"[1]. Two years later, Vonnegut further elaborated on the subject in his fourth novel, "Cat's Cradle": one of the scientists responsible for the US atomic project accepted the provocative challenge made by the military

---

[1] For a full transcript of the speech, see: https://www.archives.gov/milestone-documents/president-dwight-d-eisenhowers-farewell-address

establishment to create a substance capable of instantly solidifying water, so as to allow the Marines to land anywhere without getting wet (Vonnegut 1963). The substance is produced without concern for potentially disastrous consequences; a series of grotesque accidents will lead to its release into the oceans and to the freezing of all the water on the planet, with foreseeable consequences for life on Earth. In the same period, the danger that technocratic and military elites could lever on the destructive power of the nuclear arsenal to extend their control over society was the subject of speculation also by another cult author, Philip K. Dick, obsessed with the theme of conspiracy against ordinary citizens. "The Penultimate Truth" (1964) foreshadowed the beginning of a nuclear war between the Soviet Union and the United States for the colonial domination of Mars (a reference to the many peripheral crises of those years, such as that of Cuba). Before the conflict moved to Earth, the populations of the two Superpowers were relocated to underground cities, committed to continuing the productive effort for war purposes. In reality, the leaderships of the two countries had reached an agreement to end the hostilities but also to keep the populations in the belief that it was still raging, supported by a common and gigantic propaganda apparatus. Within a few years, the image of the Cold War as an artificial condominium of the two powers to control the population through lies and terror would enter the common language of the anti-nuclear protest movements (Cordle 2020, 147).

The full realization that the possession of the atomic bomb even by the Soviet Union was destined to change the very nature of war was at the core of "Level 7" by Mordecai Roshwald (1959), a best-seller of the time also appreciated by intellectuals such as philosopher Bertrand Russell. The protagonist recounts his promotion among the operators of the nuclear apparatus of his (never specified) country; they are forced to live in a shelter hundreds of feet underground, designed to survive the impending conflict for hundreds of years, during which time they will also become the nucleus of future humanity. The methods for their selection are indicative of the perversions imposed by the new war logic: social alienation becomes a merit since the scarcity of ties with those who remain on the surface guarantees an unhesitating execution of the final order. When this arrives, broadcasted over a loudspeaker from an unknown source, the sequence of a few buttons reduces the Earth to a radioactive wasteland in minutes. The following days are narrated by the protagonist through the growing awareness that the very concept of victory no longer makes sense in the nuclear age, until the malfunctioning of the power system would also condemn to death the occupants of the shelter which was to last for centuries. The novel, destined to remain a landmark of dystopian fiction, drew heavily on the topicality of the arms race. The placing into orbit of the first artificial satellite (Sputnik) in 1957 by the USSR produced in the USA a profound revision of the procedures for alerting and responding to a possible atomic attack, with a substantial increase in automation[2]. Roshwald's story was the first to explore in deep the psychological effect of this automation on soldiers reduced to "button press machines", totally dependent on technology. The consequences of automation were also the main focus of "Fail-Safe" (1962) by Eugene Burdick and Harvey Wheeler. The novel owed its notoriety to the incredible coincidence between its serial publication in the "Sunday Evening Post" and the Cuban Missile Crisis (1962), which once again contributed to blur the lines between reality and speculation in the debate on nuclear dystopia (George 2013, 14). In the novel, a series of improbable but not impossible technical errors triggered the peremptory and irrevocable order for a team of US nuclear bombers to hit Moscow in response to a Soviet attack that turned out to be a false alarm. Faced with the impossibility of interrupting the automatism, the President of the United States gave the order to bomb New York as a sacrifice to appease the Soviet wrath and to avoid a general war. The dramatic humanity of some passages (such as the first horrified reaction of the Soviet leader to the offer of "exchange" or the sacrifice of the US First Lady, occasionally visiting New York) seemed designed to highlight the dehumanization entailed in the reaction protocols and

---

[2] On the Eisenhower Administration reaction to the Sputnik, see Wenger (1997, 154-ff).

in their language made of "massive retaliation", "first" and "second strike capability", and so on.

A Hollowed-Out World

The "home front" of the Cold War evoked early by Vonnegut became central in the following years, due to the attempt of the US Administrations to persuade the population that adequate preparation would make the difference in the event of an atomic attack: for this purpose, a specific federal body, the Federal Civil Defense Administration, was established in 1950[3]. The Civil Defense was first tasked with recruiting creative minds to whom it entrusted the creation of effective information material to be distributed to the population. Among these was also the science fiction author Philip Wylie, well known since the 1930s for his novels that lambasted the laxity of the national mores and the risk of new forms of tyranny (including communism) (Seed 1995, 2). Wylie's zeal pushed him beyond his duties to publish a hugely successful novel that was both moral and pedagogical. "Tomorrow!" was structured around the story of two Midwestern towns and of their different preparation in view of an atomic attack (Wylie 1954). In the novel, the term "apocalypse" recovered its etymological origin of "revelation": in the frenzy of destruction caused by the bombs, those who had trained in time to follow the procedures would have survived; the others were doomed to succumb to panic and radiation. However, in the following years, Wylie changed his ideas considerably. The disturbing data that came from the development tests of the hydrogen bomb convinced him that "no conceivable form of defense and Civil Defense would prevent such a war from pretty much wiping out life in the Northern Temperate Zone" (Seed 2013, 86). The radical change of perspective resulted in his latest editorial success, "Triumph", which indirectly criticized the recent relaunch of the Civil Defense operated by the Kennedy Administration. The story sees fourteen individuals find safety from a Soviet atomic attack in a bunker under the Rocky Mountains. The discovery that they are

---

[3] For a history of Civil Defense, see Geist (2019).

the only survivors in the Northern Hemisphere corresponds to the bitter realization that the "Triumph" of the title is meaningless in the atomic age. Wylie entrusted to the long monologue of a protagonist all his criticism of the silly optimism of the previous years, which had also been his:

> "There were also lots of prophetic books and movies about total war in the atomic age, and all of them were practically as mistaken as plain people and politicians and the Pentagon planners. In all of them that I recall, except for one, we Americans took dreadful punishment and then rose from the ground [...] and defeated the Soviets and set the world free. That one, which came closer to reality so far as the Northern Hemisphere is concerned, showed how *everybody on Earth* died." (Wylie 1963, 96)

Wylie's conversion anticipated that of the country, which polls showed increasingly skeptical about the chances of survival since the early 1960s (Spencer 2014, 3). As for the exception called into question by Wylie, it was the well-known novel "On the Beach" by British writer Nevil Shute, published in 1957 (Shute 1957) and soon translated into a Hollywood blockbuster directed by Stanley Kramer. The book departed from the canon of nuclear apocalypse since, rather than dwelling on the graphic details of the war between the two Superpowers (which remained far in the background), it followed the psychological descent into hell of the Australian population, from the hope of being spared by the fallout to the certainty of its inevitability. As mass suicide becomes a plausible option, even encouraged by the Australian authorities, the protagonists find their way from despair to resignation, sparing no invectives for what could have been done to avert catastrophe. The last one takes her own life on the beach evoked by the title that the novel shares with a well-known poem by T.S. Elliot, concluded by the lines that also open Shute's book: "This is the way the world ends / Not with a bang but a whimper". The novel and its film adaptation became a case for the Eisenhower Administration, concerned that their sense of absolute helplessness in the face of atomic attack undermined any efforts made in the Civil Defense (Seed 1999, 190). A government meeting even discussed possible measures to counter the message, except to surrender to the evidence that nothing effective could be done. Soon, "On the Beach" attracted the criticisms of the many strategists committed to making attracted also the possession of the atomic weapon palatable to the population in the framework of deterrence, or even of its limited use in the event of war. Such was the teaching of the books by Herman Kahn, one of the most iconic and notorious strategists of the time. In "On Thermonuclear War" (1960), Kahn judged "On the Beach" and its idea of ultimacy as "interesting but badly researched" (Kahn 1960, 9). Two years later, Kahn's "Thinking about the Unthinkable" accused again the novel and the film of promoting an unfounded pessimism that prevented the country from developing a rational strategy which should consider the use of atomic bombs or their credible threat, even at the cost of sacrifice of millions of men (Seed 1999, 6-7). The episode is indicative of how at the time, since the prospect of a nuclear war could only be debated on a theoretical basis, literary speculation found legitimate space alongside and in competition with the strategic-military one.

The hollowed-out word of "On the Beach", however, long remained an exception in science fiction during the 1950s and 1960s. Istead, a real "Doomsday Literature" flourished at the time, in which the survival of part of humanity was often functional to describe the biological, psychological and social consequences of an atomic war, relying on the increasing availability of scientific evidence. "Coloured by squalid truths and morbid speculations", this literature marked the climate of the time to the point that even the literary works that wanted to provide a less pessimistic vision ended up included in the general gloomy mood (George 2003, 37). Harry Hart (Pat) Frank, a journalist and government intelligence aide under various administrations, shared Wylie's concern that Americans were underestimating the need for adequate preparation for an atomic warfare. This evidence prompted him to publish in 1962 the manual "How to Survive the H-Bomb and Why", and a few years earlier his most successful novel, "Alas, Babylon" (Frank 1959). The plot revolves around a revamped mythology of the frontier, where ordinary citizens reorganize into peripheral communities (in this case, in Florida) without waiting for help from the missing central authority. Despite Frank's commitment to emphasizing the inventiveness of which the survivors proved capable in overcoming the enormous difficulties facing them, the readership was more struck by the social degeneration associated with such conditions: a "military model of human relations" pervaded by a Darwinist approach to survival itself (Porter 2004, 43). Moreover, the prospect of an international downgrade of the United States, forced to receive aid from "Third World" countries untouched by the conflict was unattractive to say the least for American readers. Frank himself seems to cede to pessimism as the book ends with the bitter acceptance that knowing that the United States had won that war no longer made any sense. A similar fate befell Dr. Bloodmoney, or How We Got Along After the Bomb, one of Dick's best-known novels published in 1965 (Dick 1965). A tragic sequence of mistakes and underestimations by the Pentagon and the reckless scientists at its service had led to a short and catastrophic nuclear exchange with the Soviet Union. From that moment on, the plot focuses on a small rural community in California. Despite tensions, violence and unmentionable secrets, the community seems to prefigure the rise of a new rural idyll, far from the corruption of the cities and the decisional centers, in which citizens give free rein to their ability to remedy the economic and technological collapse (as the memorable horse-drawn cars) and the disturbing and paroxysmal genetic mutations that have affected nature itself, including human nature. To the author's surprise, it was the latter aspect that most resonated with the readers, as well as the brutal cancellation of the comforts of modern life; Dick grew disappointed with this pessimistic interpretation and profited from the new introduction to the 1985 edition of the novel to clarify how proud he was of his characters' ability to survive "not [...] even as beasts, but as real humans doing genuinely human things" (Sutin 1995, 80-83).

Survival took the shape of a providential last call for humanity in the novel that more than any other received critical acclaim, while selling more than two million copies in the United States. Walter Miller's "Canticle for Leibowitz" (Miller 1959) revolves around the story of an abbey in the heart of the United States through three post-atomic eras, roughly identifiable as a new Middle Ages, a Renaissance, and a Modernity. Beyond the plot, the novel contains the catalog of the most recurring nightmares at that time about the post-atomic future. The monks collect, keep, and reproduce "memorabilia" of the lost world, including the instructions for the making of nuclear weapons, despite having lost the codes necessary to understand them: the atomic war had put an end to the civilization of the past and made incomprehensible even the daily life of the time. The loss of collective memory has produced a narrative of the causes of war in which natural and supernatural are indistinguishable: "fallout" is now the name of an irascible Old Testament-like demon capable of flooding the world with fire (Tietge 2008, 678-679). The laborious rediscovery of knowledge by new "sages" involves the continuous conflict with religion, represented by the abbey, which would like to impose a moral code; this does not happen and humanity bitterly reveals itself once again "a race quite capable of admiring its own image in a mirror, and equally capable of cutting its own throat before the altar of some tribal god". At the outbreak of a new atomic war, the abbey decides to send an expedition to the most remote space colonies, with the faint hope that elsewhere, history may take a different course. The inventiveness and irony of the author's language did not hide his underlying pessimism about the inability of human nature to escape its destiny of self-inflicted destruction, just as at the time the world seemed condemned to experience a new apocalypse a few years following the end of World War II, during which Miller had been among the pilots who razed the Abbey of Monte Cassino in Italy.

The Non-human Saviors of Humanity

Resignation to the inevitable disaster, be it the extinction of life on Earth or the irreversible breakdown of civilization, was so rooted in science fiction of the time that it is difficult to find narratives depicting humanity as able to prevent its annihilation. Two illustrious examples also appear to be the most significant of the need to imagine an external intervention. The aforementioned "The Penultimate Truth" was an evolution of Dick's short story "The Defenders", published in 1953 (Dick 1953). Humanity is again forced to survive to escape the consequences of a nuclear war between the United

States and the Soviet Union. They left the burden of the war to the robots, who report terrible news of a devastated and uninhabitable surface. After eight years, however, some security personnel are surprised to find that an increasing number of robots returned from the surface without showing any signs of radiations. A team decides to verify for themselves, despite the warnings of the machines. Once on the surface, the team finds a pristine paradise in place of the devastation: the robots reveal that, once left alone, they put an end to the war, not seeing any rationality in its continuation; however, they had also decided to keep humanity in a lie, waiting for it to finally be ready to evolve out of its bellicosity. For this reason, the newly emerged men will not be allowed to return and report what they have seen; rather, they are encouraged to collaborate with some Soviets who had followed the same path in running a farm, in the hope that "the working out of daily problems of existence will teach [them] how to get along in the same world". With ironic optimism, Dick believed that humanity had the potential to produce machines not only more powerful but also wiser than itself. Published in the same year, "Childhood's End" is a masterpiece by British author Arthur Clarke, which presents another form of external intervention able to save humanity from its self-destructive impulses (Clarke 1953). A fleet of flying saucers suddenly installs itself above the main terrestrial cities, with the intention of stopping the "mad race" between the United States and the Soviet Union for ever more sophisticated military technologies, which threatens to extend to space. The mysterious "Overlords" impose their supervision over human affairs; in return, they ensure a golden age of peace and prosperity. A large part of the population accept this new state; only some dissidents perceive the risk of a life deprived of culture and innovation and give birth to a "New Athens" in the middle of the Pacific Ocean. There, however, they soon discover the project that the Overlords had harbored for humanity: the newborns undergo an evolution that will lead them to evolve and to join the "Overmind", a collective cosmic intelligence freed from the limitations of material existence. Faced with the evidence that humanity is therefore doomed to disappear, the citizens of New Athens commit suicide by exploding an atomic bomb which wipes out the city; meanwhile, their children enter the new cosmic collective consciousness in a pillar of light. The only salvation for humanity, Clarke seems to suggest, would lie in an evolution that takes it out of individualism and partisan struggles but also puts an end to its existence as a species.

Even a far from exhaustive review like this shows how English-speaking science fiction soon adopted nuclear dystopia as one of its favorite themes after 1945, and why. On one hand, it offered the opportunity to fustigate the eternal self-destructive tendencies harbored by the human species, which endangered its cultural and social achievements. On the other hand, the perception of the gravity of the new risk epitomized by nuclear weaponry prompted many authors (even among those initially more optimistic) to depict in strong colors the consequences that its possession or use would have on humanity. Science fiction literature took upon itself the duty of warning citizens and of increasing their awareness. In doing so, it produced images and words that would leave a lasting mark in popular culture in the following decades, and would often clash with the discursive strategies deployed by the authorities, which in turn aimed at normalizing the presence of atomic weapons in everyday life (Schiappa 1989, 3).

References

Boyer, Paul. 1984. "From Activism to Apathy: The American People and Nuclear Weapons, 1963-1980", *The Journal of American History* 4.

Boyer, Paul. 1998. *Fallout. A Historian Reflects on America's Half-Century Encounter with Nuclear Weapons*. Columbus: Ohio State University Press.

Burdick, Eugene, and Harvey Wheeler. 1962. *Fail-Safe*, New York: McGraw-Hill.

Claeys, Gregory. 2017. *Dystopia. A Natural History*. Oxford: Oxford University Press.

Clarke, Arthur C. 1953. *Childhood's End*. New York: Ballantine Books.

Cordle, Daniel. 2020. "The Politics of Vulnerability: Nuclear Peril and the Global Imagination", *The Palgrave Handbook of Cold War Literature*, edited by Andrew Hammond. London: Palgrave.

Dick, Philip K. 1953 (January). *The Defenders*, in "Galaxy Science Fiction".

Dick, Philip K. 1964. *The Penultimate Truth*. New York: Belmont Books.

Dick, Philip K. 1965. *Dr. Bloodmoney, or How We Got Along After the Bomb*. New York: Ace Books.

Finney, Jack. 1955. *The Body Snatchers*. New York: Dell Books.

Frank, Pat. 1959. *Alas, Babylon*. Philadelphia PA: J.B. Lippincott & Co.

Geist, Edward M. 2019. *Armageddon Insurance. Civil Defense in the United States and Soviet Union, 1945-1991*. Chapel Hill: University of North Carolina Press.

George, Alice L. 2013. *The Cuban Missile Crisis. The Threshold of Nuclear War*. London: Routledge.

George, Alice L. 2003. *Awaiting Armageddon. How Americans Faced the Cuban Missile Crisis*. Chapel Hill: University of North Carolina Press.

Kahn, Herman. 1960. *On Thermonuclear War*. Princeton: Princeton University Press.

Kahn, Herman. 1962. *Thinking about the unthinkable*. New York: Horizon Press.

Malvestio, Marco. 2021. *Raccontare la fine del mondo. Fantascienza e antropocene*. Milano: Nottetempo.

Miller Jr, Walter M. 1959. *A Canticle for Leibowitz*. Philadelphia PA: J.B. Lippincott & Co.

Porter, Jeffrey L. 2004. "Narrating the End: Fables of Survival in the Nuclear Age", *The Journal of American Culture* 16 (4):41- 47.

Roshwald, Mordecai. 1959. *Level 7*. New York: McGraw-Hill.

Schiappa, Edward. 1989. "The rhetoric of nukespeak", *Communication Monographs* 56 (3): 253-272.

Seed, David. 1995. "The Postwar Jeremiads of Philip Wylie", in *Science Fiction Studies* 22 (2): 234-51.

Seed, David. 1999. *American Science Fiction and the Cold War. Literature and Film*. Edinburgh: Edinburgh University Press.

Seed, David. 2013. *Under the Shadow. The Atomic Bomb and Cold War Narratives*. Kent State: Kent State University Press, Kent State.

Shute, Nevil. 1957. *On the Beach*. Portsmouth (NH): Heinemann.

Spencer, Brett. 2014. "From Atomic Shelters to Arms Control: Libraries, Civil Defense, and American Militarism during the Cold War", *Information & Culture* 49, (3): 351–85.

Sutin, Lawrence (ed.). 1995. *The Shifting Realities of Philip K. Dick. Selected Literary and Philosophical Writings*. New York: Vintage Books.

Tietge, David J. 2008. "Priest, Professor or Prophet: Discursive and Ethical Intersections in A Cantife for Leibowitz", *The Journal of Popular Culture*, 41 (4), 676-694.

Vonnegut, Kurt. 1952. *Player Piano*. New York: Charles Scribner's Sons.
Vonnegut, Kurt. 1963. *Cat's Cradle*. New York: Holt, Rinehart and Winston.
Wenger, Andreas. 1977. *Living with peril. Eisenhower, Kennedy, and Nuclear Weapons*. New York: Rowman & Littlefield.
Wylie, Philip. 1954. *Tomorrow!*. New York: Rinehart & Company.
Wylie, Philip. 1963. *Triumph*. New York: Doubleday.

A Close Enough Dystopia? International Law and Climate Change in Kim Stanley Robinson's *The Ministry for the Future*

Mariangela La Manna

Introduction: Situating Climate-Fiction in the Framework of Dystopian Literature

Dystopian literature has often been considered as the nemesis of *serious* literature and accordingly dismissed as a somewhat lower form of literary entertainment for teenagers or, alternatively, for nerdy and scarcely mature grown-ups. Such superficial and overzealous assessment touches especially upon one particularly vituperated sub-genre of dystopian literature, namely science fiction (also known as *sci-fi*). However, there is more to dystopia and to science-fiction than meets the eye. Many dystopian novels managed, in fact, to grasp and address some among the most pressing challenges for policy-makers and scholars alike, thus stimulating a conversation on very sensitive dilemmas in ethical and political terms. This is of course true with reference to the quintessential text-book dystopian novel, namely Orwell's *1984*, that warns readers against the surveillance mechanisms of a totalitarian State, but it may also apply to more recent literary works, such as Kazuo Ishiguro's *Never Let Me Go*, that triggered a debate on the boundaries of scientific and medical progress against the backdrop of human dignity, not to mention Margaret Atwood's *The Handmaid's Tale*, which is at the very centre of the conversation on reproductive rights, or the same author's *Maddaddam Trilogy*, tackling the relationship between man and nature and the ineliminable features of the human condition.

One of the most common scenarios in dystopian fiction is the destruction of the natural environment and the subsequent adjustment of individuals and communities to the new reality. Such narrative scheme appears to be pivotal in numerous novels (suffice it to recall Ballard's *The Drowned World*, Rachel Carson's *Silent Spring*, Jeanette Winterson's *The Stone Gods*, Cormac McCarthy's *The Road* or the above-mentioned *Maddaddam Trilogy*, among many others). Within such broader framework, a more specific literary *topos* providing for context and inspiration would of course be climate change. The many threats posed by the latter for life as we know it (i.e. our lifestyle) or even human life on the planet altogether were not undetected by writers, film directors and artists, that addressed the issue either in a more or less explicit fashion (e.g. John Brunner's *Stand on Zanzibar*), or through metaphors and symbols (e.g. the meteorite in *Don't Look Up*, a proxy for climate change or possibly for the COVID 19 pandemics). All in all, thus, climate change offers the ideal framework for setting fictional works (Nicolini 2020, 1-2), so much so that the catchphrase climate fiction (or *cli-fi*) was created, encompassing a thick body of novels and short stories (Menherrt 2016), an equally vast amount of comics (among many others *Réfugiés climatiques et castagnettes*, David Ratte's two-volume dystopian account of sea level rise and climate-induced migrations, stands out), and even videogames (suffice it to mention the global warming-induced Cordyceps pandemics in *The Last of Us*, eventually featuring in a successful HBO series), which further confirms climate change's inherently transmedial nature.

Attentive commentators deem science fiction to be the one literary form capable of capturing the implications of climate change in scientific and social terms, due to this genre's confidence with scenarios that, however improbable, are nonetheless premised on entirely plausible facts and figures. It is, in fact, purported that, due to their inherent features, only two sub-genres of science fiction, namely dystopian literature, on the one hand, and post-apocalyptic accounts, on the other, can match the implications of the Anthropocene (Malvestio 2021, 19-20), the particular era we are living in, where mankind managed to alter the climate and the natural order of things. More precisely, dystopian fiction fashions cautionary tales molded on speculative accounts on the human condition in the hypothesis that some of its negative traits were to prevail. To that end, it exasperates such traits and depicts a world that, however scarcely desirable, is ultimately still entirely possible and plausible. On the contrary, post-apocalyptic fiction examines the conduct of individuals or communities following sudden and unprecedented catastrophic events of massive proportions (e.g. a nuclear catastrophe or a natural disaster). The two notions, akin to one another, can thus be distinguished by considering that post-apocalyptic novels are premised on the occurrence of a specific even triggering a structural and radical change in human life, thus separating the world *before/after* the event, whereas the main feature of dystopian literature would be the continuity flowing between our present time and the alternative present or the future envisaged in the narrative (Malvestio 2021, 21). Interestingly enough, climate-fiction situates itself at the confluence of both sub-genres, and encompasses both techniques either singly or combined (Malvestio 2021, 107), coherently with the dual nature of climate change itself, a typically slow-onset phenomenon that nonetheless triggers violent manifestations (e.g. floods, heatwaves etc.).

The same features can be detected in Kim Stanley Robinson's *The Ministry for the Future*, a welcome addition to the list of existing eco-dystopian fictional works, with its witty and intelligent depiction of the structural limitations of international organizations before the climate challenge, and its dry account of the inefficient enforcement mechanisms provided for under international law to react to internationally wrongful acts, namely the blatant (and not so) fictional violation of the 2015 Paris agreement. The present chapter wishes to critically assess the book through the lens of international law, a task that will be carried out pursuant to a *law and literature* (also *law and lit*) perspective, a sensible and common enough methodological choice in climate studies. Within the body of existing legal literature on climate change, *law and lit* accounts are, in fact, far from unheard of (Rogers 2020) as recent scholarship on the issue further confirms (Birrell and Dehm 2021). Still, for the sake of clarity, before actually resorting to the methodology under discussion, one that international legal scholarship in Italy is still somewhat skeptical of, it may be useful to have its basic features pointed out, in order to better grasp the international law insights underlying the fictional work under review, prior to offering some concluding remarks.

It will be demonstrated that, far from being a purely literary product, *The Ministry* manages to describe a future that is now menacingly approaching, all the while figuring out some among the most significant structural shortcomings of the international legal order and addressing some among the most intriguing doctrines under international law that currently happen to be at the very heart of the debate both within institutions and scholarly circles.

Methodological Insights: *law and literature*

Lawyers are known to be very grounded people, always with a foot in the real world. This is of course true with reference to practitioners, but it may also apply to academics, that like to think of themselves as no-nonsense, straight to the point scholars set on producing rational accounts of reality and keen to offer viable solutions to actual problems. Especially legal positivists (let it be known, by way of disclaimer, that the present writer should like to fit in the lot), who are extremely wary of interdisciplinarity and take great pride in the scientific nature of law, make sure to prevent as accurately as possible any contamination (Bianchi 2016, 288). Against this backdrop, one needs to appreciate the American-born approach that goes under the name of *Law and Literature*, which was first introduced in the 1920s to be eventually developed, systematized and turned into an actual field of study in the 1970s. Contrary to its detractors contention, this specific methodology is entirely premised on the idea fiction may indeed be a vector to enable a better understanding of the real world.

Law and lit is one of the many interdisciplinary approaches (*law and economics, law and sociology, law and international relations* etc.) that came about as a reaction to more traditional methodological perspectives. Such approaches, however, are not free from dangers and difficulties (Cryer 2011, 76). Misconceptions, misgivings and miscommunication are in order, and the chance for important elements to be lost in translation is very high. It is thus important to prevent any communication failure among disciplines by clarifying and keeping in mind the key concepts of each, in order to manage to speak the same language in the end. In other words, interdisciplinarity taken seriously rests on scholars' ability to resort in a confident fashion to the two or more toolboxes involved (Baron 1999, 1060). Commentators warn, in fact, against the dangers of *disciplinary tourism* (Cryer 2011, 77), the typical attitude of those scholars that approach interdisciplinarity with a hobby-like mentality, cherry-picking whatever insight they may be fascinated with, while disregarding that discipline's toolset and basic rules altogether.

However high the risks underlying interdisciplinarity, *law and literature* may perhaps be best equipped among the many *law and* approaches to minimize such risks (Yahyaoui Krivenko 2015, 103-104). After all, both disciplines are concerned with the interpretation of texts, and they also share several additional features. Besides the centrality of text, one has in fact to account for the heavy reliance on symbols and founding myths, as well as on the creative use of language for the purposes of *shaping* reality (Bianchi 2016, 287). Plus, both are *communal* in nature as they speak to specific communities, which will further the debate and interpretative practice on respective texts, based on sharing the same linguistic and cultural practice (West 1988-1989, 131).

Within the broader *law and lit* methodology, at least two different methods need to be distinguished, based on the different relationship between the two disciplines they envisage, namely law *in* literature and law *as* literature (Simpson 2021, 21-25). The latter is intuitively enough represented by the literary analysis and critique of legal texts (rules, regulations, judicial decisions…) The *law as literature* technique is, in fact, an analytical tool germane to literary critique, as it inquires how judgments are made, and how they can be made more or less persuasive, thus analyzing legal texts just as if they were literary texts. This is especially true with reference to judicial decisions, where the language and the style resorted to by judicial authorities may very well serve as a vector to transmit content (Bianchi 2012, 300-303). A scholar adopting that kind of approach would basically take a legal text and subject it to a literary analysis, examining the literary figures, the choice of words, the rhythm, the sheer number of times a term is used, the context, the presence of any references to pop culture etc. Thus, a *law as literature* approach has a lot in common with critical approaches to international law, that aim to launch an attack on the possibility of objectively interpreting written texts (Cryer 2011, 96-97). The *law in literature* approach, on the other hand, revolves around the analysis of literary works for the purposes of gaining insights possibly of use for lawyers (the same inspiration underlying the present chapter). The typical mindset of scholars pursuing *law in lit* boils down to the use of literary works in order to figure out the way in which writers relate to or represent legal matters, and, ultimately, to stimulate reflection about the law (Morgan 2007, 5), a task that may pursued by addressing classics (Meron 1998, 1; Schultz and Ost 2018, 1-2) as well as modern fiction and poetry.

The frequency the overall toolbox of *law and lit* approaches is resorted to may vary significantly from one branch of law to another, as well as from one national tradition to another. In particular, international legal scholarship in Italy was not very sensible to the promises of interdisciplinarity. However, interest for interdisciplinary approaches (especially in the forms of the *law in lit* method) is growing, as the recent publication of a collection of chapters on the law-based aspects in Dante's poetry (Casolari 2022) that also harbours quite a few chapters on international law issues (e.g. on the responsibility to protect) further confirms. Be it as it may, the whole set of *law and literature* approaches needs not to be underestimated or vilified, as it may very well help lawyers to temper the excesses of formalism and corroborate their technical assessments with some meta-legal and value-based considerations (Bianchi 2016, 308-309). It is pointed out that at the very least literature may teach layers something about the human condition (Carofiglio 2019). This should make even more sense in the domain of international environmental law, a branch of international law so technical and complex as to need to be counterbalanced with a fair amount of passion and emotion (Hilson 2022, 1).

Measuring Kim Stanley Robinson's Dystopian Scenario against the Background of Existing International Law Rules and Institutions

The present section will thus tackle *The Ministry for the Future* with a *law in lit* method, by trying to identify and assess the international law rules and institutions envisaged in the novel. Kim Stanley Robinson's fictional work is the ideal object for that sort of analysis. His previous work constituting the so-called *Mars Trilogy* was already explored from that specific perspective (Jones 2022). His work in the more circumscribed framework of *cli-fi* is just as rich and deserving of further analysis. He has in fact published two other books on the subject matter of climate change beyond the one currently under review, i.e. *New York 2140* and *2312*, that were appreciated by literary critics.

The novel is set in 2025 and the plot goes as follows: with the so-called tipping points in the rise of global temperatures reached and crossed, the management of the climate crisis is spiraling out of control. A brand new agency, shortly thereafter labeled The Ministry for the Future by journalists, is thus created as a subsidiary body for the implementation of the 2015 Paris agreement, and is given the very specific mandate of defending present and future generations. This is entirely fictional, of course, but accurately crafted to be as plausible as possible. Even the language of fictional COP 29 mirrors the typical language resorted to by actual Conferences of Parties. It reads, in fact: "Be it resolved that a Subsidiary Body authorized by this twenty-ninth Conference of the Parties serving as the meeting of the Parties to the Paris Climate Agreement (CMA) is hereby established, to work with the Intergovernmental Panel on Climate Change, and all the agencies of the United Nations, and all the governments signatory to the Paris Agreement, to advocate for the world's future generations of citizens, whose rights, as defined in the Universal Declaration of Human Rights, are as valid as our own. This new Subsidiary Body is furthermore charged with defending all living creatures present and future who cannot speak for themselves, by promoting their legal standing and physical protection". The story then follows the deployment of every means available under science, technology, and economics to mitigate the unsustainable socio-environmental situation, some of them sensible, albeit very hard (e.g. the whole issue of carbon quantitative easing, a carrot-and-stick mechanism revolving around the notion of carbon coin, a new currency to be issued as a prize for carbon mitigation, especially crafted to incentivize actors to refrain from burning fossil fuels), others not entirely self-evident (e.g. water pumping at the very core of ice caps to prevent them from melting and slipping into oceans, further worsening sea level rise), others very debatable (e.g. the Indian sunscreen in the atmosphere mimicking the effect of volcanic eruptions to prevent sunrays to reach the surface of the planet). In the end, after many failures (the topical and most significant among them being a tragic heatwave in India causing the death of roughly 20 million) and ever-escalating social, political and diplomatic tensions, the joint efforts of the many players involved manage at last to curb emissions and to restore an environmentally acceptable global standard somewhat comparable to the one existing prior to the fossil fuel era or, possibly, even better than the one.

The muscle behind such successful mitigation strategy is the main character in the book, fictional former foreign minister of Ireland Mary Murphy, who leads the newly-created body. This character shares an uncanny resemblance with Mary Robinson, former President of Ireland and former United Nations High Commissioner for Human Rights, a key figure in the fight against climate change. The other main character, medical doctor Frank May, is the survivor of the Indian heatwave, which left him scarred in body, mind, and soul, forcing him to consider and eventually try to no avail to join a transnational eco-terrorist organization known as the Children of Kali, a well-meaning (they wish to tackle the crisis by having carbon emissions at long last curbed) yet deadly association (they complete one attack after the other against those individuals they deem to be responsible for the climate crisis due to their lifestyle, occasionally causing the death of innocent people). The two characters, very different from one another, will briefly meet in Chapter 25 when he seizes her and locks in a room with her, only to discuss the political and operational underpinnings of the fight against climate change, a scene reminiscent of Michael Fagan's intrusion in Queen Elizabeth II's private quarters in Buckingham Palace back in 1982, when the man, mentally and socially vulnerable, got to share with the Queen the problems of the working class in the United Kingdom under Margareth Thatcher's government, a scene portrayed in season 4 of the successful series *The Crown*. Besides the two main characters, several other narrators need to be accounted for. The book encompasses, in fact, different perspectives and the story is far from linear, as even non-fiction chapters are included here and there to try and break the reader on very complex issues attaining to science, politics, and economics.

International-law wise, *The Ministry* touches upon many important elements under the climate regime as well as other areas of the international legal order. Accounts of the 2015 Paris agreement (Robinson 2020, 15) are apposite and correct and even the somewhat slippery notion of Conference of the Parties (COP), a peculiar entity to be found typically in multilateral environmental agreements is adequately dealt with (Robinson 2020, 15-16). What is more intriguing, however, is the implicit assessment of the notion of sovereignty and the implications thereof, as well as the realist reading of the de-centralized enforcement mechanism of international law. Robinson cleverly shares his insights on the structural inadequacies of the international community and its legal order, by showing that there is only so much States and international organizations can do in the face of patent violations of both treaty law and customary law, absent a centralized enforcement agency. This appears clearly under Chapter 24, when Mary discusses India's decision to pursue the unorthodox solar radiation management solution to keep the temperature low following the heatwave. When she points out "There are questions of sovereignty here, I know. But India signed the Paris Agreement along with all other nations" she is met with a very dry response on the part of Indian representatives: "We may break the treaty (...) We won't allow another heatwave just so we can be in compliance with a treaty written up by developed nations outside of tropics and their dangers" (Robinson 2020, 140).

Related to that, one can detect a criticism both of the legitimacy of the UN in leading the fight against climate change and of the effectiveness of its action. More broadly Frank May conveys a great deal of skepticism on international cooperation under institutional frameworks. This can especially be gathered from the dialogue between Mary and Frank in Chapter 25, whereby he corners Mary and asks for a show of repentance, accountability, and action in whatever form necessary to prevent an impending mass extinction. He is first met with a formalistic reply on the part of Mary who points out that the Ministry is established under the Paris agreement, thus being independent and detached from the UN (Robinson 2020, 95) and then with further rebukes that, far from calming his anguish and rage, only manage to further spun his frustration ("We can only model scenarios. (...) We track what has happened and graph trajectories in things we can measure, and then we postulate that the things we can measure will either stay the same, or grow, or shrink, (Robinson 2020, 96), "We've made divisions that focus on various aspects of the problem. Legal, financial, physical, and so forth. We prioritize what we do to portion out the budget we're given, and we do what we can" (Robinson 2020, 98), culminating with Mary's firm and principled rejection of targeted assassinations of individuals most responsible for triggering the climate crisis (Robinson 2020, 99). The faith in multilateralism and international cooperation is eventually restored later in the story by Mary herself and by her quest for the issuance of the carbon coin currency (Robinson 2020, 188-189).

The most interesting element from the perspective of an international lawyer, however, is perhaps the author's treatment of some of the allegedly fundamental values under the international legal order, such as solidarity, which is taken into consideration in its numerous dimensions. The most strikingly evident aspect of solidarity dealt with in The Ministry would certainly be its intergenerational nature. The book's emphasis on future generations is abundantly clear in the titular choice, but also further developed in the story thanks to the character of Tatiana, a friend and colleague of Mary's, who is eventually killed. Tatiana is said to be very keen of finding "allies and legal means to advance the cause of defending the generations to come" and not alien to the technical issues involved in the task, namely legal standing in proceedings "for people who don't exist yet" (Robinson 2020, 35). Intergenerational solidarity or equity is currently at the very centre of the debate, especially in light of the *Sacchi et al. v. Argentina et al.* petition brought before the UN Committee on the Rights of the Child, the treaty-monitoring body competent to monitor the implementation of the 1989 Convention on the Rights of the Child, which was declared inadmissible due to lack of the requirement of the exhaustion of local remedies, the *Duarte Agostinho v. Portugal et al.* case, currently pending before the European Court of Human Rights and expected to be heard late in September, the 2021 *Neubauer* decision of the German Constitutional Court, and the recent request for an advisory opinion formulated by the General Assembly to the International Court of Justice, where the interests of future generations are explicitly mentioned and taken into account.

All in all, international law is always very present throughout the book and, even if its inefficiencies and failures are depicted for everyone to see, one can nonetheless gather a certain amount of faith in the rule of law, its structures and mechanisms, especially in the final part of the dialogue between Mary and Tatiana under Chapter 9. When a dismayed Mary, facing the collapse of the whole conventional climate regime, asks Tatiana "So what do you think we can do to improve that situation?", her friend replies "Rule of law is all we've got. (…) We tell people that and then try to make them believe it" (Robinson 2020, 35).

Concluding Observations

Amitav Ghosh is a vocal opponent of climate fiction set in the far distant future, guilty of allegedly absolving current societies from their responsibility in the causation of the climate crisis. This criticism does not apply to the book under review for two reasons: *i)* the story is set in a near future, only marginally distant from our present, thus creating a familiar and plausible imaginative landscape, which makes it all the more terrifying (e.g. the initial sequence culminating in the heatwave scene in India appears to be disquietingly similar in nature—though luckily not so much in its outstanding proportions—to scenes we struggle with every so often in the news); *ii)* the narrative shows in an abundantly clear manner that our everyday actions and inactions are just as effective in triggering the dystopian scenario depicted in *The Ministry* as are the (scarcely effective) environmental policies adopted and implemented by domestic and supranational institutions or the conduct of corporate actors, especially the so-called *Carbon Majors*. The compelling narrative makes readers just uncomfortable enough as to start thinking how to change their habits in order to better deal with the issue of climate change, thus fulfilling the inherent agenda of dystopian fiction, i.e. depicting a world one would never want to live in, so as to warn individuals of the impending risk of such scenario coming into being and trigger a cultural change (Malvestio 2021, 19). This adequately serves the pedagogical aspirations underlying eco-dystopian fiction (Rigby 2015, 2).

However gloomy, though, *The Ministry* is a somewhat uplifting piece of literature. One of the book's main features is, in fact, its underlying optimistic stance, that appears in a more prominent fashion in the last chapters. *The Ministry* conveys a message of hope by showing the potential of mankind not only to overcome a potentially life-ending crisis, but also to take the opportunity to turn the world into a better place, by establishing a post capitalistic, more just, equal, and sustainable society, thanks to a wide array of strategies adopted in different regions of the world (sustainable agriculture in India, a new economic model in Spain, the sensible and accurate groundwater management in California). Contrary to a first impression, thus, *The Ministry* is not a work of dystopian fiction properly meant, though one can be forgiven for branding it a dystopian novel at first sight. The reaction of single individuals, communities, States and international institutions to the catastrophe of climate change and the joint efforts to mitigate its consequences, thus overcoming societal shortcomings and selfish attitudes, make *The Ministry* an example of utopian fiction instead.

Bill McKibben, an authoritative writer and the author of a thorough and insightful review of Robinson's work in *The New York Review* does not seem to share this assessment. He points out that

The Ministry "is not utopian, it's anti-dystopian, realist to its core" and further adds "…there's still money and still nation-states and still central banks, and change comes from riot and occupation and protest…". Without resorting to those analytical categories, Bill Gates acknowledged the same, by saying that *The Ministry* is a scary but hopeful novel about climate change. Be it as it may, experts emphasized that optimism may prove more effective a narrative than pessimism, and that emphasizing successes in the protection of the environment, rather than failures, is more inspiring for individuals (Boyd 2015). One thing is, however, beyond dispute: what Amitav Ghosh termed *the unthinkable* is all too thinkable now and we should all roll up our sleeves to meet the challenge.

References

McKibben, Bill. It's Not Science Fiction, The New York Review, 17 december 2020 issue

Menherrt, Antonia. *Climate Change Fictions. Representations of Global Warming in American Literature*. London, New York; Palgrave Macmillan, 2016.

Baron, Jane. 1999. "Law, Literature, and the Problems of Interdisciplinarity.", *The Yale Law Journal* 108, no. 5: 1059-1085.

Bianchi, Andrea. 2012."Il tempio e i suoi sacerdoti. Considerazioni su retorica e diritto a margine del caso *Germania c. Italia.*" *Diritti umani e diritto internazionale* 6, no. 2: 293-309.

Bianchi, Andrea. 2016. *International Law Theories. An Inquiry into Different Ways of Thinking*. Oxford: OUP.

Birrell, Kathleen, and Julia Dehm. 2021. "International Law and the Humanities in the Anthropocene." In *Routledge Handbook of International Law and the Humanities*, edited by Shane Chalmers and Sundhya Pahuja, 407–421. London and New York: Routledge.

Boyd, David. 2015. *The Optimistic Environmentalist. Progressing Towards a Greener Future*. ECW Press: Toronto.

Carofiglio, Gianrico. 2019. *La misura del tempo*. Einaudi: Torino.

Casolari, Federico et al., eds. 2022. *Dante e Diritto Un cammino tra storia e attualità*. Modena: Mucchi Editore.

Cryer, Robert et al., 2011. *Research Methodology in EU and International Law*. Oxford: Hart Publishing.

Ghosh, Amitav. 2016. *The Great Derangement. Climate Change and The Unthinkable*. Chicago: The University of Chicago Press.

Hilson, Chris. 2022. "The Role of Narrative in Environmental Law: The Nature of Tales and Tales of Nature", *Journal of Environmental Law* 34: 1-24.

Jones, Henry. 2021. *International Law and the Production of Resources: Lessons from the Colonization of Mars.*" In *Routledge Handbook of International Law and the Humanities* edited by Shane Chalmers and Sundhya Pahuja, 302-311. London and New York: Routledge.

Kaplan, Ann. 2016. *Climate Trauma. Foreseeing the Future in Dystopian Film and Fiction*. New Brunswick, New Jersey and London: Rutgers University Press.

Malvestio, Marco. 2021. *Raccontare la fine del mondo. Fantascienza e Antropocene*. Milano: Nottetempo.

Markley, Robert. 2019. *Kim Stanley Robinson*. Champaign: University of Illinois Press.

Meron, Theodore. 1998. *Crimes and Accountability in Shakespeare*, *American Journal of International Law* 92, no. 1: 1-40.

Morgan, Ed. 2001. "The Other Death of International Law." *Leiden Journal of International Law* 14, no. 1: 3-24.

Morgan, Ed. 2007. *The Aesthetics of International Law*. Toronto: University of Toronto Press.

Nicolini, Matteo. 2020. "Law and the Humanities in a Time of Climate Change", *The Cardozo Electronic Law Bulletin* 26, no. 1: 1-29.

Ratte, David. 2020. *Réfugiés climatiques et castagnettes*. Paris: Grand Angle.

Rigby, Kate. 2015. *Dancing with Disaster. Environmental Histories, Narratives and Ethics for Perilous Times*, Charlottesville: University of Virginia Press.

Afterword

Massimo Scaglioni

Mapping the Dystopian Narratives: The Project of the "Atlas of Dystopian Storytelling"

The contemporary audiovisual scenario is characterized by a growing proliferation and fragmentation of platforms, products and narratives, and as a consequence, by high hybridization of genres, languages and consumption practices. In this rich and diversified environment, the theme of dystopia has increasingly developed, due to a redefinition of classic anxieties that cross our fragile societies. We are now facing an overabundance of content, rhetoric and production models where it's not always easy to find a correct and linear way; thus, within the project dedicated to the study and the analysis of dystopias in the 21st century, an "Atlas of Dystopian Storytelling" (www.unicatt.it/atlantedelledistopiemedi
ali) has been created, aimed at providing a diachronic overview of representation of dystopias through media such as movies, TV series and videogames, a sort of a multimedia cartography of fears of contemporary society. Following a wide approach to the concept and label of "dystopia" (containing also apocalyptic, post-apocalyptic, uchronic narrations), the Atlas is built alongside two methodological pillars: on one hand, historical and geographical references with a focus on places and times of production and representation as central keys to highlight how dystopias are related or not to specific countries and cultures, and on the other hand the emphasis on the concept of "transmediality" since many dystopian media products have been variously adapted in different languages (from novels to audiovisual products, for instance) revealing the strength and the longevity of this kind of narrations.

At present time, the database composing the Atlas consists of over 500 products among movies, Tv series and videogames produced since the beginning of the new century and it is constantly updated. On of the most original activities characterizing the Atlas is the attempt to individuate the main topics through which contemporary dystopian narratives could be developed: a perimeter that has been divided in six area, often intertwining among them: a) *natural disasters and environmental catastrophes*: media products that are centered on the fear of a degeneration of the conditions of the Earth and the planet and denounce the approaching of a fatal point of no return for our ecosystem due to the devastating consequences of nuclear catastrophes and global warming; b) *human-technology relations*: stories and narratives that emphasize the coexistence between man and machine and its drift towards a world dominated by technological tools; c) *epidemics/health emergencies*: the *topos* of the fear of contagion has been often present in literature and narratives throughout the centuries. This topic is often the pre-condition of a dystopian narrative, and represents the starting point through which people in the story change their perspectives and relations in an apocalyptic or post-apocalyptic world; d) *migrations*: migratory flows is another issue defining dystopian media products. The control of borders, the clash between two different cultures, the de-humanization of the figure of the migrant, the need to move from one's own land are aspects upon which many dystopian audiovisual narrations are built; e) *consipracy theories*: some variations of dystopian narratives take root in certain niches of our societies, especially in online communities, in which the paranoid idea of an hypotetical grey eminence who works to subvert the order is spread. This topic is developed in movies and TV series often inspiring by social movements; f) *crisis of democratc societies*: the loss of freedom and the collapse of democratic institutions are constantly present in our lives as fears and inspire the *what if* mechanism and the consequent dystopian narrations. The Atlas also provides a geographical distribution of the richness of production and, alongside the six thematic areas, it identifies six zones to list the products: North America, Latin America, Europe, Nordics, Middle-East, Asia-Pacific. Each of them is characterized by specific interests and ways of representation: dystopias are global, but their storytelling is strictly tied to specific cultures as the outcome of history, traditions, social and political past. Thus, the Atlas aims to act as a useful tool for those interested to study dystopian media products and their impact on culture and society.

About the Autors

Stefania Antonioni | *Università di Urbino Carlo Bo* | Italy
stefania.antonioni@uniurb.it

Stefania Antonioni is Associate Professor of Television Studies at the University of Urbino Carlo Bo. Her research interests include Television serial narratives, Audience reception online and offline, Promotional Strategies and Paratexts. She edited the volume (with Marta Rocchi), *Investigating medical drama TV series. Approaches and perspectives* (2023) and several articles.

Luca Barra | *Università di Bologna* | Italy
luca.barra@unibo.it

Luca Barra is Full Professor at the Department of the Arts of University di Bologna, where he teaches Television and Digital Media, Contemporary TV Series, and TV Production Cultures, and leads the MA in Information, Cultures and Organization of Media (INCOM). His research mainly focuses on television production and distribution cultures, the international circulation of media products (and their national mediations), comedy and humor genres, and the evolution of the contemporary media system.

Giovanni Bernardini | *Università di Verona* | Italy
giovanni.bernardini@univr.it

Giovanni Bernardini is Researcher in Contemporary History at the University of Verona, Italy. His research focuses on planning policies in Western Europe during the 20th Century, the containment of Bolshevism in Europe after 1917, West German foreign policy during the "Cold War", the history of the South Tyrol question, the mediatization of history. Among his latest publications are: *Parigi 1919. La Conferenza di pace* (Il Mulino, 2019), *La medialità della storia. Nuovi studi sulla rappresentazione della politica e della società* (Il Mulino, 2019), co-edited with C. Cornelissen.

Anja Boato | *Sapienza Università di Roma* | Italy
anja.boato@uniroma1.it

Anja Boato is a Ph.D. candidate in Music and Performing Arts at Sapienza University of Rome. Her research topic focuses on cinematic virtual reality (Cine-VR) and its application to immersive experiences at film festivals. She has written about transmedia storytelling, fandom studies, and popular culture in edited books, essays, and a book (*Shipping. Uno sguardo sociologico sui fandom romantici*, Edizioni Epoké, 2022).

Valerio Alfonso Bruno | *Università Cattolica del Sacro Cuore Milan* | Italy
valerioalfonso.bruno@unicatt.it

Valerio Alfonso Bruno is Research Fellow at Università Cattolica del Sacro Cuore, where he collaborates with Polidemos (Center for the Study of Democracy and Political Change) and fellow at the Far-Right Analyis Network (FRAN). Bruno is a specialist on the Italian far-right and has recently contributed to the *Routledge Handbook of Far-Right Extremism in Europe* and the *Handbook Non-Violent Extremism*. His online analyses have appeared, among others, on Al Jazeera, Financial Times, The Economist, France24.

Antonio Campati | *Università Cattolica del Sacro Cuore Milan* | Italy
antonio.campati@unicatt.it

Antonio Campati is Assistant Professor at Università Cattolica del Sacro Cuore (Milan). He is a member of the Editorial Board of *Rivista italiana di filisofia politica* and *Power and Democracy*. His research interests mainly focus on the transformations of political representation, the role of elites and the theories of democracy. On these issues, he has written essays published in journals and collective volumes.

Daniela Cardini | *Università IULM Milan* | Italy
daniela.cardini@iulm.it
Daniela Cardini is Associate Professor at IULM University, Milan. Her research is focused on television studies, in particular on seriality in television narratives and production. Among her publications: *La canzone nelle serie tv. Forme narrative e modelli produttivi* (Pàtron 2021, with Gianni Sibilla); *Long TV. Le serie televisive viste da vicino* (Unicopli 2017); *La lunga serialità televisiva. Origini e modelli* (Carocci 2004); "Il telecinefilo. Il nuovo spettatore della Grande Serialità televisiva", *Between* (2014); "Serial contradictions. The Italian debate on television series", *SERIES - International Journal of Television Narratives* (2016).

Paolo Carelli | *Università Cattolica del Sacro Cuore Milan* | Italy
paolo.carelli@unicatt.it

Paolo Carelli PhD is Assistant Professor of Media Theory at Università Cattolica del Sacro Cuore where he also teaches Broadcasting History. Senior Researcher at CeRTA (Research Center on Television and Audiovisual Products), he is didactic coordinator of Master "Fare TV. Gestione, Sviluppo, Comunicazione".

Manuela Ceretta | *Università di Torino* | Italy
manuela.ceretta@unito.it

Manuela Ceretta is Rector of the Università della Valle d'Aosta – Université de la Vallée d'Aoste and full professor of History of political thought at Turin University. Her research interests focus on dystopian tradition and particularly on the relationship between power, domination and voluntary submission. She edited two collections of essays on George Orwell (2007) and Aldous Huxley (2019) and published several peer-reviewed articles like: *Sulla distopia* (2012); *Esorcizzare la paura, invocare le paure: utopia e distopia di fronte a una passione antica* (2016); *Non è un paese per bambini? Cenni su alcune recenti trasformazioni della letteratura distopica* (2018); *Immaginario distopico e crisi europea* (2022).

Patricia Chiantera-Stutte | *University of Bari* | Italy
patricia.chiantera@uniba.it
Patricia Chiantera-Stutte is Full professor of History of Political Thought at the University of Bari. Her research interests are: History of historiography, populism, theory of civilization, geopolitics, biopolitics. She published on many international reviews, including "Storia del pensiero Politico", "Tocqueville Studies", "Journal of Social Theory"- and with Maria Pia Paternò she edited the issue on dystopia and Europe for the review "Storia del pensiero politico". Some of her works are: Von der Avantgarde zum Traditionalismus (2002, Campus), Delio Cantimori (2011, Carocci), Il pensiero geopolitico (2014, Carocci), Denken Im Raum (with U. Jureit, Nomos, 2021).

Raffaele Chiarulli | *Università Cattolica del Sacro Cuore Milan* | Italy
raffaelerosario.chiarulli@unicatt.it

Raffaele Chiarulli is Research Fellow at Università Cattolica del Sacro Cuore, Department of Communication and Performing Arts. His research focuses on screenwriting history, narrative theories and links between theatre, film and literature. In 2021, he won the SRN Award for Best Journal Article about screenwriting. In 2023 Along with Armando Fumagalli and Eva Novrup Redvall, he edited *The Children are Watching Us. Exploring Audiovisual Content for Children*, monographic issue of the Journal of Media, Performing Arts and Cultural Studies.

Fabio Ciammella | *Sapienza Università di Roma* | Italy
fabio.ciammella@uniroma1.it

Fabio Ciammella is a Research Fellow in Sociology of Cultural and Communicative Processes at the Department of Communication and Social Research (CoRiS), Sapienza University of Rome. His research interests include: transmedia studies, internet and social media studies, participatory culture, media practices, information disruption, distributed creativity, storytelling and the imaginary. Recent publications include: *Transmedia Activism* (2022).

Paola Dalla Torre | *Università LUMSA, Roma* | Italy
p.dallatorre1@lumsa.it

Paola Dalla Torre is Associate Professor of Film History at LUMSA in Rome. Part of her studies are devoted to contemporary cinema and especially science fiction, with a particular focus on the relationship between cinema and bioethics. In this regard, the following texts are worth mentioning: *Sognando il futuro* (Rubbettino, 2012), *Cinema contemporaneo e questioni bioetiche* (ed., Studium 2010).

Lorenzo Denicolai | *Università di Torino* | Italy
lorenzo.denicolai@unito.it

Lorenzo Denicolai is a researcher at the University of Turin, where he teaches Media Anthropology and Applied Informatics in Multimedia Communication. He deals with audiovisual media, media literacy, human-technology relations and robotics. He is the author of scientific articles in national and international journals and of the monographs *Scritture mediali. Riflessioni, rappresentazioni ed esperienze mediaeducative* (2017) and *Mediantropi. Introduzione alla quotidianità dell'uomo tecnologico* (2018).

Alessandro Dividus | *Università di Torino* | Italy
alessandro.dividus@unito.it

Alessandro Dividus holds two PhDs in Political Sciences (University of Genoa; University of Pisa). He is actually a Post-doc researcher with a project on contemporary dystopian literature and meritocracy, and an Adjunct Professor of history of political thought at the University of Turin. His research areas include history of political thought, utopian and dystopian studies, political philosophy, epistemology and ethics. He published several articles and essays, a monograph *Politica e Coscienza. Il Liberalismo Sociale di T. H. Green* by GUP (Genova University Press), and attended numerous international conferences.

Vassilis Galanos | *University of Stirling* | United Kingdom vassilis.galanos@ed.ac.uk

Vassilis Galanos is Lecturer in Digital Work at the University of Stirling's Management School and Associate Editor of *Technology Analysis and Strategic Management* (Taylor & Francis). Vassilis has worked with the University of Edinburgh's Science, Technology and Innovation Studies department, the Edinburgh Futures Institute, and the Bridging Responsible AI Divides (BRAID) UK programme. Vassilis is working on historical sociologies of artificial intelligence and internet technologies and is the author, with Dr James K. Stewart, of the forthcoming book *Internet, AI and Society: A Guide for the Perplexed* (Wiley Blackwell, Inc).

Luca Gendolavigna | *Sapienza University of Rome* | Italy
lucagendolavigna@gmail.com

Luca Gendolavigna holds a PhD in Nordic Languages and Literatures at the Department of Literary, Linguistic and Comparative Studies of the University of Naples "L'Orientale". He currently works as adjunct professor at the Department of European, American and Intercultural Studies (SEAI) at Sapienza University of Rome. His research interests are migration and postmigration literature in Scandinavia, literary multilingualism and the recent dystopian turn in contemporary Swedish literature. In 2023, Luca Gendolavigna published a monograph entitled *Storie d'identità - La Svezia postmigrante* (*Stories of Identity: Postmigrant Sweden*) for the Italian publisher Aracne.

Ivo Stefano Germano | *Università del Molise* | Italy
ivostefano.germano@unimol.it

Ivo Stefano Germano is an Associate Professor of Sociology of Digital Media, University of Molise, SUSef department. Topics of research concerns: Sociology of culture, Sociology of Digital Media, Sociology of journalism and sports. His main pubblications are: *Tribuna Stampa: storia critica del giornalismo sportivo da Pindaro a Internet* (con I. Cucci, 2003); *La società sportiva: significati e pratiche della* *sociologia dello sport* (2012); *Il calcio in fuorigioco? Indagine sulla disaffezione del pubblico italiano nei confronti del sistema calcio* (con P. Aroldi e G. Gili, 2017).

Mariangela La Manna | *Università Cattolica del Sacro Cuore Milan* | Italy
    mariangela.lamanna@unicatt.it

Mariangela La Manna is an Assistant Professor of International Law at the Catholic University. She has written on universal jurisdiction in the prosecution of international crimes, State immunity from foreign civil jurisdiction, self-determination of peoples, and the international climate regime, among other things. Her current research focuses on environmental protection in the event of an armed conflict.

Silvia Leonzi | *Sapienza Università di Roma* | Italy
    silvia.leonzi@uniroma1.it

Silvia Leonzi is full Professor of Sociology of Cultural and Communication Processes at the Department of Communication and Social Research at Sapienza University of Rome. She is the President of the Master's Degree Program in 'Media, Digital Communication and Journalism'. Her research is focused on media studies, cultural consumption, imaginary, storytelling and transmedia. Among her publications: *Lo spettacolo dell'immaginario* (2009), *Homo Communicans* (con G. Ciofalo, 2013) and *Transmedia Studies. Logiche e pratiche degli ecosistemi della comunicazione* (2022).

Jovana Malinarić | *Università di Bologna* | Italy
    jovana.malinaric2@unibo.it

Jovana Malinarić is a performing arts dramaturg and PhD researcher in Theatre and Performance Studies at the University of Bologna in collaboration with the University of Utrecht. Her research presents innovative approach on a contemporary dramaturgy as a practical knowledge. Among her main publications are:

Un'etnografia del folle: Poor Tom dall'isolamento al teatro elisabettiano; Dare forma all'incontro. Gli aspetti relazionali della drammaturgia contemporanea.

Emiliano Marra | *Indipendent Researcher* | Italy
emiliano.marra@gmail.com

Emiliano Marra teaches humanities in a junior high school. He graduated in Comparative Literature in Padua and he was awarded a PhD in Italian Studies at University of Trieste in 2015. In the following years, relating the topic of Italian alternative history tales, he published some papers and he also attended some conferences. He is a contributor to the web magazine Pulp Libri. Among his latest pubblications: "Mussolini nella letteratura ucronica italiana" in *Rivista di Politica* (2022).

Ivana Mette | *Università degli Studi Roma Tre* | Italy
ivana.mette@uniroma3.it

Ivana Mette is a PhD student in "Landscapes of the contemporary city. Policies, techniques and visual studies", Cinema and Visual Culture curriculum at Roma Tre University. Her study interests concern, reception studies, neuroscience and cognitivism in cinema, but mainly virtual reality and its transmedia implications, with a focus on direction and storytelling in VR. She has published articles for magazines such as *Imago - Studies of cinema and media*.

Marco Milani | *Università di Bologna* | Italy
marco.milani6@unibo.it

Marco Milani is Assistant Professor of History and Institution of Asia at the Department of Arts, University of Bologna. His main research interests include contemporary Korean history and society, North and South Korean foreign and security policy, inter-Korean relations and contemporary Korean cultural production. He has published numerous articles and book chapters on North and South Korea's foreign policy, inter-Korean relations and contemporary Korean history and cultural production. He is co-editor of the book on South Korea's foreign policy titled *The Korean Paradox: domestic political divide and foreign policy in South Korea* (Routledge, 2019).

Damiano Palano | *Università Cattolica del Sacro Cuore Milan* | Italy
damiano.palano@unicatt.it

Damiano Palano is Full professor of Political Philosophy, Director of Political Sciences Department at Università Cattolica del Sacro Cuore and Director of Polidemos (Center for the Study of Democracy and Political Change). He is currently engaged in a research project on the transformation of democracy and on the rise of populism. Recent publications include the books: *Bubble democracy. La fine del pubblico e la nuova polarizzazione* (Scholé-Morcelliana, 2020); *State of Emergency. Italian democracy in times of pandemic* (EDUCatt, 2022; ed.) and *Animale politico* (Scholé-Morcelliana, 2023).

Massimiliano Panarari | *Università degli Studi di Modena and Reggio Emilia* | Italy
massimiliano.panarari@unimore.it

Massimiliano Panarari is Associate Professor of Sociology of Communication at Università degli Studi di Modena and Reggio Emilia (Department of Communication and Economics). His research topics include: Sociology of Media; Political Communication; Sociology of Culture; Journalism Studies; Social Theory. Among his main publications: *La credibilità politica* (con Guido Gili, 2020); *Uno non vale uno* (2018); *Poteri e Informazione* (2017); *Elogio delle minoranze. Le occasioni mancate dell'Italia* (con Franco Motta, 2012); *L'egemonia sottoculturale* (2010).

Romina Perni | *Università di Perugia* | Italy
romina.perni@unipg.it
Romina Perni teaches History and Philosophy at Liceo 'Donatelli' in Terni. She was a Research Fellow at the Department of Political Science of the University of Perugia. She is interested in publicity

and transparency of power, especially related to Kant's political philosophy. Among her publications: *Pubblicità, educazione e diritto in Kant*, Firenze University Press, Firenze 2023; *République, usage public de la raison et éducation chez Kant*, in "Cités", vol. 93, no. 1, 2023, Traduit de l'italien par Emmanuelle Bouhours, pp. 153-166 ; *La deformazione distopica. Raccontare il tempo presente con Francis Bacon*, in "Cosmopolis", n. XVI, 1.2019.

Miriam Petrini | *Sapienza Università di Roma* | Italy
   miriam.petrini@uniroma1.it

Miriam Petrini is a PhD student of Sapienza University. Her PhD research deals with EIAR's radioplays and particularly Federico Fellini's radiodramas. Her research studies radioplays produced by EIAR focusing on writers who would become the main authors of Italian Cinema in the 20th Century. Among her works: "Federico Fellini all'Eiar (1940-1943). Tra l'evoluzione del radioteatro e la nascita del «felliniano», L'avventura" (Il Mulino, 2021).

Andrea Piano | *Sapienza Università di Roma* | Italy
   andrea.piano@unroma1.it

Andrea Piano is a PhD candidate at the University of Rome "La Sapienza". The topics he is interested in are game studies, cultural heritage, sociology of culture, mythology and environment. Main publications are: "The PAC-PAC Authoring Environment for Game Design Teaching: Two Learning Experiences Compared", with Argiolas and Cuccu (2021) and "Mythopoiesis and Collective Imagination in Videogames". Proceedings of the ARQUEOLÓGICA 2.0 - 9th International Congress & 3rd GEORES, with Ceccherelli and Ilardi (2021).

Grazia Quercia | *Sapienza Università di Roma* | Italy
   grazia.quercia@uniroma1.it

Grazia Quercia, PhD in Communication, Social Research and Marketing at Sapienza University of Rome, is Adjunct Professor of the

Transmedia Design Lab at Guglielmo Marconi University. Her research interests include cultural and creative industries, digital media, seriality, transmedia studies, and gender representation. Latest publications include: "La forza vitale dell'universo narrativo di "Doctor Who"", in *Mediascapes Journal* (2019) with Antenore and Ciofalo and "The Toon Gaze. La rappresentazione del femminile nei cartoni animati prescolari", in *OCULA* (2021), Ciofalo and Leonzi.

Matteo Quinto | *Università di Bergamo* | Italy
matteo.quinto@unibg.it

Matteo Quinto is a PhD candidate at the University of Bergamo. His research interests concern fantastic narratives, intermediality and non-fiction in cinema and literature. He is currently researching nostalgia, cultural memory and ecocriticism in animated cinema. His publications include essays on Antonio Franchini, Jonathan Littell, Marco Bellocchio, Brian De Palma, Miyazaki Hayao, Ari Folman, on posthuman identity and on children-parents relationships in animated cinema. He is the editor of books on Erich Auerbach (Pavia University Press 2018), Dario Fo (Pavia University Press 2018), Pier Paolo Pasolini ('Autografo' 61, Interlinea 2019) and on Italian female writers of the 20th century (Mimesis 2023).

Enrico Reggiani | *Università Cattolica del Sacro Cuore Milan* | Italy
enrico.reggiani@unicatt.it

Enrico Reggiani is Full Professor of *English Literature* at the Faculty of Linguistic Sciences and Foreign Literatures of the Università Cattolica del Sacro Cuore. He has published widely on a) W. B. Yeats and other Irish writers; b) writers of Catholic origin, culture and background; c) interdisciplinary relationships between literature and economy/economics. At present, the transdisciplinary relationships between literature and music are his main research area and he has recently been defined as an international scholar "with a high profile in the relevant field". He is also the director of the Studium Musicale di Ateneo.

Massimo Scaglioni | *Università Cattolica del Sacro Cuore Milan* | Italy
massimo.scaglioni@unicatt.it

Massimo Scaglioni is Full Professor of Media History and Media Economics at Università Cattolica del Sacro Cuore. He is also Adjunct Professor of Transmedia Narratives and Television: Industry and Languages at Università della Svizzera Italiana (USI) in Lugano. He is the co-founder and current director of Ce.R.T.A. (Research Centre for Television and Audiovisual Media at Università Cattolica) and director of the Master's course "Fare TV. Gestione, Sviluppo, Comunicazione" at ALMED. Massimo Scaglioni is the author of several books on media and broadcasting history and industry, including: *La televisione nella pandemia. Intrattenimento, fiction, informazione e sport nell'anno del Covid-19. Annuario 2021* (Carocci, 2021); *A European Television Fiction Renaissance: Premium Production Models and Transnational Circulation* (Routledge, 2021, with L. Barra); *Cinema Made in Italy. La circolazione internazionale dell'audiovisivo italiano* (Carocci, 2020).

Anna Sfardini | *Università Cattolica del Sacro Cuore Milan* | Italy
anna.sfardini@unicatt.it

Anna Sfardini is Assistant Professor at Università Cattolica del Sacro Cuore, where she teaches "Intercultural Communication" and "Research Methods on Media Production and Consumption." She is Senior Researcher at Ce.R.T.A. (Centre for Research on Television and Audivisual Products), and didactic director of the Master "Fare Tv. Gestione, Sviluppo Comunicazione.". Her principal filed is media and television studies with a focus on media convergence, audiences, Tv genres, mediatization of politics, tv for women and for kids. She is the author of several papers and books including *Reality Tv* (Unicopli, 2009), *La tv delle donne. Brand, programmi e pubblici* (Unicopli 2015, with C. Penati), *La politica pop* (Il Mulino, 2009 with G. Mazzoleni), *La televisione. Modelli teorici e percorsi di analisi* (Carocci, 2017, with M. Scaglioni).

Gianni Sibilla | *Università Cattolica del Sacro Cuore Milan* | Italy
gianni.sibilla@unicatt.it

Gianni Sibilla PhD, teaches at the Università Cattolica del Sacro Cuore where since 2000 he is the director of the post-degree course Master in Music Communication. In the same university he teaches Music media and markets. He also teaches at IULM University. He published several essays and books on the relation between popular music and the media and on the cultural industry, among which *I linguaggi della musica pop* (Bompiani, 2003) and *Musica e media digitali* (2008), *La canzone nelle serie TV. Forme narrative e modelli produttivi* (2021, with Daniela Cardini).

Mario Tirino | *Università di Salerno* | Italy
mtirino@unisa.it

Mario Tirino is a researcher at the University of Salerno, where he teaches Television and New Media, Sociology of Youth Cultures, and Media Communication and Sport. His topics of research include the sociology of digital cultures, the mediology of literature and comics, and the sociology of sports cultures. He is the author of *Postspettatorialità. L'esperienza del cinema nell'era digitale* (2020) and of over one hundred articles published in national and international scientific journals. He directs the scientific series "L'Eternauta. Studies on Comics and Media" (with G. Frezza and L. Di Paola) and "Binge Watchers. Media, sociology and history of seriality" (with M. Teti).

Joseph Trotta | *University of Gothenburg* | Sweden
joe.trotta@sprak.gu.se

Joseph Trotta is an associate professor and distinguished teacher of English Linguistics at the Department of Languages and Literatures, University of Gothenburg, Sweden. Joe is a lapsed Chomskyan, his research focus has shifted over time from theoretical approaches to English syntax toward the use of English in popular culture. Trotta's academic interests are eclectic and varied; most of his recent publications are interdisciplinary and deal with issues of identity and linguistic representation in mediatized language such as TV dialogs, music lyrics, online games, etc. In 2019 he was the chief editor of the anthology *Broken mirrors: Representations of apocalypses and dystopias in popular culture*.

Maria Teresa Zanola | *Università Cattolica del Sacro Cuore Milan* | Italy
    mariateresa.zanola@unicatt.it

Maria Teresa Zanola is Full professor of French Linguistics, Director of the Observatory of Terminologies and Language Policies, Università Cattolica del Sacro Cuore, Officier dans l'Ordre des Arts et des Lettres and Member of the Accademia della Crusca. Topics of her research include: Specialised languages and terminologies in diachronic and comparative perspectives; Language Policies in Higher Education; Principal Investigator of the 2020 PRIN project FLATIF "Fashion languages and Terminologies across Italian and French". Main publications are: *Arts et métiers au XVIIIe siècle* (L'Harmattan, 2014); *Che cos'è la terminologia* (Carocci, 2018; Ma hwa eilm almustalahat, arabic edition); (ed.) Terminologie diachronique. Méthodologies et études de cas, *Cahiers de Lexicologie* (2021).

ibidem.eu